Routledge Revivals

Economic Nationalism of the Danubian States

Economic Nationalism of the Danubian States (1928) examines the economic situations in the newly-configured countries of the basin of the Danube. The First World War and its following peace treaties saw this region's map completely redrawn, and this book looks at the economic consequences and the new countries' economic policies.

Economic Nationalism of the Danubian States

Leo Pasvolsky

Routledge
Taylor & Francis Group

First published in 1928
by George Allen & Unwin, Ltd.

This edition first published in 2025 by Routledge
4 Park Square, Milton Park, Abingdon, Oxon, OX14 4RN

and by Routledge
605 Third Avenue, New York, NY 10017

Routledge is an imprint of the Taylor & Francis Group, an informa business

Publisher's Note
The publisher has gone to great lengths to ensure the quality of this reprint but points out that some imperfections in the original copies may be apparent.

Disclaimer
The publisher has made every effort to trace copyright holders and welcomes correspondence from those they have been unable to contact.

A Library of Congress record exists under LCCN 29002355

ISBN: 978-1-032-90574-7 (hbk)
ISBN: 978-1-003-55860-6 (ebk)
ISBN: 978-1-032-90575-4 (pbk)

Book DOI 10.4324/ 9781003558606

ECONOMIC NATIONALISM OF THE DANUBIAN STATES

BY

LEO PASVOLSKY

London

GEORGE ALLEN & UNWIN, Ltd.

Ruskin House, 40 Museum Street, W.C. 1

1928

PRINTED IN THE UNITED STATES OF AMERICA

STATEMENT

Each investigation conducted under the auspices of The Brookings Institution is in a very real sense an institutional product. Before a project is undertaken it is given thorough consideration, not only by the Director and the staff members of the Institute in whose field it lies, but also by the Advisory Council of The Brookings Institution. When an investigation is begun it is placed under the supervision of a special Committee consisting of the Director of the Institute and two or more selected staff members.

It is the function of this supervising Committee to advise and counsel with the author in planning the analysis and to give such aid as may be possible in rendering the study worthy of publication. The Committee may refuse to recommend its publication by the Institution, if the study turns out to be defective in literary form or if the analysis in general is not of a scholarly character. If, however, the work is admittedly of a scholarly character and yet members of the Committee, after full discussion, cannot agree with the author on all phases of the analysis, the book will be published in the form desired by the author, with the disagreeing Committee member, or members, writing a criticism for publication as an appendix.

After the book is approved by the Institute for publication a digest of it is placed before the Advisory Council of The Brookings Institution. The Advisory Council does not undertake to revise or edit the manuscript, but each member is afforded an opportunity to criticize the author's analysis and, if so disposed, to prepare a dissenting opinion.

DIRECTOR'S PREFACE

This volume differs from others in the Institute's series of European studies in that it is concerned not with a single country but with a geographic region embracing a number of states linked together by common economic bonds. At the end of the World War, Austria, Hungary, Czechoslovakia, Rumania, and Yugoslavia were separated from old alignments and set up as independent political and, presumably, economic entities. After ten years of reconstruction and of endeavor to achieve economic independence, these nations remain parts of an economic empire, and there is relentless pressure in the direction of economic solidarity.

Part I of this study sets forth the pre-war economic status of Austria-Hungary and of Rumania and Serbia and discloses the immediate economic consequences of the dissolution of the old Hapsburg empire. In Parts II to VI the author presents a concise yet authoritative analysis of the post-war economic history, respectively of Austria, Hungary, Czechoslovakia, Rumania, and Yugoslavia. Part VI —Nationalism vs. Unity—surveys the maladjustments and difficulties from which this economic region as a whole has suffered since the Great War and discusses the possibilities of future improvement along lines of economic co-operation.

The preparation of this volume has been under the supervision of a Committee consisting of the Director, and Robert R. Kuczynski, Thomas Walker Page, and Cleona Lewis of the staff of the Institute.

HAROLD G. MOULTON,
Director.

Institute of Economics,
June, 1928.

AUTHOR'S ACKNOWLEDGMENTS

WHEREVER possible, documentary data were used in the preparation of this study. They were supplemented with other reliable materials in printed or manuscript form. Such materials are not, however, as yet available on all points discussed in this book, and much of the information contained in it or used as the basis for the author's conclusions had to be obtained in conversation or correspondence with informed observers in each of the countries.

The author wishes to express his deep appreciation of the assistance rendered him by the representatives of the United States Departments of State and Commerce, stationed in various European countries, and by various persons and institutions in a number of European countries. He is under special obligation to Messrs. A. Loveday, J. Chapman, and P. Jakobsen, of the Economic and Financial Section of the League of Nations Secretariat; M. Pierre Quesnay, of the Banque de France; Professor M. Frère, formerly of the Reparation Commission; Professor Friedrich Hertz, of the Federal Chancellor's Office, Vienna; Dr. Richard Schüller, of the Austrian Foreign Office; Dr. Otto Rosenberg, of the Austrian Union of Bankers; M. J. Dvorácek, former Czechoslovak Minister of Commerce; Dr. A. Basch, of the Czechoslovak National Bank; Professor Macek, of the Prague University; Dr. A. Szaboky, Hungarian Undersecretary of State for Finance; Professor F. von Fellner, of the University of Budapest; Dr. V. V. Badulesco, Secretary-General of the Rumanian Ministry of Finance; Mr. G. Boncesco, Financial Counsellor of the Rumanian Legation in Washington; Professor I. Angelesco, former Secretary-General of the Rumanian Ministry of Commerce; Mr. Š. Sećerov, head of the Yugoslav delegation to the International Economic Conference; Mr. D. Stošovic, Editor of *The Belgrade Economic Review;* Professor M. Nedeljković of Belgrade University; and others.

Dr. M. Nadler, Assistant Director of the Institute of International Finance, New York, has read the manuscript and has made many valuable suggestions. Cleona Lewis, of the Institute of Economics staff, contributed greatly to the organization of the material and the presentation of statistical data. R. P. Ward, also of the Institute staff, prepared the maps.

LEO PASVOLSKY

Washington, D. C.,
June, 1928.

CONTENTS

CHAPTER III

CHAPTER IV

PART II

AUSTRIA'S EXPERIENCE SINCE THE WAR

CHAPTER V

CHAPTER VI

CHAPTER VII

CHAPTER VIII

CHAPTER IX

PART III

CZECHOSLOVAKIA'S EXPERIENCE SINCE THE WAR

CHAPTER X

CHAPTER XI

CHAPTER XII

CHAPTER XIII

CHAPTER XIV

PART IV

HUNGARY'S EXPERIENCE SINCE THE WAR

CHAPTER XV

CHAPTER XVI

CHAPTER XXI

CHAPTER XXII

CHAPTER XXIII

CHAPTER XXIV

PART VI

YUGOSLAVIA'S EXPERIENCE SINCE THE WAR

CHAPTER XXV

CHAPTER XXVI

CHAPTER XXVII

CHAPTER XXVIII

CHAPTER XXIX

PART VII

NATIONALISM VERSUS UNITY

CHAPTER XXX

ECONOMIC NATIONALISM
OF THE DANUBIAN STATES

INTRODUCTION

To no part of Europe did the World War bring such far-reaching and important changes as to the countries which lie, wholly or in part, in the basin of the Danube River. There were five Danubian countries before the war; Austria and Hungary—the two nations that made up the Dual Monarchy—Serbia, Rumania, and Bulgaria. The treaties of peace, which redrew the map of Europe, changed almost beyond recognition the configuration of all of these countries, with the exception of Bulgaria. They left six countries in the basin of the Danube: Austria, Hungary, Czechoslovakia, Rumania, Yugoslavia, and Bulgaria. The first five of these are the Danubian States with which this book is concerned.[1]

Together these five countries constitute an important portion of Europe. Their combined territory is 850,000 square kilometers, and their population 58 millions. Next to Russia, the Danubian basin is the largest granary of Europe. It possesses immense timber resources and very considerable mineral

[1] Bulgaria is not discussed in this study, principally because she was not involved in the dismemberment of the Austro-Hungarian Monarchy and is not directly concerned in the plans for the creation of an economically unified territory comprising the other five Danubian States. Her economic experience since the war will be the subject of a separate study at a future date.

wealth. It lies in the very heart of the European continent, and is traversed by all important trade routes from the West to the East. What happens to these countries is a matter of close concern to the rest of Europe and, consequently, to the whole world.

Prior to the war, the Austro-Hungarian Monarchy was the predominant factor in the valley of the Danube. In the course of centuries, its dynasty had become master of numerous nations and races, until the whole country was nothing but a patchwork of racially and linguistically different groups. This agglomerate gradually evolved into the form of a Dual Monarchy, in which the realm of the Habsburgs existed at the time of the outbreak of the World War. As a result of an arrangement made in 1867, the Germans in the Empire of Austria and the Hungarians in the Kingdom of Hungary mutually recognized each other as the dominant group in its respective half of the Monarchy. The other groups in each of the halves, although they exceeded in aggregate numbers the dominant groups, were made subject to the latter.

This arrangement cut across racial and linguistic frontiers both within the Monarchy and outside. It inevitably resulted in discontent and irredentism, which acted as disruptive influences. The Czechs in Austria and the Slovaks in Hungary, originally of common stock and language, worked for liberation and unification. The Rumanians in Bukowina (part of Austria) and Transylvania (part of Hungary) worked for unification with the Rumanians organized into an independent Kingdom, just outside the frontiers of the Monarchy. Similarly, the Slovenes and the Dalmatians in Austria and the Croats in Hungary were working toward unification, in an independent State, with the other branch of the southern Slavs—the Serbs—whose Kingdom also touched the frontiers of the Monarchy.

The World War provided an opportunity for the realization of these political ambitions on the part of the subject national groups of the Dual Monarchy. Even before hostilities came to an end, the Austro-Hungarian Monarchy had already ceased to exist and the Habsburg dynasty had lost its ancient throne. In a brief space of time the Galician section of the Monarchy broke off to become a part of reconstituted Poland, the lands occupied by the Czechs and the Slovaks united into a newly-created country, the Rumanians of the Monarchy united with those of the pre-war Kingdom of Rumania, the southern Slavs formed the State of Yugoslavia, and several important territories in the western part of the Monarchy were joined to Italy. What was left of Hungary became an independent State, while the remaining remnant of the Dual Monarchy became new Austria.

The treaties of peace applying to these countries merely put a stamp of international approval upon what had already been accomplished in practice by the series of revolutions which shattered the very structure of the Austro-Hungarian Monarchy. There were two such treaties: that of St. Germain with Austria and that of Trianon with Hungary. These treaties regularized the frontiers of the reconstituted and the newly created states, defined their obligations toward each other and toward the other belligerents, and left them to the task of organizing themselves into nations.

Coming into existence as a result of the violent disruption of old relationships, in a strained atmosphere of war and revolution, the new Danubian countries could not escape extreme manifestations of political nationalism, which was intensified by the fact that large numbers of Hungarians and of Austrian Germans found themselves, after the war, in the condition of minorities in the newly created states. And side by side with this aspect of their new nationhood these countries were confronted with economic problems of great magnitude and complexity. Political subjection had too long been identified in their minds with economic domination, and political nationalism found an equally distinct counterpart in economic nationalism, which was stimulated, and in some instances even dictated, by the general economic situation obtaining in Europe immediately after the war.

Three new states—new Austria, new Hungary, and Czechoslovakia—were carved wholly out of the territory of the Dual Monarchy. Portions of the former Habsburg domains were joined to Rumania,

Serbia, Poland, and Italy. The frontiers thus set up became economic frontiers, behind which each of the newly created or reconstituted States set to work creating an economic organization coterminous with its territory.

These countries have now had almost a decade of experience as national entities. So great have been the difficulties confronting them during these post-war years, that the question has naturally arisen in the minds of students and observers all over the world as to what the future holds in store for them. By easy analogy with pre-war conditions, the thought naturally occurs that the sane and most hopeful road for these countries to pursue is the one which leads to some sort of economic unity among them. Can they and will they follow such a road?

This book is devoted primarily to a consideration of this question. Its purpose is to set forth the basic elements in the post-war situation of the Danubian countries, to analyze the experience of each of these countries within its present frontiers, and to appraise the factors involved in, and the various plans proposed for, a solution of the question: "Nationalism or unity?"

Part I presents a discussion of the process by which the Danubian States came into being. It consists of an analysis of the pre-war economic situation in the Austro-Hungarian Monarchy and in the Kingdoms of Rumania and Serbia, a description of the economic and financial dismemberment of the Monarchy, and a consideration of the newly created and reconstituted states as national entities.

In Parts II to VI an analysis is given of the experience since the war of Austria, Czechoslovakia, Hungary, Rumania, and Yugoslavia. An examination is made of the currency and fiscal condition, the international trade and financial position, the basic productive activities, and the economic policy of each of them, and an attempt is made to present, as far as possible, the point of view of each of these countries with regard to the need, the feasibility, and the desirability of some sort of economic unity within the Danubian group of states.

Finally, in Part VII, an analysis is made of the factors involved in the Danubian situation, both from the point of view of the Danubian States themselves and of other European powers, and an appraisal is given of the various possibilities for future development.

PART I

THE EMERGENCE OF THE DANUBIAN COUNTRIES

CHAPTER I

AUSTRIA-HUNGARY'S INTERNATIONAL ECONOMIC POSITION

THE Austro-Hungarian Monarchy consisted of two autonomous halves, the Empire of Austria and the Kingdom of Hungary. The formal connection between them was dynastic, the Emperor of Austria being at the same time the King of Hungary. This relationship was fixed by the so-called "Compromise of 1867," which was a compact between the two nations, determining the individual status of each of them.

Under the terms of the Compromise, each half of the Dual Monarchy had its own administration and its own state budget. Their military and diplomatic affairs, however, were conducted in common, and each of them contributed to the maintenance of the Court and of certain imperial institutions. They also had joint control over the provinces of Bosnia and Herzegovina. In trade matters they were organized as a customs union: commerce between them was free of any formal encumbrances and was facilitated by the fact that they had a common currency. The development of the two countries was, therefore, intimately interrelated, although, as we shall see later on, there were definite and serious conflicts of policy between them.

During the last decade before the World War, important changes took place in the economic position of the Monarchy. The war found it in a state of economic transition, confronted by a number of serious and pressing problems. While the need of solving these particular problems was obviated by the dismemberment of the Monarchy after the war, the conditions which created some of them were, indirectly, bequeathed by the former members of the dual state to their successors.

In its foreign trade and other international transactions, the Monarchy faced a condition which forced it to increase its already enormous foreign indebtedness. In its government finance, it was confronted likewise by a necessity of covering a part of the budgetary expenditures with borrowed funds. In its general economic situation it was face to face with the problem of a rapidly growing population, whose requirements could be satisfied only by industrial development and a general intensification of economic activities—a process that was impeded by internal political difficulties. In this chapter we shall examine these salient features of the economic position of the Austro-Hungarian Monarchy.

I. THE INTERNATIONAL ACCOUNTS

The Austro-Hungarian Monarchy began the twenty-year period preceding the World War with an accumulation of public and private foreign indebtedness. The Monarchy had been a heavy foreign borrower for almost two centuries. Numerous and often disastrous wars in which the Habsburgs had engaged were exceedingly costly and entailed borrowing in other countries. The construction of railways and the financing of economic development generally had to be done with foreign capital.[1]

Interest obligations on accumulated foreign indebtedness required large annual payments. The total foreign indebtedness of the Monarchy in 1890 was about 9 billion crowns.[2] By the end of 1913, it was 9,760 millions. These debts were classified in the official statistics of the Monarchy into three categories: the Austrian debts, including those owed in common by both halves of the Monarchy; the Hungarian debts; and the debts of Bosnia-Herzegovina.

On the eve of the war the foreign obligations of Austria amounted to 5,876 million crowns, of which 2,778 millions represented state debt, including the common debt of the Monarchy. Of the remaining 3,098 millions, foreign holdings of railroad bonds amounted to 1,963 millions, while foreign-held bonds and stocks of various industrial, banking, and commercial enterprises made up the other 1,135 millions. Thus state and railroad bonds constituted more than 80 per cent of Austria's foreign obligations. In the

[1] See Reinitz, Max, *Das oesterreichische Staatsschuldenwesen,* Leipzig, 1913.

[2] The crown was equal to $0.2026.

case of Hungary the situation was somewhat different. Of that country's total foreign obligations on the eve of the war—amounting to 3,784 million crowns—2,273 millions, or only 60 per cent of the total, represented foreign holdings of state and railroad bonds. The foreign debt of the provinces of Bosnia and Herzegovina amounted on the eve of the war to 100 million crowns.[3]

On the other hand, Austria-Hungary had investments in other countries. These investments were estimated at about one billion crowns, and consisted of foreign securities, held mostly by the great Vienese banks. The largest holdings represented German and American securities, next to which in importance came Japanese and Chinese, Turkish, Russian, British, Bulgarian, Rumanian, and French securities.[4]

During the two decades preceding the war, the payments of interest and dividends on Austria-Hungary's foreign obligations were equal to between 300 and 350 million crowns a year. The returns on Austro-Hungarian investments in other countries were estimated at about 40 million crowns. The net outgo for debt payments had to be covered by means of foreign trade balances and income from service operations.

During the twenty years prior to the war Austria-

[3] The debt figures given here are taken principally from Bartsch, Franz, *Statistische Daten über die Zahlungsbilanz Oesterreich-Ungarns vor Ausbruch des Krieges*, Vienna, 1917, pp. 5-45.
[4] *Statistische Daten über die Zahlungsbilanz*, etc., p. 38.

Hungary's trade balance shifted from an export to an import surplus. The table below shows the Monarchy's merchandise trade and specie movement for this period: [5]

AUSTRO-HUNGARIAN FOREIGN TRADE, 1894-1913
(In millions of crowns)

Year	Merchandise [1]			Bullion and Specie			Net Balance
	Exports	Imports	Balance	Exports	Imports	Balance	
Average for 1894–1898	1,554	1,482	+ 72	83	114	− 31	+ 41
1899–1903	1,946	1,711	+235	65	108	− 43	+192
1904	2,182	2,111	+ 71	53	110	− 57	+ 14
1905	2,391	2,213	+178	60	56	+ 4	+182
1906	2,598	2,411	+187	53	43	+ 10	+197
1907	2,658	2,587	+ 71	79	44	+ 35	+106
1908	2,389	2,467	− 78	67	84	− 17	− 95
1909	2,475	2,821	−346	128	237	−109	−455
1910	2,588	2,930	−342	81	43	+ 38	−304
1911	2,582	3,275	−693	133	41	+ 92	−601
1912	2,927	3,670	−743	179	20	+159	−584
1913	2,988	3,509	−521	107	35	+ 72	−449

[1] The figures for 1894-1903 refer only to the special trade of the Austro-Hungarian Customs Union. The figures for 1904-1913 include not only the special trade but also the returns of the so-called "improvement" trade.

During the years 1894-1898, the imports of the Austro-Hungarian customs union averaged 95 per

[5] Figures from *Statistik des auswärtigen Handels,* official annual publication of the Austrian Ministry of Commerce; *Statistical Abstract of Principal and Other Foreign Countries,* Vols. 28 and 38; and Bartsch, Franz, *Statistische Daten über die Zahlungsbilanz,* etc.

cent of the exports. During the following five years the imports were only 88 per cent of the exports. After that, however, the situation began to change. Between 1904 and 1913, the imports increased from 2,111 million crowns to 3,509 millions, or by 1,398 million crowns. At the same time the exports rose from 2,182 millions to 2,988 millions, an increase of only 806 million crowns. In 1904 the imports were 97 per cent of the exports; in 1913 they were 118 per cent.

During the same period Austria-Hungary shipped abroad considerable amounts of gold. Of the ten years only three showed an excess of imports over exports in the movement of gold and specie. The other seven showed net exports, ranging from 4 million crowns in 1905 to 159 million in 1912. The gold reserves of the Austro-Hungarian Bank decreased between 1909 and 1913 from 1,713 million crowns to 1,563 millions.[6]

The income from international service operations increased steadily between 1894 *and* 1913. There were four main sources of such income: (1) emigrant remittances; (2) tourist trade; (3) banking profits and trade commissions; and (4) transit traffic.

Emigrant remittances represented the most important source of international service income. During the decade 1901-1910 alone, over 2,100,000 persons emigrated from the Monarchy to the United States, besides those who went to Canada, Argen-

[6] *Statistische Daten über die Zahlungsbilanz*, etc., p. 91.

tina, and other countries. These emigrants sent large sums of money back to their native land. In 1909 the sums thus transmitted amounted to no less than 200 million crowns. By 1913 the amount had doubled, reaching in that year 408 millions.

Besides these more or less permanent migrations, there was a considerable movement of seasonal labor to Germany. It is estimated that no less than a half-million laborers annually, left the country for a few months. Returning to their native land, they brought back their savings, aggregating, on the average, about 35 million crowns a year.[7]

Income from the tourist trade was also important. Certain portions of the Monarchy, especially Bohemia, contained world-famous health resorts, such as Karlsbad, for example. They drew annually thousands of foreigners. The same was true of certain portions of the Tyrol and of the other mountainous parts of the country. Although there was an offsetting item in the expenditures of Austrians and Hungarians travelling abroad, nevertheless the balance of the tourist trade was in favor of Austria-Hungary, ranging, during the ten-year period preceding the war, between 75 and 100 million crowns a year.

Another important source of international income consisted of banking profits and trade commissions. The Viennese banks did considerable business for various Balkan countries. In many cases they acted

[7] *Statistische Daten über die Zahlungsbilanz,* etc., pp. 65-75.

as commission agents. The sale of goods on commission was done also by some of the large trading firms. These commissions and profits brought into the country considerable amounts of foreign bills of exchange. Altogether, during the years immediately preceding the war, the Monarchy derived from all these sources no less than 100 million crowns a year.[8]

Transit traffic was still another source of revenue. The territory of the Austro-Hungarian Monarchy was crossed by many important trade routes. Vienna and Budapest were great railway centers as well as large Danubian ports. A considerable amount of international traffic passed through them and through a number of other centers. Moreover, Austria-Hungary had a mercantile marine, which was operated at a profit. These transportation operations resulted in net international income for the Dual Monarchy amounting in 1907 to 37 million crowns, and in 1908 to 34 millions. In 1909, the figure rose to 56 millions, and in 1911 it reached 72 millions.[9]

Income from trade and services fully offset the interest obligations only from 1899 *to* 1908. In the following summary statements we bring together all of the principal items of international income and outgo by five-year periods from 1894 to 1913.[10]

[8] This estimate is based on the author's conversations with several bankers in Vienna.

[9] *Statistische Daten über die Zahlungsbilanz*, etc., pp. 58-65.

[10] The estimates given in this statement are based on the data

AUSTRIA-HUNGARY'S INTERNATIONAL INCOME ACCOUNT, 1894-1898
(Totals for the five-year period, in millions of crowns)

Net income from:		
Balance of merchandise trade and gold and specie movement	205	
Emigrant remittances	150	
Tourist trade	200	
Banking profits and trade commissions	200	
Transit traffic	100	
		855
Net outgo for:		
Interest and dividends on foreign indebtedness	1,550	
Less returns from foreign investments.	120	
		1,430
Net outgo for all items		575

Thus for the five-year period from 1894 to 1898, the excess of exports over imports and the net income from service operations was insufficient to cover the interest and dividend payments on the foreign debts. There was a net deficit of 575 million crowns, which was covered by means of foreign borrowing.[11]

During the next five-year period, the situation was different, as may be seen from the following table:

presented above; also on the investigations made by Dr. Ignatz Gruber and published in *Tabellen zur Währungsstatistik,* Part II, Vol. 3, an official publication of the Austrian Ministry of Finance; and *Statistische Daten über die Zahlungsbilanz,* etc.

[11] Dr. Gruber, in a paper read before the Tenth Session of the International Institute of Statistics, estimated the amount borrowed abroad by Austria-Hungary during the decade from 1892 to 1901 at 768 million crowns. See *Bulletin de l'Institut International de Statistique,* Vol. XV, London, 1906, Part II, p. 122.

Austria-Hungary's International Income Account, 1899-1903

(Totals for the five-year period, in millions of crowns)

Net income from:		
Balance of merchandise trade and gold and specie movement	960	
Emigrant remittances	200	
Tourist trade	250	
Banking profits and trade commissions...	300	
Transit traffic	150	
		1,860
Net outgo for:		
Interest and dividends on foreign debts...	1,750	
Less returns from foreign investments..	150	
		1,600
Net income from all items		260

The international accounts for the years 1899 to 1903 showed a net surplus. This was due to a large increase in the excess of exports over imports. An even larger net surplus was shown by the accounts for the next five-year period.

Austria-Hungary's International Income Account, 1904-1908

(Totals for the five-year period, in millions of crowns)

Net income from:		
Balance of merchandise trade and gold and specie movement..................	405	
Emigrant remittances	700	
Tourist trade	350	
Banking profits and trade commissions...	400	
Transit traffic	180	
		2,035
Net outgo for:		
Interest and dividends on foreign debts...	1,750	
Less returns from foreign investments..	150	
		1,600
Net income from all items		435

The increase in the net surplus during the years 1904-1908 was not a result of the trade balances. On the contrary, the total excess of exports over imports was smaller during these five years than during the preceding five-year period. But during the years 1904-1908 there was an increase in emigrant remittances and in other service items, which was more than sufficient to offset the decrease in the trade balance.

During the years 1909-1913 the international accounts again showed a large net deficit:

Austria-Hungary's International Income Account, 1909-1913
(Totals for the five-year period, in millions of crowns)

Net income from:			
Emigrant remittances		1,500	
Tourist trade		500	
Banking profits and trade commissions		450	
Transit traffic		250	
			2,700
Net outgo for:			
Balance of merchandise trade and gold and specie movement		2,400	
Interest and dividends on foreign debts	1,750		
Less returns from foreign investments	200		
		1,550	
			3,950
Net outgo for all items			1,250

During these five years also, there was a very large expansion of income from emigrant remittances. But at the same time, the balance of trade became heavily adverse, with the result that a net deficit of over a billion crowns during this period had to be made up by means of new foreign borrowing.[12]

The change from an export to an import surplus presented a very serious problem to Austria. With an export surplus of about 200 million crowns a year in the period 1899 to 1903, the Dual Monarchy had no difficulty in meeting its foreign payments without resort to borrowing. The diminished excess of exports in 1904-1908 was offset by the increase of emigrant remittances. But in the last five years before the war even the continuing and rapid increase in emigrant remittances proved insufficient to cover the export deficiency.

The primary cause of the steady increase in imports was to be found in the rapid growth of population during this period. As we shall see in the last section of this chapter, it was the growth of population which led to increased consumption requirements and to the inauguration of the program of industrial expansion. The shifting internal situation in its relationship to the changing balance of trade was the subject of much discussion in Austria during this period.[13]

[12] According to *Das Handelsmuseum,* Vienna, May 8, 1913, the Austro-Hungarian borrowings abroad during the years 1911 and 1912 alone amounted to 660 million crowns.

[13] See, for example, Wekerle, Alexander, *Die passive Handelsbilanz,* Vienna, 1913; von Böhm-Bawerk, Eugen, "Unsere passive Handelsbilanz," in *Neue Freie Presse,* Vienna, January 6-8-9, 1914.

II. THE BUDGET AND THE CURRENCY

Austria and Hungary maintained separate budgets, each of them contributing to the common or imperial expenditures and to the service on the imperial debt. Each had an ordinary and an extraordinary budget, the expenditures under the latter being mainly for railroad construction and military needs.

Total budgetary expenditures in Austria and Hungary almost always exceeded government revenues. It is true that the ordinary budgets were drawn up in such a way as to show a balanced condition or even a surplus. But revenue from taxation did not provide the means necessary for covering the extraordinary expenditure.

The table on page 16 shows typical ordinary budgets for both halves of the Monarchy during the twenty-year period preceding the war.[14]

The surpluses yielded by the ordinary budgets were absorbed by extraordinary outlays. But they amounted to only a small part of these special requirements.

During the first half of the period under consideration, the extraordinary expenditures averaged over 250 million crowns a year. During the second half, they amounted to over 400 millions a year. For the whole period, the extraordinary outlays of Austria and Hungary exceeded 6.5 billion crowns,

[14] Figures from *Statistical Abstract for Principal and Other Foreign Countries,* Vols. 28 and 38.

Ordinary Budgets of Austria and Hungary
(In millions of crowns)

I. Austria

Year	Revenues	Expenditures	Surplus
1894	1,321	1,280	41
1897	1,482	1,417	65
1900	1,586	1,585	1
1905	1,815	1,720	95
1908	2,247	2,153	94
1911	2,830	2,653	177

II. Hungary

Year	Revenues	Expenditures	Surplus
1894	951	872	79
1897	1,022	911	111
1900	1,042	957	85
1905	1,015	1,049	34[a]
1908	1,409	1,320	89
1910	1,543	1,419	124

[a] Deficit.

and the major portion of them was covered by means of loans. Between 1894 and 1913 the total government debt of Austria and Hungary (domestic and foreign) increased by 6.2 billion crowns, or by about 50 per cent.

The currency of Austria-Hungary was on a gold basis, although a full gold standard was never in operation. The Austro-Hungarian Bank, under a charter from the governments of Austria and of Hungary, acted as the bank of issue, and upon it devolved the task of maintaining the exchange value of the crown. It did this by means of extensive operations in foreign bills.[15]

The Austro-Hungarian currency was put on the gold basis by the legislation of 1892, which, however, did not go into full effect until 1900. From that time on, the exchange value of the currency was maintained in a fixed relationship with gold, although specie payment did not exist.

The Bank acted for both halves of the Monarchy, which thus had in practice a single currency. Theoretically the two currencies were separate and distinct, the basic unit being officially known as the *krone* in Austria and the *korona* in Hungary.

The Bank was obligated by its statutes to maintain a gold cover of not less than 40 per cent. The remainder of the circulation had to be covered by means of bills of exchange, stocks or shares, deposits of precious metals or paper securities, and foreign bills or notes. Government bills could be discounted only if they bore the signatures of at least two endorsers known to be solvent. The Bank was not permitted to grant any credits or loans to the government.

During the last ten years before the war, the note

[15] For a good description of the Austro-Hungarian Bank and its currency system and operations see *Banking in Russia, Austro-Hungary, the Netherlands, and Japan,* prepared by the National Monetary Commission, 61st Congress, 2nd Session, Senate Document No. 586, Washington, 1911; for a brief history of the Bank see Zeuceanu, A., *La Liquidation de la Banque d'Autriche-Hongrie,* Vienna, 1924, pp. I-XVI.

circulation of the Bank never exceeded 2,800 million kronen, and the metal cover was never under 53.5 per cent.[16] The statutes of the Bank contained a provision whereby the government could compel it to maintain an adequate gold cover. The Bank was obliged to pay a 5 per cent tax on all bank note circulation in excess of the gold cover plus 600 million kronen.[17]

III. THE TREND TOWARD INDUSTRIALIZATION

During the decade preceding the Great War the Austro-Hungarian Monarchy followed a program of industrial expansion. The primary motivating force was the increase in population. As in other European countries, a growing population on a limited area appeared to necessitate an expansion of industry as a means of providing gainful occupation. The national resources of Austria-Hungary were, moreover, such as to favor a policy of industrialization.

The growth of population was outstripping economic opportunity. While the Monarchy possessed large agricultural resources, the increase of rural population could not be absorbed in agricultural pursuits, particularly in view of the restriction of opportunity by the existence of the system of large

[16] Rosenberg, Wilhelm, "The Problem of the Austrian Krone," in *Manchester Guardian Commercial: Reconstruction in Europe Series*, 1922, pp. 147-8.

[17] Rašín, Alois, *Financial Policy of Czechoslovakia during the First Year of Its History*, Oxford, 1923, p. 8.

landed estates. We have seen that during the last decade, emigration to the United States alone averaged over 200,000 a year, while something like one-half million laborers annually sought seasonal employment beyond the country's frontiers. Although some of this emigration was prompted by political causes, the bulk of it was clearly economic in character. The Austrians and the Hungarians were fully conscious of the applicability to their situation of the famous dictum of the German Imperial Chancellor Caprivi, who said on the occasion of his negotiations for some trade agreements, "We must export either goods or men." [18]

Migration did not, however, entirely relieve the population pressure. Additional internal employment opportunities appeared to be necessary, and industrialization provided these opportunities.

The natural resources of Austria-Hungary favored her industrial development. She had the advantage of being practically self-sufficient so far as her basic food-supply was concerned. The two halves of the Monarchy were really economically complementary, and were organized as a customs union. The fertile fields of Hungary produced a substantial surplus of foodstuffs, for which a ready market was found in the industrialized sections of Austria. Hungary shipped 72 per cent of her exports to Austria, and received from the latter 71.5 per cent of her imports.

[18] Hertz, Friedrich, *Die Productionsgrundlagen der oesterreichischen Industrie vor und nach dem Kriege, insbesonders im Vergleich mit Deutschland,* Vienna, 1917, pp. 72-74.

This made it possible for the industrialized sections of the Monarchy to be independent of food imports from outside the frontiers of the customs union, as well as to have an important internal market.

Austria-Hungary was also fairly well supplied with mineral wealth and was not greatly dependent on the outside world for raw materials originating in mining. Her principal imports in the raw material group consisted of textile materials, rubber, hides, and bristles.

Of the separate articles imported by Austria-Hungary, the textile group, consisting principally of cotton and wool, headed the list. This group constituted well over a quarter of the total imports. Then, in the order of importance, came metals and metal manufactures, special foodstuffs and tobacco, hides and leather, and fuels.

Foodstuffs, mostly prepared, rather than raw, constituted the largest single export group, with refined beet-sugar heading the list. The second largest export group consisted of timber and wood products.

But while the industrial development of Austria-Hungary, aided by favorable conditions with regard to natural resources, proceeded at a fairly rapid rate, the domestic requirements of the Dual Monarchy consumed a considerable proportion of the increased output. The growing excess of imports over exports was clearly indicative of this state of affairs.

Austria-Hungary's industrial development just before the World War was very marked. Between

1903 and 1913 the number of factories increased by 40.6 per cent, while the number of industrial workers grew by 45 per cent. The consumption of coal during the same period increased in Austria by 54 per cent and in Hungary by 93 per cent. The consumption of raw iron rose by 90 per cent for Austria and by 83 per cent for Hungary. This expansion of industrial activity in Austria-Hungary compared favorably with the tempo of growth even in such a rapidly developing country as Germany, in which the number of industrial workers increased during the same period by 41 per cent, while the consumption of coal rose by 61 per cent and that of raw iron by 91 per cent.[19]

This rapid industrialization of the country was reflected in the commodity composition of the Austro-Hungarian foreign trade. The table on page 22 shows the development of Austro-Hungarian trade during the years 1904-1913, classified into raw materials, semi-manufactures and finished products, and showing the relation of exports to imports in each group.[20]

It is clear from this table that the imports of raw materials were increasing much more rapidly than the exports. While the former grew during the decade by 747 million crowns, the latter increased by only 58 millions. On the other hand, as

[19] Hertz, Friedrich, *Die Productionsgrundlagen der oesterreichischen Industrie,* etc., pp. 5-13.

[20] Figures from *Statistische Daten über die Zahlungsbilanz,* etc., p. 52.

COMMODITY COMPOSITION OF AUSTRO-HUNGARIAN FOREIGN TRADE, 1904-1913

Broad Classes by Years	Exports		Imports		Balance in Millions of Crowns
	In Millions of Crowns	*As Percentage of Total Exports*	In Millions of Crowns	*As Percentage of Total Imports*	
I. RAW MATERIALS					
1904	861	*41.2*	1,250	*61.0*	− 389
1909	875	*37.8*	1,604	*58.4*	− 729
1913	919	*33.2*	1,997	*58.6*	−1,078
II. SEMI-MANUFACTURES					
1904	314	*15.0*	257	*12.6*	+ 57
1909	406	*17.5*	435	*15.8*	− 29
1913	528	*19.0*	499	*14.7*	+ 29
III. FINISHED PRODUCTS					
1904	914	*43.8*	540	*26.4*	+ 374
1909	1,037	*44.7*	707	*25.8*	+ 330
1913	1,323	*47.8*	911	*26.7*	+ 412

regards semi-manufactures and finished products, the exports and the imports increased almost at the same rate.

The great Vienna banks played a peculiar rôle in the industrial development of Austria-Hungary. Vienna had been for centuries a great trading center and developed financial institutions of considerable importance and extended international connections. When the need of modernizing the economic life of the country led, in the second half of the past century, to the establishment of industry, the savings of the country were too meager to provide the necessary capital. Industry had to be established with foreign capital, which entered the country through the intermediary of the banks of Vienna, the financial center of the Monarchy.

A situation was thus created in which the banks became the controlling element in the industrial life of the country. They continued to retain this rôle, especially since the accumulation of capital within the country was very slow and almost every important step in the industrial expansion of the Monarchy had to be based on the utilization of the international resources and connections of the great banks. But even in these conditions, when the banking interests, because of their very nature, were bound to lay special emphasis on the foreign trade angle of the industrial situation, the Austro-Hungarian exports did not keep pace with the industrial development.

Conflicts of economic policy between Hungary and Austria complicated the process of industrialization. Although the two halves of the Dual Monarchy were organized as a customs union, they did not constitute a real economic entity. Conflicts of regional interests often arose very sharply and were not always easy to compose.[21]

[21] Debates on economic policy in the Parliaments of Vienna and Budapest furnish ample material on this subject. Even within Austria and Hungary there were many conflicts of regional interests, as between Bohemia and Vienna, for example, or between Croatia and Budapest. But the conflict between

Hungary, although primarily an agricultural country, was developing a definite trend in the direction of industrialization. Both the desire to achieve more than a one-sided economic system and a pressure of population were pushing her in the direction of the establishment of her own industries. She was building up a textile industry. Her machine industry, especially in the field of electrical appliances, was rapidly developing an export trade. As we saw above, the rate of increase in her consumption of coal was much greater than Austria's, while the rate of growth in her consumption of raw iron was only slightly less than that of Austria. Direct government subsidies and discriminatory railroad rates were the principal means of stimulating domestic industry.

Side by side with this industrial development, Hungary was also interested in maintaining in Austria a protected market for her foodstuffs and the other products of her agriculture. She was, therefore, always on the side of high agricultural tariffs for the whole Austro-Hungarian customs union.

Austria, on the other hand, having large industrial centers, was watching with growing apprehension the industrialization of Hungary. While she could not prevent it, she was eagerly seeking ways of counteracting its effects upon her own industries.

Vienna and Budapest, as the two capitals of the Dual Monarchy, was clearly the most important of these regional clashes.

There was, for example, a growing body of opinion in Austria in favor of a decrease of agricultural protection.

There was also a latent but very real rivalry between the banking institutions of Vienna and of Budapest. The latter were very eager to establish their own international connections and were often successful in this. At regular intervals agitation flared up in Hungary for the establishment of a National Bank, independent of the Austro-Hungarian Bank.

On the eve of the Great War, the general economic situation in the Austro-Hungarian Monarchy was far from sound. The rapid growth of population increased consumption requirements, and led to a program of industrial expansion which necessitated a great increase in imports. The growth of imports, unaccompanied by an expansion of exports, produced a deficit in the country's international accounts, caused a notable diminution of the gold stock of the Bank of Issue, and necessitated new foreign borrowings. The growth of militarism accentuated the difficulties both in connection with the international accounts and the internal budget situation.

Austria-Hungary sought the way out of this situation through the industrialization of the country. But the process proceeded slowly and was impeded by internal political difficulties and clashes of regional interests which obstructed a free play of economic forces.

Conflicts of policy between the two halves of the Monarchy played an exceedingly important rôle in the situation. While formally united, Austria and Hungary were drifting into a relationship which was bound, sooner or later, to cause very serious economic friction between them. Whether or not they would have been able, in the end, to compose their differences is an open question. The World War and its consequences made it unnecessary for them to face the issue.

The dismemberment of the Austro-Hungarian Monarchy, which we shall discuss in the next chapter, also disposed of most of the other economic problems which confronted the country on the eve of the war. But the problem of population still remained, transferred to each of the new states that rose out of the ruins of the Monarchy.

CHAPTER II

ECONOMIC AND FINANCIAL DISMEMBERMENT OF AUSTRIA AND HUNGARY

THE World War destroyed the Austro-Hungarian Monarchy. Not only did the two halves of the dual state separate from each other, but the Empire of Austria and the Kingdom of Hungary themselves fell apart. Three new states were carved entirely out of the territory of the former Monarchy. These were the new Austria, the new Hungary, and Czecho-slovakia. Besides that, important portions of Austrian and Hungarian territory were joined to Rumania, Serbia, Poland, and Italy. The resources and the liabilities of the Monarchy were partitioned among these seven countries.

In this chapter we shall discuss the various phases of this economic and financial dismemberment of Austria and Hungary, centering our discussion particularly on the three Danubian countries which were carved wholly out of Austro-Hungarian territory. In the next chapter we shall discuss the emergence of the two Danubian cessionaries of Austria-Hungary: Greater Rumania and Yugoslavia.

I. EFFECTS OF THE WAR ON THE AUSTRO-HUNGARIAN MONARCHY

The World War placed a terrific strain on the economic resources of the Dual Monarchy. All the Central Powers operated virtually as component parts of a mammoth war machine, controlled principally from Berlin. Cut off from the rest of the world, they had to rely almost exclusively on their own resources.

Deprived of their imports of raw materials, the industries of Austria-Hungary functioned weakly, except for those branches which supplied war needs. Even so far as food supply was concerned, in which the Monarchy had always been self-sufficient, the war had brought about grave difficulties. The conscription of farm labor and the lack of imported fertilizers resulted in decreased output. At the same time, Germany, finding herself cut off from her Russian and overseas sources of food, was compelled to make pressing demands for food on the Dual Monarchy. All this brought about a shortage of food within Austria and Hungary themselves.

The war caused an almost complete disorganization of Austro-Hungarian finances. In spite of the financial assistance which Germany gave her ally and of the numerous war loans issued by the governments of Austria and of Hungary, the Monarchy found itself compelled to finance the war, to an appreciable extent, by means of the printing press.

One of the first actions of the Austro-Hungarian

government after the outbreak of the World War was the inauguration of a number of exceptional measures with regard to the Austro-Hungarian Bank. By the decree of August 4, 1914, the statute provisions regarding Bank loans to the government and the maintenance of the gold cover were suspended. Bank note circulation increased very rapidly, while the Bank's stocks of gold were used for purchases abroad. The results of this may be seen from the following table.[1]

CIRCULATION AND COVER OF THE AUSTRO-HUNGARIAN BANK, 1914-1918

Date	Circulation in Millions of Kronen	Percentage of Gold Cover
July 23, 1914	2,130	74.6[a]
December 31, 1914	5,137	23.4
" " 1915	7,162	11.5
" " 1916	10,889	3.2
" " 1917	18,440	2.0
October 26, 1918	33,529	1.0

[a] It is interesting to note that the gold cover was still very large at the outbreak of the war, in spite of the heavy exports during the years immediately preceding the war.

At the end of the war 86.7 per cent of the note circulation of the Austro-Hungarian Bank represented loans to the government and about 12 per cent advances to private individuals on war loans. The Bank was obligated to advance to private indi-

[1] Rosenberg, Wilhelm, "The Problem of the Austrian Krone," *Manchester Guardian Commercial,* cited above.

viduals 75 per cent of the par value on the war loan bonds—a practice which proved very embarrassing after the end of the war when the market value of the bonds fell to 60 per cent of par. The Bank was thus, in effect, converting war loans into currency, merely increasing the volume of circulation.

The superabundance of currency in circulation had the effect of destroying all credit transactions. Private borrowings were reduced to a minimum, and there was an enormous increase of deposits in the banks. The interest rate on deposits fell at first to 1 per cent and finally to 0.5 per cent. The government attempted to ease this situation by permitting the Bank to issue 4 per cent Treasury bills. But the proceeds of these issues were turned over to the Treasury and again set into circulation by the latter.[2]

Apart from economic and financial strain, the Monarchy was beset by many difficulties of political and moral character. Made up of a large number of racial and national groups that had, for generations, opposed the policies of Vienna, the Monarchy could not possibly count on the undivided loyalty and support of its people.

The Czechs in Bohemia and Moravia were working for national independence. Their movement was active both within the country and outside. It undoubtedly exerted a very great disruptive in-

[2] Eventually, in 1919, these bills, to the amount of 6.6 billion kronen, were paid off by the Bank by means of freshly issued notes.

fluence upon the affairs of the Monarchy, not only within the country but even in its foreign relations.[3] A similar movement was in progress among the Yugoslavs of Croatia and Slovenia. Moreover, there was a good deal of disaffection against the imperial rule among the Hungarians. The Austro-Hungarian Monarchy held together only as long as the outcome of the war was at all doubtful.

The defeats suffered by the armies of the Central Powers caused the break-up of the Austro-Hungarian Monarchy. The Habsburg dynasty received its death blow on October 22, 1918, when Hungary declared herself independent of the Habsburg Crown. This was followed by similar declarations on the part of the Czechs and Slovaks, and several days later on the part of the southern Slavs. The declaration of independence on the part of the Czechs and the Slovaks disrupted not only the Austrian Empire, but also the Kingdom of Hungary. Of the three principal divisions of Czechoslovakia, two, Bohemia

[3] Dr. Stephen Osuský, the Czechoslovak Minister in Paris, tells in his pamphlet, *George D. Herron; Jeho Práca v Našej Zahraničnej Revolúcii* (Brno, 1925), of secret negotiations conducted in Switzerland in October, 1918, between the Austro-Hungarian Chancellor Lammasch and President Wilson's personal representative, Professor George D. Herron. In the course of these negotiations, Chancellor Lammasch, in the name of Emperor Charles, proposed what amounted to a separate peace between the Dual Monarchy and the Allied and Associated Powers, on the basis, however, of the preservation of the territorial integrity of the Monarchy. These proposals were rejected by President Wilson, because their acceptance would have constituted a violation of pledges given by him to the Czechs. For an English translation of a portion of Dr. Osuský's pamphlet see *The Slavonic Review,* London, March, 1926.

and Moravia, had formerly been parts of Austria, and one, Slovakia, had been incorporated in Hungary.

The political dissociation of the two parts of the Austro-Hungarian Monarchy, thus begun, proceeded very rapidly. Galicia broke away from Austria and was finally included in Poland; Bukovina was similarly severed from Austria to become a part of Rumania; Transylvania passed from Hungary to Rumania; Sub-Carpathian Russia from Hungary to Czechoslovakia; the Hungarian territories of Banat and Baczka passed partly to Rumania and partly to Yugoslavia, the latter receiving also Croatia-Slovenia which had been a part of Hungary, as well as Dalmatia and what is now known as Slovenia, which had been included in Austria, and Bosnia and Herzegovina, formerly held under joint Austro-Hungarian control. Istria, Trentino, and portions of the Tyrol became part of Italy.

II. DIVISION OF AUSTRIAN AND HUNGARIAN RESOURCES

As a result of its dismemberment, the Austrian Empire lost nearly three-quarters of its territory and almost four-fifths of its population. Similarly, the Kingdom of Hungary lost two-thirds of its territory and three-fifths of its population. The following table indicates the disposition of Austrian and Hungarian territory and population.[4]

[4] Exclusive of Bosnia-Herzegovina, ceded entirely to Yugoslavia.

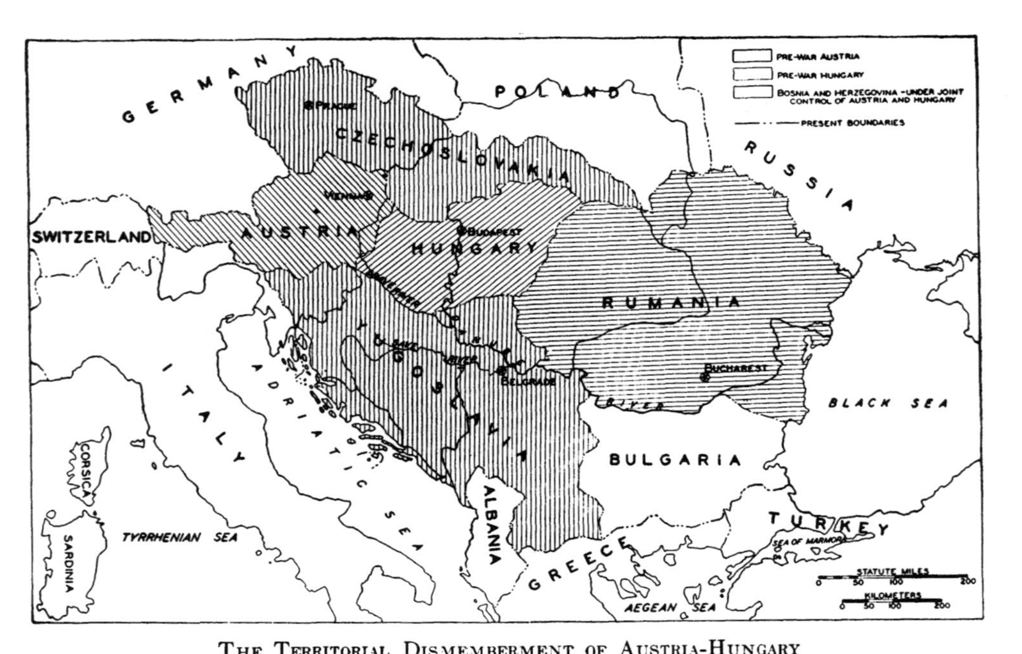

THE TERRITORIAL DISMEMBERMENT OF AUSTRIA-HUNGARY

Division of Austro-Hungarian Territory and Population

Country	Territory in Square Kilometers	Population in Thousands
I. Austrian Empire[1]	300,004	28,572
Retained by present-day Austria.	79,580	6,572
Ceded to Czechoslovakia........	77,834	9,843
" " Rumania	10,441	800
" " Yugoslavia	29,256	1,680
" " Poland	80,309	8,352
" " Italy	22,584	1,544
II. Kingdom of Hungary[2]	324,411	20,886
Retained by present-day Hungary	92,720	7,946
Ceded to Czechoslovakia........	62,937	3,576
" " Rumania	102,787	5,265
" " Yugoslavia	66,497	4,071
" " Austria	5,055	392
City of Fiume..................	21	44

[1] Decoudu, Jean, *Le Partage des dettes publiques autrichiennes et hongroises,* Paris, 1926, p. 15.
[2] *L'Annuaire général de la France et de l'Etranger,* Paris, 1923, p. 867.

Thus Czechoslovakia and Poland received the largest shares of Austria's territory and population. Rumania was the largest recipient of Hungarian territory and population, Yugoslavia and Czechoslovakia coming next.

Austria and Hungary had large and varied economic resources. The national wealth of Austria was estimated at 87 billion crowns, and that of Hungary at 50 billions.[5]

[5] Von Fellner, Friedrich, *Das Volksvermögen Oesterreichs und Ungarns,* Vienna, reprinted from *Rapports de la XIVe Session de l'Institut International de Statistique à Vienne.*

Austria had large coal fields in Bohemia, Moravia, and Silesia, and extensive deposits of iron ore in Styria. Her principal timberlands were in the Tyrol, and her oil fields in Galicia. In the northern and eastern parts of the Empire, principally in Bohemia, Moravia, and Galicia, she had important grain lands and sugar-beet plantations.

On the basis of these resources, Austria built up her industries, locating them largely with respect to natural advantages. Her two great industrial areas were in the vicinity of the Bohemian, Moravian, and Silesian coal fields, and around Vienna and the Styrian Mountains. These were the two principal centers of metallurgy. The textile industry was also centered in Bohemia, Moravia and Silesia, and in Vienna.[6]

Hungary's natural resources, apart from her soil, were not extensive. In her Danubian lands she had some of the finest grain lands in the world and fairly extensive sugar-beet plantations. She also had considerable amounts of timber, principally in the mountains of Slovakia and Transylvania. Neither her coal nor her iron deposits were very large. Coal (principally lignite) was mined mainly in the territory of present-day Hungary and in Transylvania, and iron mostly in Transylvania and Slovakia.

Her industry was located largely in the territory of present-day Hungary, centering around the city

[6] See Layton, W. T., and Rist, C., *The Economic Situation of Austria*, Geneva, 1925, p. 49.

of Budapest. This was true particularly of machine construction, stone, and chemical industries. The textile industry was divided between the city of Budapest and Slovakia, the latter being also the principal center of the paper industry. The wood-working industry was largely in Transylvania.[7]

The pre-war national income of Austria was 14.5 billion kronen, and of Hungary, 7.5 billion. Industry, trade, and transportation furnished two-thirds of Austria's income, and agriculture one-third. On the other hand, agriculture was responsible for about 60 per cent of Hungary's income.[8]

No estimates have been made for the division of this income as between present-day Austria and the new states. For Hungary, it has been estimated that the territory comprising present-day Hungary retained 39 per cent of the national income of the pre-war Kingdom, while Czechoslovakia received 17 per cent, Rumania 22 per cent, and Yugoslavia, 20 per cent. The remaining 2 per cent went to Austria and the City of Fiume.[9]

Czechoslovakia received the largest single share of Austro-Hungarian resources. Within her frontiers

[7] Based on *Mémoire du Gouvernement Royal hongrois concernant la répartition de la dette publique de l'ancienne Hongrie,* Budapest, 1922.

[8] Von Fellner, Friedrich, *Das Volkseinkommen Oesterreichs und Ungarns,* Vienna, 1917, p. 113.

[9] Von Fellner, Friedrich, "Die Verteilung des Volksvermögens und Volkseinkommens der Länder der Ungarischen Heiligen Krone," in *Metron,* Vol. III, No. 2, 1923.

are comprised a little less than one-quarter of the total territory of the former Monarchy and over one-quarter of the whole population. She has the important coal basin of Austria-Hungary and by far the more important of the two industrial areas. The forest wealth of Slovakia is hers, and the sugar plantations of Bohemia and Moravia. She also has some of the best cultivated arable land of the former Monarchy.

Before the war the territories now comprising Czechoslovakia contributed as follows to the total production in Austria-Hungary of the commodities specified:

Commodity	Percentage of Total Value Produced
Sugar	92
Alcohol	46
Beer	57
Malt	87
Chemical products	75
Metals	60
Porcelain	100
Glass	92
Cotton products	75
Woolen products	80
Jute products	90
Leather	70
Gloves	90
Footwear	75
Paper	65

Altogether Czechoslovakia inherited a very large part of the total industrial equipment of the former

Monarchy and a substantial share of Austro-Hungarian natural resources.[10]

Austria and Hungary became mere fragments of their former selves. Together with their losses of territory and population, they also lost some of their most valuable natural resources. Each of them retained an industrial center—Austria, in Vienna and Lower Austria, and Hungary, in and around the city of Budapest—but found itself cut off from sources of principal raw materials and fuel.

The new Austria retained large deposits of iron ore and extensive timber areas. But her metallurgical industry was deprived of its supply of coking coal. The new Hungary retained productive grain lands, but lost all of her timber resources.

Important economic resources were acquired by the four cessionary states. The rich grain lands of Banat and the forests of Transylvania and Bukowina were ceded to Rumania. With Transylvania, that country received also some mineral wealth of various kinds, principally coal, iron, manganese, and salt.

Yugoslavia's share of Austro-Hungarian resources was mainly in the form of grain lands and forests. Her portion of the former territory of the Monarchy contains also some mineral wealth and industrial equipment.

The oil fields of the Austro-Hungarian Monarchy

[10] Císař, J., and Pokorný, F., *The Czechoslovak Republic*, Prague, 1922, Part II, Chapter IV.

went to Poland. The great Adriatic ports became Italian.

III. SEPARATION OF THE CURRENCIES

After the break-up of the Dual Monarchy, the Austro-Hungarian Bank still continued to function, pending the decisions of the Peace Conference. It continued to make 75 per cent advances on war bonds, which sold at a much lower rate in the market, justifying this practice by the fact that it had a guarantee of the Austro-Hungarian government for reimbursement on account of losses incurred in such operations. It even continued to advance newly printed currency to the governments of Austria and of Hungary.

The post-war position of the Austro-Hungarian Bank was extremely anomalous. It was characterized as follows by Dr. Rašín, the Czechoslovak Minister of Finance, in his reply to the Bank's protest against Czechoslovakia's decision to establish its own currency: [11]

> The Austro-Hungarian Bank has become merely a printing press for bank notes, and has ceased to be a bank of issue, whose duty it is, in accordance with the spirit of its Articles, to further the business life of the country.

An attempt to remedy the situation was made when, on the initiative of Dr. Rašín, an agreement was negotiated between the Bank and the govern-

[11] Rašín, A., *Financial Policy of Czechoslovakia,* etc., p. 30.

ments of the new states, under which each of these states received the right to appoint a government commissioner to superintend the affairs of the Bank, while the Bank undertook to grant no state loans without the consent of all the commissioners. Efforts were also made to obtain the Bank's promise to make no more advances on war bonds, but to this it would not agree.

The Bank's persistence in advancing on war bonds more than their market value on the basis of an obligation of a no longer existing government to reimburse its losses, foredoomed the agreement to failure. And when on top of that the Bank agreed to print for the Austrian government 2 billion kronen of new currency, over the protest of some of the other new states, the situation became thoroughly untenable. Without waiting for the decisions of the Peace Conference, the new states decided to take the situation into their own hands and to proceed with the creation of their own currencies.[12]

The first attempt to establish a currency independent of the Austro-Hungarian Bank was made in Yugoslavia. On January 8, 1919, the Ban (Governor) of Croatia issued a decree, ordering the stamping of all the bank notes circulating in the territory under his control.[13]

Czechoslovakia was, however, the first country in

[12] Rašín, A., *Financial Policy of Czechoslovakia,* pp. 16-19.

[13] Steiner, Fritz G., "Vienna as the Exchange Market for the Succession States," in *Manchester Guardian Commercial: Reconstruction in Europe Series,* 1922, p. 37.

which the stamping of the currency to establish its separation was carried out thoroughly and on an extensive scale. Very elaborate preparations were made for the process. On February 25 the Czechoslovak National Assembly in a secret session passed a law empowering the Minister of Finance to stamp all Austro-Hungarian notes in circulation in the country. That night the Czechoslovak frontiers were placed under military guard to prevent the smuggling of notes, and all postal communications with foreign countries were suspended for two weeks.

The actual stamping of the notes took place between March 3 and 9. From that time on only stamped notes were legal tender on Czechoslovak territory. At the same time the Czechoslovak government took over the branches of the Austro-Hungarian Bank found on its territory, and the separation of the Czechoslovak currency from the Austro-Hungarian Bank was complete in practice, although the legal basis for the establishment of a separate Czechoslovak currency was provided only by the law of April 10, 1919.[14]

One of the results of the stamping of currencies in Yugoslavia and Czechoslovakia was an influx of unstamped notes into Austria, which compelled the Austrian government to take a similar step several days after the process was completed in Czechoslovakia. Hungary followed suit several months

[14] For a graphic description of the stamping process see Rašín, A., *Financial Policy in Czechoslovakia,* pp. 25-43.

later, upon the collapse of her Soviet régime. Poland did the same at the beginning of 1920.

The Peace Conference formally approved the separation of the currencies. By the time the Conference reached in its discussions the question of the disposition of the Austro-Hungarian Bank, the separation of the currencies was an already accomplished fact, and nothing remained for it but to provide for the liquidation of the Austro-Hungarian Bank.[15] This was done by Article 206 of the treaty of St. Germain and Article 189 of the treaty of Trianon.

The treaties provided that the liquidation of the Austro-Hungarian Bank was to begin on the next day after the treaties went into effect. In view of the delay in the ratification of the treaty of Trianon, the liquidation did not actually begin until September 1, 1920, when the receivers appointed by the Reparation Commission, under the authority of the treaties, formally took control of the affairs of the Bank.

The work of liquidation lasted almost four years. It was only on July 31, 1924, that the liquidation accounts were finally closed and the Austro-Hungarian Bank officially ceased to exist.[16]

[15] For an authoritative study of the Austro-Hungarian currency situation during and immediately after the war by a former Governor of the Austro-Hungarian Bank see Popovics, Alexander, *Das Geldwesen im Kriege*, Vienna, 1925.

[16] Zeuceanu, A., *La Liquidation de la Banque d'Autriche-Hongrie*, is a detailed and authoritative narrative of the long and complicated work of the Bank's liquidation by one of the receivers appointed by the Reparation Commission.

IV. DISTRIBUTION OF THE PRE-WAR DEBTS

The dismemberment of the Austro-Hungarian Monarchy necessitated a distribution of its huge public debt among the states which had arisen on its territory and the states which had received parts of its territory. As we have already seen, each half of the Monarchy had its own public debts. Then there were debts for which Austria and Hungary were jointly responsible. Finally, the debts of Bosnia-Herzegovina were in a special category. Distribution had to be made of both the foreign and the domestic debts in all four of these categories.

The basic principles for the distribution of the debts were laid down by the treaties of peace. In almost identical language, the treaties of St. Germain and of Trianon made provisions for the determination of the amounts to be distributed, and the assessment of liability as among the seven states responsible for the debts.[17]

War debts were left out of account entirely. Only the pre-war debts were considered as subject to distribution. These debts were divided into secured and unsecured, and special provisions were made for the treatment of each category.

Secured debts, that is debts for which railways or

[17] See Article 203 and Annex of the treaty of St. Germain and Article 186 and Annex of the treaty of Trianon. The seven states in question are Austria, Hungary, Czechoslovakia, Rumania, Yugoslavia, Poland, and Italy, the first two known officially as the "Succession," and the last five as the "Cessionary," states.

similar properties had been specifically pledged, were to be charged against the states on whose territory the pledged property happened to be. If a certain property securing a certain debt was located entirely on the territory of a single state, then that state was to assume sole responsibility for the debt. If a property, such as a railway, for example, stretched across frontiers, then each of the states involved was to assume responsibility for a portion of the debt corresponding to the actual share of the property found within its frontiers.

Unsecured debts were to be divided among the various territories on the basis of the contribution made by each territory before the war to the revenues of the Austro-Hungarian Monarchy. In this manner each of the seven succession and cessionary states would become responsible for a certain percentage of each debt. But this responsibility would be only nominal, an important modification of it being introduced by a further provision of the treaties.

Each of the states was obligated by the treaties to call in for stamping all the bonds of the Austro-Hungarian Monarchy found within its territory. Each of the states then was to become responsible to its citizens for all the bonds held within its territory. The actual responsibility of each of the countries was then to be fixed on the basis of a comparison, for every debt, between the amount of the bonds stamped in any given country and the general percentage of liability assigned to that country by the method described above.

The actual work of distributing the debts was left by the treaties of peace to the Reparation Commission. In the performance of this task, the Commission was guided as far as possible by the principles laid down in the treaties, although in many instances it had to exercise its own discretion.

The problem of dealing with secured debts was comparatively simple. Whenever any particular pledged property was found entirely within the frontiers of a single country, the whole debt based on the pledge was assigned to that country. In the case of railways, the kilometric length of all the lines involved was used as the basis of distribution.

The problem of unsecured debts was much more complicated. The treaties provided that the distribution of these debts should be in accordance with "the ratio between the average for the three financial years, 1911, 1912, and 1913, of such revenues of the distributed territory and the average for the same years of such revenues of the whole of the former Austrian (or Hungarian) territories as in the judgment of the Reparation Commission are best calculated to represent the financial capacity of the respective territories." The Reparation Commission based the apportionment of liability on the principal direct and indirect taxes of Austria and Hungary, on stamp and registration duties, and, in the case of Hungary, also on the salt monopoly.

As a result, liability for the Austrian debts was apportioned as follows:

Austrian Republic	36.827	per	cent
Czechoslovakia	41.700	"	"
Poland	13.733	"	"
Italy	4.087	"	"
Yugoslavia	2.043	"	"
Rumania	1.610	"	"

Similarly the debts of Hungary were distributed as follows:

Present Hungary	49.629	per	cent
Rumania	23.659	"	"
Czechoslovakia	17.384	"	"
Yugoslavia	6.800	"	"
Austria	1.716	"	"
State of Fiume	0.812	"	"

In exchange for all the Austro-Hungarian bonds presented to it for stamping, the government of each succession or cessionary state gave new bonds issued by itself. These new bonds were in the currency of the issuing country. For Austro-Hungarian bonds expressed in crowns the rates of exchange were fixed as those existing for each particular country at the date of the establishment by it of a separate currency. Austro-Hungarian bonds expressed in foreign currencies or in gold were exchanged for bonds similarly expressed.

Each government issued bonds to the full amount of the percentages apportioned to it. If the amount of bonds stamped by it was less than that, the excess was delivered to the Reparation Commission, which distributed these excess bonds among those countries in which the amount of stamped bonds exceeded the new issue based on the apportioned percentages.

The interests of foreign holders of Austro-Hungarian bonds were handled by the Innsbruck and Prague Conferences. The protocols signed at these conferences settled the question of the amounts to be paid to foreign holders, the manner in which payments are to be made, and the agency through which these payments are to be distributed.

The Innsbruck protocol, signed June 29, 1923, dealt with one Austrian and one Hungarian gold annuity and one Austrian and two Hungarian loans expressed in various currencies. For the gold annuities it provided a reduction of interest payments to 32 per cent of the original amounts, and for the loans in various currencies to 27 per cent of the gold value. These reductions are to apply until 1931, when they may become subject to revision.

The protocol also dealt with the service on the bonds originally issued by the Chartered Company for the Austrian and Hungarian State Railways (STEG). It provided a scheme whereby interest and amortization payments on three bond issues of the Company would be assured for all holders, even the nationals of the succession and cessionary states.

The collection of interest payments on all these loans and their distribution among the holders of bonds were placed by the protocol in the hands of a

Joint Office of Foreign Holders of Bonds of the Austrian and Hungarian Pre-War Public Debts. This Joint Office is located in Paris and is financed by contributions from the seven debtor states.

The Prague protocol, signed November 14, 1925, constituted agreement on the apportionment of liability for the debts covered by the Innsbruck protocol as proposed by the Reparation Commission. It also amended the Innsbruck protocol in certain letails.[18]

[18] For the details of the work of the Reparation Commission with respect to the distribution of the Austro-Hungarian debts, see the following publications of the Commission: *Distribution of the Pre-War Austrian and Hungarian Debt*, Document VII, and *Accord de Prague;* for a critical study of the principles laid down in the peace treaties with regard to the apportionment of liability, see Sack, A. N., *Le Mode de répartition des dettes autrichiennes et hongroises,* Paris, 1927; also the same author's "Die Verteilung der Schulden der oesterreichisch-ungarischen Monarchie," in *Zeitschrift des Instituts für Weltwirtschaft und Seeverkehr,* April, 1926; and Decoudu, Jean, *Le Partage des dettes publiques autrichiennes et hongroises.*

CHAPTER III

RUMANIA AND SERBIA BEFORE AND AFTER THE WAR

In the preceding chapter we discussed the dismemberment of the Austro-Hungarian Monarchy and described, in general outlines, the size and resources of the New Austria, the New Hungary, and Czechoslovakia—the three states which were carved entirely out of the territory of the Austro-Hungarian Monarchy. In this chapter we shall deal with Rumania and Yugoslavia, each of which originated primarily in a union of a small pre-war Kingdom and portions of the territory of the former Monarchy.

The pre-war Kingdoms of Rumania and Serbia were of recent origin. For centuries they had been parts of the Ottoman Empire and were under Turkish overlordship until formally freed by the Congress of Berlin in 1879. As a result of the World War each of them received important cessions of territory from both Austria and Hungary. Rumania acquired also the Russian province of Bessarabia, while Serbia received a small strip of Bulgarian territory and absorbed also the Kingdom of Montenegro. While from the point of view of international law, Greater Rumania and Yugoslavia are thus merely expansions of pre-war Rumania and Serbia, economically they are entirely new countries in which the original small kingdoms have become parts of larger national units.

I. RUMANIA

Rumania began her independent existence in a very primitive economic condition. A predominantly agricultural country, endowed with fertile soil, she nevertheless experienced great difficulties because of a lack of economic organization and especially of means of transportation. Almost immediately after securing political independence, Rumania began to seek foreign loans which would provide her with the means of building up her economic life. "Rumania is borrowing for the purpose of making herself independent," was the way the Rumanians formulated their policy when they opened the negotiations for their first railroad loan.[1]

Rumania was a foreign borrower from the early eighties to the outbreak of the World War. The construction of railways and the general economic development of the country required large imports of machinery and materials, especially during the last two decades of the nineteenth century. The exports during this period were insufficient to pay

[1] Badulesco, Victor V., *Les Finances publiques de la Roumanie*, Paris, 1923, p. 54.

for the imports, and the deficit was covered by means of foreign borrowing. After the turn of the century, exports began to exceed imports, but at so slow a pace that the accumulation of foreign indebtedness necessitated outlays for payments of interest and amortization, which usually exceeded the export surpluses.

The following table shows Rumania's foreign trade during the thirty-five-year period immediately preceding the World War: [2]

RUMANIA'S FOREIGN TRADE, 1890-1914
(In millions of lei)

Year	Exports	Imports	Balance
Average for			
1880–84	215	291	− 76
1885–89	260	312	− 52
1890–94	300	407	−107
1895–99	249	344	− 95
1900–04	325	275	+ 50
1905–09	469	394	+ 75
1910	617	410	+207
1911	692	570	+122
1912	642	638	+ 4
1913	671	590	+ 81
1914	452	504	− 52

Thus the total excess of imports over exports between 1880 and 1899 was 1,650 million lei. The government debt contracted during this period

[2] Figures from *Les Forces économiques de la Roumanie*, Bucharest, 1920, and the *Statistical Abstract for the Principal and Other Foreign Countries*, Vols. 17, 28, and 38. The Rumanian currency was the *leu* (plural *lei*), equal to the gold franc.

amounted to about 1,300 millions.[3] The remainder of the trade deficits and the interest payments on the debts during this period were probably made up out of the proceeds of private investments in Rumania and of floating indebtedness.

By 1914 the total foreign debt of the Rumanian government was between 1,500 and 2,000 million lei.[4] Foreign private investments in Rumania were estimated at about 500 millions.

The reason for this increase in the foreign debts lay in the fact that the export surpluses were too small to cover all foreign payments. These payments, during the years immediately preceding the war, were as follows: [5]

Interest on foreign debt	100
Dividends on foreign investments	75
Tourist and other expenditures	45
Total	220

The amount indicated above was offset somewhat by the country's income from emigrant remittances

[3] According to Freiherr von Brackel, *Rumäniens Staats-Kredit*, Munich, 1902, pp. 82-3, the consolidated government debt of Rumania on March 31, 1902, was 1,358 million lei.

[4] Dr. S. Radulescu, in his *La Politique financière de la Roumanie depuis 1914*, Paris, 1923, Vol. I, p. 88, and Dr. Badulesco, in his *Les Finances publiques de la Roumanie*, p. 54, place the total debt at about 1,500 million lei; in *Les Forces économiques de la Roumanie* the total debt is estimated at 1,800 millions; Professor I. N. Angelescu, in his essay on "Public Finance and the Monetary Situation in Rumania," published in *The Economic Situation and Organization of Rumania in 1926*, places the total debt at about 2 billions.

[5] G. Cioriceanu, in *Revue Economique Internationale*, March 10, 1925, estimates the interest payments on the foreign debt at 80 million lei. This figure appears to be too low.

and foreign expenditures in Rumania. But even so, it was only in such exceptional years as 1910, when the favorable balance of trade was about 200 million lei, that the country could meet out of its own resources all of its foreign obligations. Generally speaking, resort had to be had to new borrowings.

The budgetary situation was satisfactory only during the decade immediately preceding the war. Up to 1905 expenditures exceeded revenues almost every year. From 1905, however, until the outbreak of the war the ordinary budget was not only in balance, but even showed annual surpluses, as may be seen from the table given below.

RUMANIAN BUDGET, 1905-1914 *
(In millions of lei)

Year	Revenues	Expenditures	Surplus
1905	279	233	46
1906	292	239	53
1907	308	216	92
1908	446	395	51
1909	459	418	41
1910	507	448	59
1911	575	465	110
1912	567	488	79
1913	609	512	97
1914	568	540	28

* Figures from *Les Forces économiques de la Roumanie.*

These surpluses were absorbed by extraordinary and supplementary credits. But on the whole,

Rumania was not confronted by any fiscal difficulties during the years immediately preceding the war.[6]

Rumania continued until the World War to be primarily an agricultural country. The production of foodstuffs constituted the occupation of the bulk of her population, while shipments of cereals and their derivatives represented about two-thirds of her total exports. In 1913 her principal exports were as follows, in millions of lei:

Cereals and derivatives	448
Petroleum products	131
Vegetables and fruit	34
Timber products	24
Other exports	34
Total	671

Petroleum products appeared among Rumania's exports only a comparatively short time before the war. The petroleum industry was, however, expanding rapidly. Side by side with the development of the petroleum industry there was also in Rumania a growth of other industrial activities, such as flour-milling, etc. This was reflected in the imports of metals and machinery. Between 1890 and 1913 the value of this import group increased almost tenfold. So rapid was the expansion of metal and machinery imports on the eve of the war that their amount doubled between 1910 and 1913.[7]

[6] For a discussion of Rumania's pre-war budgetary situation see Radulescu, S., *La Politique financière de la Roumanie,* Vol. I.

[7] A part of this increase was due, no doubt, to the requirements of the Balkan wars.

The following table shows, in millions of lei, Rumania's principal imports in 1913:

Metals and machinery	232
Textiles, clothing, etc	136
Chemicals and explosives	45
Wooden wares	23

The total imports for the year were 590 million lei. Therefore metals, machinery, and textiles accounted for almost two-thirds of the country's imports.

The World War crushed Rumania, but out of it emerged Greater Rumania, the largest of the Danubian countries. Rumania did not enter the war until 1916, but it was, soon after that, overrun by the armies of the Central Powers. At the request of the Allied Powers, the Rumanian government ordered the destruction of the oil wells in order that they should not fall into the hands of the invaders. The major portion of the Rumanian gold reserve was removed to Moscow for safe keeping; it fell later on into the hands of the Soviet government and became lost to Rumania. Supplies of food and all other materials that could be utilized for war purposes were seized by the invaders.

The occupation authorities paid for all requisitions with paper money which they themselves issued. In this manner the country became flooded with worthless paper currency.[8]

[8] For the condition of Rumania during the war see Berindey, Alexandre, *La Situation économique et financière de la Roumanie sous l'occupation allemande,* Paris, 1921.

Greater Rumania, as she emerged from the war, includes the old Kingdom of Rumania, portions of Hungarian and Austrian territory, and the Russian province of Bessarabia. She has a territory of 294,-892 square kilometers and a population of over 17 millions. The table below shows the territory and population of each of these parts of the new Kingdom:.[9]

TERRITORY AND POPULATION OF GREATER RUMANIA

Components	Territory in Square Kilometers	Population in Thousands
GREATER RUMANIA	294,892	17,154
Old Kingdom	137,903	7,897
Transylvania and Banat	102,125	5,488
Bessarabia	44,422	2,957
Bukowina	10,442	812

The economic wealth of Greater Rumania is large and varied. To the agricultural resources of the old Kingdom have been added the rich grain fields of Bessarabia and Banat. Bukowina and the mountains of Transylvania contain extensive forests. Transylvania also contains many minerals and some industrial equipment, which, together with the oil fields of the old Kingdom, give Greater Rumania some basis for industrial development.

[9] Figures from Bell, H. T. Montague, *The Near Eastern Year Book,* London, 1927. For general information about Rumania see also Bowman, Isaiah, *The New World,* Chapter XV, and Szende, Julius, *Die Successionstaaten,* Budapest, 1924.

II. SERBIA

Like Rumania, Serbia began her independent existence in a very primitive economic condition. Also an overwhelmingly agricultural country, she lacked everything that would help in the utilization of her soil. But she faced an added handicap in the fact that her economic life was dominated by an outside power. Serbia's whole history, from the time of her liberation from Turkey to the outbreak of the World War, was taken up with a bitter struggle against determined attempts made by the Austro-Hungarian Monarchy to absorb her economically.

For the first twenty-five years of her independent existence Serbia was under Austro-Hungarian economic domination. Prior to her achievement of political independence in 1879, Serbia's foreign trade was under the virtually monopolistic control of Austria-Hungary—this state of affairs having resulted from the latter's arrangements with Turkey. Almost 100 per cent of Serbia's imports and about three-quarters of her exports passed through the hands of her powerful northern neighbor. And even after 1879, the Monarchy never ceased in her attempts to maintain this control.[10]

One of Serbia's first actions after securing her independence was the conclusion, in 1879, of a

[10] This sketch of Serbia's economic history is based principally on Stojanović, Costa, *La Serbie économique à la veille de la catastrophe de 1915*, Paris, 1919; the same author's *The Commerce of Serbia; a Historical Sketch and Survey*, Rome, 1919; and Nestorović, Ivan Z,, *Der Aussenhandel Serbiens*, Leipzig, 1913.

provisional trade agreement with Great Britain on the basis of most-favored-nation treatment. Austria-Hungary protested against this agreement, demanding for herself special trade privileges and threatening Serbia with reprisals in the form of a 10 per cent duty on all Serbian products imported into the Monarchy. After some struggle, Serbia satisfied the Austro-Hungarian demands, and in 1880 a treaty was concluded between the two countries, which was accompanied by a secret convention whereby Serbia undertook to conclude no trade treaties without the consent of Austria-Hungary. This clause was somewhat modified later on, but it virtually dominated Serbia's foreign trade relations until 1906. Thus there was practically a customs union between the two countries, Austria-Hungary enforcing her position by a repressive use of veterinary inspection against Serbian livestock exports whenever Serbia exhibited any signs of freeing herself from control.

From 1906 *to* 1911 *Serbia was in a state of commercial war with Austria-Hungary.* During the year preceding the outbreak of this war, Serbia made her first attempt to break away from Austro-Hungarian control. While negotiating with the Monarchy for a new commercial treaty, she also entered into negotiations with Bulgaria for the formation of a customs union between them. These latter negotiations were successful, and a convention was drawn up which was promptly ratified by the Bulgarian

Parliament. When this fact was announced, however, Austria-Hungary broke off her negotiations with Serbia, demanding from the latter a choice between herself and Bulgaria. In response to this demand, Serbia rejected the Bulgarian convention and resumed negotiations with Austria-Hungary. But the negotiators failed to reach an agreement, and in the summer of 1906 the Austro-Hungarian frontiers were closed to most Serbian products. This embargo lasted for two years.

Negotiations were inaugurated once more in 1908 and resulted in the signing of a convention, which was followed by a reopening of the Austro-Hungarian frontiers. But the convention failed of ratification, the Austro-Hungarian frontiers were closed to Serbia once more and the new embargo lasted until January 1, 1911, when a commercial treaty between the two countries was finally concluded and went into effect.

The period of commercial war with Austria-Hungary proved to be a turning point in the economic life of Serbia. During these five years, she succeeded in concluding commercial treaties with nearly all European countries and in effecting profound changes in both the commodity composition and the geographical distribution of her foreign trade.

During the three decades under review the predominance in Serbia's export trade shifted from livestock to cereals. The following table indicates these changes in the composition of Serbia's export trade.

COMPOSITION OF SERBIA'S EXPORT TRADE
(Figures are in percentages of total values)

Broad Classes	1881–1893	1894–1905	1906–1911
Livestock	42.2	38.2	10.0
Animal products	8.8	13.1	15.5
Fruit	24.9	18.3	17.7
Cereals	19.5	22.6	39.7

Up to the time of Serbia's break with Austria-Hungary, livestock played a predominant rôle in Serbian exports. This was due to the requirements of the Austro-Hungarian market. But the situation changed radically after that market was closed to Serbia. Livestock constituted 42.2 per cent of the total exports in 1881-1893, and 38.2 per cent of the total for 1894-1905; but in 1906-1911 it was only 10 per cent of the total exports. On the other hand cereals, which during the first decade and a half of Serbia's independent existence furnished only 19.5 per cent of the country's exports, contributed almost 40 per cent after the establishment of the Austro-Hungarian embargo.

The shift in markets was also marked. In 1881-1893, Austria-Hungary's share in Serbia's foreign trade was 93 per cent of exports and 60 per cent of imports. In 1894-1905, it was 84 per cent of exports and 66 per cent of imports. But between 1906 and 1911 it was only 30 per cent of exports and 35 per cent of imports. Even in the year 1911, when full trade relations were re-established between Serbia and Austria-Hungary, the latter's share in Serbian foreign trade was only 48 per cent of exports and 47 per cent of imports.

A considerable part of Serbia's exports shifted to Germany, which in 1911 took 29 per cent of the total. Similarly some of Serbia's purchases also shifted to Germany, the latter's share in Serbian imports in 1911 being 31 per cent.

On the import side of the principal commodities were manufactured goods, among which textiles and machinery were the most important.

Serbia was generally able to meet her foreign obligations out of her own resources. From the early nineties to the outbreak of the Balkan wars, her exports exceeded her imports, as may be seen from the following table: [11]

Serbia's Foreign Trade, 1881-1911
(In millions of dinars)

Year	Exports	Imports	Balance
Average for 1894–1905..........	61	46	+15
1906..............	72	44	+28
1907..............	82	71	+11
1908..............	78	76	+ 2
1909..............	93	74	+19
1910..............	98	85	+13
1911..............	117	115	+ 2

[11] Serbia's unit of currency was the *dinar,* equivalent to the gold franc.

Thus the excess of exports over imports fluctuated between 2 and 28 million dinars, depending upon crop conditions so far as grain was concerned, and the operation of the Austro-Hungarian veterinary inspection in the case of livestock. Prior to the nineties of the past century, Serbia's imports exceeded her exports, although the adverse balance of trade was not very large. From 1881 to 1893 the adverse balance of trade averaged one million dinars a year.

At the outbreak of the World War, Serbia had a foreign debt of about 850 million dinars. A part of it had been inherited from the Ottoman Empire, and this debt together with the various borrowings of the early years of the country's independent existence, was consolidated by means of a Conversion Loan, issued in 1895 for 355 million dinars. For over a decade after that, Serbia's foreign borrowings were very small, but in 1909 she floated a loan of 150 million dinars for the purpose of railroad construction and army equipment. Finally, in 1913 she borrowed 250 million dinars for the purpose of liquidating the costs of the Balkan wars.[12]

The payments on Serbian foreign loans prior to 1909 amounted to a little over 20 million dinars a year. After that year they were slightly in excess of 25 millions. The favorable balances of trade and emigrant remittances were generally sufficient to

[12] Nedeljković, M., "The Public Debt of Yugoslavia," *The Near East Year Book*. See also Simić, Milan, *La Dette publique de la Serbie de l'origine à la guerre de 1914*, Paris, 1925.

cover these payments, other items in the Serbian international accounts being practically negligible.

Serbia faced a difficult budgetary situation during the years preceding the war. Her total expenditures, ordinary and extraordinary, usually exceeded her revenues, and the deficits had to be made up by means of borrowing, principally in the foreign markets.

The following table shows the total revenues and expenditures in the ordinary budget for the Kingdom of Serbia: [13]

SERBIAN BUDGET, 1901-1911
(In millions of dinars)

Year	Revenues	Expenditures	Balance
1901	74.0	73.1	− 0.9
1902	70.6	73.0	− 2.4
1903	70.6	73.0	− 2.4
1904	89.2	89.1	+ 0.1
1905	88.0	87.6	+ 0.4
1906	89.2	89.0	+ 0.2
1907	90.5	90.5	0.0
1908	95.8	95.8	0.0
1909	103.6	103.3	+ 0.3
1910	115.3	115.1	+ 0.2
1911	120.1	120.1	0.0

No figures are available as to the extraordinary budget, which comprised principally expenditures for military equipment and for the waging of wars. There is no doubt that the outlays for these purposes

[13] Figures from Stošović, D., *Godišnjak Kraljevina Srba, Hrvata i Slovenaca,* Belgrade, 1926.

were very considerable. They were principally responsible for the creation of the state debt.

Serbia emerged from the World War a component part of the Kingdom of Serbs, Croats, and Slovenes. When the war broke out, the lines of her own economic development had not as yet been clearly determined. She had passed successively through a period of political subjection to Turkey, of economic vassalage to the Austro-Hungarian Monarchy, of a bitter commercial struggle with her powerful northern neighbor, and of the two Balkan wars. She emerged from these wars with her territory increased by 80 per cent and her population by 50 per cent. She was just at the beginning of the process of welding her old and her new territories into an economically united whole, when the first shot fired upon her capital by the Austrian batteries from across the Danube served as the signal for the World War.

Early in the war the territory of Serbia was completely overrun by the armies of the Central Powers, which remained in occupation until the Armistice. This long period of occupation completely disorganized the economic life of the country, and its re-establishment became a part of the process of economic organization in the new triune kingdom.

This new country, which is popularly known as Yugoslavia, or the land of the southern Slavs, is a patchwork of territories formerly held under several sovereignties. It has an extent of 248,987 square kilometers, and a population of about 12 millions. It consists of the old Kingdoms of Serbia and Montenegro, portions of territory acquired from Austria and from Hungary, and Bosnia and Herzegovina, formerly held jointly by Austria and Hungary. The territory and population of each of these parts of the new Kingdom are shown below: [14]

TERRITORY AND POPULATION OF YUGOSLAVIA

Province	Territory in Square Kilometers	Population in Thousands
YUGOSLAVIA	**248,987**	**12,017**
Serbia	95,667	4,130
Montenegro	9,668	200
Bosnia and Herzegovina	51,199	1,890
Dalmatia	13,245	650
Croatia	43,309	2,711
Slovenia	16,197	1,056
Voivodina	19,702	1,380

The economic character of Yugoslavia is predominantly agricultural. In the mountainous portions of the country there are considerable timber and mineral resources. In Croatia, Yugoslavia has a certain amount of industrial equipment.

[14] Figures from Bell, H. T. Montague, *The Near Eastern Year Book*. For general information about Yugoslavia see also Bowman, Isaiah, *The New World*, Chapter XIV, and Szende, Julius, *Die Successionstaaten*.

CHAPTER IV

DANUBIAN STATES AS NATIONAL ENTITIES

THE circumstances under which the new Danubian States were formed determined, to a large extent, the general lines of the national policies pursued by each of them. Three of these states—Czechoslovakia, Rumania, and Yugoslavia—were on the side of the victors in the war, and were, therefore, the gainers as a result of the treaties of peace. The other two—Austria and Hungary—were among the defeated nations and, consequently, the losers. In the nature of things, the first three countries have been vitally interested in maintaining the situation produced by the treaties, while the latter two have been just as vitally interested in changing it.

The outcome of the war and the revolutionary explosion which broke up the Austro-Hungarian Monarchy left behind them an atmosphere of bitterness and mutual distrust which found expression in definitely nationalistic and isolationist policies. Many factors of both political and economic character played an important part in the shaping of these policies. In this chapter we shall examine these factors and their bearing on the development of the

Danubian States as national entities, as well as the efforts which have been made for the establishment of closer economic relations among these states.

I. FACTORS MAKING FOR NATIONALISM

Czechoslovakia, Rumania, and Yugoslavia, the three victor countries of the Danubian group, were, from the very beginning, imbued with fears lest their new status might not prove permanent. These fears permeated their whole national life, and they were enhanced by the spirit which was only too apparent in the defeated countries.

The defeated countries showed no signs of accepting the peace settlements as final. Austria, Hungary, and Bulgaria signed the treaties of peace under protest. And although this spirit of resentment and opposition took different forms in each of the three countries, the attitude of all of them was disquieting to their victorious neighbors.

Resentment against the peace settlements was sharpest in Hungary. The separation of Slovakia and especially of Transylvania was a great blow to Hungary, particularly because each of these territories contains large numbers of Hungarians—over a million and a half in Transylvania alone. For several years after the signing of the peace treaties, Hungary refused even officially to consider these territories as permanently lost to her. For example, the official statistics of Hungary's trade with Rumania and Czechoslovakia distinguished between trade with "territories separated from Hungary" and "the rest of Rumania" or "the rest of Czecho-slovakia." Hungary was bitterly outspoken in her determination to regain the lost territories.

In Austria the opposition to the treaties of peace centered around the conviction that the Republic of Austria created by the treaty of St. Germain was not capable of independent existence. Austria had no hopes of a territorial adjustment that would enlarge her as a country. Her desires were directed rather toward a union with Germany, which was forbidden by the treaty, except by consent of the League of Nations Council, and opposed by the victor countries.

With this as the spirit of the defeated countries, the victors felt their position as far from being secure, in spite of the fact that the effective disarmament of the defeated countries made any actual military danger practically non-existent. Hungary, with her violent and undisguised opposition to the peace settlements, was the focal point of their apprehensions, especially since Hungary became the center of the efforts made for the restoration of the Habsburg dynasty.

Fear of Habsburg restoration stimulated nationalist policy in the victor countries. Ex-Emperor Charles made no effort to restore the Austrian throne. But he made two definite attempts, in 1921, to regain the throne of Hungary. The victor countries felt that with a Habsburg monarch again on her throne, Hungary would be an even more insistent claimant for the return to her of the territories which had been separated from her by the treaties of peace.

Under the shadow of this fear, the victor countries applied themselves with great vigor to the creation of military establishments. Moreover, by means of a series of defensive alliances among themselves, Czechoslovakia, Rumania and Yugoslavia created a loose political organization known popularly as the Little Entente, the main purpose of which is to maintain among the Danubian States the situation created by the treaties of peace.[1]

Military considerations increased the intensity with which the victor countries developed their nationalist policies. The newly created countries sought safety in isolation from their former overlords and in the development of a strong nationalist spirit. The necessity which confronted each of them of welding into a unit more or less heterogeneous territories and groups of population also urged them in the same direction.

The pressure of domestic problems in the new countries played an important part in the development of intense nationalism. The territories which comprise Czechoslovakia had formerly been under two sovereignties; those which make up Rumania, under three; those which are incorporated in Yugoslavia, under five. While in each of these countries, the majority of the population is of similar racial

[1] See Mousset, A., *La Petite Entente*, Paris, 1923; also "The Foreign Policy of the Little Entente," in *The Slavonic Review*, April, 1927.

stocks, the influence that had been exerted on the various groups, even of the same racial stock, by different former masters was great enough to necessitate considerable adjustment. Moreover, each of the countries acquired more or less significant racial minorities—Germans, Hungarians and Ruthenians in Czechoslovakia; Hungarians, Germans, Russians, and Ruthenians in Rumania; a large number of groups in Yugoslavia. It was no easy matter to make nations out of all these groups, and their very heterogeneity made the majority group in each country all the more determined on an intensely nationalist policy.

The territories which each of the new countries acquired from different sovereignties had been part and parcel of the national life of the countries to which they had belonged. All their activities had been oriented in the same direction as those of their former masters. Their schools, for example, had been parts of the educational systems of the countries of their former allegiance; so that it became necessary for each of the new countries to create its own national system of education. Similarly all cultural institutions had to be redirected.

Even more important problems confronted the new countries in the sphere of economic activity. This was equally true of the victorious and the defeated nations. Each of the former found itself compelled to create a new economic organization out of the various segments of its territory; each of the latter faced the necessity of adjusting its economic life to its contracted territory and resources.

The problem of communication presented an outstanding difficulty. In Czechoslovakia, for example, the railroads of the territories that had formerly been parts of Austria were directed generally toward Vienna, while those in the territories that had been Hungarian were directed toward Budapest. Both groups of railroad lines had to be reoriented mainly toward Prague. The situation in Rumania and Yugoslavia was even worse. Similarly the channels through which the component parts of the new countries had directed their trade had to be changed. Their financial affiliations had to be transferred to the banking centers of the countries of which they had become parts. All these stupendous tasks of internal reorganization had to be carried on in conditions of economic and financial disorganization which the new countries had inherited from the war and the break-up of the Austro-Hungarian Monarchy.

In nationalism the new countries sought salvation from economic disorganization. The war had exhausted them. Its strain had been felt in all parts of the former Monarchy, as well as in the two Balkan kingdoms. Financially, each of the new countries inherited an empty treasury. Economically, each took over a badly operating equipment, broken up into artificial parts as a result of the new territorial adjustments.

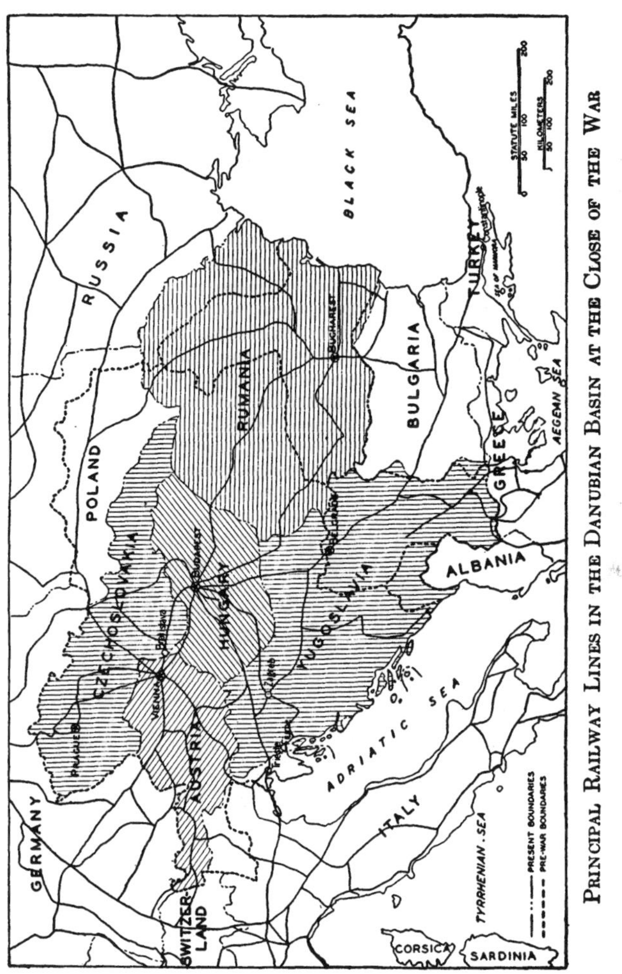

PRINCIPAL RAILWAY LINES IN THE DANUBIAN BASIN AT THE CLOSE OF THE WAR

The new countries, victors and vanquished alike, found themselves compelled to close their frontiers against each other so far as the movement of essential commodities was concerned. In this they were merely following the system which had become established in the Austro-Hungarian Monarchy during the war. For some time before the end of the war, the Monarchy had really split up into territories in each of which local authorities did everything in their power to impede the outflow of commodities, especially foodstuffs and raw materials. So scarce were supplies in all the new countries that the governments saw as their best policy the retention within their borders of whatever stocks were found there.[2]

For reasons of financial adjustment also a policy of isolation was deemed best by the governments of the new countries. The task of establishing new currencies and of maintaining some sort of control over foreign exchanges was felt to be facilitated by strict mutual isolation.

In this, as in everything else that the new countries did during the initial stages of their independent existence, the atmosphere of mutual distrust and of political fears played an exceedingly important rôle. In the minds of the racial groups which broke away from the Habsburg dynasty and consti-

[2] Austria, although, as we shall see from our discussion of her situation in Chapters V-IX, opposed to isolationist policies, was also compelled, by force of circumstances, to adopt most of the measures employed by the other states.

tuted themselves independent states, political independence appeared most precarious without economic independence. Beyond the pressing economic and financial needs of the moment, which forced them into a condition of almost complete isolation from each other, they saw, as a vital necessity, such an economic organization as would leave each of them more or less independent of Vienna, which to them had been not only the political, but also the all-powerful economic and financial capital of the Monarchy.

Desire to break away from the economic domination of Vienna was another powerful stimulant toward a policy of nationalism. The fear of Vienna as a dominant economic and financial center was felt in Hungary, as well as in Czechoslovakia, Rumania, and Yugoslavia, although in the three latter states there was in addition also a desire to break the connection between those portions of their territory which had been taken from Hungary and the banking influence of Budapest.

The policy of "nostrification" was adopted by the three victor states. Under this policy, an attempt was made by the governments of these countries to free all enterprises found within their frontiers from the control of Vienna and Budapest. This was done by making it illegal for any enterprise operating, for example, in Czechoslovakia to have its managing seat located in Vienna, as had been the common practice in the Monarchy.

It was particularly in the field of banking that special efforts were made to apply this policy. Each of the new countries was eager to have its own financial center, free from the powerful influence of Vienna, in order that the economic life of the country would not be dominated from abroad.

Ideas of economic self-sufficiency found ready acceptance in the new countries. There is, no doubt, a close connection between the policy of "nostrification" and the determination on the part of the non-industrialized countries of the Danubian group to build up their own industries, although the greatest impulse to this development probably grew directly out of the policy of economic isolation which was pursued by the new countries at the beginning of their independent existence.

As we saw above, the great industrial centers of the former Monarchy had been located in Bohemia and in the Vienna district, with a smaller center in and around Budapest. Of the new states, therefore, Czechoslovakia and Austria retained the bulk of the industrial equipment. But this equipment found itself cut off from a large part of its former market. The policy of economic isolation which was pursued by the new countries at the beginning of their independent existence prevented both the flow of foodstuffs and raw materials from the agricultural to the industrialized countries, and the flow of manufactured goods in the opposite direction. Industries sprang up almost sporadically in the Danubian territory in localities other than the great industrial centers of the former Monarchy.

The notion that political independence was incompatible with economic dependence on foreign countries took deep root in the new Danubian countries. It acted as a powerful stimulus to industrial development in the primarily agricultural countries of the Danubian group, and found its principal expression in the commercial policies of these countries.

II. DEVELOPMENT OF COMMERCIAL POLICY

The new states came into existence in a condition of almost complete chaos so far as trade was concerned. As a matter of fact, toward the end of the war trade had become almost non-existent, and the exchange of prime necessities of life was handled by governmental authorities. This system was inherited by the new states and continued by them for several months. It applied not only to domestic distribution, but also to foreign trade. Only gradually did it give way to a system of government regulation in trade, and finally to the re-establishment of ordinary processes of trade. Thus there have been three distinct stages in the development of commercial policy among the Danubian States.

Intergovernmental barter took the place of international trade during the initial period of the existence of the new states. Dearth of supplies was one of the reasons for this continuation of the system that had become established during the war. But there were other reasons, too. Almost a year elapsed between the end of the war and the definite fixing of the new countries' frontiers. This rendered exceedingly difficult the establishment of customs administrations. Moreover, each of the countries had to create or entirely reorganize its institutions of government, and it appeared that the control of the movement of commodities from one country to another could best be handled by means of direct distribution from the centers. Finally, the chaotic condition of currency and exchange rendered trade almost impossible.

Exports and imports were handled by governments directly in agreement with other governments. This system extended to all the countries of Central and Eastern Europe. For example, Austria agreed to supply Czechoslovakia with magnesite and certain manufactures, in exchange for which Czechoslovakia agreed to supply Austria with sugar; Poland and Czechoslovakia agreed to exchange oil and potatoes for sugar and manufactured articles; Yugoslavia and Poland arranged for an exchange of tanning materials for oil. It was in effect a system of barter among governments.

This system lasted through the year 1919. It could not, of course, continue long, because as conditions of life became better organized the system of intergovernmental barter proved to be less and less adequate to supply the needs of the population.

In 1920 it gave way to another method of governmental regulation of foreign trade.

Quota agreements characterized the second stage in the development of commercial policy among the new states. Direct government handling of exports and imports was gradually discontinued, and a system of licences was introduced in its place. In this manner the governments still retained a rigid control over the amounts and character of goods entering and leaving their respective countries, but left the actual process of importing and exporting the commodities to merchants. The volume of trade between countries was regulated by agreements, which specified the kinds and the amounts of goods for which licences were to be issued.

Trade among countries was thus re-established, but was regulated on a different basis from that which had existed before the war. Under pre-war conditions, foreign trade was considered free, except as it was obstructed by customs duties and by regulations of public safety and sanitary nature. Under quota agreements in the new states, trade was forbidden, except as it was specifically allowed by means of licences issued by the respective governments.

Customs tariffs as means of regulating foreign trade were still in the background. But as the various countries perfected the organization of their domestic affairs, the way was opened for a return to the system of foreign trade regulation that had existed before the war. Although keeping in force many of the trade restrictions established under the system of quota agreements, the new countries began to introduce effective tariff legislation.

By 1921 *the Danubian countries definitely returned to the system of customs tariffs and ordinary commercial treaties.* This was the beginning of the third stage in the development of their commercial policy. By that time, Czechoslovakia and Austria had done a great deal toward the removal of the artificial trade restrictions which had characterized the first two stages in the development of their commercial policy. Other countries, notably Hungary, on the contrary, introduced still further restrictions. Nevertheless, the year 1921 definitely marked a return to the tariff system.

Czechoslovakia, Austria, and Hungary continued the old Austro-Hungarian tariff, modifying it to the extent of mechanically increasing customs duties in accordance with their respective exchanges. Yugoslavia adopted the old Serbian tariff, with some modifications, while Rumania reintroduced the tariff system of the pre-war kingdom, also adjusting duties to the exchange.

These were admittedly merely makeshift arrangements. The Austro-Hungarian tariff had been designed to satisfy the economic needs of the whole Monarchy in its relations with the rest of the world. As re-enacted by the three states that had been carved out of the territory of the former Monarchy, and applied by them against each other, it could scarcely answer their requirements. Similarly, differences in the economic character between Yugoslavia and the pre-war Kingdom of Serbia, and between Greater Rumania and the pre-war kingdom, rendered the old Serbian and Rumanian tariffs scarcely suited to the needs of the two new states. But such as they were, the tariffs introduced by the Danubian States in 1921 marked real progress over the primitive systems of barter and quota agreements, and opened the way for the development of a real commercial policy.[3]

The change from quota to customs regulation of foreign trade was very gradual. It required several years for the Danubian countries to work out new tariff systems in which the duties would be more or less well adjusted to the actual economic conditions. In most of the countries new tariffs were introduced in 1924 and 1925. In the meantime many restrictions continued to be maintained, some of them being in force even to this day.

The Brussels and the Genoa conferences played an important rôle in the restoration of normal commercial practices. These two parleys, held respectively in 1920 and 1922, were convoked for the purpose of examining the abnormal economic conditions created in Europe by the war and its after-

[3] See Hodač, Francis, "The Tariff Arrangements of the Succession States," in *The Manchester Guardian Commercial: Reconstruction in Europe Series,* July 27, 1922; and Hantos, Elemér, *Die Handelspolitik in Mitteleuropa,* Jena, 1925.

math. Their discussions and resolutions went far toward directing the fiscal and commercial policies of the new states into the channels of time-tested practices.

The International Financial Conference held in Brussels dealt principally with questions of currencies and government budgets. But it also called attention to the fact that the financial recovery of Europe would be impossible without far-reaching economic adjustments in the domain of both production and trade. In its resolutions on international trade, the conference stated that "improvement of the financial position largely depends on the general restoration as soon as possible of good-will between the various nations." In stating this, the conference had in mind particularly the new states of central and eastern Europe. It devoted a good deal of attention to the situation in these countries, which had already caused considerable worry to the Allied Supreme Council, and endorsed the following declaration made by the Council on March 8, 1920:

> The states which have been created or enlarged as a result of the war should at once re-establish full and friendly cooperation, and arrange for the unrestricted interchange of commodities in order that the essential unity of European economic life may not be impaired by the erection of artificial economic barriers.

Two years later, the League of Nations, which was the initiator of the Brussels Conference, followed up the work done in Brussels by sending out a questionnaire addressed to all the participating powers, in which information was asked as to the application of the recommendations made by the conference. The answers to these questionnaires received from the Danubian countries indicate the extent to which the work of the Conference influenced commercial policy in most of them.[4]

The Genoa Conference was equally outspoken in urging upon the new countries a policy of greater trade facilities. Neither of these conferences had a decisive effect on the commercial policy of the Danubian countries, but they both, nevertheless, exerted an influence in the direction of treaty arrangements looking toward freer trade intercourse.

The Danubian tariffs are partly protectionist and partly "bargaining" in character. They differ from country to country, but on the whole each of them represents protectionist tendencies, although some countries are much more insistent in this respect than others. Broadly speaking, the tariffs of Czechoslovakia, Austria, and Hungary have been directed primarily toward protection of industry, while the tariffs of the other states have had in view the protection of currency as well. They all, however, have been drawn up on the basis of high levels of duties with the frank intention of using these levels for bargaining purposes in the negotiation of trade agreements and commercial treaties.

[4] See *Brussels Financial Conference: The Recommendations and Their Application,* League of Nations document, Geneva, 1922.

In later chapters, in connection with each of the Danubian countries, we shall discuss the peculiarities of the various Danubian tariffs and of the commercial treaties concluded on the basis of them. The negotiation of these treaties has had an important influence on the question of whether or not the isolationist policies of the Danubian countries can give way to closer and more amicable relations among them.[5]

III. EFFORTS TOWARD CLOSER RELATIONS

Side by side with the development of isolationist policies in the Danubian States, several attempts have been made to establish more friendly relations among them. The initiative in this movement has come primarily from Austria. Many groups in the remnant of the former Austrian Empire which has become the Republic of Austria were convinced from the start that their country if more or less isolated from its neighbors, is incapable of independent economic existence. The Austrian representatives at the Peace Conference urged this view on the Allied Powers in an attempt to obtain their consent for a union between Austria and Germany.

[5] For a general discussion of the Danubian tariffs and commercial treaties see Layton, W. T., and Rist, C., *The Economic Situation of Austria*, Part II, Chapter III; Hantos, Elemér, *Die Handelspolitik in Mitteleuropa*, Chapters II and III; and annual *Reports* on commercial and financial conditions in the various Danubian countries, published by the British Department of Overseas Trade. See also Page, T. W., *Memorandum on European Bargaining Tariffs*, Document of the Preparatory Committee for the International Economic Conference, Geneva, 1927.

Failing in this, they turned their attention to the possibility of reconstructing some sort of economic unity for the territories that had formerly comprised the Austro-Hungarian Monarchy.

The treaties of peace made provision for the establishment of close economic relations among some of the new states. By the economic clauses of the treaties of St. Germain and Trianon, Austria and Hungary are obligated to grant complete equality of commercial treatment to the Allied and Associated Powers, but there is an important exception made in this connection in favor of their relations with each other and with Czechoslovakia. This exception is stated in the following terms in the treaty of St. Germain: [6]

> Notwithstanding the provisions of Articles 217 to 220, the Allied and Associated powers agree that they will not invoke these provisions to secure the advantage of any arrangements which may be made by the Austrian government with the governments of Hungary or of the Czechoslovak State for the accord of a special customs régime to certain natural or manufactured products which both originate in and come from those countries, and which shall be specified in the arrangements, provided that the duration of these arrangements does not exceed a period of five years from the coming into force of the present treaty.

This provision of the peace treaties was never invoked in the case of Hungary. Austria and

[6] Article 222, which is identical with Article 205 of the treaty of Trianon, except that in the latter the words "Hungarian government" are substituted for the words "Austrian government" and vice versa.

Czechoslovakia made an unsuccessful attempt to apply it almost at the end of the period specified in the treaties. But there is no doubt that the existence of this provision, coupled with other circumstances, opened the way for the discussion of the problem of closer economic relations among the Danubian States.

The possibility of a Danubian economic union began to be discussed soon after the war. At the beginning, the union was generally regarded as more or less in the nature of a forlorn hope. The whole trend of developments seemed to be in precisely the opposite direction. The intense nationalism of the victor states and their ever-present fears of a possible resumption by Vienna of a dominant economic and financial rôle, beyond which they saw the dangers of renewed political control, loomed up as insuperable obstacles to any possible success of the scheme. At the same time Hungary was becoming more and more determined in her policy of remaining aloof from Austria, which she had regarded as an enemy in the past, and from the three victor states, which she considered as her despoilers and consequently as her enemies.

But in the meantime there developed a growing realization among the new states of the fact that whatever advantages there may be in the policy of severe trade restrictions, that policy also carries with it very serious disadvantages. After all, whatever the policy, the Danubian countries had to trade with each other. They had always exchanged products, and they still needed each other as markets. Gradually it became possible for the groups which were working for closer economic relations to convince the governments of the new states that the question of the removal of some of the restrictions was at least worth discussing in a conference comprising the representatives of all of them.

The Portorose Conference of November, 1921, was the result. While the questions on the agenda of the conference were very largely of a technical and detailed nature, hope was expressed in many quarters that the outcome of the discussion would be some progress in the direction of an economic unification of the Danubian countries.

The Portorose Conference was the first important attempt to establish better economic relations among the Danubian States. It consisted of representatives from Austria, Hungary, Czechoslovakia, Rumania, Yugoslavia, Poland, and Italy—the heirs of the former Austro-Hungarian Monarchy—as well as from Great Britain and France. The United States was represented by an observer.[7] It was called for the purpose of considering the questions of commercial relations, including import and export

[7] The conference was largely due to the energetic initiative of the American observer, Colonel Clarence Browning Smith, who, as the American representative on the Reparation Commission in Vienna, had long urged upon the governments of the new states the necessity of such a meeting. See Shotwell, James T., "The Portorose Conference," in *International Conciliation,* July, 1922.

prohibitions, postal and telegraph relations, and transport.

The conference drew up a general protocol, and a number of agreements, arrangements, and recommendations. Of by far the greatest importance among the instruments negotiated at Portorose was the general protocol, which embodied the principles on which the economic relations among the new states were to be based. Article I of this protocol reads as follows:

> The governments of the States represented by the signatory delegates shall, as soon as possible, take the steps necessary to re-establish freedom of imports and of exports in the relations between their several countries. In any case, they shall abolish all import prohibitions or restrictions on July 1, 1922, at the latest, and shall, before that date, make arrangements among themselves to fix, by common consent, a date whereon all export prohibitions, control, or other restriction affecting the exportation of any merchandise, shall be abolished.* * * It is agreed, moreover, to avoid customs legislation which would establish customs duties or other taxes, equivalent to actual import or export prohibitions.

The protocol provided for exceptions to this general principle by recognizing restrictions imposed for motives of public safety and for sanitary reasons, as well as for reasons "emanating from the relations of the above indicated States with other States." It also recognized the validity of restrictions for goods subject to a state monopoly or to domestic measures. The states signatory to the protocol further agreed to enter into negotiations with each other for the purpose of concluding commercial treaties "based, in principle, on commercial freedom," not to impose any further trade restrictions, and, pending the abolition of restrictions, to inaugurate measures looking toward the mitigation of the existing conditions.[8]

The Portorose protocol failed of ratification by the states whose representatives had negotiated it. In this manner the conference disappointed both the immediate and the larger hopes of its initiators. No such concerted action for the abolition of trade prohibitions and restrictions and for the inauguration of negotiations for commercial treaties as was envisaged by the conference took place. As we have already seen, some of the new countries had already begun to abolish or mitigate trade restrictions; they continued their activities in this direction. Some of the others, on the contrary, placed new restrictions in the way of their export and import trade.[9] On the whole, the Portorose Conference left the relations among the Danubian States very much as they had been before it met. The three victor states, although bound together politically by the Little

[8] For the text of the protocol and of the other decisions of the Portorose Conference see *International Conciliation,* July, 1922.

[9] See page 369. The Hungarian government, for example, in its reply to a questionnaire sent out by the Secretariat of the League of Nations, stated: "Up to the present, no other Succession State has ratified, still less put into force, the agreements (of the Portorose Conference), and Hungary cannot be expected to take the initiative in this respect, on account of her exceedingly serious economic position." See *Brussels Financial Conference: The Recommendations and Their Application,* p. 92.

Entente, still continued to be more or less isolated from each other economically. And the relations between them, on the one hand, and Austria and Hungary, on the other, continued to be unfriendly both politically and economically.

In the course of the years 1922-1924, however, a series of important events took place, which served to improve very appreciably the relations among the Danubian States. The financial collapse of Austria and Hungary resulted in a direct intervention in the Danubian affairs of the League of Nations, and this proved to be an extremely important factor.

The intervention of the League of Nations in Austria and Hungary helped to improve relations among the Danubian States. In order to bring about their financial reconstruction, it was necessary that the two countries be freed from their reparation obligations. Any action along these lines undertaken by the Reparation Commission had to be approved by Czechoslovakia, Rumania, and Yugoslavia. All this required a change of general attitude as between the victorious and the defeated Danubian countries.

Austria, in order to secure international financial assistance, had to renew her solemn pledge, already made under protest at St. Germain, not to seek union with Germany, or with any other power. The unreconciled attitude of Austria on this matter had been a source of considerable worry to her victorious neighbors, who were apprehensive lest Austria by making an attempt to unite with another power should upset the *status quo* established by the treaties of peace.[10] The terms on which Austria accepted the League's assistance served to calm down at least this phase of the strained atmosphere pervading the Danubian States.

Similarly, Hungary, as a part of the terms on which she received international financial assistance, renewed her pledges not to seek territorial changes. This also served to assuage the fears on the question entertained by the victor states. Altogether the relations between Hungary and her neighbors improved very noticeably as a result of the terms on which her financial reconstruction had been accomplished.

Two attempts to improve relations among the Danubian States were made in 1925. Both originated in Austria. One was an attempt made by the Austrian government, through the instrumentality of the League of Nations, to establish a preferential customs régime between Czechoslovakia and Austria. The other was the convocation in Vienna of an unofficial conference for the purpose of discussing the pressing economic problems of Central Europe.

The negotiations for a preferential customs régime between Austria and Czechoslovakia were directly in line with the provisions of the peace treaties

[10] Just before the League intervened in her affairs, Austria made an attempt to negotiate an economic union with Italy.

which we noted above. True, the attempt was made at the very end of the five-year period specified in the treaties, but it was a movement in the same direction. There was, however, a complicating element in the fact that Italy insisted on also being party to the arrangement. The principal discussions took place at Geneva, and the scheme under consideration involved the establishment of a preferential customs régime between Austria and Italy, and between Austria and Czechoslovakia. Thus two separate agreements were proposed, the result being that the relations between Italy and Czechoslovakia were left out of account. The negotiations failed completely.

The Central European Economic Conference, held in Vienna September 8-9, 1925, was an attempt to push to the fore the question of the necessity for the countries of Central Europe of some sort of an economic arrangement that would make for closer relations. The conference passed a resolution on the subject, in which it declared:

> The Central European Economic Conference considers as one of the principal evils of the central European economic situation the continuing isolation of the economic systems of small States.

The conference proposed the creation of a permanent commission which would make a thorough study of the whole complex question of economic relations of central European States and prepare the ground for the creation of a central European economic union.[11] Since 1925 several similar conferences have been held.

Such, in general outlines, have been the principal efforts to establish better and closer relations among the Danubian States. As we examine, in the chapters which follow, the problems and the experience of the individual states, we shall describe the part that each of them played in these various efforts and its particular attitude towards the whole question of economic nationalism and economic unity.

[11] For a description of the conference see Dolberg, Richard, *Die Mitteleuropäische Wirtschaftstagung*, Vienna, 1925.

PART II

AUSTRIA'S EXPERIENCE SINCE THE WAR

CHAPTER V

THE PROBLEMS OF AUSTRIA

THE Republic of Austria began its existence under a number of extremely heavy handicaps. Its share of the Austrian Empire's territory was 26.5 per cent, and of the Empire's population, 23 per cent. With almost one-third of its population compressed in the city of Vienna, with every phase of its economic life disrupted, the new country faced what appeared to be insurmountable economic difficulties, which were further complicated by veritable political chaos.[1]

The break-up of the Austro-Hungarian Monarchy left the territory of the new Austria in a tragic economic condition. For over a year prior to the Armistice, this territory, especially the city of Vienna, had been experiencing a chronic food shortage. The Imperial government, which had been steadily growing weaker, found its authority less and less effective for compelling Hungary and the other granaries of the Monarchy to ship food to the capital and its adjacent territory. This process of already

[1] For a description of the changes produced in Austria by the process of dismemberment, see Bowman, Isaiah, *The New World*, Chapter XI.

developing economic dissociation was completed by the political break-up of the Monarchy.

When the new states, as one of their first acts of political self-assertion, closed their boundaries to any exports of food and other necessities of life, the territory of the Austrian Republic found itself cut off from some of its most important sources of supplies. Austria's supply of coal had been derived from the mines of Silesia and Bohemia, while her requirements of petroleum had been filled from the oil fields of Galicia. All these sources of fuel suddenly became almost inaccessible to her by the closing of the new Czechoslovak frontiers. The same was true of many of the basic raw materials needed in her industries.

Bad as was the situation in the whole of Austria, the condition of the city of Vienna was even worse. As the political and economic center of the whole Monarchy, the huge capital city had aroused special enmity on the part of the formerly subject—now liberated—national groups. Whereas formerly it had extended its power and influence over the whole territory of the Monarchy, it now found itself suddenly isolated. Even in the rest of the Austrian territory, there existed this same feeling against Vienna. The provinces of the new Austrian State themselves erected barriers against a flow of supplies into their own capital.

The situation in Vienna was still further aggravated by the influx of Austrians who had formerly occupied administrative and other positions in those portions of the Empire which had seceded from it. While this influx was counter-balanced by an exodus from Vienna of hundreds of thousands of Czechs, Hungarians, Croatians, etc., who hastened to join their respective liberated national groups, it nevertheless added to the population of the capital considerable numbers of impoverished refugees.

The economic life of Austria was practically at a standstill. Industry, trade, and transportation were all badly affected. Unemployment was almost universal, and starvation could be prevented only by assistance from abroad, with the central government assuming the duty of providing for the population at least a minimum maintenance. Relief credits were granted by the Allies, principally Great Britain and the United States, as well as by some of the neutrals, and aggregated, during the first two years of new Austria's independent existence, over $100,000,000.[2] The feeding of the population, undertaken by the state, constituted a truly crushing burden on the government budget.

The principal political difficulty that confronted Austria was the antagonism between Vienna and the provinces. Racially an almost homogeneous state, the Austrian Republic faced at the beginning a con-

[2] These credits came in 1919 from individual governments and in 1920 through the International Committee of Relief Credits, established in Paris in April of that year. According to the *Minutes* of the Meetings of the Committee (Vol. II, p. 155), the total credits extended amounted, at the exchange rate of October, 1921, to a little over 26 million pounds sterling.

flict of sectional interests. It required a great deal of effort to work out an arrangement whereby a central government could be set up in Vienna. The country was finally organized into a federal republic, and the weakness of the central government has had a profound influence on Austrian affairs.

It was only gradually that the chaos of the first few months following the end of the war gave place to more orderly conditions. During the years 1920 and 1921 the political system of the new Austria became more or less consolidated, but the economic situation in the country was steadily going from bad to worse. These economic difficulties finally culminated in the crisis of 1922, which was followed by intervention by the League of Nations, and the inauguration of the League scheme for the financial salvaging of the country. Finally, in 1926, the League control was withdrawn and Austria regained most of her economic freedom.[3]

During the first nine years of its existence (1919-1927), the Republic of Austria faced five major economic problems. These were: (1) a continuous excess of outgo over income in its international accounts; (2) unemployment; (3) currency disorganization; (4) an unbalanced budget; and (5) shortage of operating capital. Some of these pressing current problems she has now solved, but back of

[3] For a vivid description of the economic plight of Austria during the first years of the country's existence see Bauer, Otto, *Die Oesterreichische Revolution;* also, de Bordes, J. van Walre, *The Austrian Crown,* London, 1924, Chapter I.

them there has ever loomed up the question of whether or not Austria, as organized by the treaties of peace, is capable of independent economic existence. After the transformation of the large Austrian Empire into the tiny Austrian Republic, the conviction became widespread in Austria that the country could not exist economically. Prior to the signing of the treaty of St. Germain, the Austrian leaders made earnest attempts to achieve a union between their country and Germany. Their attempts failed, and the Republic of Austria was formally proclaimed. But the question still remained, and it has flared up at intervals. The whole economic policy of the Austrian Republic has been dominated by this outstanding question, closely connected with which has been the peculiar problem presented by the city of Vienna, the disproportionately large capital of the country.

CHAPTER VI

AUSTRIA'S FISCAL AND CURRENCY REHABILITATION

THE most spectacular features of Austria's experience have been in connection with the country's currency. In Part I we discussed the financial dismemberment of the Austro-Hungarian Monarchy and the process by which separate currencies were established in the various Danubian States. We saw there that the currency of the Austrian Republic came into existence in March, 1919, when the stamping of the Austro-Hungarian notes circulating on its territory was completed. In this section we shall examine Austria's monetary history since that date.

From the first half of 1919 to the second half of 1922 Austrian currency was continuously depreciating. During some parts of this period depreciation proceeded slowly; at other times, the exchange value of the crown fell with a catastrophic rapidity. All through this period it was the state budget that constituted the principal, though not the sole, cause of constantly expanding circulation and the consequent depreciation of the currency. The currency question in Austria, is therefore, inextricably tied up with that of the budget, and the two are examined together in this chapter.

There have been so far two great periods in the vicissitudes of Austrian public finance. The first extends to the end of 1922, when the League of Nations reconstruction scheme began to be put into effect; the second begins with the inauguration of the League scheme and extends until the present time. As regards the currency, the first period is one of depreciation, while the second is one of stabilization. As regards the budget, the first period is one of constantly increasing deficits covered by means of new issues of paper money, while the second is the period of gradual attainment of budgetary equilibrium.

I. STATE BUDGET AND CURRENCY DEPRECIATION

The budgetary situation of the Austrian Republic during the first four years of its existence may be seen from the table on page 102, in which the total figures for receipts, expenditures, and deficits are expressed in paper crowns.[1]

During the first three years of the existence of the Austrian Republic budgetary revenues were never sufficient to cover even one-half of the expenditures of the State. During the first six months of 1919 only one-third of the expenditures were covered by actual revenues. During the next twelve months, the ratio between receipts and expenditures

[1] De Bordes, J., *The Austrian Crown*, p. 22.

AUSTRIAN BUDGETS, 1919–22
In millions of paper crowns

Period	Receipts	Expenditures	Deficit	*Percentage of Expenditures Covered by New Issues of Paper Money*
January 1–June 30, 1919 [a]	1,339	4,043	2,704	*67*
July 1, 1919–June 30, 1920	6,295	16,873	10,578	*63*
July 1, 1920–June 30, 1921	29,483	70,601	41,118	*58*
July 1–December 31, 1921 [a]	24,075	49,496	25,421	*51*
January 1–December 31, 1922	209,763	347,533	137,770	*40*

[a] Period of six months.

rose slightly, as it did also during the twelve months following. During the last six months of 1921 there was a rather sharp change in the relation between receipts and expenditures, the former rising to as much as 50 per cent of the latter, while in 1922 the ratio was still higher. Difficulties of tax collection, as well as large expenditures were responsible for the deficits.

Social burdens undertaken by the state constituted the principal cause of the huge budgetary deficits. There were several such burdens which weighed heavily upon the state budget. These were: unemployment and food relief, low prices of commodities sold by the state, low fares charged by the state railroads and the maintenance of a large number of government officials.

Unemployment was especially heavy in Austria during the first half of 1919. In May of that year the number of persons receiving government aid was 186,000—a figure never exceeded during the following five years.[2] This number decreased by the end of the year to 87,000, and continued to decrease thereafter, until in November, 1921, it reached its lowest ebb—8,700. Unemployment doles were thus a very heavy burden on the budgets of the first two years.

Food relief constituted an even heavier burden. The system became necessary as a result of the condition in which Austria found herself immediately after the war with respect to the other new states. Foreign relief credits brought food into the country, and these supplies were distributed by the government almost gratuitously. Political conditions prevented even a gradual increase in the price of foodstuffs thus distributed by the state. The government was weak, the whole situation uncertain, and the spectre of Bolshevism loomed up from across the Hungarian frontier.

The magnitude of the burden thus carried by the state may be seen from the fact that in December, 1921, for example, over half of the total expenditures of the government resulted from food subsidies. And it was not until the end of 1921 that the govern-

[2] See p. 161.

ment began seriously to consider the need of abolishing this system of almost gratuitous feeding of the population. Food prices immediately began to rise rapidly, and there were riots in Vienna. Nevertheless, the government persisted in its policy of relieving the budget from the burden of food relief, and the system was finally abolished early in 1922.

The same considerations that had led the government to continue food relief accounted for its failure to raise the prices of other commodities which were sold by state agencies. For example, the tobacco monopoly, which before the war and again, after the beginning of reconstruction, constituted an important source of revenue, was, during this period, a source of deficit. Tobacco rose in price, but cigars and cigarettes were sold at very low prices, the losses thus produced entering into the budgetary deficits.

Next, the railroads, which are owned by the state, contributed appreciably to the budgetary deficits. Again because of the government policy of attempting to maintain low prices, railroad fares remained excessively low in the face of a disproportionate rise in other prices. At one time railroad fares calculated in gold were scarcely equal to one-tenth of the pre-war fares.

Finally, overabundance of government officials weighed inordinately upon the budget of the new state. The Austro-Hungarian Monarchy always had an excessive administrative apparatus. With the break-up of the Monarchy, Vienna, now the capital of a country of 6.5 million inhabitants, was left with an administrative personnel which had been excessive for a country of 30 millions.[3] It is true that this administrative apparatus was somewhat relieved by the withdrawal to their own countries of the nationals of the new Danubian States, but on the other hand it was augmented by the need for providing employment for Austrian officials who had been driven out of the territory of these other states. The salaries of government officials, low as they were, vied in their totality with the food relief as a burden on the state budget and the cause of huge budgetary deficits.

By the time the League stepped in with its program of reconstruction, two of these causes of budgetary deficit were no longer operative. Food relief had been abolished, and unemployment doles were at a very low ebb. But railroad and government monopolies were still operated at a great loss to the state, and the administrative personnel still remained out of all proportion to the size of the country. It was with these two factors that the League had to deal especially in working out a scheme for the financial salvaging of Austria.[4]

The budgetary deficits were covered by new issues of constantly depreciating paper money. There

[3] Hungary was governed from Budapest.

[4] See Annex II of the *Report of the Delegation Sent to Vienna by the Financial Committee of the League of Nations;* also de Bordes, *The Austrian Crown,* pp. 17-22.

really was no other resource left to the government but the printing press, which ground out paper currency in ever increasing amounts.

As far as its financing went, the government of Austria during the first few years of the country's existence was truly fantastic. The Ministry of Finance had no control whatever over the expenditures of the various Ministries. Budgets were voted by the Parliament, but they meant nothing. It is said that during one of the years the total budget voted by the Parliament was spent during the first month of the year for which it was to provide.[5] After that the government lived on a system of extraordinary credits. Each of the ministries and state enterprises was expected, as far as possible, to cover its expenditures out of its own receipts. The expected deficits were reported at short intervals (once or even twice a week) to the Ministry of Finance, which provided funds by means of newly printed notes supplied by the Bank of Issue.

Under this purely chaotic scheme, not only was it impossible to make any attempts to curb unnecessary expenditures, but no one actually knew how much was being spent by the government as a whole, until months after, when the various ministries and enterprises would finally turn in their accounts to the Ministry of Finance.

One thing alone was certain: the printing presses of the currency engraving bureau worked at top

[5] De Bordes, J., *The Austrian Crown*, p. 21.

speed, while the notes they turned out depreciated almost as fast as they were shoved into circulation. And as the notes depreciated, the expenditures of the government increased, at least so far as the number of paper crowns required was concerned. The revenues of the government also rose in terms of the number of paper crowns received. But while the ratio between receipts and expenditures rose very slowly, the number of crowns required to cover the deficits increased from month to month and almost from week to week.

Budgetary deficits, necessitating new issues of paper money, constituted a very important factor in the depreciation of the Austrian currency. But there were other contributory causes, each of them sufficiently important in itself.

A deficiency of international income and the "flight from the crown" contributed to the depreciation of the currency. As we shall see in the next chapter, Austria had through this period a large excess of imports over exports which could not be covered by her income from service operations. The offer of paper crowns in payment of international obligations caused their depreciation by affecting adversely the rate of exchange. The "flight from the crown," a phenomenon common to all countries that have passed through currency depreciation, began in Austria very early, almost immediately after the end of the war, under the influence of a number of special conditions.

As we have already indicated, the political situation in Austria during the first months of the country's existence was most uncertain. The widespread conviction that the remnant of the old Austrian Empire which was to constitute new Austria was incapable of independent existence undermined all confidence in anything connected with the country. This was especially true with regard to the currency. The outbreak of Bolshevism in Hungary and the possibility of its spread into Austria still further depressed this waning confidence. Those who had savings sought for means of safeguarding them, and stable foreign currencies provided the most convenient method.

Everybody who could possibly do so attempted to convert crowns into dollars, pounds, Swiss francs, or any other currencies that promised safety. The demand for these currencies increased enormously, and since their available supply was too small even to meet current foreign payments, there was a concomitant offer of Austrian crowns in foreign markets. The result of these two parallel processes was a powerful downward pressure on the exchange value of the crown. This was accompanied by an upward pressure on the price level within Austria.

As prices rose, the "flight from the crown" gained new impetus. It pressed on the budget by expanding the deficits and forcing the government to issue ever larger amounts of paper money—a procedure certainly not conducive to a restoration of confidence. It pressed also on the balance of payments, since an appreciable part of the export proceeds never found its way into the country, but remained on deposit in foreign banks. The vicious spiral of currency depreciation that figured so prominently in the deliberations of the Brussels Financial Conference of 1920 was in full operation in Austria.[6]

The depreciation of the Austrian currency proceeded faster than the increase of the circulation. The currency of new Austria came into existence early in 1919. On February 19 and 27 of that year decrees were issued providing for the stamping of all notes in circulation in the territory of the Republic. The stamping was done between March 12 and 24. The stamped notes were to be exchanged for new Austrian notes.

On March 23, 1919, the circulation of the Bank of Issue was 4,804 million crowns, and the exchange value of the crown in Zurich was 21.5 Swiss francs for 100 Austrian crowns. This was a trifle over one-fifth of the par value (100 gold crowns are equal to 104.5 Swiss francs). After that the circulation began to increase and the exchange value to fall.

The following table shows the development of the bank note circulation of the Austrian Bank of Issue[7] and the concomitant changes in the Zurich

[6] The proceedings of the Brussels Conference, published by the League of Nations, contain very important materials on the processes involved in the Austrian and other European instances of post-war inflation.

[7] When the stamping of notes was completed, the Austro-Hungarian Bank began to issue special notes for the account of

rate of exchange of the Austrian crown, expressed in Swiss francs: [8]

AUSTRIAN CIRCULATION AND EXCHANGE

Date	Millions of Crowns	Number of Swiss Francs Equal to 100 Crowns	Value of Total Circirculation (in Swiss Francs)
March 23, 1919......	4,804	21.50	1032.86
December 31, 1919...	12,134	3.15	382.22
December 31, 1920...	30,645	1.55	475.20
December 31, 1921...	174,114	0.20	348.23
April 15, 1922........	321,925	0.06	193.16

During the nine months of 1919 immediately following the establishment of the new Austrian currency, the fall in the exchange of the crown was so precipitous that at the end of the period the value of the total circulation in Swiss francs fell to only 37 per cent of what it was at the time when the stamping of the old Austro-Hungarian notes was completed. During the year 1920 the fall in the exchange was not nearly so precipitous. In the

the Austrian Government. On January 1, 1920, the Bank was placed in liquidation, and its Austrian division, known as the *Oesterreichische Geschäftsführung,* took over the functions of the old bank and became the Austrian Bank of Issue. It existed until the creation of the Austrian National Bank under the League of Nations reconstruction scheme. See *European Currency and Finance:* Foreign Currency and Exchange Investigation for the United States Senate Commission of Gold and Silver Inquiry, 1925, Serial 9, Vol. 2, p. 12.

[8] Rosenberg, Wilhelm, "The Problem of the Austrian Krone," *Manchester Guardian Commercial,* cited above. Column III is obtained by multiplying Column I by Column II and dividing by 100.

course of that year the circulation increased two and one-half times, yet at the end of the year the total circulation was worth 46 per cent of its value in March, 1919. After that the fall in the exchange began to outstrip the increase of the circulation. During the year 1921 the total circulation increased nearly six times, but its value at the end of that year was only 34 per cent of the March, 1919, figure. During the first three and one-half months of 1922—the circulation nearly doubled, but its total value, at the end of that period, was only 19 per cent of the above figure. Thus in the course of four years the total circulation increased more than sixty-fold, but its total value decreased by four-fifths.

II. FOREIGN FINANCIAL INTERVENTION

During this whole period Austrian hopes rose and fell with the outlook for assistance from abroad. And it was foreign financial intervention that finally saved the Austrian situation.

The solution of Austria's pressing financial problems was impossible without foreign intervention. There were several reasons for this. In the first place foreign loans were imperatively needed for the balancing of both the government budget and the international accounts. These loans could come from either foreign governments or foreign private capitalists. But they could not be arranged because under the treaty of peace the Reparation Commission held a blanket mortgage on all the resources of

Austria. Financial relief from abroad could come only through a series of agreements involving both the Reparation Commission and the various Allied governments. Moreover a complicated system of priorities had been set up for the relief credits granted to Austria, and the possibilities of loans abroad were tied up with agreements concerning these priorities.

Austria began to plead for foreign financial intervention only a few months after the signing of the treaty of St. Germain. The first plea was made in 1919, when Dr. Renner, the Austrian Chancellor, went to the Supreme Council to plead for the establishment of an Austrian Section of the Reparation Commission in Vienna. The result of this plea was not only the establishment of such a section, but the submission of the Supreme Council, in the fall of 1920, of the so-called "Goode Scheme" for the rehabilitation of Austria, named after the Chairman of the Section, Sir William Goode.

The "Goode Scheme" proposed the granting to Austria of a loan aggregating 250 million dollars principally by the Allied governments. This sum was to be used for the rehabilitation of Austrian finance and the general economic development of the country. The proposal was rejected by the Supreme Council in January, 1921, and a specially appointed committee was charged with a further study of the Austrian problem. Out of this new inquiry grew the so-called "Loucheur Scheme."

This new proposal envisaged the creation of a private company with a capital of 200-250 million francs, which was to undertake the economic development of Austria with the assistance of the Allied governments. The "Loucheur Scheme," which was in effect an attempt at establishing a colonial régime for Austria, never received really serious consideration and was quickly abandoned.

In March, 1921, Austria made another attempt to secure assistance from the Supreme Council. In reply to a plea presented by Austrian Chancellor Mayr, the Council turned the whole matter over to the Financial Committee of the League of Nations.

A delegation sent to Vienna by the Committee completed its investigation by the end of May, and a few days later its reports were approved by the Council of the League of Nations. The plan proposed by these reports provided for a stabilization of the Austrian currency by means of a foreign loan, to be used for covering budgetary deficits, up to such time as the budget could be balanced by means of a thorough reorganization of the whole system of public finance.

The new plan could not, however, be put into operation, before the obstacles presented by the claims of the Reparation Commission and of the powers that had granted relief credits could be definitely removed. While the Reparation Commission was willing to act, some of the governments were not. Particularly was this true of the United States, where the waiving of priority with regard to Austrian relief credits required an act of Congress, and that was not obtained until the spring of 1922.[9]

As the negotiations for foreign assistance dragged out, the Austrian situation grew worse and worse. In fact it had become so bad that at the end of 1921 Great Britain and France granted Austria credits to the extent of 250,000 pounds sterling each. Other credits were promised for 1922, including a British credit of 2,250,000 pounds sterling, a Czechoslovak credit of 500,000,000 Czechoslovak crowns, and some credits from France and Italy. The French and Italian credits were never granted. Most of the Czechoslovak credits were used to pay outstanding accounts due to the importation of coal. A large part of the British credits was used up in an unsuccessful attempt to stabilize the crown. By the early summer of 1922 all hope based on these sporadic acts of foreign aid was dissipated, and Austria was in the throes of a spectacular crash of her currency.

At the beginning of May, 1922, the dollar was quoted in Vienna at a little over 8,000 paper crowns. By the middle of June, it was quoted at 21,500 crowns. By the middle of July it rose to 37,000

[9] The joint Congressional resolution, which authorized the President to take the necessary measures in the matter of Austrian priorities, was not ready for President Harding's signature until April 6, 1922. For the text of the resolution see Moulton, H. G., and Pasvolsky, L., *World War Debt Settlements* (Investigations in International Economic Reconstruction, Institute of Economics), Washington, 1926.

crowns. A month later it stood at 59,000 crowns. Finally on August 25 it reached its maximum at 83,600 crowns. The price level kept full pace with this depreciation, rising as fast as the exchange fell, while note circulation lagged far behind.

Early in August, 1922, the Austrian government made its last appeal to the Supreme Council, asking for a credit of 15,000,000 pounds sterling. In a letter addressed to that body on August 7, the Austrian Minister in London said:

> If against all expectations this last hope were also to prove chimerical, the Austrian government, knowing that to save the situation they had tried in vain all means which lay in their power and which constituted the utmost exertion of the people, would have to call together specially the Austrian Parliament and to declare, in agreement with it, that neither the present nor any other government is in a position to continue the administration of the State.

Even so worded, the Austrian plea was refused by the Supreme Council on the ground that the Allied governments "do not feel that they would be justified in calling upon their heavily burdened nationals to assume further obligations for the benefit of Austria, which has, in the few years since the war, already received so much from them with such disappointing results." The Austrian government was referred to the Council of the League of Nations.

It was during this period that Monsignor Seipel, the Chancellor of Austria, began his pilgrimage to Czechoslovakia, Germany, and Italy, in the hope of obtaining some economic arrangement with Austria's most powerful neighbors that would promise that country financial relief even at the price of its political sovereignty. His pilgrimage finally brought him to London and Geneva, i.e., to the Council and the Assembly of the League of Nations, and in the end resulted in the signing, on October 4, 1922, in Geneva of the three protocols embodying the scheme for an effective foreign intervention under the guidance of the League of Nations.

The Austrian crisis was checked by the action of the League of Nations. The moment the Council of the League decided to take up in earnest the question of Austrian reconstruction, there was immediately a widespread conviction that the solution of the problem was at hand. This conviction communicated itself first of all to that delicately adjusted mechanism, the international exchange market. Nearly two weeks before Chancellor Seipel officially laid the Austrian question before the Council of the League, on August 25, the foreign exchange rate ceased to soar and began to decline, the internal price level following suit three weeks later. The printing presses in Austria were still grinding out new currency; the various Ministries were still dispersing this new currency through the country by means of continuing budgetary deficits. Yet the rate of exchange was slowly declining. The crisis was checked.

Other events connected with foreign financial intervention moved fast after this. The League sent a delegation to Vienna to work out in detail the measures which were to be inaugurated. A new bank of issue was organized and its statutes approved by the Austrian Parliament on November 14. Four days later, on November 18, the printing of uncovered paper money ceased. On November 26 the Austrian Parliament conferred extraordinary powers upon the government; on December 2 it ratified the Geneva protocols, and on the day following adopted the program of reforms prescribed by the scheme. On December 15 Dr. A. R. Zimmermann, the Burgomaster of Amsterdam, arrived in Vienna and immediately took up his duties as the Commissioner General of the League of Nations. Finally, on January 2, 1923, the Austrian National Bank opened its doors.

The actions taken abroad were equally prompt. On October 27 the Reparation Commission freed from its claims the Austrian assets which were to serve as security for short-term loans, then under negotiation. By December 15 similar action was taken by the powers which had granted relief credits. The Geneva protocols were fully ratified by the beginning of January.

Pending the flotation of the reconstruction loan, temporary credits were granted to Austria. The French and Italian credits originally promised in the spring of 1922 were now made available. A loan of 3,500,000 pounds sterling in the form of one-year

Austrian Treasury bills was issued in six countries. These loans provided Austria with necessary resources until in the summer of 1923 the reconstruction loan was finally floated, and means were permanently provided for the program of reconstruction involved in the League scheme.[10]

The League of Nations reconstruction scheme for Austria was embodied in three protocols, signed in Geneva on October 4, 1922. Protocol No. I consisted of a declaration made, on the one hand, by the governments of Great Britain, France, Italy, and Czechoslovakia, and on the other hand by the governments of Austria, whereby "the political independence, the territorial integrity and the sovereignty of Austria" were made inviolate. Austria undertook specifically "not to alienate its independence" and to "abstain from any negotiations or from any economic or financial engagement calculated directly or indirectly to compromise this independence." She did retain, subject to the treaty of St. Germain, "her freedom in the matter of customs tariffs and commercial and financial agreements," provided, however, that her economic independence should in no way be violated or impaired "by granting to any State a special régime or ex-

[10] For further details of this story of foreign financial intervention in Austria see the League of Nations publications on the subject, notably *The Restoration of Austria: Agreements Signed at Geneva on October 4, 1922;* and *The Financial Reconstruction of Austria,* Geneva, 1926; also O. S. Phillpott's *Reports* to the British Department of Overseas Trade, and de Bordes, J., *The Austrian Crown,* pp. 22-32.

clusive advantages calculated to threaten this independence."

Protocol No. II dealt with the reconstruction loan to be arranged for Austria. It set forth the condition under which this loan was to be floated and the system of control that was to be set up to supervise the administration of the loan. It contained also an undertaking on the part of the four signatory governments (Austria is not a signatory to this protocol) to guarantee the annuities under the loan.

Finally Protocol No. III, signed by Austria alone, contained the obligations assumed by the Austrian government. In this protocol the Austrian government undertook to draw up a program of reforms to cover a period of two years; to steer through the Austrian Parliament a draft law conferring upon any governments that may be in power during this two-year period plenary powers for carrying out these reforms; to accept the nomination of a Commissioner General appointed by the Council of the League of Nations, responsible to it, and removable by it; to furnish securities necessary for the guarantee of the reconstruction loan. The Austrian government stipulated that all these measures "are conditional and shall not become finally binding until the British, French, Italian, and Czechoslovak governments have confirmed their promised guarantees by the approval of their respective Parliaments." [11]

[11] For full details of the reconstruction scheme see the following publications of the League of Nations: *Financial Reconstruction of Austria; Report of the Financial Committee of the Coun-*

The reconstruction scheme followed very closely the Report of the Financial Committee of the League of Nations. In its report submitted to the Supreme Council of the Allies on June 3, 1921, the Committee laid down the following two conditions as prerequisite to any restoration of Austrian finance:

1. The suspension, for a period of at least 20 years, of the liens on Austrian assets in respect of reparation and of relief credits; and
2. The adoption by Austria herself of the most stringent measures for the improvement of her internal financial situation.

With the first of these conditions met by the action of the Reparation Commission and of the individual governments concerned with relief credits, the reforms inaugurated under the reconstruction scheme were designed to bring about two specific results: the stabilization of the currency and the gradual balancing of the State budget.

III. THE NATIONAL BANK AND THE STABILIZATION OF THE CURRENCY

The Financial Committee laid down the principle that a permanent stabilization of the Austrian currency, which involved its effective reform, could not be accomplished without the establishment of a new Bank of Issue.

cil; The Restoration of Austria: Report of the Provisional Delegation of the League of Nations at Vienna; and the *Monthly Reports* of the Commissioner General.

The creation of a Bank of Issue was the first task undertaken and carried out in the process of Austrian reconstruction. The new bank, which became known as the Austrian National Bank, was secured, so far as possible, against suffering the fate of the old Austro-Hungarian Bank in having its issue functions seized by the government for the purposes of fiduciary inflation. (See p. 29.) By necessary amendments to the Banking Law of July 24, 1922, and by its own statutes—both the amendments and the statutes were approved by the Austrian Parliament on November 14, 1922—The National Bank was made practically independent of the government.

The shares representing the capital of the Bank, a total of 30 million gold crowns, were offered for private subscription, and of this total, 22 millions were supplied by the public. The rest was paid in by the government. The Bank is thus practically a non-official institution, its sole official function being the note issue monopoly, under conditions, however, rigidly prescribed by its statutes.

Only one official of the Bank, its President, is appointed by the government. The other members of the managing board are elected by the shareholders, and no official of the State can be a member of the board.

The Bank is specifically forbidden to give the government—national, provincial, or municipal—recourse to any of its funds, without receiving in exchange gold or other acceptable securities. The government cannot, therefore obtain banknotes in exchange for its own Treasury bonds or bills. The Bank is obligated to maintain a metallic cover equal, during the first five years, to no less than 20 per cent of its total banknote circulation plus current accounts, less the amount of the State debt to the Bank.[12] The rest of the circulation and of the sight liabilities of the Bank must be covered by discounted bills. The cover is to be increased gradually to 33⅓ per cent.[13]

By governmental decree of December 29, 1922, the National Bank was authorized to take over all the affairs of the *Oesterreichische Geschäftsführung,* which had been functioning as the Bank of Issue and was to cease to exist on January 1, 1923. By the same decree, the Bank was authorized to take over the affairs of the Austrian Central Office for the Circulation of Foreign Paper, known as the *Devisenzentrale.*[14]

[12] The State debt to the Bank consists of the Treasury bonds handed over to the Bank's predecessor in exchange for the banknotes issued to cover budgetary deficits. Since the Bank is not allowed to accept any Treasury bonds and since provision is made for the extinguishing of the State debt, for example by applying to it the State's share in the profits of the Bank, the portion of circulation covered by Treasury bonds is bound to decrease gradually.

[13] *Report of the Provisional Delegation of the League of Nations at Vienna,* pp. 4-5.

[14] The *Devisenzentrale* dates back to a war measure adopted in February, 1916, when a special central office was created, as a part of the Austro-Hungarian Bank, to handle payments from and to foreign countries. This central office was reorganized into an independent institution in April, 1919, under the direct author-

The merging of the *Devisenzentrale* with the new National Bank was dictated by practical considerations. The realizable resources of the *Oesterreichische Geschäftsführung* were practically negligible. Its last balance sheet (December 31, 1922) showed a total circulation of 4,080 billion paper crowns and current accounts of 328 billions, and gold resources equivalent to less than 5 billion paper crowns. On the other hand, the *Devisenzentrale* had in its possession a comparatively enormous supply of foreign currency, which was constantly increasing during the later months of 1922, because of the reappearance of hoarded resources.

The first balance-sheet of the National Bank represented a totally different picture from that indicated by the last balance-sheet of the *Oesterreichische Geschäftsführung.* With bank-note circulation equal to 4,054 billions and current deposits aggregating 417 billions, it showed realizable assets equal to 1,195 billions. As a matter of fact these assets were even greater, by no less than 8 or 10

ity of the Ministry of Finance, and was used as a means for regulating foreign exchanges. The *Devisenzentrale* was expected to handle all the foreign exchange coming into the country and passing out of it. It was never quite successful in having complete control of foreign exchange operations, although up to October, 1920, the government imposed severe restrictions on private purchase and sale of foreign exchanges. For a little over a year after that the government allowed considerable freedom in foreign exchange transactions, but in December, 1921, restrictions again began to be introduced, with the result that by the time its functions were taken over by the National Bank, the *Devisenzentrale* was in fair control of foreign exchange operations. See de Bordes, J., *The Austrian Crown,* pp. 108-13.

per cent, on account of the fact that they were calculated on the basis of the average exchange for the second half of 1922. The merging of the Bank of Issue with the *Devisenzentrale* made it possible for the new National Bank to begin its existence with a 26.7 per cent cover of its total circulation, which meant, considering the fact that over half of the circulation represented State debts to the Bank, two and one-half times the cover required by the statutes of the Bank[15]

When the National Bank began operations the Austrian crown had already reached a fair degree of stability. In November, 1922, the average exchange rate of Vienna on New York was 71,400 crowns to the dollar; in December, it was 70,025; in January, 1923, 71,500. Then it gradually declined, until in July it became 70,760, and remained practically at that level until the new currency unit was introduced.[16]

The stabilization of the crown was thus achieved in a very short period of time. The task of maintaining its stability devolved upon the National Bank, which had, from the start, ample resources for this purpose.

Up to the beginning of 1925, however, the Bank exercised very rigid control over all transactions in foreign currency. It was only at the end of March, 1925, that all foreign exchange market restrictions

[15] First *Monthly Report* of the Commissioner General of the League of Nations. [16] *European Currency and Finance.*

were removed, and Vienna became once more a free market for international financial transactions. This action on the part of the Austrian government was, however, preceded by another very important step.

At the end of 1924 a new currency unit was introduced in Austria. The gold value of the new unit, known as the *schilling,* was fixed on the basis of the exchange value of the crown that had been maintained without interruption for the preceding year and a half. The schilling is equal to 10,000 paper crowns and is worth 0.21172086 grammes of pure gold, or $0.1412.

The new currency, which has now been substituted for paper crowns, while expressed in gold, is not, strictly speaking, a gold currency. The National Bank is not obliged to redeem its bank notes in gold, nor have any gold coins been put into circulation, although the resumption of specie payment is provided for in the statutes of the Bank at a future date. Parity is, therefore, maintained by the practical expedient of the Bank's purchasing all the foreign currency offered to it and selling all the foreign currency demanded from it at the fixed rate of exchange. In 1925, however, the Bank relaxed its rigid stabilization of the exchange rate by permitting a small margin between buying and selling prices, corresponding to import and export gold points.[17]

[17] Layton, W. T., and Rist, C., *The Economic Situation of Austria,* p. 112.

IV. THE STATE BUDGET UNDER THE LEAGUE CONTROL

Next to the stabilization of the currency, the balancing of the State budget was to be the basis of the Austrian financial reconstruction. The Austrian government undertook to make no further resort to new isues of paper money for the purpose of making up budgetary deficits, and agreed to take a number of measures which would bring its expenditures within the scope of its revenues.

The reconstruction scheme envisaged the balancing of the Austrian budget within a period of two years. This was to be accomplished by vigorous action in several directions. Expenditures were to be diminished and revenues increased.

The principal device for decreasing expenditures was a drastic reduction of the administrative personnel. Under the scheme the Austrian government undertook to discharge gradually a total of 100,000 State officials, including employes on the Federal railways. Strict economies were to be practiced in other directions, as well.

Revenues were to be increased by a more efficient handling of the already existing apparatus of collection. Deficits in the operation of State enterprises were to be eliminated by a gradual increase of prices in the case of monopolies and of rates in the case of the railways. Other means of increasing revenue were a recalculation of customs duties on a gold basis, the introduction of new indirect taxes, and the increase of some of the already existing ones.

The following table shows the condition of the Austrian budget since 1923, the estimates contemplated by the reconstruction scheme being set side by side with the actual results achieved: [18]

THE AUSTRIAN BUDGET, 1923-25
(In millions of schillings)

Item	1923		1924		1925	
	Estimates	Closed Accounts	Estimates	Closed Accounts	Estimates	Closed Accounts
Total revenue	524.1	697.4	659.7	900.6	726.7	908.5
Current expenditures	709.4	779.6	647.0	810.0	706.6	741.4
Deficit (—) or Surplus (+)	—185.3	— 82.2	+12.7	+90.6	+20.1	+167.1
Capital expenditures	80.0	76.0	79.6	103.6	77.3	90.6
Total balance	—265.3	—158.2	—66.9	—13.0	—57.2	+ 76.5

The budgetary estimates under the reconstruction scheme contemplated a deficit due to current expenditures in 1923 equal to 185.3 million schillings, or a total deficit, including capital expenditures, of 265.3 millions. Although the actual current expenditures for the year exceeded the estimated ex-

[18] Based on Layton, W. T., and Rist, C., *The Economic Situation of Austria*, pp. 152-3; the *Monthly Reports* of the Commissioner General of the League of Nations; and the League of Nations *Memorandum on Public Finance*, 1927.

penditures by 70 million schillings, the excess of actual over estimated revenues was so great that the total deficit for the first year of Austrian reconstruction was 158.2 million schillings, or over 100 million less than had been anticipated.

For the year 1924 the reconstruction scheme contemplated a small surplus of revenues over current expenditures and a total deficit of 66.9 million schillings. The current expenditures for that year exceeded the estimates by 163 millions, yet the excess of revenues over expenditures was 90.6 millions, with the result that the total deficit was only 13 millions.

The Austrian budget was balanced in 1925. The closed accounts for that year show a surplus of 76.5 million schillings, the revenues for the year being sufficient to cover both the current and the capital expenditures. The Treasury returns for the first ten months of 1926 again indicated a fully balanced budget, the revenues exceeding all expenditures by 7 million schillings.

The capital expenditures in the Austrian budget are of three general groups. The bulk of outlays under this head—70-75 per cent—is for the need of the railways. Then there are outlays for other public undertakings, and finally new investments in State monopolies.

A large foreign loan was one of the indispensable elements in the scheme for Austrian financial reconstruction. Pending the flotation of the loan, however, temporary arrangements had to be made to carry on the expenses of government without recourse to the printing press, the printing of new paper currency for the purpose of covering budgetary needs having been definitely discontinued on November 18, 1922. These temporary arrangements comprised an internal gold loan, taken up by the great Viennese banks; direct foreign credits; and a short-term foreign loan.

The reconstruction loan was floated in the summer of 1923. It was a twenty-year loan, intended to yield about 950 million schillings. The annual payments on the loan were guaranteed by the gross receipts of the Austrian customs and of the tobacco monopoly, the proceeds of these two sources of revenue being turned directly over to the Commissioner General of the League who was to return to the Austrian Treasury amounts in excess of the sums required for the debt service. Moreover, in accordance with the Geneva Protocol No. II, the governments of Great Britain, France, Czechoslovakia, and Italy guaranteed the service on the loan to the extent of 84 per cent. In addition, four other countries adhered later on to Protocol No. II and undertook a share in the guaranteeing of the loan, with the result that 90 per cent of the loan carries full guarantee of foreign governments.[19]

Indirect taxation is the largest source of govern-

[19] For the details of the flotation of the loan and the disposal of the funds obtained, see *The Financial Reconstruction of Austria*, Geneva, 1926.

ment revenue. It is followed in importance by direct taxation and by the government monopolies. The following table indicates, in percentages of the total revenue for the year, the principal items of revenue in the Austrian budget for 1925:

Austrian Budget Revenues, 1925
(In percentages of the total for the year)

Indirect taxes:		
Customs duties	15.06	
Duties on articles of consumption	6.36	
Duties on business transactions	25.70	
		47.12
Direct taxes		20.92
Government monopolies		12.93
Employers' and workmen's contributions to the unemployment fund		7.50
Miscellaneous receipts		11.53
Total		100.00

Thus indirect taxation yields almost half of the total revenues of the state. The yield of direct taxation is only slightly over one-fifth of the total. The yield of the four government monopolies—tobacco, salt, lotteries, and explosives—is given here as the net profit accruing to the government, rather than as gross receipts.

Contributions to the provinces, pensions, and debt payments constitute the chief items of expenditure. The table on page 131 shows, in percentages of the the total for the year, the various items of expenditure in the Austrian budget for 1925:

AUSTRIAN BUDGET EXPENDITURES, 1925
(In percentages of the total for the year)

Contributions to the provinces	20.53
Pensions	17.68
Payments on the public debt	12.74
Unemployment doles and other social expenses	9.58
Financial and economic administration	7.76
General administration	11.36
National defense	5.50
Public instruction and religion	4.14
Capital expenditures for public enterprises	7.62
Miscellaneous expenditures	3.09
Total	100.00

Thus pensions and unemployment doles still weigh heavily on the Austrian budget. Altogether these two items of expenditures constitute 27.36 per cent of the total. If we omit from the budget the contributions of the provinces, then pensions and unemployment doles constitute a third of the total budget expenditures.

The national income of the country is estimated at about 1,100 schillings per head.[20] All taxation, national and local, amounted, in 1924 and 1925, to about 190 schillings per head. This would give Austria a burden of taxation equal to slightly over 17 per cent of the national income.

During the three and a half years of control by the League of Nations, Austria achieved complete

[20] In Layton, W. T., and Rist, C., *The Economic Situation of Austria*, pp. 163-65, the per capita income is calculated at 770 gold crowns.

financial stability. Her currency was reformed and placed on a virtual gold basis. Her State budget reached a condition of equilibrium. The achievement of these results led to the withdrawal of the League control, which became effective June 30, 1926.

The terms under which the League control was withdrawn were so designed as to insure continued financial stability. The League retains the right to re-establish control "if the proceeds from the assigned revenues are insufficient to cover the service of the (reconstruction) loan or if the equilibrium of the budget is seriously endangered." [21] Moreover, the Austrian National Bank continues to have a foreign adviser, appointed by the League Council. But the continuation of this stability depends to a large extent upon the country's international financial position, to which we can now turn our attention.

[21] For the documents relating to the withdrawal of the League control, see *The Financial Reconstruction of Austria*, 1926.

CHAPTER VII

AUSTRIA'S INTERNATIONAL ACCOUNTS

A CONTINUED maintenance of fiscal and currency stability in Austria is directly dependent upon the country's international financial position. In the preceding chapter we saw that deficits in the international income of the country, as well as unbalanced budgets, have been responsible for currency depreciation. In this chapter we shall summarize Austria's international financial transactions, which have been affected by currency difficulties, and have, in turn, exercised a great influence upon monetary conditions.

There is scarcely another country in the world in which exports pay for so small a part of imports as is the case with Austria. There is scarcely another country, therefore, in which service and financial operations constitute such an important factor in offsetting the trade deficit. In this chapter we shall examine Austria's exports and imports, as well as the other items of her international revenue and expenditures, in order to see in what manner the large deficits which have characterized the foreign trade of the Austrian Republic have been covered.

From 1920 to 1926 Austria was annually buying abroad more than she could pay for with her commodity exports. The treaty of St. Germain, which determined the frontiers and the general international status of the Austrian Republic, was signed on September 10, 1919. The year 1920 was, therefore, the first calendar year during which the new country was fully organized. The table on page 135 shows the total exports and imports of Austria during the period from 1920 to 1926, expressed in Austrian schillings, the new currency introduced in 1924.[1] For the years prior to 1924, the paper-crown values used in Austrian statistics have been converted to schillings at the average rate of exchange for each of the years under consideration.[2]

The table shows the extent of Austria's foreign purchases in comparison with her sales to other countries. In 1920 and 1921 she paid with her exports for only a little more than half of her imports. In 1922 the proportion was slightly higher. Both the exports and the imports increased by comparison with 1921, but while the former rose by about 300 million schillings, the latter grew by less than 100 millions. The following year, however, exports in-

[1] See p. 125.

[2] Official statistics of the Austrian foreign trade appear in *Statistik des auswärtigen Handels Oesterreichs,* published by the Austrian Ministry of Commerce, and currently in *Statistische Nachrichten* of Vienna. The conversions into schillings used here are based on the *Memorandum* submitted to the International Economic Conference by the Austrian Delegation to the Conference.

AUSTRIA'S FOREIGN TRADE, 1920-1926
(In millions of Austrian schillings)

Year	Exports	Imports	Adverse Balance of Trade	*Exports as a Percentage of Imports*
1920.........	1,347	2,453	1,106	*54.9*
1921.........	1,311	2,448	1,137	*53.6*
1922.........	1,600	2,530	930	*63.2*
1923.........	1,626	2,768	1,142	*58.7*
1924.........	1,988	3,473	1,485	*57.2*
1925.........	1,954	2,891	937	*67.6*
1926.........	1,728	2,805	1,077	*61.6*

creased by 26 millions, while imports rose by 238 millions. As a result, the adverse balance of trade during that year was larger than in any of the preceding three years.

The "replenishing" year 1924 was the high water mark of the adverse balance of trade. During the following year the imports showed a sharp decline. Austria's purchases abroad in 1925 were half a billion schillings less than in 1924. The exports during that year were maintained on almost the same level as during the preceding year. As a result the adverse balance of trade in 1925 was only two-thirds of the 1924 balance. In 1926 imports were somewhat below the 1925 figure, but exports showed a contraction by comparison with the preceding two years. The adverse balance of trade increased again.

Present-day Austria is thus a country with a substantial and persistent excess of imports over exports. The best she was able to do during the years 1920-26 was to raise the value of her exports to slightly over two-thirds of her imports. This was in 1925. As a rule her export-import ratio was appreciably below that.

Austria has indeed a smaller export-import ratio than almost any other country. During the seven-year period under consideration, her total imports were 19,368 million schillings, while her total exports were only 11,554 millions. Exports paid for only about 60 per cent of the imports. In the year 1925 Austria's exports were 67.6 per cent of her imports. During the same year, Great Britain's exports constituted 66 per cent of her imports; Italy's, 70 per cent; Germany's 71 per cent; Switzerland's 77 per cent; Belgium's, 86 per cent; and Hungary's, 93 per cent.

The foreign trade deficit is the largest but not the only net item of international expenditure for Austria. She has also to make payments abroad on account of her public and private foreign debts. On the other hand she has large income from her own investments abroad and from a number of service operations.

Austria's income from foreign investments is much larger than the annual outlays for interest on her foreign debts. The debt of the Austrian government consists primarily of the League of Nations reconstruction loan and of the Austrian share of the pre-war debts of the Austro-Hungarian Monarchy, as allocated by the Innsbruck and Prague protocols. Long-term municipal and private indebtedness is small in amount. But there is a comparatively large short-term debt, accumulated as a result of unfavorable trade balances. Interest or principal payments on all these debts aggregate an appreciable annual sum.

Austrian citizens, however, participate in the ownership of various industrial, trading, and banking enterprises, and of landed properties in other countries. The returns from these investments comprise, therefore, profits from such enterprises, as well as dividends, directors' fees, and bonuses resulting from ownership and control of foreign stocks and bonds.

Before the war the amount of funds coming to Vienna and the rest of the territory of present-day Austria as a result of these investments was much larger than it is today. Some of the holdings were sold during the years immediately following the war, and although a part of these losses have since been recovered through repurchase, the net diminution of holdings has been very considerable. The policies pursued by the new states in which Austrian investments were located, have caused the removal from Vienna to their own capitals of the directing seats of many enterprises partly owned by Austrians. The agrarian reforms instituted by most of these new states greatly decreased Austrian land holdings.

International service operations bring Austria an appreciable net income. The city of Vienna is still an important financial and trading center for the countries of south-central Europe and the Balkans. It is true that each of the new states, for whose territory Vienna formerly served as such a center, has developed its own banking system and is making every effort to establish its own international connections. Nevertheless, the great prestige and the long-established international connections of the Viennese banks still afford them an opportunity to handle many of the international, financial, and commercial transactions in which its neighbors are concerned. These operations represent a source of international income for Austria.

With Vienna still the great scientific, artistic, and cultural center of south-central Europe, and with the mountainous portions of Austria, especially the Tyrolean Alps still constituting one of the most important vacation areas of Europe, Austria attracts every year a large number of foreigners. This tourist traffic constitutes an important source of international income.

The tourist traffic in Austria is a larger source of revenue than merely the living and travelling expenditures of the foreigners. In Vienna many articles of apparel and numberless specialties attract the attention of the tourists, and Vienna has enormous facilities for catering to this sort of trade. To the visitors coming from the countries to the south and east of Austria, Vienna offers a large assortment of articles which are either unavailable in their own countries or else very much more expensive. This "pocket" or "trunk" export escapes inclusion in the general export figures; yet it represents a fairly considerable item of revenue.

Emigrant remittances and the earnings of Austrian musicians, actors, scientists, etc., add to Austria's international revenue. Railroad and river transit services also represent income for Austria.

Austria's service earnings have not been sufficient to cover her trade deficits. The summary statement on page 140 shows the country's international income and outgo since the stabilization of the currency, that is, during the four-year period from 1923 to 1926. We have not attempted any evaluation for the pre-stabilization period, because of the uncertainty introduced into any calculations that might be made by the fluctuations of the currency. There is sufficient evidence, however, to show that the deficits during the years 1919-1922 were very substantial.

Thus during the four years since the stabilization, service earnings and net income from foreign investment covered only 60 per cent of the trade deficits.

Exports of capital and foreign borrowings serve to cover the trade and service deficit. During the pre-stabilization period Austria could not borrow abroad, and was compelled to make her payments chiefly by the transfer of property. After the stabilization,

Austria's International Income Account, 1923-1926
(Totals for the four-year period in millions of schillings)

Net outgo for:				
Foreign trade deficits			4,641	
Losses on franc speculation[a]			100	
				4,741
Net income from:				
Interest:				
Income from foreign investments		1,600		
Less outgo on foreign indebtedness:				
Public	630[b]			
Private	200			
		830		
			770	
Trade commissions and banking profits			800	
Tourist trade			800	
Emigrant remittances			120	
Transit traffic			400	
				2,890
Net deficit, all items				1,851

[a] Principally in 1924.
[b] Included in this figure is a small amount repaid on the principal of the debts.

foreign loans furnished her with the means of payment.

In 1920-1922 relief credits represented the only foreign funds obtained by Austria in the form of loans. They amounted, for that period, to about 350 million schillings. The remainder of the deficit, which was apparently quite large, was covered by the sale abroad of paper crowns, of Austrian holdings of foreign securities, and of Austrian real estate and shares in Austrian enterprises.

The sales of paper crowns were, indeed, much larger than the actual requirements of international payments. Almost from the very end of the war, because of political uncertainty and monetary disorganization, there was an almost continuous flight of capital from Austria. This flight assumed two forms. In the first place, crown holdings were converted into stable foreign currencies, and in the second, a part of the proceeds of the export trade were kept abroad, thus necessitating additional sales of paper crowns or of property and securities.

After the stabilization of the currency, most of the capital that had fled from Austria returned to the country. This inflow of funds served to cover a part of the net outgo during the years 1923 and 1924. Some of these funds were used for the repurchase of securities sold by Austrians during the preceding years. The net amount which returned to the country was, probably, in the neighborhood of half a billion schillings.

The remainder of the deficit was covered by means of foreign loans. The League of Nations reconstruction loan, exclusive of the part sold within Austria, furnished the country with about one billion schillings' worth of foreign currencies. The long term loans during these years brought in a little over 200 million schillings. The remaining part of the deficit, about half a billion schillings, was covered by means of short-term loans.

The total amount of short-term borrowing was

probably a billion schillings. During the same period the National Bank increased its gold and foreign currency assets by 430 million schillings, only a small part of which came from domestic hoarding. Moreover, Austrian exporters have resumed to some extent their practice of extending liberal payment terms to their foreign customers.[3]

If Austria is to achieve exchange stability and get on without a constant increase of foreign indebtedness, she will have to increase the ratio of exports to imports. The deficit in her international income account as a whole amounts to about 450 million schillings a year—the net income from services, amounting to approximately 700 millions a year, being much more than offset by the trade deficit.[4] Among the service items, net income on interest account cannot be expected to show any increase; and trade commissions, banking profits, and income from the tourist trade can increase only slowly. To balance the account, the trade deficit must be reduced either through curtailing imports or through expanding exports. The difficulties involved in lessening the trade deficit are indicated in the following chapter.

[3] For the sources of the estimates given here and details of foreign borrowings see Appendix, pp. 582-92.

[4] Figures based on table on p. 140 above.

CHAPTER VIII

TRADE, PRODUCTION, AND BANKING IN AUSTRIA

THE reasons for Austria's continued excess of outgo over income in her international accounts must be sought in the general economic condition of the country, especially in the character of its foreign trade and its productive activities. The present chapter is devoted to an analysis of these important elements of the Austrian situation.

I. CHARACTER AND DIRECTION OF FOREIGN TRADE

Austria depends upon the rest of the world for a large part of her food supply, for practically all of her mineral fuel, and some of the basic raw materials she needs in her manufacturing industries. Her exports to the rest of the world consist almost exclusively of manufactured goods and of timber. The table on page 144 shows the principal groups of Austria's imports and exports during the years 1922-25.

Generally speaking there have been very few changes in the relative importance of the various import and export groups. On the import side, there has been a noticeable increase in the relative

COMMODITY GROUPS OF IMPORTS AND EXPORTS
(In percentages of total values of imports or exports for the year)

Groups	Imports				Exports			
	1922	1923	1924	1925	1922	1923	1924	1925
Live animals	5.0	6.4	6.9	9.0	0.8	1.3	0.8	1.5
Articles of food and drink	25.6	26.1	26.9	26.6	2.0	1.5	2.3	1.9
Raw materials and semi-manufactures	31.0	31.5	29.4	29.6	15.4	15.5	18.1	20.1
Manufactured goods ..	38.3	35.9	36.0	32.3	81.1	81.0	77.9	73.3
Gold and silver........	0.1	0.1	0.8	2.5	0.7	0.7	0.9	3.2

importance of live animals and a decrease in the importance of manufactured products. On the export side there has been an increase in the importance of raw materials and semi-manufactured goods, and a decrease in the importance of manufactured goods. These changes do not, however, indicate any distinct tendencies, although an examination of the foreign trade by the more important articles does show quite well defined lines of development.

Austria has been increasing her imports of unworked foodstuffs and decreasing those of worked food products. The importation of cereals increased from 413,000 metric tons in 1922 to 646,000 metric tons in 1925. At the same time the importation of flour dropped from 211,000 to 109,000 metric tons. The number of cattle and pigs brought into the country in 1922 was 301,000; in 1925 it was 973,000.

On the other hand the importation of edible fats and greases dropped from 58,000 metric tons in 1922 to 32,000 in 1925.

The imports of vegetables have also decreased appreciably between 1922 and 1925. But on the other hand, the imports of sugar increased during the same period by 50 per cent, while the amount of other foodstuffs brought into the country doubled.

The imports of coal have shown a definite downward tendency. In 1922, 5,812,000 metric tons of coal and coke were brought into the country; in 1925 the amount was only 5,272,000. At the same time, however, the imports of petroleum and oil products increased from 104,000 to 131,000 metric tons. The imports of chemicals rose from 83,000 to 115,000 metric tons.

In textiles there has also been a shift from worked to unworked materials. The imports of raw cotton increased from 28,000 to 38,000 metric tons, but the imports of cotton manufactures decreased appreciably.

There has been a general shift in the relative importance of exports from the metal to the textile groups. In 1921 and 1922 the metals and metal manufactures group occupied the most important place on the export list, with textile and textile manufactures holding the second place. In 1923 the two groups became equal in importance, while in 1924 the position was completely reversed. In 1921 the metals group accounted for 33.40 per cent of

Austria's exports, and in 1924, for only 27.62 per cent. On the other hand, the textile group rose from 23.21 per cent in 1921 to 34.72 per cent in 1924. Approximately the same relationship existed in 1925.

Construction timber has shown the largest increase in Austria's exports during this period. Its shipments increased from 771,000 to 1,775,000 metric tons. At the same time the exports of paper and paper products rose from 169,000 to 257,000 metric tons. There have also been some increases in the exports of pig and bar iron, and of stone and cement. On the other hand, the exports of machinery and of metal manufactures generally have shown a downward tendency.

Austrian foreign trade has been shifting away from the Danubian countries. The table on page 147 shows the geographical distribution of Austria's exports and imports in 1922 and 1925.

It is clear from the table that the importance of the Danubian countries as markets for Austrian exports declined noticeably between 1922 and 1925. While Austrian exports to Czechoslovakia and Bulgaria increased somewhat, the exports to Hungary, Rumania, and Yugoslavia decreased. On the other hand, the percentage of Austrian exports going to other European countries, especially in Western Europe, and to countries overseas increased noticeably. There has been a similar shift in the import trade, though not on as large a scale. In 1926 there

GEOGRAPHICAL DISTRIBUTION OF AUSTRIA'S FOREIGN TRADE, 1922 AND 1925

(In percentages of total values for the year)

Country of Source or Destination	Austrian Exports		Austrian Imports	
	1922	1925	1922	1925
ALL DANUBIAN STATES ..	43.2	38.8	41.5	44.1
Czechoslovakia	10.3	12.0	23.6	19.9
Hungary	12.9	10.1	11.1	13.1
Rumania	6.4	6.5	1.4	4.8
Yugoslavia	12.5	8.9	4.1	6.0
Bulgaria	1.1	1.3	1.3	0.3
ALL OTHER COUNTRIES ..	56.8	64.3	58.5	60.1
Germany	14.7	15.1	22.4	15.8
Poland	9.2	8.4	9.2	8.4
Italy	10.2	10.4	5.1	5.7
Switzerland	4.7	4.8	5.1	4.4
United Kingdom	3.5	3.6	2.4	3.6
France	1.2	2.6	1.2	1.9
U.S.A.	1.4	2.2	8.2	7.7
Others	11.9	17.2	4.9	12.6

was a slight increase in Austria's imports from the agricultural countries of the Danubian group. This was due to an increase in her imports of foodstuffs, resulting from poor crops.

Czechoslovakia, the most important of the sources of Austria's imports, supplies that country with the bulk of its foreign purchases of textiles, coke, and minerals. She also ships to Austria considerable quantities of iron manufactures and some vegetables. Czechoslovakia buys from Austria the bulk of the latter's exports of silk goods and raw metals. Hungary's sales to Austria are restricted mainly to flour, living animals, and animal products. Her purchases from Austria are largely textiles and paper. Yugoslavia sells to Austria chiefly living animals and animal products. She buys from Austria a large variety of manufactured articles, chiefly textiles and clothing, paper goods, machinery and instruments of all kinds. Rumania is a purveyor of oil to Austria, mostly in the form of lubricants. Her principal purchases from Austria consist of machinery.

Germany supplies Austria with a variety of products. Her principal sales to Austria consist of iron ware and other metal manufactures, including a considerable amount of machinery. Besides, she sells to Austria large amounts of chemicals, fats and greases, and rubber. Her purchases from Austria consist mainly of timber, iron manufactures, and chemicals. Poland is Austria's chief purveyor of coal and oil. Her purchases from Austria are mainly textiles, rubber and leather goods, and various kinds of machinery. Italy supplies Austria with fruits, vegetables and beverages, and buys from her timber and paper pulp.

American sales to Austria, comprising a little over 6 per cent of that country's total purchases abroad, consist mainly of raw cotton and lard. The United States buys from Austria chiefly glass ware and novelties, and some minerals.

II. AGRICULTURAL PRODUCTION AND REQUIREMENTS

Austria has considerable and varied agricultural resources. In spite of the fact that large portions of the country are mountainous, altogether unproductive lands constitute but a small percentage of the whole area, although the amount of arable land is also not very large. More than a third of the total area—38 per cent—is covered with forests; 22.5 per cent are arable land; 16 per cent are mountain pastures; 12 per cent are meadows; 1.5 per cent are gardens and vineyards; and approximately 10 per cent of the total area entirely unproductive.[1]

Austria grows all four of the principal cereals—wheat, rye, oats, and barley—as well as root plants and vegetables. As a matter of fact, agriculture plays a more important part in her economic life than is generally supposed, and the country is able to supply a considerable portion of its food requirements.

The post-war recovery of crop yields has not been as rapid as of the planting area. In 1924 the area sown to rye was 83 per cent of the pre-war area; the oats area was 85 per cent of the pre-war; the wheat area, 83 per cent; and the barley area, 88 per cent. Burgenland (ceded to present-day Austria by Hun-

[1] The statistical data given in this section are based mainly on Layton, W. T., and Rist, C., *The Economic Situation of Austria*, pp. 61-75; Basch, A., and Dvořáček, J., *Austria and Its Economic Existence*, Prague, 1925, pp. 19-25; *Wirtschafts-Statistisches Jahrbuch*, 1924, pp. 169-173; and *Agricultural Survey of Europe*, Bulletin 1234 of the Department of Agriculture, 1924.

gary) added somewhat to the whole planting area. On the other hand, the total crop yield for rye was, in 1924, only 68 per cent of the pre-war yield; for oats, 78 per cent; for wheat, 75 per cent; and for barley, 83 per cent. In 1925, an exceptionally good crop year, the output of cereals approached much nearer the pre-war figures, but in 1926 it again dropped almost to the 1924 level of production. This slowness of yield recovery has resulted principally from shortage of livestock and difficulties of obtaining adequate amounts of artificial fertilizers.

The post-war recovery of root crops in Austria has been much more rapid than of cereal crops. The potato area (exclusive of Burgenland) was, in 1924, 97 per cent of the average for the last five years before the war; the sugar-beet area was 94 per cent. Both the potato and the sugar-beet crops, however, were no less than 114 per cent of the pre-war. To these amounts Burgenland added very appreciably, especially in the case of sugar-beet.

On the whole, Austria's own crops can satisfy the major requirements of her population. This is certainly true in the case of three of the principal cereals, and of potatoes. Only in the case of wheat have the imports far exceeded home production. The following table indicates the consumption of cereals in Austria during the cereal year 1924-25 (i.e., July 1, 1924—June 30, 1925) and the origin of the cereals consumed:

AUSTRIA'S CEREAL CONSUMPTION, 1924-25
(In thousands of metric tons)

Cereal	Net Imports	Production	Consumption	*Production as Percentage of Consumption*
Wheat	441	231	672	*34*
Rye	102	411	513	*80*
Oats	97	332	429	*77*
Barley	85	157	242	*65*

If the crops of 1924 had been equal to the average of the last five pre-war years, Austria would have been able, during the cereal year 1924-25, to satisfy all her requirements of rye and even have a small export surplus; she would have just about satisfied all her requirements of oats; she would have been short of about 20 per cent of her requirements of barley and of 55 per cent of her requirements of wheat.

The potato crop of 1924 was sufficient to satisfy the requirements of the country. The sugar-beet crop, however, sufficed for barely a third of the total sugar consumption; the imports of sugar during the year were more than double the home production.

Austria imports about half of the meat she consumes. The country has favorable conditions for livestock raising. It is abundantly supplied with fodder, almost two-thirds of the total area devoted to agricultural purposes being used for the growing of products which are fed to animals. The recovery of livestock since the war has been fairly rapid. Nevertheless, Austria is still not in a position to supply her own requirements of meat and dairy products. The following table shows the livestock population of Austria in 1923 in comparison with 1910, again exclusive of Burgenland:

Austria's Livestock Population
(In thousands of head)

Livestock	1910	1923	*1923 as a Percentage of 1910*
Horses	298.3	264.7	*89*
Cattle	2,222.5	2,036.8	*92*
Pigs	1,846.1	1,379.6	*75*
Sheep	296.4	591.1	*200*
Goats	234.3	374.1	*160*

For the whole country we must add to the above figures for 1923 the following livestock population of Burgenland: 17.8 thousand horses; 124.9 thousand head of cattle; 92.7 thousand pigs; 6.3 thousand sheep; and 8.1 thousand goats.

Austrian cattle are, generally speaking, of higher quality than the cattle in the countries lying south and east of Austria. This is especially true of the cattle raised in the Austrian Alpine lands. Certain quantities of this cattle are exported for breeding purposes. On the other hand, the meat requirements of the eastern part of Austria, particularly the city of Vienna, have to be met by the importation of slaughter animals.

Austria is also an importer of dairy products, as well as of poultry and eggs, and of vegetables. Her own production along these lines is not sufficient to meet her requirements.

It is not impossible for Austria to increase her agricultural production. The general character of Austria is very much similar to that of Switzerland, yet the agricultural output of the latter is considerably larger. For example, the yield of the principal cereals in the two countries, in quintals per hectare, were as follows in 1923: [2]

	Wheat	Rye	Barley	Oats
Switzerland	20.6	21.5	16.1	21.6
Austria	12.6	10.0	12.7	11.6

The livestock population of the two countries per square kilometer of productive land is as follows: [3]

	Horses	Cattle	Cows	Pigs
Switzerland	41.8	44.5	23.3	19.5
Austria	37.5	28.7	14.2	19.5

Austria cannot, in all probability, become entirely self-sufficient as far as her food supply is concerned. There seems no doubt, however, that she may, through an intensification of her agriculture, diminish appreciably the volume of her food imports.

[2] Basch, A., and Dvořáček, J., *Austria and Its Economic Existence,* p. 70. [3] Ibid., p. 71.

III. INDUSTRIAL PRODUCTION AND REQUIREMENTS

The urban population of Austria depends for its livelihood upon the industries of the country and its transport, commercial, and banking organizations. The industrial position of the country is not unfavorable, except for the lack of fuel which constitutes the only real element of weakness.[4]

Austria has a large and varied industrial equipment. No industrial census of Austria is available, but some idea of the relative importance of the various industries may be obtained from the number of workmen employed in each of the branches. Here we have figures only for those workmen whose conditions of work are regulated by collective agreements. The number of workmen thus registered is 880,699 and their distribution among the various branches of industry is shown on page 155.[5]

If we add to the above, 200,191 other employes of various kinds, i.e., clerks in various industrial, commercial, and banking enterprises, professional offices, etc., and 94,868 employes in hospitals, theaters, barbershops, etc., we obtain a fairly good idea of the various groups of employment among the urban population of Austria.

[4] The statistical data in this section are based mainly on Layton and Rist, *The Economic Situation of Austria*, pp. 49-60; Basch and Dvořáček, *Austria and Its Economic Existence*, pp. 9-18; *Wirtschaft-Statistisches Jahrbuch;* the files of the *Statistische Nachrichten;* and a study by Dr. Friedrich Hertz, entitled "Die Entwicklung der oesterreichischen Industrie, 1923-26," kindly placed at our disposal in manuscript form.

[5] Figures prepared by the Austrian Statistical Office and published in *Statistische Nachrichten*, March 25, 1925.

Distribution of Workmen in Austria by Branches of Industry

Industry	Number Employed	*Percentage of Total*
Metallurgy and engineering.........	188,532	*21.4*
Building	140,541	*16.0*
Clothing and shoemaking...........	75,644	*8.6*
Wood	70,946	*8.1*
Textiles	67,476	*7.7*
Food	60,397	*6.9*
Commerce and transport............	58,413	*6.6*
Mining	52,998	*6.0*
Hotels, etc.	35,659	*4.1*
Paper	30,060	*3.4*
Chemicals	26,778	*3.0*
Printing, etc.	25,683	*2.9*
Stone and earthenware, etc..........	24,537	*2.8*
Leather	13,166	*1.5*
Rubber	5,660	*0.6*
Electrical supply	3,209	*0.4*
Total.............................	880,699	*100.0*

Metallurgy and industries based on metallurgy constitute the basis of Austria's industrial development. Their output enters largely into the export trade of the country, and they provide employment for the largest group of the industrial population of Austria.

The metallurgical industry of Austria enjoys the advantage of large iron ore resources. One of Europe's largest iron ore deposits is located at Eisenerz, in Styria. On the other hand, the industry is handicapped by the absence of coking coal.

Austria's total coal production has increased considerably since the war. In 1913 the territory of present-day Austria produced 87,000 tons of coal and 2,621,000 tons of lignite, or a total, calculated in coal values, of 1,397,000 tons. In 1924 the production of coal was 172,000 tons and that of lignite was 2,770,000 tons, or a total, in coal values, of 1,560,000 tons. The 1924 production exceeded that of both 1913 and 1923. It was, however, smaller than the production of 1922, when the output of lignite was so great that the total coal value produced was equal to 1,734,000 tons. In 1925 the production of coal was 145,000 tons, but that of lignite was 3,012,000 tons.

This production is not nearly sufficient for the country's requirements. The consumption of coal, in coal values, was, in 1924, 6,900,000 tons, or more than four times the country's own production.

The production of pig iron is considerably below the pre-war figure. In 1913 Austria produced 607,000 tons of pig iron. In 1923, the production of pig iron was 344,000 tons. In 1924 it dropped again to only 267,000 tons, but rose in 1925 to 380,000. In 1926 it was 333,000 tons. The production of steel, which was 499,000 tons in 1923, also dropped, in 1924, to only 370,000 tons, but rose again to 464,000 tons in 1925 and 474,000 in 1926.

Besides iron ore, Austria has other mineral resources of considerable value. Her magnesium, copper, lead and zinc mines produce fairly large quantities of these metals. Finally, she is a producer of graphite, gypsum, and salt.

Austria's metal working and engineering industries have had a long and successful development. She produces high grade steel and many varieties of steel manufactures, especially construction materials, machinery and machine parts of various kinds, and tools. Almost half of the engineering enterprises of the former Austrian empire are lo-

Austria's Principal Resources

cated in present-day Austria. Among them are five locomotive works, eight automobile factories, several bicycle factories, and many shops for the production of engines of every description.

The textile and clothing industry follows metallurgy in importance. The development of its various branches is not, however, uniform. The cotton industry is overdeveloped so far as spinning is concerned, and underdeveloped as regards weaving. The reason for this lies in the uneven distribution of spindles and looms in the former Austrian empire as between Austria and Bohemia. Present-day Austria has retained a much larger proportion of spindles than of looms, although her weaving industry has been considerably extended since the war by the addition of no less than 5,000 looms. The woolen industry is far behind the cotton. Other branches of the textile industry include the manufacture of silk, jute, and hemp, as well as the production of large quantities of felt and knitted goods, and of various articles of haberdashery.

The tanning and leather industry represents an important item in the industrial system of Austria. Not only does it produce large quantities of footwear, but it is also responsible for a very lucrative trade in leather specialties, which are purchased largely by foreign tourists.

Industries based on timber are important for Austria. Almost two-fifths of the total area of Austria is under forests, and the annual lumber production is 9.5 million cubic meters. A considerable part of this timber is used for fuel. The timber industry is well developed. Tree-cutting, work in the sawmills, and the production of such by-products as resins, tanning materials, and charcoal, employ no less than 120,000 men. These timber resources constitute the basis of a well developed wood-working industry, as well as of a large paper industry. Furniture and many other kinds of wood products are turned out in large quantities. Paper of almost every description is manufactured.

Austria has a group of agricultural industries. Chief among these is the sugar refining industry. It is followed in importance by beer-brewing and the production of alcohol.

Besides these, there are in Austria several smaller industries. The manufacture of rubber goods, chemicals, earthenware, cement, enamel, and glass is carried on in the country.

Austria's industries are not adjusted primarily to the needs of the country. They grew up when the Vienna district was one of the two principal industrial centers of the Austro-Hungarian Monarchy. They developed in conditions of full collaboration with industrial plants located in other parts of the Monarchy. During the war Vienna was the great center of war industry, which resulted in a large expansion of Austrian metallurgy and engineering. And when the Monarchy fell to pieces, Austria found herself with some branches of industry developed far beyond the requirements of her own territory but cut off from their former markets, and with some branches developed far below the country's requirements. The metal trades represent an outstanding example of the first, and textiles of the second.

During the period of inflation there was an appreciable industrial expansion in Austria. Between 1919 and 1923 the number of factories in the country increased from 6,283 to 7,645. Altogether it is estimated that the total productive capacity of

Austria's industrial equipment at the present time is no less than 20 per cent greater than it was before the war.

But this expansion was merely a development along already existing lines, rather than an adjustment to new conditions. Austria's imports of cotton manufactures, for example, still exceeded her exports of these commodities in 1925 by 100 million schillings, while her exports of cotton yarn exceed her imports by 81 millions.

Austria's industrial output has not reached the pre-war level, and unemployment is one of the major economic problems confronting her. It is estimated that the industrial output of Austria in 1924-26 was between 75 and 80 per cent of the pre-war capacity, which would make it about two-thirds of present-day capacity. This figure, however, is a general average. For some of the important industries, notably metallurgy, the percentage is appreciably lower. This low level of production finds its reflection in the condition of employment within the country.

No exact figures are available for the total number of unemployed. But we have fairly complete statistics for the number of unemployed receiving doles, and these figures indicate with sufficient accuracy the rise and fall of unemployment.

The year 1919 began with very heavy unemployment which reached its highest point in May of that year, when 186,000 persons were receiving unemployment benefits. Then the number of recipients of such benefits began to recede, and continued to do so through the year 1920, by the end of which year it dropped to only 16,000. This reduction in the number of persons receiving unemployment relief continued through the year 1921, reaching its lowest level in November of that year, when only 8,700 persons were on the doles list. Then the number began to rise again. In December, 1922, the number of unemployed on the doles list was almost 83,000. In March, 1923, it was 167,000. After that it declined again, dropping to 76,000 at the beginning of November, when it began to rise once more. It was 126,000 at the beginning of March, 1924; 64,000 at the beginning of July of that year; 189,000 at the beginning of March, 1925. After that it gradually declined once more, and was 112,000 at the beginning of August, 1925. By December, 1926, it was well over 200,000.[6]

We thus see that unemployment in Austria was particularly heavy during the first half of 1919; during the first half of 1923; during the winter and early spring months of 1924-25; and again in 1926. It was lightest through the year 1921. The periods of heavy unemployment mark the hardest crises in the post-war Austrian situation.

Considerably more than half of the total number of unemployed are usually found in the city of Vienna and its suburbs. At various times the

[6] Figures from *Statistische Nachrichten.*

Vienna district has been responsible for as much as two-thirds of the total unemployment. The heavy unemployment in the city of Vienna is due not only to the low level of the utilization of the industrial, commercial, and banking equipment, but also to the fact that there are in the city large numbers of former government officials, army officers, etc., who are now compelled to seek other occupations.

As a general thing the occupational groups in Vienna which suffer the largest degree of unemployment are as follows: the metal-working and machinery industry; the building trades; the textile and clothing trades; and bankers', merchants', hotel, etc., clerks. Some of these groups, the building trades, for example, are highly seasonal. For example, on March 31, 1925, the number of unemployed in the building trades receiving doles was 32,000; on June 30 of that year it was only 9,000.

IV. BANKING AND CREDIT SITUATION

The currency débâcle in Austria affected profoundly all phases of the country's life, but its most outstanding consequence has been the destruction of liquid capital. The currency depreciation wiped out savings and the operating funds of industrial enterprises. Under its influence the holders of paper money made every effort to convert their holdings into safer values, represented especially by industrial stocks and foreign currencies. This resulted in a tremendous expansion of banking activities, only in part liquidated since the stabilization of the currency.

The close and intimate connection between industry and banking, which, as we saw in Part I (pages 1-26), constituted one of the characteristic features of the economic organization of the Austro-Hungarian Monarchy, is even more pronounced in present-day Austria. And just as in the old Monarchy the Vienna banks had a virtual monopoly of the financing functions of the whole country, so now these same banks occupy a predominant position with regard to the rest of present-day Austria.

Even more than before the war the financing of industry in Austria is done through the Vienna banks. Originally this condition grew out of the circumstances which attended the industrial development of the country. When Austrian industry began to develop early in the second half of the past century, it found itself seriously handicapped by the paucity of liquid funds accumulated in the country. Savings were very small, and industry had to be financed to a large extent by foreign capital. The channel through which this capital flowed into the country was the great Viennese banks. In this manner the great banks of Vienna not only determined the manner of industrial development, but they also acquired direct or indirect control of the ownership and management of industrial enterprises. This resulted in the accumulation in the great Vienna banks of enormous resources, which were not greatly impaired by the war, since their direct advances to the government in war times were repaid by the State Bank, while their holdings of the government war bonds were very skillfully disposed of to the general public.

On the other hand, industry came out of the war and faced the first years of the post-war period in greatly weakened condition. Under the influence of inflation, industrial enterprises found themselves forced more and more to go to the banks for financial assistance, with the result that at the present time the control exercised by the banks over industry is even greater than it was before the war.

The inflation period was characterized by an expansion of banking and by speculative booms. While the nine great Vienna banks still continue to be the dominant factor, the increase in the number of banks during the decade following the beginning of the war has been very marked. In 1913 there were on the territory of present-day Austria 26 large banks and 150 smaller or private banks. On January 1, 1924, the number of the larger banks was 61, while that of the smaller was 260. Since then there has been a considerable reduction, especially in the number of the smaller banks. In August, 1925, there were only 175 of these smaller banks, and 59 of the larger ones.

This growth of the number of banks prior to 1924 was due to a number of reasons. Two of these were particularly important. They were: first, a series of stock exchange booms, and second, speculation in foreign currencies.

Several stock exchange booms were the direct result of currency depreciation. Under conditions of rapid inflation, bank deposits at any reasonable rate of interest became a disastrous method of employment for savings, and the funds which would otherwise have gone into bank deposits were diverted to the stock exchange. This resulted in a spectacular speculative activity in the securities market.

Various mining stocks stood out through this whole period as the prominent object of speculation. In January, 1922, their index was more than five times the general index of all the other securities. In the course of that year, while the index for all the other securities increased by 324 points, the index for the mining stocks went up by over 13,000 points. This skyrocketing of the mining stocks continued even more rapidly in 1923: during that year the index increased by over 20,000 points. All the other stocks also mounted rapidly during that year, their general increase being almost 1,200 points.[7]

Simultaneously with speculation in domestic securities there was also violent speculation in foreign currencies. This phase of speculative activity began as one of the consequences of the monetary dismemberment of the former Monarchy (see Chapter II). For some time after the creation of separate

[7] Figures from *Statistische Nachrichten.*

currencies in the new states, Vienna continued to be the exchange market for all these countries.[8] Then came the Austrian "flight from the crown." Foreign currencies vied with domestic industrial securities as methods of investment for funds which otherwise would have gone into savings. Speculation in foreign currencies was particularly violent during the period preceding the stabilization of the currency; after stabilization, the country turned to speculation in industrial securities. Speculation in foreign currencies continued, however, even after stabilization and, as we shall presently see, was principally responsible for the collapse of the stock exchange boom, which is plainly indicated in the above figures by the securities index figures for 1924.

These two groups of speculation provided a powerful impetus for the creation of new banking houses. The possibilities of profit were so great that the old and the new banks competed vigorously for deposits, in some cases offering 60 per cent and more on deposits. During 1923, when the stock exchange boom was at its height, it was further stimulated by the abundance of funds provided by the influx of foreign capital and the liberal discount policy of the National Bank. The discount rate all through this period remained at the comparatively low level of 9 per cent, and the Bank loaned quite freely.

[8] See Steiner, F. G., "Vienna as an Exchange Market for the Succession States," in *Manchester Guardian Commercial: Reconstruction in Europe Series,* p. 37.

The collapse of the last frenzied boom on the stock exchange brought on a severe panic which helped to deflate the banking situation. This occurred during the early months of 1924, when many of the large Vienna banks were caught in the meshes of the franc speculation. The sudden reversal of the movement of French exchange which resulted from the Morgan loan to France, brought enormous losses to those of the Viennese banks which were heavily engaged in speculating on a further drop of the franc. As a consequence of these losses, one large bank and many small ones closed their doors, while many other banking houses were seriously embarrassed. All this precipitated a panic, which led to a rapid deflation of stock exchange values.

There was one feature of this financial panic of 1924 which presented particular danger. A good deal of the stock exchange speculation during the boom period was conducted with foreign capital brought into the country for that express purpose. After the collapse of the boom, this foreign capital began to leave the country. There was danger for a time that the demand for foreign currencies produced by this withdrawal of foreign capital might affect adversely the stability of the Austrian currency. These fears, however, proved to be unfounded, for the Austrian National Bank weathered the storm quite successfully.

The panic of 1924 had a profound effect on the policy of the National Bank. The Bank came in for a great deal of criticism because it failed to make any attempts at stemming the tide of speculation prior to the crash. Although the securities index was rising with a terrific rapidity all through the year 1923, the Bank's discount rate remained at the comparatively low level of 9 per cent, and its loaning policy continued to be very liberal. The Bank has also been criticized, though not so generally, for not tightening its credit policy until after the crisis was practically over: the first alteration in the bank rate—its raising from 9 to 12 per cent—came only on June 5, whereas the crisis began in April; the rate was further raised to 15 per cent on August 12; several weeks after that a system of credit rationing was adopted.

But whether or not the Bank was wrong in not tightening credit during the speculative boom, and whether or not it was right in not succumbing to the temptation of locking the stable door after the horse had been stolen and contracting credit during the panic, everything points to the fact that the Bank had learned its lesson. Its whole credit policy today is closely attuned to market conditions.[9]

The discount rate of the National Bank has been gradually coming down. During 1925 it decreased to 9 per cent. By the end of 1926 it was 7 per cent.

[9] In his conversations with responsible officials of the National Bank the author gathered the impression that next to the maintenance of the exchange rate within the limits of the gold points, the greatest concern of the Bank is the prevention of stock exchange speculation.

The principal effect of the panic on the banks of the country generally has been the weeding out of many of the mushroom-growth banks of the inflation period. During the year immediately following the panic the number of small private banks decreased by 30 per cent. In spite of this reduction in the number of banks, the banking equipment of the country still remains much too large for its needs, and this fact finds an interesting reflection in the credit situation through the margin between interest paid on deposits and interest charged on overdrafts.[10]

The cost of banking credit is very high in Austria. Such credit has always played an exceedingly important part in the economic life of Austria. Austrian industrial enterprises are financed in such a way that they operate with very limited resources of their own. Not only the capital required for improvement and extension, but also a considerable part of the working capital is usually furnished by the banks. This was one of the principal reasons why interest rates were high in Austria before the war in comparison with the industrial countries of Western Europe. But high as was the cost of capital before the war, it is much higher at the present time. This is due to a large number of reasons.

The high level of banking charges is one of these reasons. Before the war the margin between the

[10] An excellent discussion of the banking and credit situation in Austria is contained in Chapters V and VI of Part II of Layton, W. T., and Rist, C., *The Economic Situation in Austria.*

interest paid on deposits and the interest and commissions charged on overdrafts varied between 2 and 4 per cent. In 1925 it was almost twice that, and it has been as high as 11½ per cent.

In 1926 the interest rates decreased very markedly, but the margin between deposits and overdrafts still remained very large. The interest paid on savings deposits in December of that year was 4.5 per cent, but the interest charged for overdrafts was about 8 per cent, which, together with the banks' commission still make the margin very large.

This wide margin in favor of the bank is explained by the fact that the expenditures of the banks at the present time are disproportionate to their turnover. For example, the balance sheets of eight large Viennese banks show that between 1913 and 1924 the administrative expenses of these banks increased by 83 per cent; the taxes paid by them increased by 50 cent; while the amount of business done by them in 1924 was scarcely 30 per cent of the 1913 figure.[11]

Shortage of liquid funds is another important reason for the high cost of credit. One of the inescapable consequences of inflation is the destruction of working capital, and Austria has gone through this process. During the inflation period savings in the ordinary sense became impossible. Funds which might have been used for building up bank balances went into speculation, or were utilized for

[11] Basch, A., and Dvořáček, J., *Austria and Its Economic Existence,* p. 47.

extending plant and equipment without reference to needs. Scarcity of capital found a direct reflection in the rise of interest rates, which were pushed up still farther by the need of insuring the lender against continued currency depreciation.

Even after the stabilization of the currency the process of employing savings for bank deposits was not resumed. The stock exchange booms prevented this. Instead of easing the credit situation, stabilization brought with it new difficulties. Industry found itself compelled to compete with speculative investment brokers, and interest rates mounted in consequence.

An appreciable growth of savings did not begin until after the collapse of the stock exchange boom. At the beginning of January, 1923, the deposits in the nine large commercial banks of Vienna and in the savings banks of Vienna and the provincial capitals equalled 11 million schillings. By the end of that year they increased to only 55 millions. By the end of 1924, however, the total deposits increased to 184.1 millions; by the end of 1925 they were equal to 455.1 millions; while by the end of 1926, they were equal to 702.2 millions.[12]

The "rent" law is responsible for a peculiar deficiency in the credit structure of Austria. The city of Vienna still has on its statute books and in actual operation a law for the protection of tenants, introduced early in the post-war period. Under this law

[12] *Statistische Nachrichten,* January 25, 1927.

practically no rents are paid in the city, and real estate mortgages have practically ceased to exist as an instrument of credit.

Finally, the preponderance of short-term, rather than long-term credit, is an important factor in the Austrian credit situation. So far the bulk of foreign credits extended to Austria has been in the form of short-term loans or bank deposits.

Austrian industries and agriculture are in need of long-term credits. Such credits are exceedingly scarce. On the one hand, neither industrial nor agricultural enterprises are willing to saddle themselves with long-term obligations at the high rates of interest charged for capital at the present time. On the other hand, neither the domestic nor the foreign lenders are willing to accept the lower rates of interest which go with long-term loans, as long as short-term credit transactions continue to offer extremely lucrative returns.

The accumulation of liquid funds within Austria, in spite of the marked increase of savings deposits, is still insufficient to provide the country with adequate operating capital. For her economic development Austria needs long-term loans from abroad, and so far the amount of capital thus imported into the country has been very small.[13] The Council of the League of Nations, in withdrawing its control, authorized the Austrian government to use the unexpended remainder of the reconstruction loan for

[13] See Appendix, p. 586.

long-term productive credits. But Austria needs larger amounts of long-term investments than she has already received.

Since these investments would go directly into private productive enterprises, the government budget would not be involved in the payment of interest on them or in their eventual repayment. But these payments would constitute a new element in the international accounts of Austria. The country's ability to meet these payments would depend upon whether or not it succeeds in increasing its trade and service operations sufficiently to develop an adequate excess of income over outgo. As matters stand today, her international income is insufficient even for her present needs. This fact renders decidedly precarious the fiscal and currency stability which she has achieved.

The reasons for the continuance of Austria's unfavorable trade balances are apparent from the above discussion. Not abundantly supplied with agricultural resources and with what resources she has poorly developed, Austria is compelled to devote nearly a third of her foreign purchases to various articles of food. On the other hand she has an industrial productive capacity far in excess of the consumption requirements of her population. The operation of these industries requires the importation of fuel and certain raw materials, these imports constituting almost 30 per cent of the country's foreign purchases. Austria's industries supply four-fifths of the country's exports, but at the same time about one-third of Austrian imports consists of manufactured goods.

This situation is the result of the fact that while Austria's industrial equipment is comparatively large, it was not originally designed to satisfy primarily the needs of the territory in which it is located. It was a specialized part of the industrial equipment of pre-war Austria, other parts of which were located in Bohemia and elsewhere. It now supplies the country with an abundance of some of the primary commodities, and fails to supply it with many others.

This fact in itself would have presented no special anomaly had Austria an opportunity of disposing of her surplus industrial production outside her frontiers. But that has not so far been the case for reasons which we shall discuss later on when we come to deal with the international aspects of the Austrian situation.[14] In the meantime we must turn to a consideration of Austria's economic policy, on which the factors noted here have exercised a profound influence.

[14] See Part VII.

CHAPTER IX

AUSTRIA'S ECONOMIC POLICY

THE economic policy of the Republic of Austria has been dominated, from the very start, by the view that, as constituted by the treaties of peace, the country must either grow progressively poorer, or else obtain a larger scope for its economic activities. At times this view has taken the extreme form of a conviction that Austria is incapable of independent economic existence, and must, therefore, become a part of a larger economic territory. At other times it has found expression in efforts to open up adequate markets for Austrian industries. At all times Austria's policy has been directed toward breaking up the condition of virtual isolation in which the country found itself as a result of post-war conditions and policies.

As we have seen from the analysis contained in the last three chapters, Austria faced, during the first eight years of its existence, five major economic problems. Two of these problems have now been solved. The other three still remain.

Financial instability, which was so pressing a danger to Austria at the beginning of the country's existence, has now ceased to be a problem. The equilibrium of the budget is not likely to be threatened, unless the Austrian government chooses to expand the administrative personnel, which is now undeniably small, or unless it finds itself compelled to increase greatly the salaries of its officials, which are also undeniably low. Nor is the stability of the currency likely to be endangered, unless the international accounts take a turn for the worse, and foreign loans are not available to fill in the gap. But the problem of the international accounts still remains as pressing as ever. While it is not impossible of solution, it is greatly complicated by that of unemployment, which also still remains unsolved.

Austria may conceivably decrease her foreign trade deficits and thus close the gap in her international accounts either by diminishing her imports or by increasing her exports, or both. The first is not impossible. For example, by intensifying her agriculture, Austria can increase considerably her production of foodstuffs and thereby diminish her imports. Again, by developing waterpower, she can cut down her foreign purchases of coal. Finally, by changing somewhat her industrial equipment she can produce within the country some of the manufactured goods that she now brings in from abroad. But these changes would still leave it difficult for her to solve her unemployment problem, since it would involve a reduction of exports as well as of imports. Closely bound up with these two unsolved problems is the third, that of operating capital and long-term foreign credits.

These are the outstanding features of Austria's first eight years of post-war experience. They indicate clearly the economic character of present-day Austria, and the conditions which they represent have shaped the commercial and the general economic policy of the country. This policy has been very largely influenced by the existence of the special problem presented by the city of Vienna. Before we discuss the various features of Austria's economic policy, we must consider first the rôle played by the huge capital city in the life and policy of Austria.

I. THE PROBLEM OF VIENNA

Vienna contains nearly one-third of the population of Austria. It has almost two million inhabitants out of the country's total of about six and one-half millions. It is an important industrial center, with a much larger industrial equipment than is required by present-day Austria. It is also a great commercial and financial center, again with an equipment which is too large to satisfy the needs of Austria alone. Taken by itself, it is a community that can live only by exporting its surplus of industrial production and its services not only to the rest of Austria, but also to other countries.

For present-day Austria, Vienna can be either a liability or an asset. It forces upon the country the problem of its own maintenance, but does not, under existing circumstances, yield proportionate economic returns. It makes Austria primarily an industrial country, badly adjusted to its own resources, dependent upon an extensive foreign trade for the maintenance of a fair standard of living for its whole population.

We have already noted that the majority of Austria's numerous unemployed is usully found in the city of Vienna. It is Vienna's industries that are largely responsible for the country's burdensome unemployment problem, and the reason for this situation lies in the fact that these industries cannot export a sufficiently large volume of finished goods to keep them working to capacity. This insufficiency of exports results in large trade deficits, since imports must still be maintained at a fairly large volume to provide the population of the country with the necessities of life.

Nor are the services which Vienna renders to other countries sufficiently remunerative under present conditions to make up the differences. It is true that the capital city provides Austria with the bulk of the country's international income from service operations. But its activities as a commercial and banking center are limited by the policies of Austria's neighbors, who are determined to win for themselves a position in which they would have their own facilities for the performance of such services.

Before the war, the industries of Vienna were a part of the industrial equipment of a country with a population of 52 millions. The capital city was the undisputed commercial and financial center of that country. Its industries and its commercial and financial institutions were built up to serve the functions which it fulfilled in the Austro-Hungarian Monarchy. While popularly Vienna was regarded in many parts of the former Monarchy as a parasite, there is no doubt that its functions were genuinely important and useful in the economic life of the country, at the same time that they were profitable to itself.

Vienna can be a real asset to present-day Austria only if it is again afforded a larger scope for its economic activities than that provided by the Austrian Republic alone. It has retained to some extent the rôle it had played in the economic affairs of the Danubian territory, but not sufficiently to justify economically the size of its industrial and service equipment.

The problem of Vienna is the real core of the whole Austrian situation. It has exerted a profound influence on the development of the country's economic policy. It has dictated in a large degree, the position which Austria has occupied since the war in the affairs of central Europe.

The question of whether or not present-day Austria is capable of independent existence, is, in reality, the question of whether or not the city of Vienna can be maintained merely as a part of Austria's present economic system. And there seem to be two possible answers to this question. Either Vienna must regain a larger scope for its economic activities, or it must be reduced in size and changed in character to fit the requirements of the country for which it serves as the capital city.

The second of these two solutions of the problem of Vienna is, theoretically, not impossible of achievement. We have already seen that the resources of Austria are probably sufficient to support the population of the country, but that if this is to be achieved, the Austrian economic system has to be reorganized with this end in view. A considerable portion of Vienna's population has to be moved to the rural districts. The whole industrial equipment has to be placed on a somewhat different basis than at the present time.

The effort involved in the reduction of the city of Vienna and the reorganization of the economic system of the country is so great, that the Austrians have not as yet brought themselves to a serious contemplation of this possibility. On the contrary, they have directed all their efforts toward encompassing the first solution of the problem of Vienna, namely, an increase in the scope of its economic activities. Their whole economic policy has been focussed on this as its central point.[1]

[1] We are not here concerned with the social aspects of the Austrian situation. For a good analysis of this phase see Macartney, C. A., *The Social Revolution in Austria*, London, 1926.

II. TARIFF POLICY AND TREATY ARRANGEMENTS

Confronted with the problem of Vienna, as we have just described it, the Republic of Austria would probably have tended, under more or less normal conditions, toward free trade. Possession of a large industrial equipment and dependence on other countries for large amounts of food, fuel, and raw materials are factors which theoretically would have indicated for her the need of an extensive and unhampered trade intercourse with other countries. But in the conditions in which Austria found herself at the beginning of her post-war existence, no such policy, or even anything approaching it, was possible. Austria could not escape the régime of export and import prohibitions and restrictions which became established in all the countries of central and eastern Europe.

Austria used the policy of trade restrictions very largely for bargaining purposes. She was hard hit by the policy of export prohibitions for food pursued by her agricultural neighbors, which compelled her to purchase her cereals and meats overseas at very high prices. She was also suffering from import restrictions applied by her neighbors to manufactured goods. Her own trade restrictions were introduced primarily for the purpose of using them as arguments in her negotiations with the neighboring countries.

The proposals of the Portorose Conference regarding the abolition of export and import restrictions found a ready acceptance in Austria. But Austria felt that she could not take the initiative in inaugurating the measures proposed until there was some assurance that her action would be followed by similar action on the part of the other countries concerned. And there seemed to be no such concerted action in sight. In fact, there was definite opposition to the Portorose proposals on the part of some of the countries, notably Yugoslavia.[2]

Another reason given by the Austrians for their continued maintenance of trade restrictions was the need of preventing an influx of goods from Czechoslovakia and Germany, both of which maintained rigorous systems of import restrictions. By shutting her markets to Czechoslovak and German imports, Austria hoped to obtain from these two countries facilities for the admission of her goods to their markets.[3]

As regards export prohibitions, Austria applied them to such commodities as foodstuffs, wood, paper, hides, etc., for the express purpose of keeping the prices of these commodities low in the domestic market. In doing this, she used exactly the same arguments as those employed by her agricultural neighbors in justifying their maintenance of export prohibitions for foodstuffs. Thus, she, too, helped

[2] Phillpotts, O. S., *Report on the Economic and Commercial Situation of Austria,* London, 1922, p. 35.

[3] Philpotts, O. S., *Report on the Industrial and Commercial Situation of Austria,* 1923, p. 40.

to create the very situation which she herself bitterly criticized.

Finally currency conditions compelled Austria to regulate foreign trade by means of government control over transactions in foreign exchanges. In fact Austria was among the first of the Danubian States to move in this direction. This was done partly to protect the rate of exchange of the Austrian crown, and partly again for bargaining purposes.[4]

As she developed her tariff policy, Austria gradually gave up many of her trade restrictions. The basis of bargaining in commercial negotiations shifted to customs duties. But that was only one element in the country's tariff policy.

Austria's tariff policy has been definitely directed toward the protection of the home market. Her manufacturing interests, deprived of their protected markets in the whole territory of the Austro-Hungarian Monarchy, found themselves compelled to rely mostly on the small domestic market of the Austrian Republic. In this market, at least, they demanded protection from foreign competition.

An attempt to meet these demands was made in 1922, when the first draft of a new tariff was placed before the country. Prior to that, Austria had been applying the old Austro-Hungarian tariff of 1906, with the modifications introduced in it during the war, the most important of which was the remission

[4] In footnote on p. 122 we described this system of controlling foreign exchanges.

of duties on foodstuffs and industrial raw materials. The rates of the old tariff, expressed in crowns, were periodically adjusted to compensate for the fall in the crown exchange. But these adjustments always lagged behind the exchange, the last increase to 10,000 times the pre-war rates having been made at the time when a gold crown was worth approximately 14,000 paper crowns. In this manner the customs duties levied in the country were only about 70 per cent of the pre-war.

The draft tariff of 1922 attempted to change this situation. This tariff proposal provided for the payment of duties in gold or at the gold parity. It was based on a general level of duties considerably higher than the pre-war. These "general duties" were frankly included for bargaining purposes, the draft tariff also providing for minimum "applied rates," which, although somewhat lower than similar duties in the pre-war tariff, were still higher than those which were actually in operation at the time the tariff came under discussion.

The general effect of the new tariff would have been an increase of protection. As a result, the proposal encountered strong opposition from the commercial classes, who considered it too highly protectionist, and even more so from the agricultural groups, who feared that it would result in too large a rise in the cost of manufactured articles. Opposition from these two quarters made the proposal impossible.

For the next two years, Austria continued to apply the old Austro-Hungarian tariff with the original rates multiplied by 10,000. But a new tariff was finally worked out and enacted in the summer of 1924. It went into effect on January 1, 1925.

The tariff of 1924 represented a compromise between the industrial and the agricultural interests. It gave industry a higher protection than it had enjoyed before, but at the same time it provided for the reintroduction of agricultural duties. In 1926 the tariff was further amended in the direction of increased agricultural duties.

Thus the Austrian tariff is of a decidedly protectionist and bargaining character. While its general level of duties is lower than that obtaining in the other Danubian countries, it is slightly higher than the old Austro-Hungarian tariff, especially in the case of industrial products. Altogether, it adds 19.2 per cent to the value of imported products, as against 18.9 per cent under the pre-war tariff.[5] Its bargaining nature is apparent from the reductions made in its general rates by the commercial treaties negotiated by Austria before and after it went into effect.

Austria's commercial treaty policy has been directed toward the opening up of markets for her exports of manufactured goods. First by means of "quota" agreements, and later on by means of tariff

[5] *Zollhöhe und Warenwerte,* Memorandum prepared by the Austrian National Committee of the International Chamber of Commerce, Vienna, 1927, Table I.

treaties, she has sought consistently to obtain for her exports an entry into the neighboring states.

In 1920-1922 Austria concluded a series of trade agreements with her Danubian neighbors, as well as with Germany, Poland, and Russia. All these agreements were of the "quota" nature, according reciprocal exemptions from import and export prohibitions. They were all based on the most-favored-nation treatment principle.

In the fall of 1922, the Austrian Committee of the Council of the League of Nations, which was responsible for the financial reconstruction of Austria, recommended, as one of the means for the improvement of the Austrian situation, the conclusion by Austria of commercial treaties, based on reciprocal most-favored-nation treatment. Acting in accordance with this recommendation, the Austrian government, in December of the same year, approached all European governments with a proposal to enter into negotiations for the conclusion of such treaties.

There was, however, one important obstacle in the way of these negotiations. The treaty of St. Germain had obligated Austria to grant the Allied powers most-favored-nation treatment for three years from the coming into force of the treaty, without reciprocity on their part. This provision expired in July, 1923, and it was not until some months after the proposal made by the Austrian government that negotiations for bilateral commercial treaties really began.

The first treaty of this character was concluded with Italy in April, 1923. This was followed in the same year by treaties with France and with the Customs Union of Belgium and Luxemburg. Although these treaties do not give Austria complete reciprocity in most-favored-nation treatment, they nevertheless afford her important concessions in tariff duties.

In 1924 Austria concluded three important commercial conventions. They were the treaties with Germany and Czechoslovakia and a supplementary agreement with France. All three of these conventions went into effect on January 1, 1925, simultaneously with the putting into force of the new Austrian tariff. In fact they were worked out with direct reference to the tariff and carried with them reductions in many of the general duties provided by the new tariff.

During the next two years Austria continued her efforts to enter into commercial treaty relations with other countries. She concluded tariff treaties with Hungary and Yugoslavia, and a more or less detailed trade agreement with Rumania. She also signed twelve other treaties, all of them based on most-favored-nation treatment principle.[6]

The trade facilities afforded by these commercial treaties have not been adequate for Austria's needs. Even when enjoying a large degree of protection in

[6] For a general statement of Austria's commercial treaty policy see the *Memorandum*, submitted by the Austrian delegation to the International Economic Conference, Geneva, 1927.

the home market, Austrian industries find that their productive capacity far exceeds domestic requirements. In other words, the economic life of Austria is so organized that she has to place a comparatively large share of her production in foreign markets: otherwise she finds herself burdened with the problem of heavy unemployment. And treaty arrangements thus far made with her Danubian neighbors have not sufficed to give her relief in this direction. It is true that the conclusion of the treaties made it possible for Austria to increase her exports. But these increases have affected her exports to the Danubian States which are her principal markets, much less than her sales to other countries. As we noted in Chapter VI, the Danubian States have been playing a decreasingly important rôle as purchasers of Austrian exports. This has been due to a number of causes.

In the first place, the Danubian countries have been steadily developing their own industries under tariff protection. The result has been that the tariff concessions they have accorded Austria have been so designed as not to prejudice too much their own industrial interests. Hence the effect of these concessions has not been very great so far as Austrian exports to the Danubian countries are concerned.

In the second place, such concessions as Austria has been able to obtain have not been on any permanent basis. Her treaty arrangements are not of the long-term character. For example, in her relations with Czechoslovakia, she signed a trade agreement in 1921, a commercial treaty in 1924, a supplementary convention some time later, and was in 1927 again engaged in negotiations for a revision of the treaty. Under the circumstances, it is extremely difficult for Austrian industries to plan their activities with any degree of assurance.

In the third place, Austria does not enjoy her pre-war preferential position in Danubian markets. On the contrary, all these markets have now become world markets, in which she has to meet the competition of better organized and industrially more powerful nations. And in the world markets, her competitive position is not very strong.

It has been estimated [7] that present-day wages in Austria are below those of the German workmen, for example, although the nominal wages of skilled labor have reached the pre-war level, while those of unskilled labor have exceeded it. Real wages, too, have approximately reached the pre-war level, thanks to the operation of the "rent law." But with the normalization of the rent situation, Austria will face a condition in which either real wages have to fall below the pre-war level, or else Austrian exports will have to find themselves in an extremely difficult competitive position.

The only alternative to this situation is for Austria to acquire again the facilities of a large protected

[7] In Layton, W. T., and Rist, C., *The Economic Situation of Austria*, p. 40.

market of the kind that her industries enjoyed before the war. Hence the insistence in her economic policy on the need for Austria of a larger scope of economic activity.

III. PLANS FOR A LARGER ECONOMIC TERRITORY

Austria sees for herself two possibilities for enlarging the scope of her economic activities. One is the formation of some sort of an economic union among the Danubian countries. The other is an economic, or even a political, union between herself and Germany. Both plans have adherents and opponents in the country. Both present advantages, as well as disadvantages, and both involve great difficulties.

Generally speaking, Austria favors a Danubian economic union. The advocates of this plan maintain that the establishment of such a union would mean for her the least readjustment of her economic system. The great reservoirs of foodstuffs, fuel, and raw materials would again become open to her. Her industries would once more become a component part of the industrial system of the whole Danubian territory. The close correlation between her industrial centers and those of Bohemia would become re-established, and the combined equipment of Austria and Czechoslovakia would have an opportunity for production on a large scale.

A large domestic market would once more be created for Austrian industries. Whether in the form of a customs union or of a regional preferential customs arrangement, a Danubian economic union would involve the closing of its market to the rest of the world, just as the Austro-Hungarian market was surrounded by a protective tariff wall. In this manner Austria would escape the competitive handicaps which, under ordinary treaty arrangements, will confront her in the Danubian markets.

The commercial institutions of Vienna, it is claimed, would also profit by the establishment of a Danubian economic union. The powerful trade organization which they had developed before the war would give them a great advantage over the weaker and the more recently established trade organizations now existing in the other Danubian countries.

Similarly, the financial institutions of Vienna would obtain an opportunity for reacquiring the dominant position which they had enjoyed in the Monarchy. They are still more powerful than the similar institutions which have come into existence in the other countries, while their international contacts are still on such a strong basis that the great Vienna banks would probably have little difficulty in establishing themselves once more as the principal financial centers of the union.

There is general agreement in Austria that a Danubian customs arrangement, either in the form of a union or of a regional preferential régime, would be beneficial to Austria. But there is a division of opinion as to whether or not any such arrangement would solve all of Austria's problems.

There is strong doubt in some Austrian quarters concerning the adequacy for Austria of a Danubian customs arrangement. The groups which hold this view maintain that a customs arrangement would provide merely an alleviation, but not a solution for the difficulties which confront Austria. They argue that even the establishment of free trade among a number of sovereign states does not provide a sufficient basis for a really close economic collaboration among them, and point to Austria's experience with Hungary before the war, when even a common sovereignty did not prevent serious economic conflicts, quite apart from questions of customs tariffs.

In the opinion of these groups, any customs arrangement would be merely an extension, with some beneficent modifications, of any commercial treaty régime. Each of the countries entering such an arrangement would still be confronted by its own problems and aspirations, and would direct its policy first and foremost toward the solution of these problems and the satisfaction of these aspirations. Each of them has now attained a certain degree of industrial development, which it would be loath to give up altogether.

They point to the possibility of such means of maintaining home industries as "administrative" protection. For example, in the countries in which a machine industry has come into existence, the governments might adopt the policy of purchasing from home enterprises—rather than from similar enterprises in other parts of the customs union—supplies for the state-owned railways, for public buildings, etc. The same might be done with regard to cloth and footwear for the army and the uniformed officials. And this might be done even if the cost of domestic production is higher than the cost of importation. Pre-war history furnishes ample examples of this.

Nor are they at all certain that merely a free customs régime would suffice to restore to Vienna anything like the dominant commercial and financial position that it had before the war. Here, again, administrative protection can be invoked very effectively. They readily admit that the Vienna money market would still be of great importance to all the States in the customs union, but they doubt that the increase of its activities in this regard would be adequate to Vienna's requirements for international service operations.[8]

What Austria really needs, according to the proponents of this view, is to be permanently and completely incorporated in a larger economic territory. They turn their attention to the plan for an economic union between Austria and Germany.

Austro-German union is the alternative to the

[8] The best statement of this view is found in *Das oesterreichische Wirtschaftsproblem,* a memorandum prepared by the economic committee of the Austrian-German Union in Vienna, published in *Der oesterreichische Volkswirt,* July 18, 1925.

plan for a Danubian customs arrangement. A more or less widespread advocacy of this project has been a constantly recurring phenomenon in Austria since the very beginning of the post-war period. As a matter of fact, the idea of pan-German unity, which would involve an economic or a political union between Germany and Austria, antedated the World War by a whole century. Ever since the period immediately succeeding the Napoleonic wars, numerous attempts were made to bring it about. Had it not been for Bismarck's opposition, Austria-Hungary might have become part of the German Customs Union. During the World War, elaborate plans were worked out for the creation of an economic union between two Teutonic Empires.[9] At the end of the War, Austrian opinion was overwhelmingly in favor of union with Germany.

On November 12, 1918, the day following the abdication of Emperor Charles, the Provisional National Assembly of Austria proclaimed simultaneously the creation of the Austrian Republic and its union with Germany. In its declaration, it stated: "German Austria constitutes a part of the German Republic." The Constitutional National Assembly

[9] See Pentmann, J., *Die Zollunionsidee und ihre Wandlungen im Rahmen der wirtschaftspolitischen Ideen und der Wirtschaftspolitik des 19. Jahrhunderts bis zur Gegenwart*, Jena, 1917, Chapter I; Gratz, Gustav, and Schüller, Richard, *Die Asussere Wirtschaftspolitik Oesterreich-Ungarns: Mitteleuropäische Pläne*, Vienna, 1925; and Grossmann, Eugène, *Methods of Economic Rapprochement*, document of the Preparatory Committee for the International Economic Conference, Geneva, 1926, pp. 15-21.

officially proclaimed the union on March 12, 1919.[10] These proclamations were withdrawn at the demand of the Allied powers, but important groups in Austria have never ceased from advocating the union, especially in periods of economic crises.

Numerous and varied arguments are advanced in favor of Austro-German economic union. It is maintained that union with Germany would give Austrian industry a large domestic market, since it would become a part of the German industrial equipment. The highly specialized producers of Vienna (art goods, fine leathers, etc.) would be the largest gainers from such a change. German initiative would develop the tourist resorts of Austria. The trade apparatus of Vienna would serve as the southward outlet for German and Austrian industry. Austria would have the protection of a great power against administrative discriminations of other countries. With Austria as a part of the German economic system, Austrian industry would have access to the great money markets of Germany, while Austrian labor would have an opportunity for raising its standard of living.[11]

The arguments advanced against union with Germany are mainly on the score of the difficulties that might be encountered by Austrian industries when faced with the competition of similar industries in Germany. The tendency in Austria is to minimize

[10] De Bordes, J., *The Austrian Crown,* p. 13.
[11] *Das oesterreichische Wirtschaftsproblem,* Section VII.

this danger on the ground that the situation thus created could be adjusted along lines of greater specialization.[12]

There is no lack of realization in Austria of the fact that great difficulties are involved in the consummation of either a Danubian or an Austro-German union. Each of these projects involves serious changes in the existing situation in central Europe. Moreover, they bring into play the interests of other European powers. Nevertheless, the Austrian policy is determinedly directed toward finding some such solution of the very grave and difficult situation with which the country is confronted.

[12] For a discussion of the problems indicated here see *Für und wider die Donauföderation* (I. "Donauföderation," by J. C. Barolin; II. "Los Vom Rhein!" by K. Schechner), Vienna, 1926; and Hantos, Elemér, *Die Handelspolitik in Mitteleuropa.*

PART III

CZECHOSLOVAKIA'S EXPERIENCE SINCE THE WAR

CHAPTER X

THE PROBLEMS OF CZECHOSLOVAKIA

Czechoslovakia inherited some of the pressing unsolved problems of the Austro-Hungarian Monarchy. Austria was stripped of her racial minorities; Czechoslovakia is racially a heterogeneous state. Of her population of a little more than 13.5 millions, there are 8.5 million Czechoslovaks proper—6.5 million Czechs and about 2 million Slovaks. Of the remaining population, a little over 3 millions are Germans, three-quarters of a million are Hungarians, and almost half a million are Ruthenians. The racial conflicts of the old Monarchy became transferred to Czechoslovakia, with the Czechs playing the rôle of the dominant group, and the Germans and Hungarians as the chief and most pugnacious minorities. Moreover, Czechoslovakia inherited in some degree the population problem of the old Monarchy.

The racial question flared up in Czechoslovakia immediately after the establishment of the republic. The leadership of the country was exclusively in the hands of the Czechs and the Slovaks. The German and the Hungarian minorities were not represented in the National Assembly which drafted the constitution of the country, and refused to recognize the legality of the government thus established. They demanded, as their right under the principle of self-determination, permission to join respectively Germany and Hungary. For the first few years, the German industrial and trade interests in Czechoslovakia, which are very powerful, sought affiliations with groups in Germany, rather than in the country of which they were a part.

Gradually, however, the antagonisms subsided. The collapse of the German currency forced the German industrial and trade interests in Czechoslovakia to turn to home affiliations. Under the guidance of President Masaryk and his associates the violent factionism which characterized the political life of the country at the beginning gave way to more tolerant attitudes. The German and the Hungarian minorities entered the parliament, and in 1926, when the question of agricultural protection broke up the Czechoslovak government coalition along class lines, the German minority split up in a similar manner. In the political regroupings that followed, economic interests rather than racial solidarity became the basis. With the appointment of two German leaders as Cabinet Ministers and of a representative of German industry as one of the directors of the National Bank, the racial problem in Czechoslovakia has adjusted itself to what might be considered as a working arrangement.

Economically, the first task that confronted Czechoslovakia was one of national consolidation. One part of the country had been formerly incorporated in Austria, the other part, in Hungary. A new and unified administration and a coordinated system of transportation and communication had to be created for the country. All this placed a tremendous burden on the fiscal resources of the newly established republic.

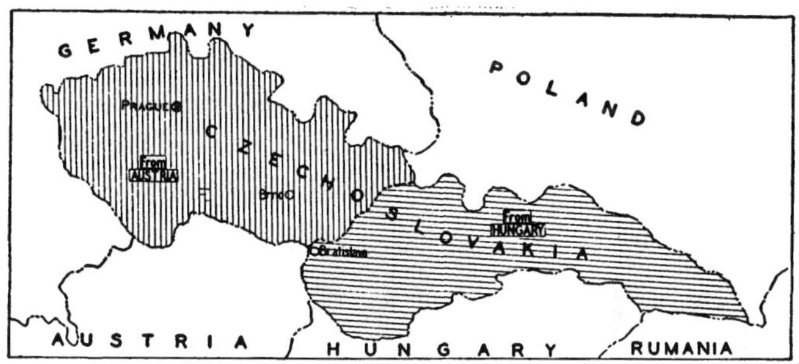

PRE-WAR SOVEREIGNTY OF LANDS COMPRISING CZECHOSLOVAKIA

Coordinated with the problem of consolidation, was the task of establishing and maintaining economic and financial stability. A new currency system had to be set up, and the government budget had to be managed in such a way as to keep Czechoslovakia from following the example of her neighbors, who were sinking deeper and deeper in the morass of monetary inflation.

Finally, the general economic life of the country had to be adjusted to Czechoslovakia's new international position. Czechoslovakia inherited a large share of the old Monarchy's industrial equipment, and only one-quarter of its population. Frontiers arose between these industries and their old-established markets. New conditions of competition came into existence and had to be faced.

From the point of view of the currency, Czechoslovakia passed through several periods. From 1919 to the middle of 1922, there was a period of depreciation; then for half a year, currency appreciation; after that, stable currency. External circumstances were principally responsible for these changes, since both the budgetary and the foreign trade situation made for stability from the very start.

From the point of view of economic adjustment, Czechoslovakia devoted the bulk of her efforts at the beginning to the task of national consolidation. The upbuilding of a unified administration and the creation of a military establishment were costly undertakings. Moreover, large outlays of capital were required for the reorganization of the railways, the postal system, the telegraph and telephone lines, and for other public works. The means for all this had to be provided out of the budget, which drew into the Treasury a relatively enormous portion of the country's national income to an almost complete neglect of the other pressing economic needs.

It was only by 1926 that the major part of this task of national consolidation was completed, and the country could turn serious attention to the problem of its general economic adjustment. The maintenance of living conditions for her population involves for Czechoslovakia a range of productive activities in both industry and agriculture which depends for its scope on many conditions outside the country's own control. Foreign markets play a rôle of utmost importance, and considerations of the country's competitive position acquire, therefore, a truly vital significance.

Czechoslovakia's pressing problems during the first eight years of the country's independent existence have thus been in the domain of national consolidation and of fiscal and currency stabilization. These problems she has now solved, but back of them lie the more far-reaching problems of the nation's general economic position, especially in the realm of world competition.

CHAPTER XI

CZECHOSLOVAKIA'S CURRENCY AND FISCAL PROBLEMS

Czechoslovakia, like Austria, faced at the beginning of her independent existence a budgetary situation in which expenditures greatly exceeded revenues. But unlike Austria, she refused from the start to succumb to the temptation of the deceptively easy way out of budgetary difficulties provided by monetary inflation. On the contrary, she exhibited a strong determination to avoid fiscal inflation at all costs.

There were several factors that worked to her advantage in this regard. As one of the victors in the war, Czechoslovakia was not burdened with an undetermined reparation claim and was not bound by a blanket mortgage to the Reparation Commission, such as deprived the vanquished states of all freedom of financial action. She had from the start a strong central government and a determined financial leadership. Moreover, the country received, in the division of Austro-Hungarian resources, extensive natural wealth and a large industrial equipment, which facilitated its general economic recovery.

Czechoslovakia achieved currency and fiscal stability earlier than any of the Danubian countries. As we saw above, she was the first of the heirs of the Austro-Hungarian Monarchy to break away effectively from the currency system of the Austro-Hungarian Bank and to establish a system of her own. For several years thereafter she led the way in the process of establishing a stable currency and in placing her budgetary practices on a sound basis. Although the whole process of fiscal and currency stabilization has not, as yet, been fully completed, the results achieved have been very significant.

I. CURRENCY STABILIZATION AND THE NATIONAL BANK

After dissociating the currency which was in circulation in her territory from the management of the Austro-Hungarian Bank, Czechoslovakia faced the problem of deciding the basis on which her monetary policy was to be constructed. There were three principal views advanced in this regard. The first was that the whole Austro-Hungarian Bank issue should be repudiated and the country should immediately proceed to the creation of a new currency. The second was that the Austro-Hungarian notes should be retained in the form of Czechoslovak notes, but that their gold parity should be legally devaluated. The third was that the pre-war parity of the Austro-Hungarian crown should be made the legal parity of the Czechoslovak crown and that the latter should be gradually restored to this parity by a process of deflation.

At the beginning Czechoslovakia chose a return to the pre-war crown parity rather than a repudiation or legal devaluation of the notes in circulation. The principal advocate of this view was Dr. Alois Rašín, Czechoslovakia's first Minister of Finance. He and his adherents argued that this course of action would necessitate the least possible general dislocation and would be the safest way of achieving financial stability, while either of the other two courses would present much greater difficulties.[1]

Dr. Rašín's policy of deflation won the day. The Austro-Hungarian notes circulating in Czechoslovak territory were stamped in March, 1919, in pursuance of the law of February 25 of that year. By the law of April 10 of the same year, these stamped notes were converted into notes of the Czechoslovak state, the unit of currency to be known as the Czechoslovak crown, abbreviated, Kč. One month later a Banking Department was established at the Ministry of Finance to act as the bank of issue, and the groundwork was laid for the process of deflation.

A drastic reduction of the volume of currency in circulation was made at the time of the stamping

[1] The policy of repudiation was advocated mainly by Dr. Jaroslav Preiss, head of the Živnostenská Banka; the policy of legal devaluation found its principal support from Professor V. Brdlík, who later on became Vice-Governor of the National Bank, and Professor J. Koloušek. See Rašín, A., *Financial Policy of Czechoslovakia*, pp. 37-9, and Koloušek, J., *Rašínova reforma měny;* Prague, 1919.

of the Austro-Hungarian bank notes. The law of February 25 provided for the retention by the government of one-half of all the notes presented, as well as of 50 per cent of the checking accounts and of the Treasury bills held by the branches of the Austro-Hungarian Bank in Czechoslovakia. Government bonds bearing interest of one per cent were given in exchange for the notes thus retained. These bonds were to be presented later on as payments on account of a capital levy, which was introduced at the same time for the purpose of extinguishing the government debt created by the taking over of the bank notes.

As a result of these operations the volume of currency in circulation was decreased by about 30 per cent. The bank notes presented for stamping and the current accounts and Treasury bills taken over amounted to 9,520 million crowns; the amount retained by the government was 2,781.5 millions.[2] When the Banking Department of the Ministry of Finance began its operations, the volume of potential currency in circulation was thus 6,738.5 million crowns. As it issued its own notes and exchanged them for the stamped bank notes, the Banking Department gradually took over this currency, in addition to which the state handed over to it the notes retained at the time of the stamping. All these notes became a part of its liabilities, balanced

[2] The amount of notes exchanged for bonds was less than one-half of the total because of exemptions for small holders.

on the asset side by a government debt to it of the same amount. By the law of April 10 the above amount was made the maximum limit of uncovered note issue. Any notes issued above this amount were to be secured by precious metals, foreign bills, commercial paper, or advances on stocks and shares.

While thus seeking to put an end to fiduciary inflation, Dr. Rašín also made strenuous efforts toward the creation of a gold fund, which would eventually permit the establishment of the gold standard.[3] As matters worked out, however, both in Czechoslovakia and in the rest of Europe, Dr. Rašín's original program could not be carried out in its entirety. His policy with regard to fiduciary inflation was continued by his successors, but untoward circumstances precluded the possibility of sufficiently rapid deflation to permit a revaluation of the crown to the pre-war parity.

The policy of a return to the pre-war parity was given up early in favor of one of stabilization at a lower gold value. A number of internal and external circumstances during the years 1919-22 carried the Czechoslovak crown through a series of fluctuations, until at last a condition of stability was reached. Chief among these circumstances were the internal price situation and the vicissitudes of the rate of exchange.

The year immediately following the war was

[3] See Dr. Rašín's own exposition of his policies and measures in his *Financial Policy of Czechoslovakia.*

characterized in Czechoslovakia, as elsewhere in Europe, by a sharp rise in prices. And this rise continued through the year 1920, although in other countries which like Czechoslovakia had given up the practice of fiduciary inflation (for example, Great Britain) the trend of prices was downward. In 1921 the Czechoslovak price index declined during the first half of the year, but rose again during the second half, reaching its highest point in December of that year and in January, 1922. From that high point the index declined gradually through the first half of 1922 and dropped rapidly through the second half. The following table shows these fluctuations is the price index.[4]

MOVEMENT OF WHOLESALE PRICES IN CZECHOSLOVAKIA, 1920-1922
(On paper currency basis; July 1914 = 100)

Year	January	June	December
1920	....[a]	....[a]	1,542
1921	1,458	1,270	1,674
1922	1,675	1,471	999

[a] No data available.

These fluctuations of the price index were due to several causes. The complicated system of trade restrictions, which characterized the situation in central and eastern Europe, was partly responsible for the high prices prevailing in 1920 and the first

[4] Mildschuh, V., "Currency Conditions," *Czechoslovakia*, New York, 1924.

half of 1921. The price index for this period would probably have been even higher, had not the government regulated the prices of the principal agricultural products. The restoration of freer trade intercourse in the first half of 1921 led to a drop in prices, but the abolition of government price regulation again raised the index in the second half of the year.

These price movements had their effect on the rate of exchange. In turn, they were, of course affected by the fluctuations in the exchange rate. The Czechoslovak crown began to be quoted on the money exchanges of other countries about April, 1919. During that month, the average rate in New York was a little over 6 cents. By the end of the year, it dropped to about 1.5 cents. In February, 1920, it reached its lowest level, and was quoted at less than one cent. By the middle of that year it recovered to over 2 cents, dropped again by the end of the year to 1.3 cents, fluctuated around that level until the middle of 1921, and then began to appreciate.

The depreciation which took place during the year 1919 is easy enough to understand. The trade balance was adverse, the general conditions all through central Europe chaotic. The fluctuations of the years 1920 and 1921, however, do not lend themselves to so simple an explanation. The balance of trade was favorable, the budgetary deficits were covered by means of domestic loans. Presumably there should have been nothing to disturb the exchange. As a matter of fact, however, the Czechoslovak crown followed during most of this period the course of the Austrian crown and the German mark. For two years, from the middle of 1919 to the middle of 1921, it was quoted in the foreign money markets above the Austrian crown and somewhat below the German mark, but it always rose and fell with these two currencies. It was only during the second half of 1921 that the Czechoslovak crown parted company with the Austrian and German currencies. The two latter then entered definitely upon a downward course, which finally ended in their complete annihilation. The Czechoslovak crown, on the other hand, began to appreciate.[5]

In one very important sense there was a direct connection between the depreciation of the Austrian and the German currencies and the appreciation of

[5] The comparative rates of exchange for the three countries are given as follows by *European Currency and Finance*, monthly averages in cents on the New York market:

Date	Czechoslovak Crown	Austrian Crown	German Mark
July, 1919	5.63	2.90	6.64
January, 1920	1.43	.47	1.69
*February "	.98	.38	1.05
July "	2.20	.66	2.53
January, 1921	1.30	.26	1.60
July "	1.31	.15	1.30
January, 1922	1.73	.0325	.52
July "	2.19	.0038	.20
†October "	3.29	.0014	.03
December "	3.10	.0014	.01

* Lowest monthly average for Czechoslovakia.
† Highest monthly average for Czechoslovakia.

the Czechoslovak crown. The German currency began to break under the burden of reparation payments imposed by the London Schedule of Payments of 1921. The Austrian currency was shattered by continuing budgetary deficits, covered by new issues of paper money, and by large adverse trade balances. In Czechoslovakia, on the other hand, the foreign trade balance continued to be favorable, while the budgetary policy rendered fiscal inflation unlikely. The result of this was that the flight of capital from Germany and Austria was directed to a considerable extent to Czechoslovakia, and the demand for Czechoslovak crowns served to raise their exchange rate.

Once having achieved freedom from the influence of the German and Austrian currencies on the international exchange markets, Czechoslovakia could turn her attention to the stabilization of her own currency. By that time it was apparent that the general trend of exchanges in the countries surrounding Czechoslovakia was distinctly downward, and that the restoration of pre-war parity was almost impossible. Seizing the opportunity presented by the period of appreciation, the Czechoslovak government decided upon a policy of stabilization.

The Czechoslovak crown was stabilized at the end of 1922. The level which the exchange rate of the crown reached by that time, about 3 cents, was taken as the basis of stabilization, and the Banking Department of the Ministry of Finance undertook to keep the rate at that level. From that time on the exchange rate of the crown has been kept roughly at one-seventh of the pre-war parity, fluctuating from a little under to a little over 3 cents.

At the beginning of the stabilization period Czechoslovakia passed through a serious exchange crisis. The rapid appreciation of the crown during the second half of 1922 was induced very largely by artificial circumstances, namely, the influx of foreign capital. There was a feeling in some economic and financial circles in the country that the rate established was too high for permanent stabilization and could not be maintained. Moreover, it was considered that the high rate of exchange would result in a very severe business depression. Finally, the impending clash between France and Germany over the reparation question, which culminated in the French occupation of the Ruhr, made the whole central European situation highly uncertain. All these factors combined to produce in Czechoslovakia in December, 1922, an unstable and panicky atmosphere, which resolved itself into a severe monetary crisis.

The form which the crisis assumed was a "flight from the crown." There suddenly developed a large demand for stable foreign currencies which threatened to depreciate once more the Czechoslovak exchange. The crisis abated, however, very quickly under the influence of a number of drastic measures taken by the Czechoslovak government.

During the year 1922 the Banking Department had succeeded in accumulating a large stock of foreign bills and currencies. On February 28 of that year these stocks amounted to 333 million crowns; by November 30 they stood at 1,541 millions. In order to prevent the depreciation of the crown, the Banking Department began selling its foreign bills and currencies. By December 31, the stocks were reduced to 658 million crowns. In this manner the exchange rate was maintained, although the sales of foreign bills had to be continued through the month of January, 1923, with the result that by January 31 of that year the stocks amounted to only 409 million crowns.

At the same time a number of regulations were introduced by the government with regard to transactions in foreign bills. During the first three years of the country's existence, Czechoslovakia, in common with all the other central European States, maintained a system of rigid government control over transactions in foreign bills and currencies. Starting with August, 1921, however, this control was gradually relaxed, and by December, 1922, it was in reality more or less nominal. During that month, however, control was re-established, and by the order of January 5, 1923, all of the existing regulations with regard to transactions in foreign bills and currencies were again put into full force. In this manner, the government found it possible to curb the speculative influences, which were very active during the crisis, and by February, 1923, the situation began to improve.

While the monetary crisis was still acute, Dr. Rašín was assassinated. But his successors at the Ministry of Finance have continued his policy of maintaining the exchange rate of the crown at the level established in 1922.

The stabilization of the currency was followed by a severe business depression. In this respect, Czechoslovakia had the same experience as all the other countries that have passed through the process. Although in her case the depressive effects were somewhat offset by the collapse of Germany and the consequent increased demand for Czechoslovak products in Germany and elsewhere, nevertheless their influence was felt very strongly.

Prior to the stabilization of the currency the Czechoslovak crown's rate of exchange did not correspond to its purchasing power within the country. All through 1920, 1921 and the first half of 1922 the crown was undervalued with respect to domestic prices. This acted as a stimulus to exports and to business activity in general. The rapid rise of the exchange rate of the crown during the second half of 1922 was not fully reflected in the internal price situation, with the result that at the end of that year and through a part of the year 1923 the crown was overvalued. This, in turn, acted as a deterrent to foreign trade and to business activity in general. As we shall see later on, the situation thus created was clearly reflected in the growth of unemployment.[6]

The under- or overvaluation of the Czechoslovak crown was particularly important with respect to Germany, which is Czechoslovakia's largest customer. During the time that the two currencies followed the same course, there was very little difference, so far as Germany was concerned, between the exchange rate and the internal purchasing power of the Czechoslovak crown. But after the mark and the crown parted company, with the former on the downgrade and the latter on the upgrade, the difference became considerable.[7] Normally this situation would have operated as an obstacle to Czechoslovak exports into Germany. But the French occupation of the Ruhr, which took place several months after stabilization began in Czechoslovakia, forced Germany to increase her imports of Czechoslovak coal and metallurgical products, in spite of the currency obstruction.

The incident of the German situation helped Czechoslovakia over the worst part of the stabilization crisis. In the course of the year 1923 the

[6] See pp. 256-58.

[7] In Mildschuh, V., *Currency Conditions,* p. 186, the undervaluation and overvaluation of the crown with respect to Great Britain and Germany are evaluated as follows, in points per thousand, the plus sign indicating overvaluation and the minus sign, undervaluation:

	May, 1921	September, 1922
Great Britain	−68	+ 34
Germany	− 7	+ 145

exchange rate and the price index became adjusted to each other, and since then the Banking Department of the Ministry of Finance has had no difficulty in maintaining the stability of the exchange rate.[8]

An independent bank of issue was not established until over three years after the stabilization of the currency. The Banking Department of the Ministry of Finance was admittedly a makeshift arrangement. The Czechoslovak leaders realized from the start the need of a real bank of issue, and as early as April 14, 1920, the Czechoslovak Parliament passed an act providing for the establishment of such a bank. Circumstances prevented the carrying out of this project, and it was not until after the passage by the Parliament of an amended Bank Act on April 23, 1925, that the creation of the National Bank became possible. The Bank began its operations on April 1, 1926.

The National Bank is a quasi-autonomous institution, and is different in this respect from the Banking Department which it superseded. It is a stock company, with a share capital of 12 million dollars (expressed in American currency), one-third of which is held by the government and the other two-thirds by private individuals. The management of the Bank is in the hands of a Governor, appointed by the President of the Republic, and a board of

[8] For the details of the process of stabilization and deflation in Czechoslovakia see Rist, Charles, *La Déflation en pratique,* Paris, 1924.

nine directors, of whom three are appointed by the President of the Republic and six are elected by the shareholders. The board of directors is authorized to coöpt a tenth member, who need not, as is the case with the rest of the personnel, be a Czechoslovak citizen—the way being thus open for the appointment of a foreign adviser. Besides its powers of making appointments, the government also reserves the right to supervise the activities of the Bank through a government commissioner, who has the power of veto over any action of the Bank which in his opinion is detrimental to the interests of the state. Moreover, all resolutions of the General Assembly of the Bank are subject to government approval, before becoming fully valid.

In its operations, the National Bank acts as the bank of issue, having complete supervision over all currency affairs. Its scope of transactions is strictly defined by its statutes. It is specifically forbidden to make direct or indirect advances to the government, although it may discount tax and customs bills and may invest one-half of its reserve funds in government bonds.[9]

The Czechoslovak currency was linked with gold, but was not placed on the gold basis with the establishment of the National Bank. The Bank Act of 1925 merely provided that the Bank is to be obli-

[9] For the details of the various provisions regarding the National Bank see Engliš, Karel, *The National Bank of Czechoslovakia,* Prague, 1925, and *Bulletin of the National Bank of Czechoslovakia,* especially Nos. 1 and 4.

gated to maintain the exchange rate of the crown on the level of the two years preceeding its establishment. The explanatory report accompanying the Act defined this level in the form of the following relation between the Czechoslovak crown and the American dollar: Kč 100 = \$2.90-\$3.03.

The Bank Act made provisions for the maintenance of a gold cover. The total amount of currency in circulation plus the sight liabilities of the Bank, but minus the state debt to the Bank on account of unsecured paper money issues, is to have a 20 per cent cover in gold and foreign bills or currencies during the first year of the Bank's existence. This cover is to be increased at the rate of 1 per cent a year during 15 years, which is the period of the duration of the Bank's charter.

It will be recalled that Dr. Rašín's original plan contemplated that the state debt created by the taking over of the Austro-Hungarian Bank notes was to be extinguished by means of a capital levy. The legislation necessary for the introduction of the levy was passed soon after the stamping of the Austro-Hungarian Bank notes, and the Banking Department was made the repository of the proceeds. As the funds collected by means of the levy came in, the Banking Department credited the government with the amount and reduced correspondingly the state debt attributable to the uncovered circulation. The original amount of the capital levy was fixed at 10 billion crowns. This amount was reduced in 1923 to 7 billions, and in 1925 a further provision was made that as soon as the receipts shall have reached 5 billions any further collections shall be applied only to the extent of one-third of the extinguishment of the state currency debt, while the other two-thirds shall be turned over to the Treasury for the purpose of extinguishing the general floating debt of the government.

The National Bank took over the functions of the Banking Department with respect to the capital levy. The collections on account of the levy reached 5 billions early in 1927, the state currency debt having been thus reduced by slightly over one-half.

On March 31, 1927, a year after the National Bank had begun its operations, the state debt to the Bank amounted to 4,745 million crowns. The total circulation of bank notes on that date was 7,028 millions, and the sight liabilities of the Bank were 1,262 millions. At the same time, the gold and silver holdings of the Bank amounted to 1,050 million crowns, and its balances abroad and stocks of foreign currencies were equal to 1,897 millions. Thus the whole circulation was covered to the extent of 35 per cent, while the portion specified in the Bank Act (total circulation less government debt) was covered to the extent of 83 per cent, instead of the 20 per cent required by law.[10]

The fact that the state currency debt is still over

[10] *Bulletin of the National Bank of Czechoslovakia,* No. 11.

half of the total circulation is the principal reason why the Czechoslovak government is reluctant to place the crown on a full gold basis. The Bank is maintaining the exchange rate at 2.96 cents to the crown, and it is expected that when the full gold standard will finally be introduced, this will be approximately the gold content of the currency unit.

II. PROGRESS TOWARD BUDGETARY EQUILIBRIUM

The Czechoslovak leaders realized from the start the need of a balanced budget, as well as of a sound currency system, and made earnest efforts toward the achievement of budgetary equilibrium. As early as February 28, 1919, Dr. Rašín said in the course of a speech delivered in the National Assembly: [11]

> We must realize from the outset that it will be impossible to maintain our Czech crown or benefit by the rise of its exchange, unless the following conditions, which I consider cardinal, are fulfilled. We must learn to balance our budget without deficit, to economize wherever possible, to spend nothing but what is essential, and to cover possible deficits with the proceeds of taxation and not by means of loans or new issues of paper money.

The first task that confronted Czechoslovakia in connection with her public finances was the creation of a budgetary form corresponding to the country's requirements. The government of the newly cre-

[11] Quoted in Rist, C., *La Déflation en pratique*, p. 107.

ated republic had inherited from the Austro-Hungarian Monarchy the budgetary experience of the pre-war years and the chaotic budgetary practices of the war period. With this as the background, the Czechoslovak government attacked the problem of creating its own budgetary practice.

The structural character of the Czechoslovak budget has passed through four stages of evolution. Starting with the form used in the pre-war Monarchy, Czechoslovakia gradually perfected its budgetary mechanism, finally reaching the form used in the drafting of her 1927 budget.

The first two Czechoslovak budgets (for 1919 and 1920) were, like the old Austro-Hungarian budgets, divided into two parts, the ordinary and the extraordinary, and included the expenditures and the gross receipts of the state railways and the other state undertakings. The only difference was that, whereas the Austro-Hungarian budgets covered fiscal years (July 1 to June 30), in Czechoslovakia the budgetary year was made to coincide with the calendar year.

In the budget of 1921 an important change was introduced. Outlays for capital investments, which had formerly been included very largely under the extraordinary budget, were presented separately. The whole budget was thus divided into administrative (subdivided into ordinary and extraordinary) and investment. While the change was primarily one of accountancy, it, undoubtedly, had an important bearing on government credit. In passing the budget, the parliament provided sufficient tax levies to cover the administrative budget. The investments were to be covered by means of loans. This meant in practice that the actual outlays for capital investments had to depend upon the general condition of the money market and the ability of the government to borrow. As a matter of fact, these outlays were always smaller than the budgetary estimates for them.

With slight modifications introduced in the administrative budget in 1923, this system lasted through 1924, when another important change was introduced. The budget for 1925 was still divided into administrative and investment, but most of the state undertakings were taken out of the administrative part. The state railways, the state model farms, and all the other enterprises owned and operated by the government were placed on a quasi-business footing. They were thenceforth to keep accounts of their own, only the net results of their operations (profit or deficit) being included in the administrative budget. Finally, in the 1926 budget, the outlays for capital investments were once more combined with the general administrative budget.[12]

The total expenditures of the Czechoslovak government exceeded its revenues up to 1926. Closed budgetary accounts are available for the period from

[12] Engliš, Karel, *The Budget for 1927,* Prague, 1926, Introduction.

1919 to 1926, and the figures for these years are given in the following table.[13]

CZECHOSLOVAK BUDGETS, 1919-1925
(In millions of Kč.)

Year	Administrative Budget*			Invest-ments	Total Surplus (+) or Deficit (−)
	Revenues	Expendi-tures	Surplus (+) or Deficit (−)		
1919	4,736	7,449	−2,713	....	−2,713
1920	11,885	13,932	−2,047	....	−2,047
1921	18,846	18,558	+ 288	1,830	−1,542
1922	20,270	20,495	− 225	1,555	−1,880
1923	16,619	18,287	−1,668	1,776	−3,444
1924	18,008	18,544	− 536	1,282	−1,818
1925	10,313	11,157	− 844	1,136	−1,980
1926	13,470	11,117	+2,353	....	+2,353

* For the years 1919, 1920, and 1926 the outlays for investments are included in the administrative budget. For the years 1919-24 the administrative budget includes gross revenues and expenditures of State enterprises; for the years 1925-26, it includes only the net results of the operation of these enterprises.

In the budgetary estimates for 1926, the administrative budget showed a surplus of 15 million crowns, while the investments were placed at 871 millions, making the total estimated deficit for the year 856 million crowns.[14] The closed account for the year, however, showed a large net surplus. The

[13] Figures from *Státní závěrečný účet Republiky Československé,* annual publication of the Supreme Audit Control Office in Prague.

[14] League of Nations *Memorandum on Public Finance.*

estimates for 1927 indicated a fully balanced budget.[15]

Thus the administrative budget has definitely tended toward a balanced condition. The large deficit of the year 1923 was the result of a falling off in revenues during the stabilization crisis and the unusually heavy repayments of maturing short-term bills. The deficit of 1925 resulted principally from an increase of expenditures for educational purposes.

The continuing excess of total expenditures over revenues was caused by the large outlays for investments. These outlays have been necessitated principally by the needs of administrative and railroad reorganization. Improvements have also had to be made in postal, telegraph, and telephone communications, in public highways, etc. All these outlays have, however, been rapidly decreasing in the last few years.

The budgetary deficits have been responsible for the creation of a large government debt. By the end of 1925 Czechoslovakia's long-term domestic debt amounted to 13,058 million crowns, and the domestic floating indebtedness was 5,810 millions. The foreign debt of the government, contracted for the purpose of purchasing military equipment and supplies, gold, etc., and for the purpose of repatriating the Czechoslovak troops in Siberia, amounted to 3,502 million crowns. In addition there were debts

[15] Engliš, Karel, *The Budget for 1927.*

contracted for investment purposes. The total indebtedness on December 31, 1925, was 26,586 million crowns.[16] Judging by these figures for the government debt, the excess of government expenditures over real revenues (apart from borrowing) must have been even greater than indicated in the above table, owing to the fact that in some of the earlier accounts no clear distinction was made between the proceeds of loans and other receipts in indicating government revenues.

By the end of 1926 the total government debt was 34,945 million Czechoslovak crowns. It was divided as follows: [17]

	Millions of Kč.
Domestic debt	24,049
Foreign debt	6,496
Debts accruing from the treaties of peace	4,400
Total	34,945

The increase was almost exclusively in the foreign debt, and was primarily the result of the assumption by Czechoslovakia of her share in the pre-war debts of the Austro-Hungarian Monarchy, as allocated by the Innsbruck and Prague protocols.

Payments on government debts and the cost of the military establishment are the largest single items of budgetary expenditures. The following table shows the various administrative expenditures

[16] *Státní záverecny účet* for 1925.
[17] Englis, K., *The Budget for 1927,* p. 62.

of the Czechoslovak government as they appear in the budget for 1926: [18]

CZECHOSLOVAK BUDGETARY EXPENDITURES, 1926

(In millions of Kč.)

President and his Secretariat	19.2
National Assembly	38.9
Prime Minister's office	58.4
Ministry of National Defense	1,935.4
" " Education	890.9
" " Social Welfare	853.6
" " Finance	803.7
" " Interior	568.7
" " Public Works	490.8
" " Justice	303.1
" " Agriculture	226.7
" " Foreign Affairs	151.3
" " Public Health	146.3
" " Commerce and Industry	37.2
" " Railways	25.5
Other Ministries and Departments	87.9
Payments on Public Debts	2,050.7
Contributions to Local Authorities	798.4
Pensions	583.6
Total	10,070.3

Thus one-fifth of Czechoslovakia's expenditures under the administrative budget goes for payments of interest and amortization on the government debts. An almost equal amount goes for the upkeep of the military establishment. Almost another fifth of the total expenditures is spent on education, social welfare, and public health, while about 6 per cent goes for pensions.

[18] League of Nations *Memorandum on Public Finance.*

It should be noted that the military expenditures have been gradually decreasing. In the budget for 1923, for example, the cost of the military establishment was estimated at 2,775 million crowns, as against the estimate of 1,935 millions in 1926. The actual expenditures for national defense in 1923 were larger than the estimates for 1926 by over 200 million crowns.

The taxation system of Czechoslovakia is in the process of reform. Generally speaking, until 1928, it was based on the system that had existed in the Austro-Hungarian Monarchy, except that the levies had been increased in the case of most taxes, while several new taxes had been introduced. There was considerable dissatisfaction in the country with the existing system of taxation, and efforts were being made to work out a system that would be better suited to the needs of the present situation.

Indirect taxes furnish the largest share of government revenues. They are followed in importance by the direct taxes and the net yields of fiscal monopolies and government enterprises. The table on page 229 shows the principal sources of government revenues, as indicated by the estimates for 1926.[19]

The largest sources of indirect taxation are the turnover tax (15.89 per cent of the total revenue), customs duties (8.06 per cent), and the transport tax (6.31 per cent). The income tax accounts for about half of the revenue from direct taxation. The

[19] League of Nations *Memorandum on Public Finance.*

CZECHOSLOVAK BUDGETARY REVENUES, 1926

Classification	In Millions of Kč.	*As Percentage of the Total*
Indirect taxes	5,764.8	*57.20*
Direct "	2,085.7	*20.69*
Net yield of fiscal monopolies	1,092.5	*10.84*
" " " public domains and government enterprises	569.6	*5.65*
Miscellaneous receipts	566.1	*5.62*
Total	10,078.7	*100.00*

fiscal monopolies are five in number, namely, tobacco, salt, saccharine, explosives, and lotteries, and the profits of the tobacco monopoly account for nearly the whole of the revenue from this source. The railroads are run at a profit, and the postal, telegraph, and telephone system also yields the government net revenue.

The system of taxation in Czechoslovakia has been exceedingly complicated. There are, for example, nineteen direct taxes, and a large number of indirect ones. This system has been greatly simplified by the tax reform which went into effect on January 1, 1928.[20]

One of the reasons why tax reform has been delayed has been the difficulty of fitting it into the administrative system of the country. Czechoslovakia started with a strongly centralized administrative system. She has recently, however, modified

[20] For the text of the law see *Sbìrka zákonu a narízení Státu ceskoslovenského,* No. 37 for 1927.

it in favor of greater provincial autonomy, and fiscal reforms are directed toward meeting the requirements of this new situation.

There is another important angle from which the Czechoslovak government is approaching the problem of tax reform. Under the present system of taxation, a disproportionate burden falls on trade and industry, and it is felt in the country that this operates as an unfavorable factor for the export trade. Another purpose of the reform is, therefore, to adjust the burden of taxation to this important requirement.

The national income of Czechoslovakia is calculated at 60 billion crowns.[21] Taking into account the taxation revenues of the central government and of the local authorities, the amount paid in taxes is approximately 20 per cent of the national income.

Thus from the point of view of her currency and fiscal problems, Czechoslovakia may be considered as having reached a state of equilibrium. The currency has been stable for several years, and the new National Bank apparently has at its disposal ample means for maintaining the exchange rate at the present level. With the gradual disappearance of the need for large investment outlays, the government budget has been balanced, and the way has been opened for the much needed reform of the taxation system. So far as the budget is concerned,

[21] Engliš, Karel, *The Budget for 1927,* p. 34.

there appears to be nothing in the currency and the fiscal aspects of Czechoslovakia's situation to cause her any apprehensions. In the next chapter we shall see what her condition is as regards her international financial position.

CHAPTER XII

CZECHOSLOVAKIA'S INTERNATIONAL ACCOUNTS

THE continued stability of the Czechoslovak exchange over a period of more than five years indicates that she has experienced no difficulty in meeting her international obligations. We must turn to her international accounts, however, in order to determine whether this has been achieved with her own resources or with borrowed funds.

Czechoslovakia inherited from the Austro-Hungarian Monarchy a large portion of the latter's industrial equipment, but she did not inherit complete ownership of these enterprises. Vienna and, to a smaller degree, Budapest retained part ownership. This fact necessitates annual payments of large sums in interest, dividends, and other forms of profit. While Czechoslovakia has some investments abroad, the returns from them are insufficient to cover her own debt payments, which therefore have to be offset by income from service and trade operations.

Between 1920 *and* 1926 *Czechoslovakia's merchandise exports have invariably exceeded her imports.* The following table shows her foreign trade, inclusive of bullion and specie movement, during the first eight years of the country's existence: [1]

Czechoslovakia's Foreign Trade and Bullion and Specie Movement, 1919-1926
(In millions of Kč.)

Year	Exports	Imports	Balance
1919..............	5,324	6,555	− 1,231
1920..............	27,569	23,384	+ 4,185
1921..............	27,311	22,433	+ 4,878
1922..............	18,086	12,695	+ 5,391
1923..............	12,573	10,222	+ 2,351
1924..............	17,035	15,855	+ 1,180
1925..............	18,799	17,594	+ 1,205
1926..............	17,848	15,262	+ 2,586

The year 1919 was one of economic dislocation following the organization of the country. Large imports of foodstuffs and the disorganized condition of the exporting industries were responsible for the excess of imports over exports during that year. During the following year, however, the industries were once more in operating order, and while the vast increase in the total value of exports and imports was due largely to the depreciation of the currency, the existence of a very substantial export surplus showed clearly that the exports increased faster than the imports. In 1922 the total value of

[1] Figures from *Mêsíční přehled zahraničního obchodu,* monthly publication of the Czechoslovak Government Statistical Office.

the exports and imports decreased owing to the appreciation of the currency, but the export surplus was even larger than during the preceding two years. The low figures for 1923 reflect the depression following the stabilization of the currency. The last three years show a fairly stable situation, with a somewhat increasing export surplus.

Interest and dividend payments on foreign investments in Czechoslovakia and other foreign debts require large annual outlays. The foreign obligations of the country are of many kinds, the bulk of them having been inherited by it. Czechoslovakia has a large private indebtedness abroad, and a considerable public foreign debt, resulting largely from the peace treaties.

Czechoslovakia could not, of course, after breaking away from the Austro-Hungarian Monarchy, wipe out the Austrian and Hungarian ownership in business and financial enterprises located on her territory. She did, however, make several efforts to minimize the sums which were bound to leave the country as a result of this situation. The "nostrification" laws, which caused the transfer of the managing seats of foreign-owned enterprises from Vienna and Budapest to Czechoslovakia, helped in this respect. The establishment of banking institutions independent of Vienna and Budapest were moves in the same direction. The agrarian reform, introduced for social and political reasons, operated in the direction of decreasing the profits of foreign owners of agricultural estates and enterprises. Moreover, every effort has been made to repurchase Czechoslovak securities owned by foreigners. Nevertheless, the amounts which still have to leave the country on account of foreign investments are comparatively very large.

In addition to this private indebtedness, Czechoslovakia has also inherited responsibility for her share of the Austro-Hungarian pre-war debts, as allocated by the Innsbruck and Prague protocols. She assumed responsibility for these debts by virtue of the provisions of the peace treaties, which also imposed upon her the so-called "liberation" payments, to correspond with the reparation obligations assessed against the new states of Austria and Hungary. She has not as yet made any payments on account of this "liberation" debt.

Finally, the process of organizing the new country required considerable foreign borrowing, especially during the first few years of the country's existence. In this manner a certain amount of public foreign debt was created.

All these forms of foreign indebtedness require annual payments to be made outside the country's frontiers. They constitute claims against Czechoslovakia's export surplus, which are offset only to a small degree by the income from the country's own foreign investments.

Other service operations bring Czechoslovakia a small net income. The various international services rendered by Czechoslovakia to other countries are offset largely by services which are rendered to her by other countries, but in the final account they leave her a small surplus.

Czechoslovakia's railways carry extensive transit traffic, and from this source of revenue the country receives a net income. Similarly, emigrant remittances yield her a net income. As against these sources of revenue she has net expenditures on account of commissions, insurance, and several other smaller items. Moreover, Czechoslovak tourists spend in other countries more than foreign tourists spend in Czechoslovakia. It is true that Czechoslovakia's important health resorts, among which are the famous Karlsbad, or Karlovy Vary, and Marienbad, or Marianske Lazne, attract large numbers of tourists. But on the whole the expenditures of foreigners in Czechoslovakia are not as large as the expenditures of Czechoslovaks in other countries. However, the net income from transport traffic and emigrant remittances is more than sufficient to cover all these expenditures.

Czechoslovakia's trade and service income during the years 1922-26 was more than sufficient to cover her payments on account of foreign indebtedness. The following table shows the principal groups of net income and outgo during the five years from 1922 to 1926: [2]

[2] For the sources on which these evaluations are based see Appendix, pp. 592-94.

CZECHOSLOVAKIA'S INTERNATIONAL INCOME ACCOUNT, 1922-1926

(Totals for the five years, in millions of Kč.)

NET INCOME FROM:		
Foreign trade in commodities	12.7	
Transit traffic	2.1	
Emigrant remittances	1.5	
		16.3
NET OUTGO FOR:		
Payments of interest, dividend, and profits on public and private foreign indebtedness	7.0	
Tourist expenditures	1.8	
Commissions, insurance, and other smaller items	1.5	
		10.3
Net income from all items		6.0

Thus for the five-year period from 1922 to 1926, Czechoslovakia had a total net income from her transactions with other countries equal to 6 billion crowns. A part of this net income was used for the building up of cover reserves at the Banking Department and, later on, at the National Bank. The remainder was used for the repurchase of domestic securities and properties held abroad and, to some extent, for investments in other countries.

Czechoslovakia's payments of interest, dividends, and profits on her existing foreign indebtedness amount to approximately 1.4-1.5 billion crowns a year. And since her income and outgo for other service operations are practically in balance she needs an excess of commodity exports over imports equal to at least this amount if she is to meet her foreign obligations without recourse to borrowing. As we saw on page 233, her export surplus since 1920 has exceeded this amount every year, with the exception of 1924 and 1925, when it fell slightly below the above figure.

CHAPTER XIII

TRADE, PRODUCTION, AND BANKING IN CZECHOSLOVAKIA

Czechoslovakia inherited some of the richest and some of the poorest sections of the Austro-Hungarian Monarchy. As we have seen, a large part of the industrial equipment of the Monarchy is located in her territory. There are also large and varied mineral resources within her frontiers, and some of the best developed agricultural sections of the former Monarchy. On the other hand in parts of Slovakia and especially in Sub-Carpathian Ruthenia, she has some economically poor and backward sections.

The existence of a comparatively immense industrial equipment determines the general economic character of the country. Czechoslovakia is primarily an industrial country, although her agriculture is also very important to her. In her industrial activities she is decidedly an exporting country.

All these factors have exerted a profound influence on Czechoslovakia's economic experience as an independent nation. In this chapter we shall examine Czechoslovakia's general economic situation, especially from the point of view of the character of foreign trade and of agricultural and industrial production.

I. CHARACTER AND DIRECTION OF FOREIGN TRADE

Foreign trade is an exceedingly important element in Czechoslovakia's economic life. Comprising the most important industrial center of the Austro-Hungarian Monarchy, the present territory of Czechoslovakia is virtually dependent upon foreign trade for the utilization of the industrial equipment that had grown up in it during decades preceding the war. The economic character of the country which is determined by this situation is clearly reflected in the Czechoslovak foreign trade.

Czechoslovakia is primarily an importer of raw materials and an exporter of manufactured goods. The table on page 241 shows the composition of the country's imports and exports.[1]

It is clear from this table that the commodity composition of Czechoslovakia's foreign trade does not vary greatly from year to year. On the export side the increase of the relative importance of the foodstuff group has been due to the recovery and expansion of the beet-sugar industry. On the import side, the relative importance of the commodity groups in 1926 is practically identical with that in 1922.

[1] Figures for 1922 from League of Nations *Memorandum on Balance of Payments and Foreign Trade Balances, 1911-25,* Vol. II; figures for 1924 and 1926 from *Mesícní prehled zahranicního obchodu.*

COMPOSITION OF CZECHOSLOVAKIA'S EXPORTS AND IMPORTS
(In percentages of the respective yearly totals)

Classification	Exports			Imports		
	1922	1924	1926	1922	1924	1926
Live animals	0.3	0.3	0.3	4.1	5.2	3.9
Articles of food and drink	12.5	18.7	18.8	22.5	25.1	22.4
Raw materials and semi-manufactures	21.3	21.7	19.4	47.1	48.1	47.2
Manufactured goods ...	64.7	59.0	60.8	26.0	21.6	26.4
Gold and silver.........	1.2	0.3	0.7	0.3	0.0	0.1
All classes	100.0	100.0	100.0	100.0	100.0	100.0

Czechoslovakia's largest export group is the textiles. They account for one-third of the total exports. Next in importance comes sugar, the exports of which constitute about 12 per cent of the total. Metals and machinery account for about 9 per cent of the total. Then come timber and paper, coal, glassware, and a large variety of manufactured products.

On the import side, the textile group is also by far the most important. Brought in mostly in the form of raw and semi-manufactured materials, the various textile products constitute over one-third of the total imports. Cereals and flour account for only about 10 per cent of the total imports; vegetables and fruit, for 3 per cent; livestock and meat products, for about 7 per cent. The remainder of the imports is made up of a large variety of raw and semi-manufactured materials required in industry, and of manufactured goods not produced in the country.

Czechoslovakia's trade is with the countries of western and northern Europe, rather than with the Danubian States. The following table shows the geographical distribution of Czechoslovakia's exports and imports in the years 1922, 1925, and 1926:

GEOGRAPHIC DISTRIBUTION OF CZECHOSLOVAKIA'S EXPORTS AND IMPORTS

Country of Source or Destination	1922		1925		1926	
	In Millions of Kč.	*As Percentage of Total*	In Millions of Kč.	*As Percentage of Total*	In Millions of Kč.	*As Percentage of Total*
I. EXPORTS						
To ALL DANUBIAN STATES	**6,863**	**37.94**	**6,101**	**32.42**	**5,927**	**33.21**
Austria	3,969	*21.95*	3,252	*17.28*	2,902	*16.26*
Hungary	1,589	*8.78*	1,178	*6.26*	1,228	*6.88*
Rumania	523	*2.89*	850	*4.52*	834	*4.67*
Yugoslavia	782	*4.32*	821	*4.36*	963	*5.40*
To ALL OTHER COUNTRIES ...	**11,223**	**62.06**	**12,720**	**67.58**	**11,921**	**66.79**
Germany	3,407	*18.84*	4,233	*22.49*	3,552	*19.90*
Poland	605	*3.34*	658	*3.49*	363	*2.03*
United Kingdom	1,347	*7.45*	1,534	*8.15*	1,540	*8.63*
Italy	663	*3.67*	756	*4.02*	441	*2.47*
France	868	*4.80*	267	*1.42*	254	*1.42*
Switzerland	285	*1.58*	557	*2.96*	516	*2.89*
United States ..	932	*5.15*	756	*4.02*	845	*4.74*
Other Countries.	3,116	*17.23*	3,959	*21.03*	4,410	*24.71*
TOTAL FOR ALL COUNTRIES	**18,086**	**100.00**	**18,821**	**100.00**	**17,848**	**100.00**

Geographic Distribution of Czechoslovakia's Exports and Imports—*Continued*

Country of Source or Destination	1922		1925		1926	
	In Millions of Kč.	*As Percentage of Total*	In Millions of Kč.	*As Percentage of Total*	In Millions of Kč.	*As Percentage of Total*
II. IMPORTS						
From All Danubian States ..	**3,365**	**26.50**	**3,286**	**18.65**	**3,219**	**21.09**
Austria	1,983	*15.62*	1,294	*7.34*	1,125	*7.37*
Hungary	684	*5.39*	1,121	*6.36*	1,028	*6.73*
Rumania	430	*3.38*	369	*2.10*	482	*3.16*
Yugoslavia	268	*2.11*	502	*2.85*	584	*3.83*
From All Other Countries ...	**9,331**	**73.50**	**14,332**	**81.35**	**12,043**	**78.91**
Germany	3,536	*27.85*	5,497	*31.20*	3,238	*21.22*
Poland	324	*2.55*	1,238	*7.02*	1,096	*7.18*
United Kingdom	652	*5.14*	653	*3.71*	602	*3.94*
Italy	296	*2.33*	726	*4.12*	337	*2.21*
France	445	*3.51*	692	*3.93*	677	*4.44*
Switzerland	169	*1.33*	331	*1.88*	327	*2.14*
United States ..	2,286	*18.01*	1,117	*6.35*	760	*4.98*
Other Countries.	1,623	*12.78*	4,078	*23.14*	5,006	*32.80*
Total for All Countries	**12,696**	**100.00**	**17,618**	**100.00**	**15,262**	**100.00**

Thus only about one-third of Czechoslovakia's exports go to the Danubian countries, mostly to Austria and Hungary, and even the percentage of her total exports which goes to these two countries diminished perceptibly during the five years from

1922 to 1926. While she increased somewhat her exports to Rumania and Yugoslavia, the total percentage of Czechoslovakia's exports going to the Danubian States decreased from 37.94 in 1922 to 33.21 in 1926.

Germany is a more important purchaser of Czechoslovak exports than any of the Danubian States,[2] and Great Britain is more important than Hungary, Rumania, or Yugoslavia. Generally speaking, the Czechoslovak exports, are, even less than the Austrian, confined to the Danubian territory. On the contrary, they go all over the world, reaching out for Western European and overseas markets.

The Danubian countries play an even less important rôle in Czechoslovakia's import trade than they do in her export trade. In 1925, for example, the imports from Germany alone greatly exceeded the imports from the whole Danubian group, though in 1926 the four Danubian countries supplied the same percentages of exports as Germany.

With foodstuffs playing a secondary rôle in Czechoslovakia's imports, her purchases of these products from the agricultural countries of the Danubian basin cannot be very extensive. From Austria she buys primarily iron ore and manufactured products.

[2] To some extent the large share of Czechoslovak trade attributable to Germany is due to the fact that a part of the goods passing through Hamburg is classified with exports to and imports from Germany proper.

II. AGRICULTURAL PRODUCTION AND REQUIREMENTS

While the economic organization of Czechoslovakia has a pronounced industrial character, the country also has a well-developed agriculture. Arable land constitutes 45 per cent of the total territory of Czechoslovakia; meadows and pastures take up 18 per cent; forests, 33 per cent; and unproductive lands constitute but 4 per cent.[3]

The percentage of the arable land in Czechoslovakia used for the various crops is as follows:

Rye	17
Oats	15
Barley	14
Wheat	11
Maize	3
Potatoes and other vegetables	15
Sugar-beet, hops, etc.	12
Fodder crops	6
Fallow lands	7

With 60 per cent of her total arable land under cereals, Czechoslovakia devotes a larger percentage of her arable land to cereals than either France or Great Britain, and approximately the same as Germany. Her varied agriculture gives her an opportunity for producing comparatively large amounts of food.

The total area under cultivation in Czechoslovakia is still smaller, but the yield per unit is larger

[3] The data presented in this section are taken largely from Brdlík, V., "Agriculture," *Czechoslovakia;* and *Agricultural Survey of Europe.*

than before the war. The area planted to cereals before the war was 3.9 million hectares; in 1925 and 1926 it was about 3.4 millions.[4] On the other hand, the figures of total production for the four principal grains in 1925 and 1926, as compared with the pre-war figures, are as follows:

Grain Production in Czechoslovakia
(In millions of quintals)

Grain	Pre-war	1925	1926
Wheat	10.3	10.7	9.7
Rye	15.5	14.8	12.6
Barley	13.0	12.5	11.2
Oats	9.6	13.0	13.1
Total	48.4	51.0	46.6

Thus in 1925 the total production of the four principal grains exceeded the pre-war output by about 5 per cent, whereas the planting area was only about 87 per cent of what it was before the war. The year 1925, however, was an exceptional one. But even in 1926, when the crops were much poorer than in 1925, the total production was still 96 per cent of the pre-war amount, while the area under cultivation was only 87 per cent. This means that the yield per hectare was considerably higher in 1925 than it had been before the war, and somewhat

[4] The pre-war figures given here are based on the calculations made in *Agricultural Survey of Europe;* the post-war figures are from *Bulletin of the National Bank of Czechoslovakia,* No. 2.

higher even in 1926. In the case of wheat, the pre-war yield was 14.7 quintals per hectare, while that for 1925 was 17.5 and for 1926, 15.6. For rye, the pre-war yield was 14.9 quintals per hectare, while the 1925 yield was 17.6 and the 1926 yield, 15.2 quintals.

The above table also indicates interesting shifts in the relative importance of the various grains. The production of wheat is approximately the same as the pre-war, but the production of rye and barley has decreased, while that of oats has increased very markedly. The reason for this lies in the fact that since the war there has been a noticeable increase of livestock, and production has been expanded not only in the case of oats, but also in the case of all the other fodder foods.

The following table shows the increase of livestock in Czechoslovakia during the post-war period, according to the censuses taken on December 31, 1920, and December 31, 1925: [5]

LIVESTOCK POPULATION OF CZECHOSLOVAKIA
(In thousands)

Livestock	1920	1925
Horses	591	740
Cattle	4,377	4,691
Pigs	2,053	2,539
Sheep	985	861

[5] Adams, A. A., *Report on the Industrial and Economic Situation in Czechoslovakia*, London, 1927, Appendix II.

The increase of horses by more than one-quarter, indicated in the table, accounts for the expansion of the oat crop, while the similar increase in the number of pigs and small increase in the number of cattle account for the increase of the other fodder crops.

Czechoslovakia is very nearly self-sufficient in basic foodstuffs. Outside of colonial products and food luxuries, her own production supplies about 90 per cent of her food requirements, and of some of the foodstuffs she produces she even has an exportable surplus.

So far as cereals are concerned, the territory of Czechoslovakia was, before the war, a surplus producer of all the grains, with the exception of wheat. It brought in from the other parts of the Austro-Hungarian Monarchy about one-third of the amount of wheat required for consumption. Today, Czechoslovakia imports both wheat and rye. She still has a surplus of oats and barley.

Czechoslovakia produces enough potatoes and other vegetables to satisfy her own requirements. She is a surplus producer of such industrial plants as sugar-beets, hops, etc. She is a large exporter of sugar, hops, alcohol, and beer.

Czechoslovakia was before the war, and still is today, short of meat and fats. She has to import about one-tenth of her meat requirements and about one-quarter of her requirements of lard and other animal fats.

With the restoration of her area under cultivation

to its pre-war size, Czechoslovakia's home production of foodstuffs probably will be nearly sufficient to fill her requirements. Wheat and meat are likely to be the only food products of which she will not produce enough, especially in view of the fact that the per capita consumption of these products is likely to increase with the general rise in the standard of living.

The agrarian revolution has undoubtedly served to increase somewhat the consumption requirements of the agricultural population. Czechoslovakia has carried out a comprehensive land reform. Prior to the end of the war, 28 per cent of the total area of the territory now comprising Czechoslovakia were owned by 151 families, while in Bohemia, for example, seven-eighths of the population owned no land whatever. By means of the agrarian reform, the Czechoslovak government expropriated most of the large estates and has divided these lands among small holders and people owning no land at all. The former owners were compensated for their land, and the new owners paid for the land they received. In this manner, Czechoslovakia has become a country of medium and small land holdings.[6]

As the increase in the yield per unit indicates, the breaking up of the large estates has been beneficial, rather than otherwise, in its effects on agricultural

[6] For the details of the agrarian reform see Vondruska, E., "Czechoslovak Land Reform," *Social Policy in the Czechoslovak Republic,* Prague, 1924, and Pavel, A., "Land Reform," *Czechoslovakia.*

production in Czechoslovakia. While the possession of larger holdings has served to augment the consumption of the agricultural population, the possibilities of increased production still make the country almost self-sufficient from the point of view of the basic food supply.

III. INDUSTRIAL PRODUCTION AND SURPLUS

Industrial production in Czechoslovakia is concentrated largely in those portions of the country which had formerly constituted a part of Austria, that is, in Bohemia, Moravia, and Silesia. Slovakia and Ruthenia, which had formerly been parts of Hungary, are, on the contrary, largely agricultural. The following table shows the distribution of population according to main occupational groups: [7]

Occupational Groups in Czechoslovakia
(In thousands)

Districts	Agriculture, Forestry, and Fishing	Industry	Other Occupations	Total
Bohemia	1,980	2,734	1,956	6,670
Moravia and Silesia...	1,176	1,272	887	3,335
Slovakia	1,819	530	652	3,001
Carpathian Ruthenia..	409	64	132	605
Total...............	5,384	4,600	3,627	13,611

[7] Vondruska, E., "Czechoslovak Land Reform," *Social Policy of the Czechoslovak Republic,* pp. 163-4, figures based on the census of February 15, 1921.

Thus for the whole country, agriculture gives employment to about 40 per cent of the total population, while industry provides a livelihood for only a little over 33 per cent. For Bohemia and Moravia, however, these percentages are reversed. Although industry provides a livelihood for a smaller percentage of the population than does agriculture, it accounts for a larger share of the national income. Industrial production amounts to 40 per cent of the total national income, while agricultural production amounts to only 34 per cent.[8]

Czechoslovakia's natural resources favor industrial development. This is true alike of fuel and of essential raw materials. From this point of view, the large concentration of Austro-Hungarian industries in the Bohemian and Moravian sections of the Monarchy was a logical process.[9]

Generally speaking, the Czechoslovak industries are divided into three classes: (1) those which derive their raw materials from home sources, namely, food industries, porcelain, glass, timber, etc.; (2) those which obtain only a part of their raw materials at home, namely, iron, steel, and other metal industries, chemicals, and leather; (3) those which import

[8] Figures based on calculations made by Professor F. von Fellner, used in Professor Corrado Gini's study on Czechoslovakia's national wealth and national income, kindly placed by him at our disposal in manuscript form.

[9] The data contained in this section are based largely on Franzl, K., "Industries," *Czechoslovakia;* Císař, J., and Pokorný, F., *The Czechoslovak Republic,* Part II; and *Tätigkeitsbericht,* annual publication of the German Union of Industries in Czechoslovakia.

their raw materials, namely, textiles, fertilizers, colored metals, etc.

For all these industries Czechoslovakia has more than adequate supplies of coal. Her coal deposits which are very large, are estimated at 18,119 million tons, of which 5,777 millions are black coal, and 12,342 millions are lignite.[10] Before the war, she supplied the major portion of the coal output of the whole Monarchy, and although after the war the production fell off considerably, it has now reached the pre-war level so far as black coal is concerned. The following table shows the coal production (in millions of tons) in Czechoslovakia before and after the war: [11]

	1913	1919	1925	1926
Black coal	14.3	10.4	12.8	14.5
Lignite	23.0	17.5	18.8	18.8
Total................	37.3	27.9	31.6	33.3

Czechoslovakia imports a certain amount of coal from German and Polish Silesia, but exports much larger amounts to Austria and other countries. She is a producer and an exporter of coking coal.

So far as other mineral resources are concerned, Czechoslovakia produces some petroleum, though

[10] Zulkowsky, E., *Die Kohlenbewirtschaftung in der Tschechoslovakei,* Berlin, 1921; in Petrascheck, W., *Die Kohlenlager und Kohlenbergbaue Oestereich-Ungarns,* Vienna, 1920, a somewhat larger estimate is given for the coal reserves of Czechoslovakia.

[11] Figures for 1913 and 1919 are from Zulkovsky, E., *Die Kohlenbewirtschaftung,* etc.; those for 1925 and 1926 are from *Bulletin of the National Bank of Czechoslovakia,* No. 11.

not in sufficient quantities to satisfy her requirements. Her output of iron ore is also less than her consumption. She has important silver mines, and one gold mine. Moreover, she produces small quantities of zinc, nickel, tungsten, manganese and other metals.

Czechoslovakia's Principal Resources

Czechoslovakia has large water-power resources, which she owes to the mountainous nature of some parts of the country. Her potential resources are estimated at 1,622,000 horse power, of which only 157,000, or less than 10 per cent, are now in use.[12]

The most important of Czechoslovakia's food-working industries are sugar-refining, brewing, and distilling. All of these are old-established and well organized industries, depending upon home-grown raw materials. There are also a large number of

[12] Zimmler, E., "Water Power," *Czechoslovakia.*

smaller food industries, and since the war an important flour-milling industry has grown up in Czechoslovakia.

The manufacture of glass and porcelain is one of the oldest of the Czechoslovak industries. The first glass works were founded in Bohemia as early as the eleventh century. Czechoslovakia produces all kinds of glassware. One of the interesting branches of the industry is the production of the so-called Gablonz ware, or glass jewelry. The production of porcelain is also extensive, while artistic pottery is made in many localities, especially in the peasant homes of Moravia.

Czechoslovakia has very extensive timber resources, one-third of the country's total area being covered with forests. The existence of these resources has given rise to highly developed woodworking and paper industry.

The metallurgical and machine industries are very extensive. Their requirements of raw iron are considerably beyond the country's own production, with the result that Czechoslovakia imports large quantities of iron from Germany, Sweden, and Austria. Likewise the chemical industries import a part of their raw materials.

The textile industry is of great importance to Czechoslovakia, and for this industry she has to import the bulk of the necessary raw materials. Apart from cotton, Czechoslovakia imports a part of her requirements of raw wool, flax, and jute. The leather industry, which is also well developed, requires the importation of hides.

On the whole, Czechoslovakia is very favorably situated with regard to basic raw materials and fuel and power resources. Like all highly industrialized countries, she has to import some raw materials, but the proportion of her requirements supplied from home sources compares favorably with other industrialized areas of Europe.

Czechoslovakia's industrial production is much greater than her domestic requirements. While the proportion of the annual output that has to be exported varies from industry to industry, on the whole Czechoslovakia exports no less than one-half of her total industrial output. There is scarcely an industry that does not have to depend upon foreign markets for the disposal of a substantial share of its products.

The textile industry, which represents the largest group in Czechoslovakia's export trade, can place only about 30 per cent of its output in the domestic market. The manufacturers of agricultural machinery have to export over three-quarters of their production; the manufacturers of enamel ware, between 80 and 90 per cent. The paper mills have to sell abroad about 60 per cent of their production. The manufacturers of glassware and of ceramic products have to export from one-half to three-quarters of their production.

Less than one-half of the sugar turned out by the

Czechoslovak refineries can be consumed within the country. An appreciable proportion of the beer, alcohol, and malt production has to be sold outside the country.

At the same time, Czechoslovakia is an importer of a number of important manufactured products. Her machine and engineering industry, for example, while very large, is not sufficiently specialized to satisfy the country's requirements. The table given below shows her exports and imports in several important branches of this industry.

EXPORTS AND IMPORTS OF METALWARES AND MACHINERY IN 1926
(In millions of Kc.)

Commodities	Exports	Imports	Balance
Iron wares	825.1	222.5	+602.6
Other metal wares	254.5	93.0	+161.5
Machines, apparatus, etc.	386.6	675.9	−289.3
Vehicles	110.6	200.4	− 89.8
Instruments, watches, etc.	88.7	161.3	− 72.6

On the whole, Czechoslovakia is a net exporter of metal manufactures. The maladjustment of her machine industry results from the fact that before the war her industrial system was a part of the whole Austro-Hungarian system. For the same reason, she is a net importer of textile yarns, and a large net exporter of textile manufactures.

The difficulty of utilizing fully her whole industrial equipment is reflected in Czechoslovakia's prob-

lem of unemployment. While this problem is not nearly as serious with her as it is with Austria, it is nevertheless very real. Czechoslovakia's unemployment was heaviest during the stabilization crisis of 1922 and 1923. The following table shows the number of unemployed in Czechoslovakia on July 31 and December 31 of each year from 1921 to 1926: [13]

UNEMPLOYMENT IN CZECHOSLOVAKIA, 1921-1926
(Figures in thousands)

Year	July 31	December 31
1921	96.8	78.9
1922	104.3	437.8
1923	216.7	192.0
1924	79.4	81.0
1925	42.0	48.4
1926	71.5	71.2

At the end of 1922 and the beginning of 1923 more than 20 per cent of the total number of workmen were idle; in 1925 only 5 per cent were out of work. The increase in 1926 over 1925 was due to the industrial crisis through which the country passed during that year, while the figures for 1927 again show a decrease.[14]

The above figures, however, do not indicate fully the extent of unemployment in Czechoslovakia.

[13] Figures from *Tätigkeitsbericht* for 1926.

[14] According to *Bulletin of the National Bank of Czechoslovakia*, No. 11. the number of unemployed on July 31, 1927, was, 39,382.

They do not take into account the partially employed, the number of whom is believed to be large. Nor do they reflect what some Czechoslovak observers call "hidden" unemployment, represented by the large increase of students in the universities, technical schools, etc.[15]

IV. CREDIT SITUATION AND THE PROBLEM OF CAPITAL ACCUMULATION

With her international income generally sufficient to cover her international payments, Czechoslovakia has had no pressing need for seeking foreign loans. She has, however, done some foreign borrowing for the purpose of strengthening her currency position and for investment purposes. The question of operating capital resources is a very important one in Czechoslovakia, and it is closely tied up with the whole credit and banking situation of the country.

Czechoslovakia has not, like Austria, passed through a period of violent currency depreciation and the consequent destruction of her operating capital resources. Her currency is, of course, far below the pre-war parity of the crown, and her operating capital has suffered somewhat in consequence. Moreover, the economic and financial dislocations involved in the establishment of a new country have had their effect. But on the whole, by escaping the ravages of extreme monetary inflation,

[15] See a discussion of this phase of the situation in *Tätigkeitsbericht* for 1926, pp. 64-5 and 99.

Czechoslovakia now finds herself in a stronger position from the point of view of her internal banking and credit situation than the countries which have felt the full weight of that devastating experience.

The establishment of an independent banking system has been a serious preoccupation with the Czechoslovak leaders. When Czechoslovakia became an independent country, most of the banks of the country were merely branches of the large Vienna and Budapest banks. It is true that there were several important Czech banks, notably the Živnostenská Banka, and that for nearly two decades prior to the break-up of the Austro-Hungarian Monarchy the Czechs in Bohemia and Moravia made strenuous efforts to establish their own banks, which developed considerably during the war. Nevertheless, the bulk of the banking business in the territory of the new state was in Austrian and Hungarian hands. This situation was changed radically by the measures introduced by the Czechoslovak government at the very beginning.

The policy of "nostrification" transformed the numerous branches of Vienna and Budapest banks into independent Czechoslovak banks.[16] With the separation of the Czechoslovak currency from that of the Monarchy and the establishment of a temporary bank of issue at the Ministry of Finance,

[16] Many of these branch banks were consolidated with existing Czechoslovak banks. Altogether the eight large Vienna banks had on Czechoslovak territory no less than 68 branches. See Hassinger, H., Die *Tschechoslowakei,* Vienna, 1925, p. 419.

a national Czechoslovak system of banking was established.

The reorganized banks inherited the methods and policies of their former parent banks. They are largely in control of industry, both through the granting of credits and actual participation in ownership. The Czechoslovak banks are different in one respect from those of Austria and Hungary: their shares are more widely held, since there are in the country no really large financial groups. But their organization and their business methods are of the general central European type.[17]

While the national character of the Czechoslovak banks has been fully assured, their international connections are still very weak. In this respect they have only partially freed themselves from the older banking institutions of Vienna. In many of their international transactions, they still have to depend to some extent upon the large Austrian banks as intermediaries.

The cost of credit in Czechoslovakia is high. There are many reasons for this. It is a situation which has resulted partly from the weakness of the banking system, partly from insufficiency of liquid capital resources, partly from the character of government finance.

The operating expenses of the banks are very large. As a result the disparity between the inter-

[17] For a general discussion of the Czechoslovak banking system see Karásek, K., "Banking," *Czechoslovakia.*

est paid by the banks on deposits and the interest charged by them on loans is considered excessive. While paying 4 per cent on deposits, the banks charge 7 to 7.5 per cent on loans, adding to this charge 1.5 per cent commission. There is a movement in Czechoslovakia for a general banking consolidation which would decrease the overhead expenses.

Savings and bank deposits generally have been increasing slowly. The table below shows the growth between 1923 and 1926, the figures covering only Bohemia, Moravia, and Silesia: [18]

BANK DEPOSITS IN BOHEMIA, MORAVIA, AND SILESIA
(In millions of Kč.)

Banks Classified	December 31, 1923	December 31, 1926
Savings banks	10,421	13,616
Other banking institutions	6,395	8,731
Total	16,816	22,347

Thus bank deposits have been increasing at the rate of almost 2 billion crowns a year. But this increase has been insufficient for the needs of the business community in view of the huge credit requirements of the government.

Fiscal requirements have not only absorbed a large part of the country's savings, but they have

[18] *Bulletin of the National Bank of Czechoslovakia*, No. 9-10.

also been instrumental in raising the cost of credit. The yield of the 6 per cent government flour loan, which is considered a standard investment security in Czechoslovakia, fluctuated in 1925 between 7.5 and 8.25 per cent, and in 1926 between 6.75 and 7.5 per cent; this high level of yield is indicative of the whole credit situation. The general cost of government financing in Czechoslovakia is so high that it exerts a powerful influence on the whole credit situation.

The problem of capital accumulation is very pressing in Czechoslovakia. Czechoslovakia is an exporting country, forced to compete in world markets, and she needs a large volume of productive capital investments in her industries. But as a matter of fact, such investments have been comparatively very small. The need for liquid resources on the part of Czechoslovak industries became particularly pronounced after they placed their accounts on a gold basis.

In April, 1925, the industrialists of Czechoslovakia held a conference in Prague to discuss the situation. The conference, on the motion made by Dr. F. Hodač, Secretary of the Czech Federation of Industries, adopted a resolution, in which it declared: [19]

> The conference unanimously resolves that the attention of all responsible circles should be called to the pressing need for the formation of new productive capital in ade-

[19] *Tätigkeitsbericht* for 1925, p. 36.

quate amounts and as rapidly as possible; otherwise, it may be too late to remedy the situation if the consequences of the loss of capital become apparent even to persons unversed in economic affairs.

There has been some tendency among Czechoslovak industrialists to blame the government's fiscal policies for the difficult credit situation of the country.[20] The government gave heed to the industrialists' demands, and a substantial part of Finance Minister Engliš's budget speech, delivered in the Parliament on October 14, 1926, was devoted to the relation between the budget and the general economic situation in the country.

The Finance Minister's measures for dealing with the problem of capital accumulation were a reconstruction of the budget in such a manner that the state would cease to make excessive demands upon the money market of the country, and a promise of tax reform.[21] The first measure means a contraction of government outlays for capital investments in order to give industry an opportunity to utilize to a fuller extent the savings of the country. Regretting the high cost of credit, which has an adverse effect on the competitive position of the exporting industries, the Minister stressed particularly the danger of unproductive utilization of credit resources. He said:

[20] See, for example, Janovsky, Karl, *Zur Frage der Kapitalakkumulation in der Tschechoslowakei,* Teplitz-Schönau, 1925.
[21] See p. 230.

I regard it as a dangerous policy on the part of local authorities to erect, on money borrowed at 8 per cent, town-halls and other buildings which offer no ordinary investor's return. With money borrowed at such rates it is possible only for the industries to make capital investments for buildings, etc., and, even in that case, only where rapid amortization is provided for.

The Minister also deprecated the tendency in some quarters to seek the way out of difficulty by means of foreign borrowing. He said:

We are often advised to have resort to the assistance of foreign capital. * * * Foreign capitalists seeking opportunities for investment here would not grant us credits on the terms prevailing in their own countries, but would accommodate themselves to the present situation on our money market so as to secure, without risk, large profits for the future. From the point of view of the country's economy generally, foreign credits are in principle injurious, for they provoke excessive imports and consumption and are a burden on the country's balance of payments. * * * I have therefore prohibited local authorities throughout the Republic from availing themselves of the opportunity of raising, without special sanction, foreign credits for costly investment purposes.

With these measures undertaken by the government, it is expected that the problem of productive capital in Czechoslovakia would be made easier. Her responsible leaders are determined to avoid foreign borrowing, as long as there exists an opportunity for a larger utilization of domestic resources.

CHAPTER XIV

CZECHOSLOVAKIA'S ECONOMIC POLICY

THE economic policy of Czechoslovakia was dominated from the very beginning by a determination to create within her frontiers an economically independent state, as well as a politically sovereign one. She possessed the bases necessary for such a state. For a generation prior to the outbreak of the World War, the Czechs in Bohemia were making strenuous efforts to build up in Prague a financial and business center free from the domination of Vienna. These aspirations received a full scope for their realization with the establishment of the Czechoslovak Republic.

There is no doubt that at the beginning the spirit which had won for Czechoslovakia her political independence carried the country too far on the road of economic separatism. Racial and political issues obscured economic realities. Within the country, there was a struggle between the politically weak but economically powerful German minority, and the politically all-powerful, but economically weaker Czechoslovak majority, the latter striving for economic, as well as political supremacy.[1] Outside the country, the fear of a possible restoration of the political and economic power of Vienna dictated a policy of isolation.

Gradually the general situation in the country calmed down to less and less extreme policy and outlook. In the preceding chapters we described the process by which Czechoslovakia has built up her administrative apparatus and utilized her fiscal resources almost to the point of straining them, for the purpose of binding the country together by means of a reorganized system of communications; the steps by means of which she created her own currency and a national banking system; the character of her economic organization and the problems confronting her in the domain of trade, agriculture and industry. It is clear from the manner in which these activities unfolded themselves that after the subsidence of the spirit that was dominant at the beginning, Czechoslovakia has definitely aimed not at the creation of an economically closed and self-sufficient state, but rather at assuring for herself an economic position which would enable her to make a maximum use of her resources, while at the same time preserving in a full measure her newly won independence.

[1] Very symptomatic of this situation was, for example, the accusation made against Finance Minister Rašín to the effect that his monetary policy was deliberately directed toward the destruction of German-owned industries in Czechoslovakia. See Rist, C., *La Déflation en pratique,* p. 109.

There was one very important aspect of the general situation which has proven to be of utmost significance in the process of economic adjustment and development in Czechoslovakia. At the beginning of her independent existence, under the influence of the factors which made for her policy of isolation from her immediate neighbors, Czechoslovakia turned her face to the countries of the west. She sought what might be termed a "western orientation," as one of the means of safeguarding her independence. At the same time, important economic considerations pushed her in the same direction. Chief among these was the question of currency. An island of currency stability in a sea of currency disorganization, Czechoslovakia had to seek outlets for her trade in markets whose purchasing power was less impaired than that of her immediate neighbors.

Circumstances, lying outside her own control, in addition to the tendencies that actuated her responsible leaders, have been important factors in shaping the economic policy of Czechoslovakia. As a country with an industrial equipment whose productive capacity far exceeds her own domestic requirements, Czechoslovakia has found it necessary to adapt herself to world conditions, especially to the conditions existing in the countries which surround her. The question of her competitive position in world markets has been and still is of paramount importance to her.

I. COMPETITIVE POSITION IN THE WORLD MARKETS

We have seen that from the point of view of her domestic requirements Czechoslovakia is decidedly overindustrialized. Her character as an exporter of manufactured goods is a cardinal factor in her economic life, and consequently a determining element in her economic policy. Having become an independent state, she faced the imperative necessity of working out an economic policy that would serve best her essential national interests.

There have been two distant views in Czechoslovakia with regard to the question of overindustrialization. The first is that the national interests of the country would best be served by a reduction of industrial activity and a development and intensification of agriculture. The second is that it is best for Czechoslovakia to maintain and even expand her industrial activities.

The problem of population renders it difficult for Czechoslovakia to reduce her industrial activities. Such a reduction would involve an increase of the agricultural population, and as we have seen, for the country as a whole, a larger percentage of the population are engaged in agriculture than in industry.

Czechoslovak agriculture is already well developed. The country is nearly self-sufficient so far as the essential food supply is concerned, and is, in addition, a surplus producer of sugar and of a number of other important agricultural commodities. The extension of arable lands is almost impossible on anything like a substantial scale. Totally unproductive lands now occupy only about 4 per cent of the total territory of the country, the lowest percentage in Europe. This fact sets definite limits to the possibility of increasing the agricultural population.

The agricultural population of the territories comprising Czechoslovakia was too large before the war. The growth of industries in Bohemia, Moravia, and Silesia absorbed a part of the surplus rural population, and no less than 60,000 persons emigrated annually from the present territory of Czechoslovakia, most of them from the rural districts.

The agrarian reform, which resulted in the breaking up of the great estates, has made large tracts of land available for small holders and has thus eased up the problem of surplus rural population. It has reduced the volume of emigration from the rural districts. But it has not solved the problem of surplus population.

During the first year of Czechoslovakia's existence as an independent state, there was practically no emigration from the country. On the contrary, there was a large stream of immigration. But after that, emigration began once more. Between July 1, 1920, and June 30, 1921, almost 41,000 Czechoslovak citizens entered the United States, in addition to the thousands who migrated to other countries. After the introduction of immigrant restriction in the United States, Czechoslovak emigrants turned in the direction of Canada and Argentina. Industrial depression has been largely responsible for these migrations, but the rural districts furnished over one-third of the total number of emigrants.[2]

The difficulties presented by immigration restriction in the United States have intensified the problem of surplus population in Czechoslovakia. And there seems to be very little prospect for agriculture to absorb even its own natural increase, let alone the urban surplus. Under these conditions, a maintenance and even an expansion of industrial activities seems to provide the only way out.

But the volume of industrial activity in Czechoslovakia depends upon foreign markets. And here the country encounters a number of very real difficulties.

The growth of industries in the Danubian countries represents a serious difficulty for Czechoslovakia. It affects some of the most important branches of industrial production in that country. The equipment built up originally for the internal market of the Austro-Hungarian Monarchy, and designed to meet primarily the requirements of that market, now has to supply other markets.

The textile industry, which furnishes no less than

[2] See Boháč, E., "Czechoslovak Emigration," *Social Policy in the Czechoslovak Republic.*

one-third of the total exports of the country, presents an excellent illustration of this. Textile mills have sprung up in all of Czechoslovakia's former markets, with the result that the rôle of the Danubian countries as purchasers of Czechoslovak textiles has been gradually diminishing, as may be seen from the following figures: In 1921, 79 per cent of the total textile exports of Czechoslovakia went to the Danubian countries; in 1924, 60 per cent. During the last quarter of 1925, only 51 per cent of the Czechoslovak exports of textiles went to the Danubian States.[3]

The same is true, to a larger or smaller degree, of a number of other industries. From our analysis of the geographical distribution of Czechoslovakia's foreign trade we have seen that the rôle of the Danubian States in the Czechoslovak export and import trade has been diminishing.

Not only does Czechoslovakia face the problem of decreased demand in her former Danubian markets, but she also finds herself there in an entirely different competitive position from the one she had before the war. This is due to the fact that the Czechoslovak industries and the markets for which they were originally designed no longer form a single economic territory.

The fact that the Danubian countries are now world markets constitutes another serious difficulty for the Czechoslovak industries. The tariff wall

[3] Uhlig, Karl, in *Wirtschaftsdienst,* August 6, 1926.

which surrounded the Austro-Hungarian Monarchy made the bulk of the territories comprising the present Danubian countries protected markets so far as the Czechoslovak industries were concerned. Today Czechoslovakia can enjoy only the advantages accruing from most-favored-nation treatment, which are extended equally to all countries having such treaties with the Danubian States.

Czechoslovakia's industrial exports are, for the greater part, of a highly competitive nature. This is especially true of such important export groups as textile and metal products. One of the results of the war and post-war conditions has been a large expansion in the output of these products, both in the territories that were producing them before the war and the territories which have only lately begun their development in this direction. This has inevitably led to an intensification of competition in these products.

Even with products in the manufacture of which Czechoslovakia was situated in a very favorable competitive position before the war, the present-day situation is different. In pre-war Europe, the territory of Czechoslovakia held an almost pre-eminent position so far as the manufacture of such products as glassware, porcelain, furniture, etc., was concerned. She encountered very little competition in this field. Since the war, the manufacture of glassware and porcelain has sprung up or developed in a number of other European countries. As a consequence, in this field, too, Czechoslovakia is now forced to meet serious competition.

The industrialists of Czechoslovakia are fully conscious of all these important factors. They realize that the exigencies of the difficult situation that confronts them demands a large degree of adaptation to the new conditions.

Czechoslovakia is confronted with the necessity of a far-reaching reorganization of her industrial system. There are two lines of development indicated for this reorganization. The first is the reduction of those phases of industrial activity in which international competition is strongest. The second is the expansion of those branches of production in which the difficulties of competition are likely to be small. Efforts are being made in Czechoslovakia along both of these lines.

The reduction of highly competitive branches of industrial activity involves a liquidation of a part of the existing equipment. This is being done at the present time, especially in the textile industry. Some of the textile factories that have come into existence on the territory of Czechoslovakia's Danubian neighbors, are equipped with machinery transplanted from Czechoslovakia. To some extent the same tendency appears in other branches of industry.

The expansion of less competitive branches means a greater specialization, especially in the production of goods of better quality. For example, in the textile industry the tendency in Czechoslovakia is to concentrate attention on the production of better grades of cloth for export, rather than on products of general consumption. In the manufacture of glassware, Czechoslovakia with her tradition of excellent workmanship, is in a position to produce articles of the higher quality, and reduce her production of cheaper glass.

Czechoslovakia needs, of course, to retain as much as possible of her industries, producing articles of general consumption. She needs these industries for the satisfaction of her domestic requirements as well as for her trade with the agricultural countries, but in their reduced scope, these industries must be brought up to a much higher degree of efficiency than they have at the present time, in order to meet the competition of the larger industrial countries.

All these changes necessary in the industrial system represent a costly process. They mean for Czechoslovak industries large productive investments. Hence the importance that the problem of fiscal policy and of capital accumulation assumes in the Czechoslovak situation.[4]

II. TARIFF POLICY AND TREATY ARRANGEMENTS

As a country dependent for its economic prosperity upon foreign trade, Czechoslovakia might have been expected from the start to be in favor of more or less free trade arrangements. Instead

[4] See pp. 262-64.

of that, the trend of developments during the period immediately following the war in all the countries of central and eastern Europe forced her into the path of trade restrictions, with the result that she became one of the most highly protectionist countries of central Europe. The need of strict trade regulation in her case was rendered especially acute by her determination to protect her currency at all costs.

Czechoslovakia began her independent existence with a system of very rigorous trade restrictions. As early as November 22, 1918, an Export and Import Commission was organized by the Czechoslovak government, and from that time on no goods could cross the frontiers of the country without a permit from this Commission. The work of the Commission was supplemented by that of a Central Exchange Bureau, established about the same time to control all transactions in foreign bills.

During the second half of 1919 and the first half of 1920 an attempt was made to place some of the functions of the Export and Import Commission in the hands of industrial syndicates. But this led to abuses, and in June, 1920, the Commission was reorganized into a Foreign Trade Bureau, which assumed the task of granting export and import licences.[5]

The system of trade restrictions was applied at

[5] Peroutka, Fr., "The Commercial Policy and the Tariff," *Czechoslovakia.*

first primarily for the purpose of conserving within the country supplies of essential commodities and to prevent the inflow of unessential imports. Later on, the chief purpose of the system shifted to the protection of the currency, and to its "bargaining" possibilities in negotiations for trade agreements.

Although Czechoslovakia returned comparatively soon after the end of the war to the customs tariff system, her government felt that in view of unstable currency conditions customs duties alone would not be sufficient for the regulation of foreign trade. This was especially so after the Czechoslovak currency parted company with the currencies of Austria and Germany and began to appreciate. The depreciation of currency in Austria and Germany gave these countries an advantage in their export trade, and the system of import restriction acted in Czechoslovakia as an anti-dumping measure.

Czechoslovakia signed the Portorose protocol, but like Austria refused to take the initiative in ratifying it and putting it into effect. As she perfected her customs tariff machinery, she gradually gave up the various trade restrictions, although she still maintains the licence system for some commodities —a practice which causes her difficulties in some of her commercial treaty negotiations.

In her customs tariff policy Czechoslovakia faces a conflict between the need of protecting the home market and of stimulating exports. So far emphasis has been placed on protection both for industry and agriculture. But it is now shifting to the requirements of her competitive position.

Czechoslovakia has not as yet worked out her own tariff. She is using the old Austro-Hungarian tariff of 1906, with the rates, which are in gold crowns, increased even more than the requirements of currency depreciation. The multipliers by means of which the original gold crown rates may be translated into paper crowns were fixed when the exchange value of the crown was much lower than the level at which it finally became stabilized. Moreover, the fear of dumping from Austria and Germany led to the fixing of multipliers which were larger than the ratio between gold and paper crowns. These multipliers were not adjusted after the appreciation and stabilization of the crown, with the result that Czechoslovakia has today a much higher degree of customs protection than was the case with the former Monarchy. In 1925 and 1926 this tariff structure was completed by the introduction of higher agricultural duties than had obtained in the Monarchy.

Altogether, Czechoslovakia's maximum customs tariff is almost double the old Austro-Hungarian tariff. The maximum duties represent 36.4 per cent of the total value of imports, while those levied under the Austro-Hungarian tariff represented only 18.9 per cent. The tariff on foodstuffs in Czechoslovakia is 34.1 per cent, instead of 26.4 per cent in the old Monarchy; on chemical products, it is 42.9 per cent, instead of 21.5; on textiles, it is 28.6 per cent, instead of 12; on iron and iron products, 53.3 per cent, instead of 31.7; on machinery, 46.2, instead of 17.[6]

The above percentages represent duties for the whole groups of products, although there is a wide range of variations within the groups. Generally speaking, Czechoslovakia has a low tariff on raw materials and semi-manufactures, and a high tariff on finished products. For example, the ratio between the duty on grain and that on flour is 30:70.

The stabilization of currencies in Czechoslovakia, as well as in the surrounding countries, has removed one of the principal reasons for the maintenance of high duties on industrial products. On the contrary, as the situation stands today the continuation of these duties is beginning to exercise a harmful influence on the country's competitive position and the possibility of stimulating its exports. There is growing up in Czechoslovakia a well-defined tendency toward a reduction of tariff rates, which is one of the phases of the general process of fiscal and economic reorganization of the country.[7]

[6] *Zollhöhe und Warenwerte,* Table I.

[7] For example, Finance Minister Engliš, in his budget speech cited above, says: "A state depending mainly upon export cannot afford to be permanently surrounded by a high tariff wall, enabling a higher level of economic figures, prices, profits, and earnings to be created than corresponds to the world's level of prices and the exchange rate of the currency. The production in the export industries of Czechoslovakia takes place at a higher level of such figures than exists in the countries to which the exports go for sale. High customs duties check export trade."

As a matter of fact, the commercial treaties which Czechoslovakia has negotiated have already lowered considerably many of the customs duties imposed under her tariff. They have really prepared the way for a complete revision of the Czechoslovak tariff, which, in any event, is one of the major tasks confronting that country in the near future.

Czechoslovakia has consistently sought to open up markets for her exports through the conclusion of commercial treaties. At the beginning these treaties were merely "quota" agreements, rendered necessary by the maintenance of the system of foreign trade control in all the countries of Central Europe. It was only gradually that the treaties assumed the form of regular commercial treaties, although it was not until 1923 that Czechoslovakia began to conclude treaties providing for the adjustment of tariff rates.

During the years 1919-1921, Czechoslovakia concluded trade agreements with all of her neighbors, except Hungary. She also concluded agreements with Yugoslavia, Bulgaria, Switzerland, Italy, France, and Spain. In 1922 she negotiated a provisional treaty with Russia. In 1923, commercial treaties were concluded with a number of other European countries, including Great Britain. A provisional treaty was signed with the United States. Most of these treaties were based on most-favored-nation treatment, but they contained no agreements with regard to tariff duties.

In August, 1923, Czechoslovakia signed a new commercial treaty with France, containing for the first time an agreement with regard to mutual tariff concessions. By this treaty, France granted Czechoslovakia her minimum tariff on a number of items and reductions from the general tariff on a number of others. Czechoslovakia, in return, granted reductions from her general tariff on a large number of articles exported to her by France. Since then she has completed a number of tariff agreements, the most important of these being with Italy and Austria in 1924, with Poland and Spain in 1925, and with Hungary in 1927.[8]

In this manner Czechoslovakia has built up a comprehensive network of commercial treaties, the conclusion of which has greatly facilitated her foreign trade. The tariff agreements concluded since 1923 have served to lower her level of customs duties, but they have at the same time opened up for her more fully some of her largest export markets. The only important tariff agreement which she still has to conclude is with Germany.

Czechoslovakia has experienced great difficulties in negotiating commercial treaties with her neighbors. The treaties she has concluded with Austria, Hungary, and Poland required prolonged and difficult negotiations, while the treaty with Germany is still pending.

[8] For a list of commercial treaties concluded by Czechoslovakia see *Bulletin of the National Bank of Czechoslovakia,* No. 3, pp. 36-7.

The first treaty between Czechoslovakia and Austria was merely a most-favored-nation convention. It was supplemented by three tariff agreements, concluded in 1924, 1925, and 1926. But in November, 1926, Austria denounced the three tariff agreements, and soon after that negotiations were begun for a new treaty. The final treaty went into effect on August 10, 1927. It contains a number of tariff adjustments, which are regarded by both sides as more or less satisfactory.

The commercial relations between Czechoslovakia and Hungary, which were practically without any treaty basis until the autumn of 1926, have now been completely regulated by a commercial and tariff treaty, put into effect in July, 1927. For a long time prior to the beginning of negotiations, it was felt in both countries that commercial relations had to be placed on a treaty basis, but it was the increase of agricultural duties in Czechoslovakia that served as the final spur to the opening of negotiations. By the new treaty, Czechoslovakia obtains concessions on about 200 articles, mostly manufactured goods, which constitute the bulk of her exports to Hungary. Hungary, on the other hand, has obtained some concessions on a number of food products.[9]

Czechoslovakia's commercial treaty negotiations with Poland were complicated at the beginning by

[9] See p. 375 of this book for Hungary's attitude to the treaty. For the details of the two treaties see Anglo-International Bank, Ltd., *Monthly Review of Central Europe,* No. 9 for 1927.

the differences existing between the two countries over frontier adjustments. The negotiations with Germany are still in progress, the principal stumbling block being the refusal of Czechoslovakia to accede to the German demand for the abrogation of restrictions in the importation of motor vehicles.

III. ATTITUDE TOWARD THE QUESTION OF A LARGER ECONOMIC TERRITORY

Unlike Austria, Czechoslovakia does not regard her own inclusion in a larger economic territory as indispensable for her national well-being. On the contrary, her whole economic policy is directed toward the preservation of her economic, as well as political, identity. The core of this policy is, therefore, the extension of the system of commercial treaties, which would give as wide as possible a scope for her export trade.

Czechoslovakia favors the establishment among the Danubian States of a regional preferential régime. The general feeling in the country seems to be that the establishment of an economically unified Danubian territory is an impossibility. The growth of industrial activity in the agricultural countries of the Danubian group is regarded as an almost insuperable economic obstacle to the creation of an economic union. Political considerations are regarded as even more insuperable obstacles. On the whole, Czechoslovakia inclines to the view that a preferential customs régime is the maximum of economic collaboration among the Danubian countries compatible with their national sovereignty.

The western orientation of Czechoslovakia during the first years of her existence has undoubtedly played an important rôle in the development of this situation. This orientation no doubt exercised an important influence on the policy of national isolation, which Czechoslovakia in common with the other newly organized states, pursued at the beginning. And out of these isolationist policies came important stimuli for new industrial developments, which now represent so important a factor in the possibilities of economic union.

But while averse to anything that could have even a remote bearing on a re-establishment of the prewar Monarchy—and economic union has always been regarded as a possible first step in this direction—Czechoslovakia has not been opposed to the establishment of close and friendly relations with the other Danubian countries. The creation of the Little Entente brought her into a close association with Rumania and Yugoslavia. She made two attempts, in 1921 and 1925, to establish closer economic relations with Austria. It was only with Hungary that her relations have until recently remained badly strained.

The provisions of the peace treaties with regard to preferential tariff arrangements as among Czechoslovakia, Austria, and Hungary, were never utilized by any of the three countries, except in the attempt made in 1925, which, as we saw above,[10] involved the establishment of a preferential tariff régime between Czechoslovakia and Austria, and between Austria and Italy. Czechoslovakia was responsible for the failure of these negotiations. In her opinion, the scheme proposed failed to fulfill what she considers an indispensable basic condition of any preferential régime, namely, reciprocal application of most-favored-nation principle as among the countries entering the arrangement. As the proposal stood, the privileges granted by Austria to Italy or by Italy to Austria were not to apply to Czechoslovakia, and vice versa. To this Czechoslovakia would not consent.[11]

While Czechoslovakia favors the establishment of preferential tariff régime among the Danubian countries, she is not at all certain that it would be of very great benefit to her. It would free her from the competition of other industrial nations in the Danubian markets, but it would still leave her face to face with the problem presented by the development of industry in the other Danubian countries. These countries would scarcely sacrifice their indus-

[10] See Chapter IV.

[11] Mr. J. Dvořáček, the Czechoslovak representative in these negotiations, in his essay, *Austria and Its Economic Existence,* has stated his country's position in this respect as follows: "It is certain that without a general application of the integral principle of most-favored-nation treatment *within the circle of the States participating in preference* it would scarcely be possible for the individual States to accede to the system, for differential treatment within the States enjoying preference would lead to far-reaching alterations in respect of markets."

trial equipment, unless Czechoslovakia in turn sacrifices some of her agricultural activity. Moreover, "administrative" protection for home industries would present a difficult problem to overcome.

On the whole, a Danubian preferential régime would perhaps benefit Czechoslovakia to some extent, but it would scarcely change appreciably the present tendency of Czechoslovak trade to seek general world markets rather than the Danubian ones.

The future of the Czechoslovak export trade is in central and western Europe and overseas, rather than in the Danubian States. We have already seen to what extent the relative importance of Czechoslovakia's exports to the Danubian countries has been decreasing, while that of her exports to the well-developed markets of the other parts of Europe and overseas has been increasing. There is every indication that this tendency is likely to continue.

Even within the Danubian group, Austria, the smallest of the Danubian States, is by far the largest market for Czechoslovak exports.[12] Similarly, Hungary is more important than either Rumania or Yugoslavia.

Moreover, the balance of trade as between Czechoslovakia and the other Danubian countries is very much in her favor. In 1926, for example, her sales to the Danubian countries amounted to 5,927 million crowns, while her purchases from these coun-

[12] This is true even if allowance is made for the fact that some of the products Austria imports from Czechoslovakia are resold by her to the Balkan countries and elsewhere.

tries were only 3,219 millions. It is doubtful whether Czechoslovakia can increase greatly her exports to these countries, unless she is willing to increase also her imports from them. And she is already purchasing from them the major portion of her imported foodstuffs.

As Czechoslovakia develops her output of the better grades of industrial products, she will have to seek more and more the wealthier markets of the economically advanced countries. From this point of view the fact that Germany and Austria are today her two largest markets is exceedingly significant. To some extent they act as middlemen for her products, but they are also important consumers.

In view of this, the question of a possible union between Germany and Austria is one of utmost importance to Czechoslovakia. Quite apart from the political aspects of this question, its economic bearing on the Czechoslovak situation is vital and far-reaching.

Economically, a union between Austria and Germany would present for Czechoslovakia both advantages and disadvantages. While the question of such a union is still discussed in Czechoslovakia principally from the ponit of view of its political ramifications, its economic aspects are rapidly emerging into the foreground.

Austria is an important factor in Czechoslovakia's export trade. But the continuation of this importance depends on whether Austria will become a progressively richer or progressively poorer market. There is very little tendency among well-informed observers in Czechoslovakia to dispute the Austrian thesis that only the inclusion of Austria in a larger economic territory can save her from economic retrogression. There is very little tendency, therefore, to deny that Austria might become economically strengthened by her inclusion in the German economic system. As such, she would represent a much larger market for Czechoslovak products of the higher grade than would otherwise be the case.

On the other hand, German industry, operating through Vienna, would be a more formidable competitor for other branches of industry in Czechoslovakia. This would add not only to the difficulties of Czechoslovakia's competitive position in the Danubian markets, but might conceivably threaten even an invasion of her own domestic market.

Moreover, a union between Austria and Germany might worsen rather than improve Czechoslovakia's position with regard to her export marketing facilities and international financial contacts. Even today, in spite of all efforts, Czechoslovakia still finds herself compelled to make a wide use of Germany's and Austria's commercial and financial organizations. This dependence is likely to increase, rather than diminish if Germany and Austria operate as a single economic territory.

PART IV

HUNGARY'S EXPERIENCE SINCE THE WAR

CHAPTER XV

THE PROBLEMS OF HUNGARY

HUNGARY emerged from the World War an independent and sovereign nation, very much, however, reduced in territory and population. The new Hungary retained, as we have seen, only 28 per cent of the territory and 37 per cent of the population of the pre-war Kingdom. Instead of a country with an important outlet to the Adriatic Sea—the port of Fiume—Hungary became a land-locked community. Her whole financial and economic life was disrupted by the break-up of her territory. Hungary, like Austria, began her post-war existence on the ruins of a once prosperous state.[1]

The economic experience of New Hungary has been dominated to a very large degree by internal and external political conditions. The Karolyi government, which became established immediately after the overthrow of the Royal régime, refused to accede to the territorial dismemberment of the country, and sought, through the instrumentality

[1] For a description of the changes produced in Hungary by the process of dismemberment see Bowman, Isaiah, *The New World*, Chapter XII; Teleki, Count Paul, *The Evolution of Hungary*, New York, 1922; and Buday, Ladislaus, *Dismembered Hungary*, Budapest, 1922.

of the peace negotiations, to change what had already become an accomplished fact through revolutionary action. Failing in this and losing as a result the confidence of many groups within the country, the Karolyi government gave way to a communist régime, which succeeded it in power. Karolyi sought redress against the dismemberment of Hungary through negotiation with the Allied powers of Western Europe represented at the Paris peace conference. The communist régime, led by Béla Kun, attempted to bring Hungary into the orbit of the international communist movement, which was then just coming into existence in Moscow and was hurling its defiance at the rest of the world.

As a reaction to this communist régime, there rose in Hungary a nationalist movement, which found its opportunity in an armed conflict between Hungary and Rumania over the Transylvanian frontier. The communist régime was overthrown, and a strongly nationalist government established in Budapest under the leadership of Admiral Horthy. This new government resumed the peace negotiations with the victorious Allied powers, interrupted by the establishment of the communist régime, and finally signed the treaty of Trianon.

However, the Horthy government agreed to the provisions of the peace treaty only under protest, and its attitude toward Hungary's neighbors remained essentially hostile. The strain produced by this hostility was accentuated by the two attempts made, in 1921, by the former Austrian Emperor to regain the Hungarian throne. The situation thus created was reflected in the economic and financial condition of Hungary.

The war left Hungary in an economically weakened condition. The breaking up of the pre-war economic system which resulted from the territorial dismemberment of the country created many new difficulties. The ravages of the communist régime, followed by the struggle with Rumania and a short but violent civil war, completed the disorganization. And during the period when Hungary lived in a state of hostility against her neighbors, she made but feeble efforts to adjust her economic and financial difficulties by her own efforts.

It was not long, however, before the Hungarian government realized that there was no hope of solving the country's difficulties without outside assistance. Like all the defeated belligerents, Hungary was bound hand and foot by the provisions of the reparation clauses of the peace treaties. The Reparation Commission held what amounted to a blanket mortgage on all the resources of the country, and this rendered impossible more or less normal financial intercourse between Hungary and the rest of the world. The need of coming to terms with the Reparation Commission in order to regain at least a certain degree of freedom in international intercourse was a powerful factor in Hungary's adjustment of her relations with the neighboring states.

The year 1923 marked the change in Hungary's international position. Her government, impressed by Austria's experience the year before with the Reparation Commission and the League of Nations, opened negotiations with the Commission. The successful termination of these negotiations, which led to the assumption by the League of Nations of the financial rehabilitation of Hungary, inaugurated the second period in the economic development of New Hungary.

The principal economic problems faced by the new Hungary during the first eight years of her independent existence were: (1) unbalanced budget; (2) currency depreciation; (3) adverse balance of trade and the consequent excess of outgo over income in her international accounts; (4) contraction of agricultural production; and (5) disruption of her industrial organization. Beyond these immediate problems there has constantly loomed up the more far-reaching and basic problem of the need for adjusting the economic system of the country to the task of maintaining its population.

In her efforts to solve these problems Hungary has followed a more or less clear line of national economic policy, which has led her into the paths of important developments. Free of the political sectionalism that has weighed upon Austria and of racial conflicts that have complicated the situation in Czechoslovakia, Hungary succeeded, after eight years of independent existence, in solving some of the pressing economic problems that confronted her. Other problems, however, still await solution, and the possibilities of their solution place before the country new tasks of policy and adjustment.

CHAPTER XVI

HUNGARY'S FISCAL AND CURRENCY REHABILITATION

HUNGARY'S fiscal and currency experience has been very much like that of Austria. In some respects, the situation that confronted her was even more difficult. During the year that followed the end of the war she had three different forms of government. Each of the régimes inherited from its predecessor an empty treasury and a set of chaotic budgetary practices. The Rumanian invasion and the short but violent civil war completed the disorganization of Hungary's public finances. By the time stable government was established, the process of supplying budgetary requirements by means of the printing press had definitely set in, and Hungarian finances were past repair by any ordinary means.

The conditions imposed upon Hungary by the peace treaties, especially with regard to reparation liability. further complicated the country's financial condition. They were principally responsible for rendering futile several attempts made by the Hungarian government to stem the tide of monetary inflation and financial disorganization. Up to 1924 the financial condition of Hungary was growing worse and worse. It was only in that year, because of international assistance, that Hungarian finances took a turn for the better.

Thus we have two distinct periods in Hungary's fiscal and currency experience since the war. The first is the period lasting for over five years, from the end of the war on, during which the currency of the country was constantly depreciating, while the state budget was badly out of balance. The second period starts in 1924, when the League of Nations reconstruction scheme went into effect, and is characterized by stabilized currency and balanced budgets.

I. BUDGETARY AND CURRENCY CONDITIONS PRIOR TO 1924

During the war no attempt was made by the Hungarian government to prepare regular budgets. The last budget for pre-war Hungary was for the fiscal year ending June 30, 1915, and through the subsequent years the government simply reenacted the 1914-15 budget, carrying on the finances of the state by means of spėcial appropriation bills. This practice was continued by the governments which held power during the early post-war years.

The first attempt to return to the system of regular budgets was made in 1920. But neither the 1920-21, nor the 1921-22 budgets came up properly before the Parliament, and the financial administration continued to operate on the basis of appropriation bills, voted by the Parliament from time to time.[1]

Government expenditures were greatly in excess of revenues. The Karolyi government, which lasted from October 30, 1918, to March 21, 1919, spent 4,800 million crowns, and received in revenue only 400 millions. The Soviet government, during its five months in power, spent 4,889 millions and collected in revenues 473 millions.[2] No figures, even estimated, are available for the remainder of 1919 and the first half of 1920. For the four fiscal years from July 1, 1920, to June 30, 1924, the budgetary estimates were as shown in table on page 299.[3]

No figures are available for the actual revenues and expenditures during these years. There is no doubt that the deficits were much larger than indicated by the estimates, because the depreciation of the currency made it impossible for the government to keep its expenditures within the limits indicated.

Subsidies to government employes and railway deficits were chiefly responsible for the excess of expenditures over revenues. At the beginning, interest payments on the debts accumulated during the war also constituted a heavy burden on the budget. But

[1] Görög, Frederic, "State Estimates," *Hungary of Today*, Budapest, 1922.

[2] Figures from the *Memorandum* accompanying the Budget Bill for 1920-21.

[3] Figures from *Magyar Kir. Penzügyminister*, quoted in *European Currency and Finance*, p. 124.

BUDGET ESTIMATES, 1920-1924
(In millions of paper crowns)

Year	Revenue	Expenditures	Deficit	*Percentage of Expenditures Covered by Issues of Paper Money*
1920–21......	10,520	20,210	9,690	*47.9*
1921–22......	20,296	26,764	6,468	*24.1*
1922–23......	152,802	193,455	40,653	*21.0*
1923–24......	2,168,140	3,307,099	1,138,959	*34.4*

as the value of the crown dropped, the relative importance of the debt payments decreased rapidly. In the budget of 1922-23, for example, these payments were already comparatively small. But the subsidies to government employes and the losses in the operation of state-owned railways and other enterprises represented larger sums than the total deficit for the year.

The subsidies to government employes were given "in kind." Under the 1922-23 budget, provisions were made to supply each government employe with 10 kg. of flour, 1 kg. of sugar, 1 kg. of fats, and 1 kg. of salt per month, in addition to 120 kg. of potatoes and 4 kg. of beans for the whole year. Moreover, each householder was supplied with 5 kg. of coal and an equal amount of wood during the year. Finally, each employe received a certain amount of cloth, linen, and footwear. Altogether subsidies were provided for 260,000 employes, which meant, counting their families, that no less than 750,000 persons, or 10 per cent of the population, received government aid.[4]

The reason for these subsidies "in kind" lay in the fact that the government found it impossible to provide an adequate monetary compensation for its employes. Owing to scarcity of supplies in the market and the violent price fluctuations due to inflation, the government found it easier and cheaper for itself to grant subsidies in kind than to increase salaries.

For the same reason the government also maintained a system of providing certain categories of the population with flour at very low prices. At the beginning this system applied to a very large part of the urban population. By 1922, however, only hospitals and charitable institutions, war invalids, widows and orphans, persons depending on charity, and employes in certain selected industries—altogether, about one and one-half million persons—came under the operation of the system. Of the 2.7 million quintals of grain required for this purpose, only a little more than half was purchased by the government in the open market; the remainder came out of grain retained for export and milling duties.

[4] De Kállay, Tibor, *Exposé adressé à la Commission des Reparations* (Memorandum presented to the Reparation Commission by the Hungarian Minister of Finance), May 4, 1923, Annex 6.

During the following year the amount of grain thus distributed was reduced by over one-third.[5]

Altogether, subsidies "in kind" added 26 billion crowns to the budget for 1922-23. Approximately the same amount was added by the excess of expense over receipts in the operation of the government-owned railways; this was due to the maintenance of very low fares for social reasons. The requirements of the state debt payments added about 11 billions to the budget for that year.

New issues of paper money covered the budgetary deficits. Hungary took no steps toward the stamping of the Austro-Hungarian bank notes circulating on her territory until after the collapse of the Soviet régime, that is almost a year after the establishment of the new state. In the meantime, the printing of new notes went on uninterruptedly. The Karolyi and the Bela Kun régimes, the period of the Rumanian occupation, and the civil war which resulted in the establishment of the Horthy régime, were all financed by means of the printing press.

The stamping of the Austro-Hungarian bank notes was one of the stipulations of the treaty of Trianon, and the Hungarian government, shortly after the ratification of the treaty, proceeded to carry out this provision. Profiting by the experience of Czechoslovakia,[6] the Hungarian government attempted to regulate the monetary problem by an enforced re-

[5] De Kállay, T., *Exposé*, etc., Annex 6.
[6] See p. 207.

tention of 50 per cent of the notes presented for stamping. This measure yielded the government Treasury 3,970 million crowns.[7] The owners of the notes which were retained by the government, received in exchange 4 per cent bonds, and the fund thus created was used for the purposes of the government budget.

But the amount made available in this manner was not sufficient to cover even half of the deficit during the financial year 1920-21, when the expenditures of the government exceeded the revenues by 9,690 million crowns. The notes retained during the stamping process were quickly used up, and the governments returned to the practice of issuing new notes. The Austro-Hungarian Bank was, in the meantime, liquidated, a Hungarian State Note Issuing Institute was created, and its presses supplied the government with the billions of paper crowns that were needed for the budgetary deficits.

Budgetary deficits were partly a cause and partly a result of monetary inflation in Hungary. The total amount of paper currency put into circulation was considerably larger than the aggregate deficits in the budget. This was due to several important factors.

The existence of large budgetary deficits covered by new fiduciary issues exercised a great influence on the exchange value of the Hungarian crown. As

[7] Von Fellner, F., "La Situation financière de l'état Hongrois," *Revue Economique Internationale,* July, 1924.

the needs of the government added fresh billions to the huge amounts of paper currency already in circulation, the value of the crown in the money markets of the world became smaller and smaller.

This depreciation of the crown exchange was rendered faster by the fact that Hungary's international accounts were also badly out of balance. The existence of huge deficits in the foreign trade of the country was another cause of monetary inflation. The excess of imports over exports could not be covered either by service operations or by foreign borrowing. Paper crowns had to be offered in payment, and that served as a powerful stimulus for further depreciation of the exchange.[8]

There was still another factor that accelerated the depreciation of the Hungarian currency. That was "the flight from the crown"—a phenomenon common to all countries that have passed through a currency débâcle. Many elements of political and economic nature combined to undermine the confidence in the future of the currency even within the country. People in Hungary were eager to exchange their crowns for stable foreign currencies, while exporters in many instances left portions of their proceeds on deposit in foreign banks. All this served to increase the demand in Hungary for foreign currencies and to depress the exchange value of the crown.

[8] For a discussion of Hungary's international accounts see the next chapter.

The fall in the exchange value of the crown and the appearance in circulation of an ever increasing volume of paper currency brought about a constant rise of prices. As prices rose the expenditures of the government increased. The government revenues could not keep pace with this increase, with the result that deficits mounted higher and higher, necessitating in turn new issues of paper currency.[9]

The price situation in Hungary during the period of inflation presented one very interesting phenomenon. Up to 1923 the increase in prices was not nearly as large as the depreciation of the crown. This situation, however, was due to the artificial measures adopted by the government for the purpose of keeping the domestic prices low. Export duties and restrictions represented the most important of these measures, with the result that the existence of low domestic prices did not tend to increase the country's exports and thus rectify the foreign trade situation. About the middle of 1923 the rise in prices outstripped the fall in exchange.[10]

A comprehensive attempt to reorganize the finances of Hungary was made in 1921. An experienced and well-informed financier, Dr. Roland Hegedüs, became Minister of Finance with almost

[9] It is true, of course, that in one respect the government gained by the depreciation of the currency, since it constantly decreased the value of the government debt and finally destroyed it altogether. But this gain was more than offset by the destructive effects of inflation on the general economic life of the country.

[10] For a detailed study of the process of inflation in Hungary see Mitzakis, Michel, *Le Relèvement financier de la Hongrie et la Société des Nations,* Paris, 1926, Chapter III.

dictatorial powers for one year. He made the keynote of his financial policy the stabilization and the subsequent gradual appreciation of the exchange value of the crown. He attempted to introduce a number of measures whereby the budgetary deficit would be wiped out and the international payments balanced, in which case it would be possible to stop the printing of paper money.

During Dr. Hegedüs's régime a large number of new taxes were introduced and some of the old ones were increased. The most important of these measures was the introduction of a 20 per cent capital levy on mobile and immobile property. The proceeds of this levy were to be used for the liquidation of the internal debt, while such other levies as a tax on war fortunes, a levy on share capital, increased turnover tax, stock exchange transactions tax, new and increased taxes on articles of luxury, matches, beer, wines, etc., were to be applied to the balancing of the budget.

Not the least important of the problems confronted by Dr. Hegedüs was the creation of a condition of confidence in the future of the Hungarian currency. The outstanding achievement of his régime was the fact that he succeeded in stemming the tide of the "flight from the crown" and in inspiring such confidence in his efforts that it became possible for the government to stop the printing presses in March, 1921.

At the same time the exchange value of the crown

began to appreciate very rapidly. In January, 1921, a gold crown was worth 2,100 paper crowns, in February, it stood at 2,030. In March, when the printing of paper money was discontinued, only 1,380 paper crowns were required to buy one gold crown. By May the value of a gold crown was 880 paper crowns. Starting with June, however, the situation began to grow worse again. By August a gold crown was worth 1,410 paper crowns, while in September, when Dr. Hegedüs resigned, the ratio between the gold and the paper crown went back to the low point at which it stood in January of that year.[11]

A number of factors conspired to render futile the work undertaken by Dr. Hegedüs. While it was easy enough to obtain the passage by the National Assembly of the twenty-nine financial bills submitted by him during his régime, it was very much more difficult to organize the administrative machinery for the execution of the measures introduced. The result of the drastic increases of taxes were much too slow to bear adequately upon the budgetary situation. A considerable part of the proceeds of the capital levy was diverted to budgetary purposes, to provide for increases in the salaries of some of the officials. Moreover, the political situation in the country was very unfavorable to permanent reform of any kind. Ex-King Charles's first attempt

[11] Humphreys, R. J. E., *Report on the Commercial and Industrial Situation in Hungary*, London, 1922, p. 8.

to regain the throne was made in April, 1921, and the second, in October.

The failure of the Hegedüs program of reforms clearly indicated the need for foreign financial intervention. One of the principal reasons for his failure lay in the reparation question. The treaty of Trianon had made Hungary responsible for a reparation program, in which, however, neither the total amount, nor the schedule of payments was fixed at the time. In the meantime, the reparation claim constituted a blanket lien upon all of Hungary's national resources.

One of the objects pursued by Dr. Hegedüs in undertaking drastic measures for the balancing of the budget, was to create a condition, in which Hungary might be able to raise foreign loans for the purpose of making up the deficit in her balance of payments. Such loans were unthinkable, however, as long as the reparation problem remained in the indefinite situation in which the treaty of Trianon had left it.

The whole program inaugurated by Dr. Hegedüs proved ineffective, mainly because of his inability to overcome the difficulties which lay outside Hungary's own control. His experience showed definitely that the financial rehabilitation of Hungary was impossible as long as the international position of the country remained what it was. It was not until the beginning of 1923, however, that circumstances both within Hungary and outside rendered possible the inauguration of the necessary negotiations that would open the way for effective fiscal and currency reforms. Austria's experience with the Reparation Commission and the League of Nations no doubt provided a strong impetus for Hungary in her appeal for foreign assistance.

II. INTERVENTION BY THE LEAGUE OF NATIONS

In April, 1923, the Hungarian government made a formal application to the Reparation Commission for the raising of the general lien imposed by the treaty of Trianon in order to enable it to float foreign loans. The Commission agreed to grant this request, on condition, however, that the release would be given only for definite loans, previously submitted to it, and with a further stipulation that a part of the proceeds should be applied to reparation payments. On the basis of this decision of the Reparation Commission, the Hungarian government made an attempt to open negotiations for a foreign loan, but found the principal money markets of the world unwilling to entertain the proposal.

One of the principal obstacles in the way of successful loan negotiations was the relations between Hungary and her neighbors. In July, 1923, however a conference of the Little Entente states met at Sinaïa (Rumania) and devoted a large part of its discussion to the Hungarian question. The result of this discussion was an agreement on the part of Czechoslovakia, Rumania, and Yugoslavia not to stand in the way of international financial assistance to Hungary on condition that the latter again pledge itself not to disturb political peace in central Europe.

As in the case of Austria, the League of Nations undertook the task of Hungarian reconstruction. Two months after the Sinaïa conference, at the September Assembly of the League of Nations, important negotiations took place between the representatives of Hungary, and of the Little Entente, which resulted in agreement on a number of questions that had formerly been in dispute. The consequence of this was that the League Council agreed to undertake responsibility for a scheme of reconstruction in Hungary along lines similar to those of the Austrian scheme.

The Reparation Commission gave its assent on October 17, and the Secretariat of the Financial Committee of the League began the necessary preparatory work. After a thorough investigation of the problem, the Financial Committee submitted its report to the League Council. The scheme for Hungarian reconstruction was finally worked out on the basis of this report, and was officially transmitted to the Reparation Commission on January 16, 1924, as the definitive plan proposed by the League. The Commission acted on the matter on February 21 by raising the liens on Hungary's assets as required by the scheme. At the March meeting of the League Council two protocols were signed and the Hungarian reconstruction scheme was launched.

Detailed plans for the work of reconstruction were worked out by a League delegation in Budapest. Negotiations were successfully concluded with the holders of relief bonds who yielded their priority in favor of the reconstruction loan. Finally Mr. Jeremiah Smith, of the United States, was appointed by the Council as the League's Commissioner General.[12]

The Hungarian reconstruction scheme was based on the two Geneva protocols. The first of these protocols was of a general political nature. The second was quite detailed and set forth the program of reform and the measures to be undertaken by the Hungarian government.

Protocol No. I was signed by the representatives of Great Britain, France, Italy, Czechoslovakia, Rumania, Yugoslavia, and Hungary. By it, the first six of these powers declared "that they will respect the political independence, the territorial integrity, and the sovereignty of Hungary," and "that they will not seek to obtain any special or exclusive economic or financial advantage calculated directly or indirectly to compromise that independence." Hungary, on the other hand, undertook "in accordance with the treaty of Trianon, strictly and loyally to fulfill the obligations contained in the said treaty,

[12] For the details of the negotiations see Sir Arthur Salter's Preface to *The Financial Reconstruction of Hungary*, Geneva, 1926. The volume contains all the relevant documents. See also Mitzakis, M., *Le Relèvement financier de la Hongrie*, Chapter IV.

and in particular the military clauses, as also the other international engagements."

By Protocol No. II, Hungary, which was the sole signatory, undertook to draw up and put into execution a program of fiscal and currency reforms directed toward the balancing of the budget and the stabilization of the currency. This program was to be worked out jointly by the Hungarian government and a Delegation of the Council of the League of Nations, and the former undertook to obtain for it the necessary parliamentary approval. The Hungarian government consented to the appointment of a League Commissioner General, who was to supervise the carrying out of the fiscal and currency program; of a committee of control appointed by the Reparation Commission to deal with questions of reparation payments; and of a board of trustees to represent the interests of the holders of the bonds which were to be issued as an international reconstruction loan.

As far as commercial relations were concerned, Hungary continued, by virtue of Protocol No. I, to "maintain, subject to the provisions of the treaty of Trianon, her freedom in the matter of customs tariffs and commercial or financial agreements," with the provision that she may not grant any state a special régime calculated to violate her complete independence. By Protocol No. II, Hungary undertook "to make every effort to conclude commercial agreements, in particular with neighboring states, with a view to reducing the obstacles and increasing the volume of her foreign trade."

III. CURRENCY STABILIZATION AND THE BANK OF ISSUE

While the arrangements for the reconstruction scheme were in progress, the Hungarian currency was undergoing a rapid deterioration. On January 1, 1924, the crown was quoted in New York at 22,000 to the dollar. By March 1 it had dropped to 69,000 and by June 1, to 90,000.[13] This exchange situation induced a veritable chaos in the economic life of the country. Prices were rising much faster than the exchange value fell, and the whole credit structure was completely disorganized.

Pending the results of the negotiations with the League, the Hungarian government made an independent attempt to stem the tide of depreciation. In February, 1924, a unit of accountancy, known as the "savings crown," was introduced. The "savings crown" was not a currency in any sense. It was simply a unit in which credit transactions could be expressed. Its relation to the paper crown was fixed daily by the Note Issuing Institute on the basis of the rate of exchange. Obligations incurred in "savings crowns" were thus payable in paper crowns at the rate of exchange prevailing on the date of payment.[14]

[13] Rawlins, E. C. D., *Report on the Commercial and Industrial Situation in Hungary*, London, 1925, p. 17.

[14] It will be recalled that a similar course was pursued by the

The introduction of the "savings crown" served to slow down somewhat the depreciation of the currency, but it did not result in its stabilization. Neither did the other measures attempted by the government, such as an enforced loan, etc., prove to be of any efficacy. The Hungarian exchange continued to fall, and the Note Issuing Institute continued incessantly to grind out fresh billions of paper crowns, which the government required for its expenditures.

Under the reconstruction scheme the creation of a new bank of issue was made a prerequisite to currency stabilization. Such an institution was created as the Hungarian National Bank by the law of April 26, 1924, and began its operations two months later, on June 24. The establishment of the new bank was attended by great difficulties.

The most important of these difficulties was the lack of adequate gold and foreign currency resources with which to begin operations. The Bank took over the affairs of the Note Issuing Institute with all of the latter's assets and liabilities. Moreover, it assumed the functions of the *Devisenzentrale*,[15]

German government during the period of rapid currency depreciation. For the details of the "savings crown" measure see Mitzakis, M., *Le Relèvement financier de la Hongrie*, pp. 74-76.

[15] The Hungarian *Devisenzentrale*, like the Austrian, had been organized for the purpose of controlling transactions in foreign currencies. It was the successor of the similar institution established during the war (see footnote on p. 122), which was abolished in 1920, but re-established in September, 1922, as a result of a panic on the exchange market, which occurred in July, 1922. In order to put an end to rapidly developing speculation in foreign currencies and securities, the government created this spe-

receiving the stocks of foreign currencies which that institution had at its disposal. But these combined resources of gold and foreign currencies were very meager.

The National Bank began its operations with an effective and virtual circulation of 3,770 billions of paper crowns.[16] At the same time, its metallic reserves were only the equivalent of 313 billions.[17] The very first task confronting the Bank was the acquisition of foreign currencies which would serve as the basis for its activities in maintaining stable exchange.

The plan for the creation of the National Bank under the reconstruction scheme envisaged the flotation of a foreign loan of 250 million gold crowns, the proceeds of which would serve to strengthen the resources of the Bank. There was, however, a considerable delay in the negotiations concerned with this loan. The New York bankers refused at first to undertake the placing of the *tranche* which was offered them, and while efforts were being made to adjust this difficulty, the whole reconstruction

cial organization, which was to exercise three-fold control over all exchange operations. The *Devisenzentrale* exercised technical control by reserving to itself and the State Note Issuing Institute, the exclusive right to deal in foreign currencies and securities. Secondly, it carried out financial control, by defending the exchange value of the crown from attacks at home and abroad; in these operations it acted through the Note Issuing Institute. Finally, with the aid of a special advisory commission, it controlled the volume of foreign trade.

[16] Von Fellner, F., "La Réforme monétaire en Hongrie," *Revue Economique Internationale,* November, 1925.

[17] Hantos, Elemér, *La Monnaie en Europe Centrale,* Paris, 1927, p. 174.

plan was being delayed. The critical condition of Hungarian finances rendered it necessary to find some other way of solving the problem, and this way was found when the Bank of England granted Hungary a credit of 4 million pounds sterling. This incident had a marked effect on the course of currency stabilization in Hungary.[18]

The Hungarian currency was stabilized with respect to the pound sterling, rather than gold. This was one of the conditions imposed by the Bank of England in granting the credit. And since the pound was itself at the time not on the gold basis, the Hungarian currency remained incompletely stabilized for several months. In this respect, Hungary's experience was different from Austria's, which had linked its currency to the dollar—that is, gold—and had complete stability from the start.

The linking of the Hungarian crown to the pound sterling rather than the dollar proved to be, on the whole, a favorable circumstance so far as Hungary was concerned. The ratio was fixed on the basis of a somewhat higher rate of exchange than the lowest rate reached in June, when the crown was quoted in London at 389,000 to the pound sterling. It was felt that this low rate did not correspond to the actual state of affairs, and it was not until July 31 that it was finally decided to stabilize the crown at 346,000 to the pound sterling, the exchange

[18] See von Fellner, F., "La Réforme monétaire en Hongrie"; also, *European Currency and Finance*, pp. 120-21.

rate in the meantime having found approximately that level. From that time on, the Bank has maintained the exchange at this ratio. But several months later, Great Britain returned to the gold standard, the pound sterling went back to parity, and the Hungarian crown, based on it, automatically appreciated with respect to the dollar and the other gold currencies.

From the time that the pound sterling reached parity, the Hungarian crown became effectively linked with gold. But the process of appreciation reacted very favorably on Hungary's foreign credit situation.

A new unit of currency was introduced in Hungary in 1925. This new unit is known as *pengö,* subdivided into 100 *fillér.* Opinion in Hungary was divided as to the gold value which was to be given the new unit. It was generally felt that the new Austrian currency, the schilling, was too low in value, and arguments were advanced in favor of adopting the gold content of the British shilling. The gold value of the pengö was fixed, however, considerably below the British unit, though somewhat above the Austrian. One pengö is worth 0.263157789 gramme of pure gold, and is equivalent to 12,500 paper crowns, or about 17.45 cents.

The term "pengö" is not new in Hungarian monetary history. It means literally, "ringing money," and was applied in the eighteenth century to the standard Austrian coin, in counterdistinction to the

the "convention coin." It has now been revived under somewhat similar circumstances to indicate the distinction between the new currency based on gold and the irredeemable paper crown, which this new currency supplants.[19]

The new currency is not convertible into gold, although provisions are made in the Charter of the National Bank for the establishment of the full gold standard. The Bank undertakes, however, to maintain it at a constant value in relation to gold, which makes the pengö a gold currency to all intents and purposes.

The stability of the currency is guaranteed by the freedom of the National Bank from government interference. By its Statutes the Bank is forbidden to make any advances to the government, whether central or local, except when such loans are secured by gold or foreign bills of exchange. The Bank also has the right to dissolve itself at any time that the government makes any infringements on its privileges as defined by the Statutes.

The National Bank is a private corporation, and of its fourteen directors, thirteen are elected by the stockholders. The fourteenth director, who acts as the Governor of the Bank, is appointed by the government on the recommendation of the Minister of Finance. The government participates in the profits of the Bank.

The Bank has a monopoly of note issue. Its notes

[19] See von Fellner, F., "La Réforme monétaire en Hongrie."

have the quality of legal tender, which will cease with the introduction of specie payment. The Statutes fix the minimum of reserves which must be maintained by the Bank. During the first five years of its existence, the reserves must be no less than 20 per cent of the total circulation less the government debt to the Bank. For the next five years, the minimum is 24 per cent; for the third five years, 28 per cent; and thereafter, 33⅓ per cent. After the resumption of specie payment, the cover must be no less than 40 per cent. The introduction of the gold standard cannot take place, however, until the government debt to the Bank shall have been reduced to 30 million gold crowns.

In its first balance sheet, issued for the week ending June 30, 1924, the National Bank showed a cover of 45.7 per cent. Two years later, in its balance sheet for the week ending June 30, 1926, the Bank showed a cover of 54.6 per cent.[20] Thus the Bank has been able to maintain a much larger reserve of metal and foreign bills than required by its Statutes.

IV. BUDGET EQUILIBRIUM UNDER LEAGUE OF NATIONS CONTROL

Next to the reform and stabilization of the currency, and, indeed, as a part of the process, the reconstruction scheme provided for the balancing of

[20] *Report* of the Commissioner General of the League of Nations for Hungary, Nos. 2 and 25.

the Hungarian budget. With the creation of the National Bank, all new issues of paper money for the purpose of covering budgetary deficits had to be discontinued. The government was thenceforth to rely only on actual revenues, and in case of need on regularly issued loans, for the covering of its expenditures.

Under the reconstruction scheme, the Hungarian budget was to be balanced within two and one-half years. This was to be accomplished by the following three means: (1) gradual elimination from the budget of those items of expenditures which were chiefly responsible for the deficits in the past; (2) a rigid keeping down of expenditures to the level expected to be reached during the first half of 1925; and (3) an increase of revenue, principally by means of direct taxation.

The outlays for allowances in kind, which had loomed so large before the reconstruction period, were expected to be eliminated by the second half of 1924. But at the same time the salaries of government officials were to be increased sufficiently to provide them with a living wage. The amounts allowed for the personnel of the army and the various administrative departments were to be increased from 67.2 million gold crowns during the first half of 1924 to 158.2 millions during the second half of 1926.

At the same time efforts were to be made to put the state enterprises on a self-supporting basis. This referred, of course, principally to the state railways. It was expected that by the second half of 1926 the deficit in the operation of railways would be wiped out, while the money required by them for capital investment would be obtainable by means of loans floated by them without any assistance from the government.

The budgetary estimates contained in the reconstruction scheme provided for an excess of expenditures over revenues during the fiscal years 1924-25 and 1925-26. It was expected that the budget would be actually balanced only by the second half of 1926. In the meantime, the reconstruction loan, included in the scheme, yielding about 250 million gold crowns, was to be used for covering the budgetary deficits. This loan was to be secured by the gross receipts of the customs, the tobacco monopoly, the sugar tax, and the net receipts of the salt monopoly.[21]

The fulfilment of the measures prescribed by the reconstruction scheme was to be supervised by the Commissioner General of the League of Nations. A system of monthly budgets was to be introduced, the Commissioner General passing on each budget as presented to him by the Hungarian government. All the revenues pledged as security for the loan were to be placed in his hands and applied by him to the payments of interest. The surplus of the pledged

[21] For the details of the reconstruction loan and the manner of the disposal of its proceeds, see pp. 358-59.

revenues was to be turned back by him to the Treasury.[22]

The Hungarian budget was actually balanced during the first six months of the reconstruction period. Neither the revenues nor the expenditures estimated in the reconstruction scheme proved to be large enough. During the first half of the fiscal year 1924-25, the actual expenditures of the Hungarian government were 10 per cent larger than the original estimate. But the revenues during the same period were almost 40 per cent greater than had been expected. The result of this was that instead of a deficit, the budget for the months July-December, 1924, showed a small surplus.

The same was true of the budget for the months January-June, 1925. The expenditures for this period were slightly in excess of the reconstruction scheme estimates, but the revenues were one-third greater than the estimate. The table on page 322 shows the comparison between the estimates and the results during the year from July 1, 1924, to June 30, 1925.

The figures given in the table refer to the preliminary net accounts issued by the Hungarian Treasury, as reported to the Commissioner General. When the closed accounts were completed, it appeared that the total net surplus for the year was about 63 million gold crowns, instead of a deficit of 100 millions, as expected in the reconstruction scheme.[23]

[22] For the details of the reconstruction scheme see *The Monthly Summary of the League of Nations, Supplement,* May, 1924.

[23] *Report* of the Commissioner General Nos. 8 and 15.

HUNGARIAN BUDGET, 1924-25
(In millions of gold crowns)

Period	Preliminary Treasury Accounts			Reconstruction Scheme		
	Receipts	Expenditures	Surplus (+) or Deficit (−)	Receipts	Expenditures	Surplus (+) or Deficit (−)
July-Dec. 1924.	208.0	205.9	+ 2.1	143.8	186.3	− 42.5
Jan.-June 1925.	245.1	216.9	+28.2	150.0	207.6	− 57.6
Fiscal Year 1924-25	453.1	422.8	+30.3	293.8	393.9	−100.1

The manner in which revenues were increased was different from that proposed in the reconstruction scheme. It will be recalled that the framers of the scheme laid particular emphasis on the increase of direct taxes, and their estimate of the revenue from this source was quite accurate. But they had underestimated the other sources of revenue, as may be seen from the table on the following page.[24]

It was really the heavy turnover tax and other indirect taxes, in conjunction with the very much increased customs duties, that made it possible for the Hungarian government to pass in the course of a few months from a badly unbalanced to a balanced budget. The budget for the fiscal year 1925-26 also showed a surplus, equal, in the preliminary

[24] *Report* of the Commissioner General, No. 16.

HUNGARIAN REVENUES, 1924-25
(In millions of gold crowns)

Source	Actual Receipts	Reconstruction Scheme Estimate
Direct taxes	93.1	94.6
Turnover tax	157.8	80.0
Customs	104.8	23.5
Stamp duties and consumption taxes	117.7	61.3
Tobacco monopoly (gross receipts)	89.2	51.0

net accounts, to about 62 million gold crowns.[25] It is interesting to note, however, that during the second reconstruction year the relative importance of the various sources of revenue shifted somewhat, and that further shifts are indicated by the budget for 1926-27.

The largest sources of government revenue in Hungary are direct taxes, turnover taxes, and the tobacco monopoly. The table on page 324 shows the yield from the various sources of taxation revenue during the fiscal years 1924-25, 1925-26, and 1926-27, the first two being considered as reconstruction years, and the third as the first "normal" year: [26]

During the first reconstruction year, the 3 per cent turnover tax was the largest source of taxation revenue. Next to it in importance were the customs

[25] *Report* of the Commissioner General, No. 25.
[26] "Special Memorandum on the Balancing of the Budget," in *The Financial Reconstruction of Hungary*, pp. 119-122.

COMPARISON OF TAXATION REVENUES FROM THE SEVERAL SOURCES
(In percentages of the total for the year)

Source	1924–25	1925–26	1926–27
Direct taxes	16.2	21.2	24.9
Turnover taxes	27.5	18.5	18.9
Stamp duties	10.8	13.7	11.7
Consumption taxes	10.1	11.4	10.3
Customs duties	17.7	16.2	10.6
Salt monopoly (net receipts)	2.1	2.4	2.2
Tobacco monopoly (gross receipts)	15.6	16.6	21.4
	100.0	100.0	100.0

duties, the direct taxes, and the tobacco monopoly. During the second reconstruction year, the turnover tax was reduced to 2 per cent, while at the same time the apparatus for the collection of direct taxes improved considerably. The result was that in 1925-26, direct taxes were the largest source of revenue, followed by turnover taxes, tobacco monopoly, and customs duties. In the estimates for 1926-27, direct taxes become still more important as a source of revenue, while customs duties take a decidedly secondary position.

The balancing of the budget was assisted by the reduction of the administrative personnel. The reconstruction scheme prescribed the dismissal of 15,000 officials. The actual number dismissed during the reconstruction period was much larger. The budget for 1923-24 made provision for 198,874 governmental officials, while the budget for 1926-27 showed only 160,548—a reduction of over 38,000.[27]

The salaries of the remaining officials have been gradually raised until they have reached something approaching adequate compensation. Over a third of the total budgetary expenditures goes for salaries, as may be seen from the table below.[28]

HUNGARIAN BUDGET EXPENDITURES, 1925-26

Classification	In Millions of Gold Crowns	*As Percentage of Total*
Salaries	213.0	*35.5*
Materials and supplies	190.0	*31.2*
Payments on the government debts	70.8	*11.8*
Pensions	73.1	*12.2*
Investments		
Expenditures resulting from peace	12.0	*2.0*
treaties	8.0	*1.3*
Contributions to local bodies	35.7	*6.0*
Total	602.6	*100.0*

Hungary's budgetary expenditures are considerably below the pre-war level. In 1913, if we assign 40 per cent of the total Hungarian budget to the territory of New Hungary, the expenditures for present-day Hungary were, exclusive of state enter-

[27] "Special Memorandum on Administrative Reforms," in *The Financial Reconstruction of Hungary,* pp. 122-24.

[28] Kemény, Georg, "Die Staatsfinanzen im Jahre 1926," in *Die Volkswirtschaft Ungarns im Jahre 1926,* Budapest, 1927.

prises, 642 million crowns,[29] as against about 600 millions in 1925-26. On the other hand, the budget of 1913 closed with a deficit of 180 million crowns, whereas the budget for 1925-26 showed a surplus.

The per capita national income in Hungary is about 450 gold crowns. The taxes collected during the fiscal year 1925-26, both by the central government and the local authorities, amounted to 72 gold crowns per head. This would mean a burden of taxation equal to 16 per cent,[30] or slightly less than in Austria. Since Hungary is primarily an agricultural country, with a comparatively smaller per capita income than that of much more highly industrialized Austria, her burden of taxation must therefore be considered as somewhat heavy.

The success achieved by Hungary in her fiscal and currency affairs led the Council of the League of Nations to withdraw its control at the expiration of the time set in the reconstruction scheme, i.e., on June 30, 1926. This date coincided with the withdrawal of the League control from Austria.[31]

The problems of the fiscal and currency rehabilitation of Hungary may be considered as solved for the present. Hungary has both a balanced budget and a stable currency. The foreign obligations of

[29] De Kállay, T., *Exposé,* etc., Annex 10.

[30] Compare *Report* of the Commissioner General, No. 17.

[31] See "Report of the (League of Nations) Financial Committee of June 6, 1926," and "Council Resolution of June 10, 1926," *The Financial Reconstruction of Hungary,* pp. 155-63.

the government are not large, although they may become larger if the reparation payments are increased substantially after the expiration of the twenty-year period for which they have been fixed at an annual average of 10 million gold crowns. But apart from budgetary conditions, the continuation of currency and fiscal stability depends, to a large degree, upon the country's international financial position, which we shall discuss in the next chapter.

CHAPTER XVII

HUNGARY'S INTERNATIONAL ACCOUNTS

IN Hungary, as in Austria, the international accounts have been a vital factor in the currency situation. The country's inability to meet its international obligations was quite as responsible for the collapse of the currency, as the unbalanced budgets. In this chapter we shall examine the post-war status of Hungary's international accounts.

Hungary's financial relations with the rest of the world consist predominantly of her export and import trade. Service operations play a very small rôle in her international accounts. Hungary is a net debtor country, her foreign investments being smaller than her debts abroad. Her ability to meet all of her foreign payments depends, therefore, primarily upon the relation between her exports and imports.

From 1920 to 1926, Hungary's imports were larger than her exports. The following table shows the country's foreign trade during these seven years, the year 1920 being taken as the first post-war year during which Hungary had more or less stable political conditions: [1]

[1] Figures from *Statisztikai Havi Közlemények,* official publication of the Royal Hungarian Statistical Office; from 1922 on,

HUNGARY'S BALANCE OF TRADE
(In millions of gold crowns)

Year	Exports	Imports	Adverse Balance	*Exports as of Percentage of Imports*
1920.........	164	417	253	*39.3*
1921.........	254	521	267	*48.7*
1922.........	338	539	201	*62.7*
1923.........	345	423	78	*81.6*
1924.........	576	703	127	*81.9*
1925.........	706	740	34	*95.4*
1926.........	765	851	86	*89.9*

During the first three years of the period under consideration, Hungary's adverse balance of trade was very large. In 1920 exports paid for less than 40 per cent of the imports. In 1922, exports constituted slightly over 60 per cent of the imports. Starting with 1923, however, there was a marked improvement in the situation. During that year and the year following, exports paid for about 82 per cent of the imports. In 1925, thanks to an exceptionally good harvest, the export-import ratio went up to 95.4 per cent, though it dropped in 1926 to slightly below 90 per cent.

In the year 1925 Hungary reached approximately the pre-war situation in the relation between her exports and her imports. While no official figures are available for the exports and imports of the territory constituting present-day Hungary, it has

bullion and specie movements are included in export and import figures.

been calculated that in 1913 this territory shipped outside its boundaries commodities valued at 777 million crowns and brought in commodities valued at 813 millions, giving it an adverse balance of trade equal to 36 million crowns, or an export-import ratio of 95.6 per cent.[2]

Hungary's foreign debts require increasing outlays for annual payments. There are five groups of foreign obligations on which payments have to be made. They are (1) the pre-war debts assigned to Hungary by the Innsbruck and Prague protocols; (2) foreign investments in Hungarian enterprises remaining over from the pre-war period; (3) reparation payments and other outlays connected with the execution of the treaties of peace; (4) relief credits extended to Hungary after the war, and the reconstruction loan; and (5) debts incurred since reconstruction.

We have already seen the manner in which the pre-war debts of Hungary were apportioned after the war.[3] The pre-war foreign investments are held principally by Austria and Czechoslovakia.

The reparation program imposed on Hungary has

[2] Figures from a statement prepared by Dr. Alois Szaboky, former director of the Royal Hungarian Statistical Office. In making his estimate, Dr. Szaboky based his calculations of exports on the proportion of total national output retained by present-day Hungary. For imports, he used industrial output as a coefficient of present-day Hungary's share of imported raw materials, reckoning other imported goods in proportion to the population. His calculations gave him the following results:

Exports = 40.9 per cent of the total, or 777 million crowns.
Imports = 38.3 per cent of the total, or 813 million crowns.

[3] See Chapter II.

been fixed for 20 years from the beginning of the reconstruction period. In addition to these annual payments, Hungary has also been made responsible for British, French, and Italian Clearing House payments, representing pre-war floating debts. Relief credits extended to Hungary after the war, principally by the United States and Great Britain, have been funded with fixed schedules of payments. The floating of the reconstruction loan in 1924 was followed by more or less extensive foreign borrowing on the part of Hungarian municipalities, banks, and private enterprises. All these debts require annual payments for interest and dividends, and in some cases for amortization.

Hungary has an offsetting item to her foreign debts in the form of the investments which her citizens still have in the territories that were cut off from the old Kingdom and incorporated in Czechoslovakia, Rumania, and Yugoslavia. Some of these investments have been lost as a result of the policy of "nostrification" and of the agrarian reforms carried out in these countries. But some of them still remain, although their extent is small by comparison with Hungary's own foreign debts.

Hungary's net income from international service operations is very small. The largest source of such income is represented by emigrant remittances, principally from the United States. But the amounts thus transferred are not large at best and are offset to some extent by the value of the property taken out of the country by new emigrants. Next in importance to emigrant remittances are the proceeds of the Danubian shipping and of general transit traffic. The income from these sources, after deducting Hungary's similar expenditures abroad, is still smaller than that from emigrant remittances.

Foreign tourists come to Hungary, but their expenditures are considerably smaller than the expenditures of Hungarians in other countries. Tourist trade is, therefore, an item of net outgo for Hungary. There are also several smaller items of income and outgo, such as receipts and disbursements for international post, telegraph, and telephone services, diplomatic missions, royalties on foreign films, etc., which, taken all together, represent a small net outgo for Hungary.

Hungary's international outgo has persistently exceeded her international income. For the earlier post-war years, adequate data with reference to service items are not available. The extent of the trade deficit is, however, shown in the table on page 329. In view of the larger trade deficit during the earlier post-war years, it is quite clear that the total adverse balance was larger than it has been since 1924. The summary table on page 333 shows the country's international income account during the period following Hungary's financial reconstruction, 1924-26.[4]

[4] For sources on which these evaluations are based see Appendix, pp. 594-6.

HUNGARY'S INTERNATIONAL INCOME ACCOUNT, 1924-26

(Totals for the period in millions of gold crowns)

NET OUTGO FOR:			
Foreign trade deficits		248	
Payments on public and private foreign debts[a]	308		
less returns from foreign investments	45		
		263	
Tourist expenditures		25	
Smaller items		15	
			551
NET INCOME FROM:			
Emigrant remittances		69	
Transit traffic and shipping		30	
			99
Net outgo for all items			452

[a] Including reparation payments and other outlays connected with the execution of the treaties of peace.

In the three-year period 1924 to 1926, the deficit on trade account averaged only 83 million gold crowns; but the net deficit on all accounts, trade and service, averaged 150 million gold crowns a year. Interest payments on accumulated foreign indebtedness of the country were much the largest deficit item.

The international deficit has been covered by the sale of paper crowns and by foreign loans. The large deficits in Hungary's international accounts during the pre-reconstruction period appear to have been met largely with the proceeds from the sale of paper crowns. While it is impossible to estimate the total amount of such sales, they apparently exceeded the trade deficit requirements during the period of the "flight from the crown." This is evident from the fact that when the currency of the country was later stabilized there was a considerable back flow of funds that had not been used in meeting foreign obligations.

During this pre-reconstruction period, foreign loans played a relatively small rôle. The relief credits extended to Hungary in 1920 and 1921 were not very extensive, nor were the amounts of foreign capital invested in Hungarian enterprises large. Such investments as occurred ceased in 1921, when it became apparent that the Hungarian situation was growing worse instead of better. In fact, some of the investments previously made were withdrawn, thus exerting additional pressure upon the exchanges.

Since the beginning of the reconstruction period Hungary, like numerous other European countries, has received from foreign loans sums ample to cover the deficits from trade and service operations.

To conclude this discussion of Hungary's international accounts, we find that the exchange problem presents serious difficulties. The persistent trade deficits, resulting from the steady increase of imports, coupled with interest payments on accumulated foreign indebtedness, necessitate a constant resort to new borrowing. In the absence of any substantial income from service operations, Hungary must rely solely upon an excess of exports for the discharge of her foreign obligations. To obtain an excess of exports in the face of increased import requirements for the support of a growing population and for the needs of the new industrial program presents a problem which thus far Hungary has been unable to solve.

CHAPTER XVIII

TRADE, PRODUCTION, AND CREDIT IN HUNGARY

THE economic characteristics of present-day Hungary are somewhat different from those of the pre-war Kingdom. We have already seen that as a result of the peace treaties, Hungary lost 72 per cent of her territory and 63 per cent of her population. New Hungary has, therefore, a somewhat larger population per square mile than the old Kingdom. This is due principally to the fact that the largest Hungarian city, Budapest, with a population of about one million, was retained by Hungary.

Present-day Hungary has relatively smaller agricultural resources than the old Kingdom. In the pre-war territory, landed property constituted about 40 per cent of the total national wealth, while in new Hungary it comprises only 35 per cent.[1] On the other hand, the industrial equipment of present-day Hungary is proportionately larger than had been the case with the pre-war Kingdom. At the same time, the Hungarian industries have lost an appreciable part of the home supply of their raw material requirements.

[1] Von Fellner, F., "La Situation financière de l'état Hongrois."

1. CHARACTER AND DIRECTION OF FOREIGN TRADE

The predominantly agricultural character of Hungary is plainly reflected in the commodity composition of the country's foreign trade. The following table shows the principal groups of Hungary's exports and imports in 1925: [2]

HUNGARY'S EXPORTS AND IMPORTS, 1925

Classification	Exports		Imports	
	In Millions of Gold Crowns	*As Percentage of the Total*	In Millions of Gold Crowns	*As Percentage of the Total*
Live animals	89.2	*12.6*	0.7	*0.1*
Articles of food and drink	405.7	*57.5*	60.0	*8.1*
Raw materials and semi-manufactures	89.2	*12.7*	251.2	*33.9*
Manufactured goods	116.0	*16.4*	427.7	*57.8*
Gold and silver....	5.5	*0.8*	0.8	*0.1*
	705.6	*100.0*	740.4	*100.0*

Hungary is primarily an exporter of foodstuffs and an importer of manufactured and semi-manufactured goods. Cereals and their derivatives, and cattle and meat products constitute the main articles of export, while textile products head the list of the imports.

In 1926, the exports of cereals and their deriva-

[2] League of Nations *Memorandum on Balance of Payments and Foreign Trade Balances, 1911-25,* Vol. II.

GEOGRAPHICAL DISTRIBUTION OF HUNGARY'S EXPORTS AND IMPORTS, 1921-1926

Country of Source or Destination	1921		1924		1925		1926	
	In Millions of Gold Crowns	*As Percentage of Total*	In Millions of Gold Crowns	*As Percentage of Total*	In Millions of Gold Crowns	*As Percentage of Total*	In Millions of Gold Crowns	*As Percentage of Total*
I. EXPORTS								
To ALL DANUBIAN STATES..	**200.7**	**79.04**	**411.7**	**71.60**	**493.6**	**70.50**	**502.9**	**67.07**
Austria	135.5	*53.37*	209.6	*36.45*	234.7	*33.52*	275.4	*36.73*
Czechoslovakia	40.7	*16.03*	138.3	*24.05*	168.8	*24.11*	149.6	*19.95*
Rumania	12.4	*4.88*	30.3	*5.28*	28.1	*4.02*	29.7	*3.96*
Yugoslavia	12.1	*4.76*	33.5	*5.83*	54.7	*7.81*	40.9	*5.45*
Bulgaria	....*	....	....*	....	7.3	*1.04*	7.3	*0.97*
To ALL OTHER COUNTRIES..	**53.2**	**20.96**	**163.3**	**28.40**	**206.5**	**29.50**	*246.9*	**32.93**
Germany	23.5	*9.26*	45.4	*7.90*	69.4	*9.92*	96.7	*12.90*
Italy	8.9	*3.51*	20.8	*3.62*	28.0	*4.00*	49.9	*6.66*
Switzerland	5.1	*2.01*	11.6	*2.02*	15.7	*2.24*	23.4	*3.12*
Poland	5.3	*2.08*	14.9	*2.59*	33.2	*4.74*	12.3	*1.64*
Others	10.4	*4.10*	70.6	*12.28*	60.2	*8.60*	64.6	*8.62*
TOTAL FOR ALL COUNTRIES	253.9	100.00	575.0	100.00	700.1	100.00	749.8	100.00

II. IMPORTS								
From All Danubian States	**371.0**	**71.25**	**423.1**	**60.20**	**442.9**	**59.88**	**461.5**	**56.23**
Austria	196.1	*37.66*	163.0	*23.19*	167.0	*22.58*	162.8	*19.84*
Czechoslovakia	152.6	*29.31*	176.8	*25.16*	183.6	*24.82*	192.3	*23.43*
Rumania	18.3	*3.51*	55.0	*7.83*	60.0	*8.11*	66.6	*8.12*
Yugoslavia	4.0	*0.77*	28.3	*4.03*	24.9	*3.37*	28.8	*3.51*
Bulgaria	....*	....	....*	....	7.4	*1.00*	11.0	*1.34*
From All Other Countries	**149.7**	**28.75**	**279.7**	**39.80**	**296.8**	**40.12**	**359.2**	**43.77**
Germany	67.5	*12.96*	88.1	*12.53*	111.1	*15.02*	136.0	*16.57*
Italy	25.5	*4.90*	29.5	*4.20*	33.8	*4.57*	38.0	*4.63*
Poland	9.2	*1.77*	38.9	*5.53*	36.5	*4.93*	41.8	*5.09*
Switzerland	5.5	*1.06*	26.5	*3.77*	25.4	*3.43*	32.5	*3.96*
Great Britain	8.3	*1.59*	15.3	*2.18*	23.6	*3.19*	20.6	*2.51*
United States	6.7	*1.29*	17.7	*2.52*	17.6	*2.38*	19.2	*2.34*
Others	27.0	*5.18*	63.7	*9.06*	48.8	*6.60*	71.1	*8.66*
Total for All Countries	520.7	100.00	702.8	100.00	739.7	100.00	820.7	100.00

* Not reported separately.

tives represented 30.4 per cent of the total exports. Live animals, meat products, poultry and eggs furnished 25.8 per cent of the total exports. Other foodstuffs exported by Hungary were sugar, vegetables, fruit, etc. Of the non-food agricultural exports, Hungary exported small amounts of raw wool, hides, feathers, etc.

The metal industries of Hungary contributed about 8 per cent of the total exports, principally in the form of machinery, electrical appliances, railroad supplies, and hardware. Moreover, Hungary exported a small amount of coal.

During the same year, textiles and textile materials constituted the principal import item. They represented almost 32 per cent of the total imports. Timber, timber products, and paper came next, with 17.4 per cent of the total. Raw metals and various kinds of machinery were responsible for 19.2 per cent, and coal and petroleum for about 10 per cent.

The Danubian countries play the largest, but diminishing part in Hungary's foreign trade. The table on pages 338-9 shows the direction of Hungarian exports and imports in the years 1921, 1924, 1925, and 1926, in gold crowns and in percentages of the total for the year.[3]

This table also reveals several interesting features of Hungary's trade relations with other countries. We see that her total exports to the other five

[3] Figures from *Hungarian Commerce and Industry in the Year 1926,* annual publication of the Budapest Chamber of Commerce and Industry, Budapest, 1927.

Danubian countries increased from 200.7 million crowns in 1921 to 502.9 millions in 1926. But the total increase in her export trade outstripped the growth of exports to the other Danubian States. Whereas in 1921 Hungary exported to Austria, Czechoslovakia, Rumania, Yugoslavia, and Bulgaria 79.04 per cent of her total exports, in 1926 she sent to these countries only 67.09 per cent of the total. With regard to imports, there has been an even more striking diminution in the relative importance of the other Danubian States. Although Hungary's total imports from these countries increased from 371 million crowns in 1921 to 461.5 millions in 1926, the percentage of Hungary's total imports supplied by these five states decreased from 71.26 to 56.23. In other words, Hungary's trade with the countries of the Danubian group has been developing much more slowly than her trade with the countries outside the group.

Even within the Danubian group there has not been a uniform progress or retrogression of trade relations. The most striking feature of the situation has been the decrease in the relative importance of Austria. In 1921 Austria took 53.37 per cent of Hungary's exports and supplied her with 37.67 per cent of her imports. In 1926 the percentages were 36.73 for exports and 19.84 for imports. Czechoslovakia's participation in Hungary's trade increased in importance so far as exports are concerned and decreased so far as imports are concerned. Rumania's rôle diminished as regards exports and increased as regards imports. Yugoslavia's participation increased somewhat as regards both exports and imports.

As far as other countries are concerned, Germany has been the largest gainer. Both her exports to Hungary and her imports from Hungary have steadily increased. Italy and Switzerland have become larger markets for Hungarian exports, while Poland, Switzerland, Great Britain and the United States have gained a relatively larger participation in Hungary's import trade.

Czechoslovakia and Austria supply Hungary with the bulk of her imports of textiles, iron goods, machinery, glassware, timber, paper, and chemicals. Czechoslovakia, in addition, supplies Hungary with coal, while Austria ships to her various mineral ores. Yugoslavia supplies her with some mineral ores and linen products, while Rumania's chief export is mineral oil. At the same time, Czechoslovakia and Austria are large markets for Hungary's foodstuffs, while Yugoslavia and Rumania take machinery, furniture and similar manufactured products.

Poland's chief exports to Hungary are coal and oil, and her imports machinery and appliances. Germany sells Hungary textiles, machinery, paper, glassware, and buys from her meat and animal products. Italy and Switzerland sell textiles and buy cereals. The principal import from the United States is cotton.

II. AGRICULTURAL PRODUCTION AND SURPLUS

Hungary is a country of relatively large agricultural resources. Of her total territory, 60.2 per cent consists of plow lands. Pastures occupy 10.9 per cent; meadows, 7.2 per cent; fruit orchards and vineyards, 3.4 per cent. Forests cover 11.8 per cent of her area, and unproductive lands comprise 6.5 per cent.[4]

Hungary's agricultural production has practically reached the pre-war level. The progressive recovery of crops during the post-war years may be seen from the table on page 344.

Thus the total agricultural output of Hungary for all crops reached in 1925 approximately the average figure for the five-year period from 1911 to 1915. But the production data given in the above table indicate considerable shifts in crops. Of the grain crops, the output of wheat was slightly below the pre-war, while that of rye was slightly above. Both barley and oats were produced in smaller quantities in 1925 than before the war. On the other hand, the production of maize increased by 50 per cent, and that of potatoes by 20 per cent, while the output of fodder beets decreased by almost one-third. We shall indicate below, in connection with the livestock situation, the reason for this shift in the fodder crops.

[4] The data given in this section are based on *Ungarisches Wirtschafts-Jahrbuch* for 1925 and 1926; *Hungary of Today;* and *Agricultural Survey of Europe,* Bulletin 1234 of the U. S. Department of Agriculture.

HUNGARY'S AGRICULTURAL OUTPUT
(In thousands of metric centners)

Classification	Average for 1911-1915	1920	1923	1925
ALL GRAINS	39,615	23,835	36,417	37,143
Wheat	19,924	10,322	18,427	19,507
Rye	8,033	5,143	7,944	8,262
Barley	7,128	4,719	5,938	5,537
Oats	4,398	3,238	3,985	3,706
Other grains	132	413	123	131
ALL FODDER CROPS..	87,646	73,030	51,615	89,676
Maize	15,054	12,742	12,509	22,345
Potatoes	19,420	20,722	13,342	23,095
Fodder beets	35,589	27,663	15,090	25,848
Sugar beets	15,106	6,398	8,636	15,274
Other roots	2,477	5,505	2,038	3,114
GRAND TOTAL, ALL CROPS	127,261	96,865	88,032	126,819

The year 1925 was a very good one for Hungary. The output was much smaller in 1924, and somewhat smaller again in 1926.

With pre-war output, Hungary can have a larger exportable surplus of grain than before the war. During the five-year period 1911-15, present-day Hungary's production of cereals was in excess of her requirements to the extent of 28 per cent for wheat, 50 per cent for rye, 32 per cent for barley, and 13 per cent for oats. A part of this surplus was used to satisfy the requirements of other sections of the pre-war Kingdom which were not self-sufficient so far as grain was concerned. This was done through the channels of domestic trade. With the separation of these deficit territories, the grain formerly shipped to them enters the foreign trade of Hungary.

As far as wheat was concerned, all the sections of the pre-war Kingdom of Hungary had a surplus of production over consumption, with the exception of Ruthenia (now ceded to Czechoslovakia), Croatia-Slavonia (ceded to Yugoslavia) and Transylvania (ceded to Rumania). The deficit of Ruthenia was small. That of Croatia-Slavonia was considerable. The territory of present-day Hungary had a very large surplus of wheat and the wheat deficit of Ruthenia and Croatia-Slavonia was undoubtedly made up, in part, from this surplus.

HUNGARY'S PRINCIPAL RESOURCES

With regard to rye, a similar situation obtained in the pre-war Kingdom. Ruthenia and Croatia-Slavonia were short; there was also a very slight deficit in Voivodina. All the other sections had a surplus, most of it in the territory of present-day Hungary.

On the same basis of computation, the amount of barley available for export in present-day Hungary would be approximately the same, or perhaps slightly larger, since the only section that had a substantial deficit was Transylvania, and this deficit was made up in part by the territory of present-day Hungary, and in part by Slovakia. Similarly, with regard to oats, the amounts available would be no greater than they were before the war, since all the sections of the Old Kingdom were self-supplying, with the exception of a small deficit in Croatia-Slavonia.[5]

Hungary has large livestock resources. As a result of the dismemberment of the old Kingdom, present-day Hungary retained 31.6 per cent of the horned cattle, 25.8 per cent of the sheep, 44.4 per cent of the pigs, and 39.7 per cent of the horses contained in the pre-war territory. Thus she has more pigs and horses per 1000 inhabitants than had the old Kingdom, though fewer horned cattle and sheep.

The livestock population of Hungary was as follows in 1925:

Horned cattle	1,920,000
Pigs	2,633,000
Sheep	1,891,000
Horses	875,000

[5] These computations are based on *Agricultural Survey of Europe*.

The relatively large pig population retained by present-day Hungary placed a heavy strain on the maize resources of the country, which were found insufficient. It was this fact that resulted in the shift from fodder beets to maize which we noted above.

On the whole, Hungary's exportable surplus in livestock may be considered as approximately equal to the pre-war. The relatively small proportion of the pre-war Kingdom's horned cattle and sheep retained by present-day Hungary is probably compensated by the relatively large proportion of the pig population.

III. INDUSTRIAL DEVELOPMENT AND REQUIREMENTS

While primarily an agricultural country, Hungary has a very definite tendency toward industrial development. As we saw in Chapter I, this tendency existed for a considerable period before the war in the old Kingdom of Hungary. Having become, after the war, a fully independent country, Hungary turned her face even more definitely than before in the direction of industrialization. The fact that present-day Hungary retained a larger proportionate share of the industrial equipment of the old Kingdom than either of its population, territory, or agricultural resources, was a further stimulus in this same direction.[6] But at the same time, present-day

[6] The data contained in this section are taken principally from *Ungarisches Wirtschafts-Jahrbuch* for 1925 and 1926; *Osteuro-*

Hungary is in a less favorable position for industrial development than was the pre-war Kingdom.

Present-day Hungary is not, as was the pre-war Kingdom, a well-balanced territory from the point of view of economic resources. The latter had within its own frontiers many of the essential basic raw materials that it required for industrial activity. The distribution of these resources, resulting from the dismemberment of the country, has left present-day Hungary in not nearly as favorable a condition. The agricultural resources of the country, as we saw above, are quite adequate. But the industrial equipment is considerably greater than the available supply of raw materials.

The table opposite shows the productive capacity of the equipment in various branches of industry, retained by present-day Hungary, as contrasted with the share of essential raw materials available through home production.[7] The figures are in percentages of 1913 totals for pre-war Hungary.

It is quite apparent from this table that present-day Hungary's industrial equipment is proportionately much greater with respect to the home supply of such essential raw materials as ores, timber, etc., than it was before the war. This means that if this industrial equipment is to be utilized, it is necessary

päisches Jahrbuch for 1923-24; *Hungary of Today; Hungarian Commerce and Industry* for 1925 and 1926; and *Die Volkswirtschaft Ungarns im Jahre 1926.*

[7] *L'Economiste Français,* Paris, December 22, 1923; based on studies made by M. Bernard Enzler, a Hungarian engineer.

Branch of Industry	Productive Capacity of Factories	Available Raw Materials
Food products	58	44
Metallurgy	50	10
Machinery	82	42
Textile	41	15
Chemical	40	30
Leather	58	48
Paper	20	12
Glass and stone	58	40

for Hungary to obtain large quantities of raw materials from other countries.

Before the war the Kingdom of Hungary was an importer of coal. Its total output was about 10 million tons, of which 8.9 million tons were lignite. It had no coking coal, and was importing about 4.5 million tons of coal and coke. Present-day Hungary retains about half of the pre-war coal production, which is more than sufficient to supply her non-industrial needs. But she has to continue the importation of coking coal.

As far as iron ore was concerned, pre-war Hungary was more than self-sufficient. Her total output was a little over 2 million tons, of which she exported about one-half million tons. Her consumption, together with the high-grade ores imported from abroad, was about 1.6 million tons.

Present-day Hungary has only one iron-ore mine, that of Rudobanya, left on her territory. The pre-war output of this mine was less than one-fifth of the total production of the country, and its ore is of a very inferior quality. As a result of this the present-day territory is markedly short of iron. The present territory of Hungary retains 30 per cent of the iron smelting equipment of the old Kingdom. The output of the Rudobanya mine is insufficient to supply it with the necessary raw material, necessitating considerable imports of iron ore.

The loss of timber lands has been equally important. Hungary before the war had a considerably developed wood-working industry, the products of which were to some extent, exported. The lumber required for the industry came from home production. Left now with less than 15 per cent of the pre-war timber area and with but 10 per cent of the sawmills, Hungary now has to depend entirely upon imported raw material for her wood-working industry.

Since the war, Hungary has expanded her industrial equipment, but her industrial output has not reached the pre-war level. The only exception has been the textile industry, the output of which has far exceeded the pre-war figure. The table on page 351 shows Hungary's industrial situation in 1925, as compared with the 1913 figures for the territory of present-day Hungary.

Thus between 1913 and 1925 the number of enterprises in Hungary increased by 50 per cent. Nearly one thousand new factories were constructed, many of them very small. The major part of the new construction took place during the inflation period

HUNGARIAN INDUSTRIAL SITUATION, 1913 AND 1925

Industries	Number of Enterprises		Number of Workers		Production in Millions of Gold Crowns	
	1913	1925	1913	1925	1913	1925
Iron and metal	240	264	35,627	31,817	252.5	171.7
Machine	138	181	44,595	31,543	226.2	132.6
Electric power plants	91	159	2,195	5,525	25.0	45.8
Stoneware, pottery, and glass	421	478	32,839	23,354	70.8	62.9
Wood and bone	225	339	11,990	10,794	41.4	45.2
Leather, bristles, and feathers.	48	81	5,762	5,859	44.9	57.5
Textile	125	228	16,092	32,348	82.2	215.5
Clothing	105	98	7,546	5,381	24.8	36.6
Paper	52	56	3,028	2,327	10.6	1.2
Foodstuffs	378	854	40,564	38,379	695.4	785.2
Chemical	150	202	9,784	8,548	124.5	101.9
Art	107	103	9,230	6,834	42.1	31.3
Total........	2,080	3,043	219,252	202,709	1,640.4	1,687.4

following the war, that is, prior to 1925. Since then there has been very little new construction of factories. The figures for the number of workers employed and for the total output given in the above table show that this equipment is not being fully utilized. The output in 1925 was in volume even smaller, by comparison with 1913, than is indicated by the figures in the table. The price index in 1925 was about 130; [8] therefore, the volume of total in-

[8] *Pester Lloyd* index.

dustrial output in 1925 was only about 80 per cent of the 1913 output.

Every industry, with the sole exception of clothing, has expanded its equipment since the war. Yet every industry, with the exception of textiles and electric appliances shows a diminution of output.

The growth of the textile industry has been very marked. Hungary's cotton industry was left after the war with 33,000 spindles and 4,000 looms; by the end of 1925 it had 128,000 spindles and 10,000 looms. A somewhat similar growth has taken place in the other branches of the textile industry. As a result, Hungary has been able to decrease markedly her imports of textiles. Between 1922 and 1925, for example, the importation of textiles decreased from 26.1 thousand metric tons to 19.8 thousands.

The fact that industrial production in Hungary has not reached the pre-war level has been responsible for the existence of the problem of unemployment. During the year 1925 the number of unemployed ranged around 30,000, the figure relating only to members of the Union of Socialist Workers.[9] The total number of unemployed was somewhat larger.

IV. THE BANKING AND CREDIT SITUATION

Like all countries that have passed through a period of currency depreciation, Hungary has been confronted with the problem of operating capital.

[9] According to *Report* of the Commissioner General, No. 25, the figures were: March, 36,873; June, 34,015; December, 26,711.

Monetary inflation had a number of serious effects on the economic life of the country, most of which did not become apparent until after the stabilization of the currency during the period of fiscal reconstruction. Questions connected with the credit situation constitute one of the most serious problems confronting Hungary.

Hungary has a well developed banking system, which has, however, suffered greatly during the inflation period. This system is of comparatively recent origin—the first Hungarian bank was founded in 1839—but it underwent a rapid expansion during the two decades preceding the war. In 1890, Hungary had 1,225 banking institutions, with a capital equal to 14,300,000 pounds sterling, and savings deposits of 45,700,000 pounds. By 1910, the number of banking institutions increased to 5,516, with a combined capital of 82,200,000 pounds sterling and savings deposits of 153 millions.[10]

About one-third of the banking institutions, representing fully 90 per cent of the capital and the deposits, were joint stock and savings banks, the principal difference between the two kinds being that the joint stock banks are interested primarily in industrial enterprises. The other two-thirds of the banking institutions were mostly cooperative banks, practically all of them members of the Central Co-

[10] This sketch of the Hungarian banking system is based principally on an article by Dr. Alexander Popovics, President of the Hungarian National Bank, in *The Times Trade and Engineering Supplement,* London, June 19, 1926.

operative Institution. These cooperative banks, with very few exceptions, were not allowed to make loans, except to their members. The agricultural credit of the country was handled principally by the Hungarian Land Mortgage Institute and the Mortgage Institute of Small Holders.

Generally speaking, mortgage loans have played a very important part in Hungarian banking. Even the joint stock banks whose general tendency was to interest themselves in industry by direct participation, as well as by granting credits, held in 1913 almost 25 per cent of their assets in the form of advances on mortgages.

Budapest was the financial center of the pre-war Kingdom, and present-day Hungary found itself in possession of almost 75 per cent of the banking capital of the whole country, although it retained only 40 per cent of the total number of banking institutions. But the great joint-stock banks of Budapest found themselves in a difficult situation, because of the disruption of their business and industrial connections produced by the dismemberment of the country.

The period of inflation added many new difficulties to those already confronting the banks of the country as a result of loss of territory. It destroyed the liquid resources of the banks, and introduced changes in the character of the banking business. Deals in commodities and advances in stock exchange securities took the place very largely of mortgage loans and the discounting of commercial bills. When, by the decree of December, 1925, the government ordered the banks to revalue their assets and liabilities in gold, as of January 1, 1925, it was found that their assets had depreciated to only about 15 per cent of the pre-war value.

The fiscal and currency rehabilitation of Hungary resulted in improved credit conditions. The most important evidence of this improvement was the increase in savings and in bank deposits generally. The following table shows the savings and current account deposits in the Post Office Savings Banks and the thirteen principal banks of Budapest: [11]

BANK DEPOSITS IN HUNGARY
(In millions of gold crowns)

Banks Classified	December 31, 1913	June 30, 1924	June 30, 1926
Savings deposits	865.1	3.1	158.3
Current account deposits..	738.9	73.6	357.7
Total deposits..........	1,604.0	76.7	516.0

The process of inflation had thus almost wiped out all bank deposits. But the two years of reconstruction had increased deposits almost seven-fold and had restored them to over 30 per cent of the pre-war figure. By the end of 1926, the total bank

[11] Figures from the *Economic Bulletin of the Central Corporation of Banking Companies* (Pénzintézeti Központ), Budapest, Vol. I, No. 1, and Vol. II, No. 3.

deposits increased to 633.6 million gold crowns, or to almost 40 per cent of the pre-war figure.[12]

The reappearance of deposits, coupled with the stabilization of the currency, resulted in a rapid reduction of interest rates. This reduction was stimulated also by the inflow of foreign capital which started soon after the beginning of the reconstruction period.

By the end of 1925 the interest rates dropped to about half of what they were at the beginning of the reconstruction period. In January, 1925, the interest rate on advances on commercial bills was between 20 and 22 per cent; in December of that year it ranged between 9.75 and 11 per cent.[13] In 1926 the downward trend of interest rates was arrested during the first few months by the crisis which resulted from the franc forgeries scandal and other causes. During the second half of the year, however, it was resumed, and by December, 1926, the interest rates on commercial drafts ranged between 7.25 and 7.5 per cent. These were the rates for Budapest. For provincial banks the rates were somewhat higher, ranging in December, 1926, between 10 and 12 per cent.[14]

One of the outstanding difficulties of Hungary's credit situation is the preponderance of short-term loans. This is equally true of domestic and foreign

[12] *Hungarian Commerce and Industry in the Year 1926,* p. 35.

[13] *Economic Bulletin of the Central Corporation of Banking Companies,* Vol. II, No. 1.

[14] *Hungarian Commerce and Industry in the Year 1926,* p. 35.

credits. The comparatively high rates of interest, especially during 1925, made long-term investments unattractive to the holders of funds. Moreover, the borrowers themselves have been reluctant to burden themselves with long-term obligations at the prevailing high rates of interest.

The principal danger in the situation has been in connection with short-term foreign credits. The stabilization of financial conditions in Hungary following the inauguration of the League reconstruction scheme, resulted in a readiness on the part of foreign capital to enter Hungary. But the funds thus brought in have been in the form of either short-term loans or of deposits in Hungarian banks. Such loans or deposits are, of course, subject to sudden withdrawals, a situation which creates uncertainty and is capable at times of placing the whole financial situation of the country in a precarious position.

The National Bank has been seriously concerned with this aspect of the credit situation. Through the year 1925 it directed its discount policy toward a reduction of general interest rates in the country, principally for the purpose of discouraging a large influx of foreign short-term funds. At the beginning of that year, its discount rate was 12.5 per cent. On March 27, the rate was lowered to 11 per cent; on May 28, to 9 per cent; and on October 22, to 7 per cent. The large withdrawals of foreign funds during the crisis of the first half of 1926 was one of the factors that had led the National Bank to lower its rate on August 26, 1926, to 6 per cent, in order to discourage further influx of short-term capital from abroad.

Hungary is in need of long-term investments and loans. The domestic capital resources are still very meager, in spite of the rapid growth of savings. Even before the war, when the volume of bank deposits was two and one-half times what it is today, Hungary had need of foreign funds for a full functioning of her economic life. Today the need of foreign borrowing is even more pressing and acute.

The reconstruction loan floated in 1924 provided Hungary with a comparatively large amount of funds invested for a long term. The total net yield of the loan, including exchange profits resulting from the appreciation of the crown in consequence of the restoration to parity of the pound sterling, was a little over 266 million gold crowns. Of this amount, only 69.5 million crowns were used for budget deficits and the repayment of pressing obligations in 1924. The existence of budgetary surpluses rendered a further recourse to the loan funds for budget purposes unnecessary, and arrangements were made for their productive investment.

For the fiscal year 1926-27, the Financial Committee of the League Council authorized the expenditure of 50 million crowns of the loan funds for capital investments. This money was used for such purposes as the construction of harbor facilities in Budapest, the improvement of the post, telegraph and telephone system, the construction of railways, public roads, and bridges, and loans for drainage and agricultural improvements. When the League control was withdrawn on June 30, 1926, the amount still remaining uninvested (after deduction for special reserve fund and advances made to the government for the purchase and minting of silver) was 119 million crowns.[15]

During the year 1925, only one long-term loan was extended to Hungary. It was a municipal loan for a nominal amount of 10 million dollars. During 1926, another municipal loan was floated, for a nominal amount of 6 million dollars. In addition, during that year a loan was floated in London for a nominal sum of 2.5 million pounds sterling, and one in the United States for 3 million dollars. Finally, during the same year, there were two issues of land mortgage debentures, one in England for 38.8 million gold crowns, and one in New York for 3 million dollars.

Hungary needs long-term credit facilities for agriculture, much more than for industry. The expansion of industrial equipment only a part of which is utilized today renders further investment in industry unlikely. On the other hand, Hungarian agriculture is in need of investment for the improvement of methods of cultivation and of the general equipment.

[15] *Report* of the Commissioner General, No. 25.

The internal trade, production, and credit problems of Hungary have an important bearing upon the problem of the international accounts discussed in the preceding chapter. The persistent shortage of liquid capital within the country is an impediment to industrial activity, and it constitutes at the same time an incentive to increased foreign borrowing. The inadequate production affects alike the budget and the foreign exchanges. The large import requirements cannot be met from the proceeds of exports and the interest on accumulated foreign indebtedness exerts a heavy pressure upon the exchanges. The proceeds from new borrowings alone make possible the maintenance of financial equilibrium.

A mere restoration of the pre-war scale of production and foreign trade will not be sufficient to meet the country's requirements.[16] There was an excess of imports before the war, and a mere return to the pre-war situation would not provide any means with which to meet foreign interest payments. If Hungary's financial stability is to be assured and if the general economic life of the country is to be placed on a genuinely sound basis, a thorough-going economic reorganization appears to be necessary.

[16] Compare the following statement made by Dr. Alois Szaboky in the *Pester Lloyd* of March 15, 1923:

"Even were Hungary's economic life to be completely consolidated and were her agricultural and industrial output to reach the pre-war figures, it would unfortunately be almost impossible to obtain a favorable trade balance."

CHAPTER XIX

HUNGARY'S ECONOMIC POLICY

THE economic policy of post-war Hungary has been dominated from the first by the idea that the country neither wants nor can afford to be a purely agricultural state, exporting foodstuffs and raw materials and importing manufactured goods. This tendency toward an all-rounded economic development existed in Hungary before the war. Together with factors of a political nature, it has been pushing Hungary strongly in the direction of intense economic nationalism.

Complete independence from Austria had long been ardently desired by some of the Magyar leaders, who, as we have already seen, strove to build up an economically independent state even within the political bounds of the Austro-Hungarian Monarchy. The overthrow of the Habsburg dynasty opened the way for the consummation of this aim, and that development alone would have been sufficient to give Hungarian policy a strongly nationalistic tendency. But this tendency was vastly intensified by the dismemberment of Hungary proper which accompanied the dissolution of the Dual Monarchy. New Hungary began her independent existence imbued with bitter resentment and hostility against her neighbors who had profited by the dismemberment—even against Austria, which, although she, too, had been dismembered, had also received, in Burgenland, a strip of Hungarian territory.

While refusing to accept as final the situation created by the treaties of peace, Hungary could not, of course, in the meantime fail to face the imperative necessity of organizing her national life within her new frontiers. Like Austria, she faced the problems of fiscal and currency disorganization and of economic maladjustment. Like Austria, she has now achieved through international assistance more or less complete fiscal and currency rehabilitation, but has not as yet solved her general economic problems, especially those of her international accounts and of operating capital.

The solution of these general economic problems is easier in the case of Hungary than in that of Austria. Hungary is economically a less complex national organism than Austria. Yet she faces problems and difficulties of an economic and social nature, which, together with the additional stimulus of political conditions, have dictated for her a policy of economic nationalism.

I. POPULATION PROBLEM AND THE POLICY OF INDUSTRIALIZATION

Hungary is a predominantly agricultural state, but she is not exclusively nor even overwhelmingly so from the point of view of the basic economic pursuits of her population. The data given below indicate the divisions of Hungary's population by occupational groups: [1]

Occupation	Percentage of the Total
Agriculture	54.9
Industry	20.5
Mining	1.2
Commerce	4.7
Transportation	4.1
Government officials	4.0
Servants, day laborers, etc.	5.2
Others	5.4
	100.0

Only 55 per cent of the total population of Hungary is engaged in agriculture. This agricultural population produces enough food to satisfy the requirements of the country and to furnish almost three-fifths of the total exports. Moreover, it produces some of the essential raw materials required by the industries.

The system of land tenure in Hungary comprises a considerable proportion of large landed estates. If we divide the land holdings into three groups, namely, small holdings (less than 140 acres), middle holdings (between 140 and 1,400 acres), and large holdings (over 1,400 acres), we get the picture of land tenure in Hungary presented by the table on page 364.[2]

[1] *Osteuropäisches Jahrbuch* for 1923-24, p. 574.
[2] Nagy, I. E., "Die Land- und Forstwirtschaft Ungarns," *Ungarisches Wirtschafts-Jahrbuch* for 1925, p. 51.

LAND TENURE IN HUNGARY

Holdings	Number of Holders	*Percentage of Total Area* [a]
Small [b]	754,000	*47.5*
Middle sized	9,260	*16.6*
Large estates	1,444	*35.9*
	764,704	*100.0*

[a] Including forests and unproductive lands.
[b] Approximate.

Thus more than a third of the total agricultural area of Hungary is comprised in about 1,500 large estates, while less than half is owned by about three-quarters of a million of small holders. But if all the agricultural area of the country were divided evenly among all the holders, small, middle and large, the resultant individual holdings would be about 29 acres per holder, or, exclusive of forests and unproductive lands, only about 24 acres.

The methods of agricultural cultivation in Hungary are not advanced. In wheat, for example, the yield per hectare is 14 quintals on large estates and 11.6 quintals on the peasant land, the average yield for the whole country being about 12.4 quintals.[3] In other words, Hungary, with much more productive soil than Austria has only about the same average yield per hectare. When compared with Switzerland, Hungary's yield per unit in wheat is equal to only 60 per cent.

[3] Nagy, I. E., "Die Land- und Forstwirtschaft Ungarns" in *Ungarisches Wirtschafts-Jahrbuch* for 1926, p. 22.

It is doubtful whether Hungarian agriculture can provide a livelihood for more than the present rural population plus its natural increase, unless the methods of cultivation are very much intensified. But such intensification and the consequent increase of production requires an increase in the capacity of foreign markets, since Hungarian agricultural output is too large for the country itself. Of the factors which are involved in such a development, we shall speak later on.[4]

Almost half of Hungary's population has to depend for its livelihood on other pursuits than agriculture. As we saw from the table on page 363 the system of transportation and the governmental organizations provide employment for 8.1 per cent of the population. Mining and commerce take care of 5.9 per cent. One-fifth of the population are engaged in industry, while 10.6 per cent are classified as domestic servants and the various miscellaneous groups.

With over a million and a half persons already dependent upon industry for their livelihood, and with over 800,000 in the servant and miscellaneous groups, it is clear that Hungary's policy of industrialization cannot be altogether a luxury. Agriculture, as we have already seen, cannot absorb them or their natural increase. On the contrary, unless Hungary succeeds in opening up new markets for her foodstuffs, every improvement in the methods

[4] See Chapter XXXI.

of land cultivation is likely to drive a part of the rural population to the urban centers. And in the cities nothing but industry can provide them with the means of livelihood.

The Hungarians regard the industrial development of their country as an imperative necessity from the point of view of the population problem. The pre-war channels of emigration are closed to them. Within the limits of the territory allotted to them by the treaties of peace they have to maintain a growing population. True, this increase is not rapid: it is less than 1 per cent a year. Nevertheless, year by year between 70 and 80 thousands are added to the population of the country, and productive occupation has to be found for them within the country.

An effective utilization of this available labor force is more difficult in present-day Hungary than was the employment of the non-agricultural population in the pre-war Kingdom. The industrial equipment which grew up in Hungary before the war was based, to a large extent, on the existence of domestic supplies of raw materials. Hungary's largest group of industries was concerned with the preparation of food, the raw materials for which came from home production. The metallurgical and woodworking industries were likewise based on domestic raw materials. Present-day Hungary inherited a larger proportion of the pre-war Kingdom's equipment than of its raw materials, while at the same time a proportionately larger part of its population is non-agricultural. In the pre-war Kingdom, 62.4 per cent of the population was agricultural (as against 54.9 per cent in present-day Hungary), while 17.0 per cent was industrial (as against 20.5 per cent to-day).[5]

There is still another point of difference between the pre-war and the present-day situation which makes the industrial position of new Hungary more difficult than was that of the pre-war Kingdom. The Hungarian industries had open to them the markets of the whole Austro-Hungarian Monarchy, and while in some branches of production (notably metallurgy and textiles) they had to meet sharp competition from the better developed industries of Austria and Bohemia, in others they had the advantages of a large protected market. Today, the Hungarian industries have the opportunity of securing as protected markets only those of Hungary herself. Outside her frontiers they have to meet world competition.

In spite of these difficulties, Hungary, after the securing of her independence, turned her face even more resolutely in the direction of industrialization than she did before the war. Driven by the population problem, and urged in the same direction by many other considerations, she embarked from the very beginning of her independent existence upon a policy of protection for her industries.

[5] *Osteuropäisches Jahrbuch* for 1923-24, p. 574.

II. TARIFF PROTECTION AND TREATY ARRANGEMENTS

Hungary began her independent existence in a state of almost complete political and economic isolation. She retained scarcely a mile of her pre-war frontiers. On all sides she was surrounded by territories which had formerly been united with her, and intercourse with these territories was rendered exceedingly difficult by the political circumstances attending the process of dismemberment. The establishment of the communist régime and the war with Rumania intensified this condition of isolation.

For a whole year after the war Hungary had no customs frontiers. Whatever goods entered or left the country prior to the establishment of the Horthy régime in October, 1919, were not subject to any customs formalities. Only after that event the Hungarian government began to apply the old Austro-Hungarian tariff, making the administrative boundaries customs frontiers, although even these boundaries did not become official international frontiers until the summer of 1921, when the treaty of Trianon was finally ratified.[6]

The application of the Austro-Hungarian tariff was manifestly ineffectual, because of the currency situation. The Hungarian government, shortly after its establishment, introduced the system of export and import prohibitions and restrictions,

[6] Lengyel, Géza, "The Situation of Hungary in Respect of Customs Policy," *Hungary of Today.*

which was already in existence elsewhere in Central Europe, and which lasted, with modifications, for about five years.

Hungary used the policy of export and import restrictions for both economic and financial reasons. Production within the country had been thoroughly disorganized by the chaotic economic conditions which characterized the first post-war year. Supplies were inadequate, and the government felt it incumbent to conserve them within the country's frontiers. This was true not only of manufactured goods, but also of foodstuffs. Later, when food production began to increase, the government still felt it necessary to regulate exports in order to prevent the internal prices from rising too rapidly. As regards imports, not only was there a bad shortage of the means of payment, but the system of trade regulation which existed in the whole of Central Europe rendered restrictions the only means of bargaining for opportunities of selling whatever exports Hungary could ship across her frontiers.

Hungary took part in the Portorose Conference. Her representatives signed the protocol drawn up there for the removal of trade restrictions and although her official spokesmen expressed their readiness to put the provisions of the protocol into effect, they made such action conditional on similar action on the part of the other signatories—which was not forthcoming.[7]

[7] See Hungary's reply to the questionnaire sent out by the Eco-

The foreign exchange situation played an important rôle in the application of the policy of trade restrictions. The establishment of the *Devisenzentrale* placed in the hands of that powerful body a virtual control over the volume of imports entering the country, although that control never became really effective.

But while the policy of export and import restrictions was directed primarily toward affording Hungary an opportunity for obtaining markets for her exports and toward the protection of her foreign exchange, it was also used as the means of fostering the resumption in the country of its pre-war industrial activity and of aiding further industrialization. It was clear to the Hungarian leaders that the old Austro-Hungarian tariff, even if its rates could keep pace with the depreciation of the currency, was scarcely applicable to Hungary's economic conditions. The present Hungarian government, not long after its establishment, turned its attention to the question of tariff revision. It was, however, some years before Hungary finally worked out a new customs tariff, which went into effect January 1, 1925, and superseded the import restrictions still in force at that date.

The Hungarian customs tariff is frankly protectionist in character. By the time the new tariff was

nomic and Financial Committee of the Council of the League of Nations in *Brussels Financial Conference: Their Recommendations and Their Application*, Vol. I. See also p. 87 of this book.

introduced, the general tendency of economic development in Hungary had become quite well defined. The policy of placing the country on a footing of more or less complete self-sufficiency so far as the basic industries are concerned had gained a more or less widespread acceptance. The new tariff was designed to further this policy.

The Hungarian tariff of 1925 is much higher than the old Austro-Hungarian tariff. The duties established by it add 31.1 per cent to the value of goods imported into the country, whereas the pre-war tariff added only 18.9 per cent. Every one of the tariff groups, with the exception of chemical products and ships, has a higher degree of protection than before the war.

Foodstuffs and agricultural products generally were protected in the Monarchy by a tariff of 26.4 per cent; in present-day Hungary, the protection is 32.1 per cent. The protection of textiles has been increased from 12 to 29.8 per cent; of rubber goods, from 13.2 to 29.8 per cent; of leather goods, from 7.2 to 27.5 per cent. The protection of timber and timber products has been raised from 7 to 21 per cent; of paper and paper products, from 14.8 to 26.5 per cent. Iron and iron products now carry a duty of 49.2 per cent, as against 31.7 per cent before the war; while the tariff on machinery has been increased from 17 to 33 per cent.[8]

It is clear that under the protection of her new

[8] *Zollhöhe und Warenwerte,* Table I.

tariff Hungary is determined to build up and maintain primarily the production of textile products and of machinery. She does not expect to become entirely self-sufficient in regard of either of these groups of industrial production. With respect to textiles, she now supplies about two-thirds of her own needs. It is doubtful that she can go beyond this. Her policy of protection is directed toward such an adjustment of her economic life as would provide employment for her population and at the same time would afford her some hope of balancing eventually her international accounts.

The problem of international accounts involves other considerations besides those of industrial protection. For one thing it requires, in the case of Hungary, an expansion of the exports of foodstuffs which represent the country's principal merchandise for international trade. With her dearth of raw materials, Hungary must depend on her import trade for the supply of essential raw materials required by her protected industries. And the exportation of foodstuffs is her chief means of paying for these imports.

The high level of tariff duties was dictated not only by the policy of protection, but also by "bargaining" considerations. The duties which we enumerated above represent the maximum rates under the 1925 tariff. They are subject to considerable reduction in the process of commercial treaty negotiations, and have, as a matter of fact, been considerably lowered in this manner since the tariff went into effect.

Hungary's first commercial agreement was concluded with Germany. It was signed on December 21, 1920, and was based on most-favored-nation treatment. In 1922, a similar agreement was signed with Austria, and in 1924, with Yugoslavia and Rumania. During these years several other agreements of this nature were signed.[9]

It was not until 1925 that Hungary began to negotiate commercial agreements based on mutual tariff concessions. During that year, however, she negotiated several commercial treaties of this nature, the most important of them being with Poland, France, and Italy. None of these agreements was altogether satisfactory to Hungary. In the case of Poland, the value of the concessions received was greatly diminished soon after the signing of the treaty by the general increase of the Polish tariff. In the case of France, in exchange for granting that country reductions of customs in respect of 280 items and general most-favored-nation treatment, Hungary received the benefit of the minimum French tariff on 65 items, varying reductions from the maximum tariff on about the same number of items, and most-favored-nation treatment with regard to only a few of these

[9] The limitations of unilateral most-favored-nation treatment imposed by the treaties of peace on the defeated nations were operative in Hungary for only six months after the coming into force of the treaty of Trianon; for two and one-half years thereafter they applied only to a small list of specified products. See Article 203 of the treaty of Trianon.

items. The Italian treaty was somewhat more far-reaching in its concessions.[10]

Hungary's most important commercial treaties, those with Austria and Czechoslovakia, were not concluded until 1926 and 1927, although the negotiations were begun as early as 1924. Hungary has more trade with these two countries than with any others, but at the same time she has had more differences to compose with them than with any of the other countries with which she has concluded commercial treaties.

In her commercial negotiations, Hungary has aimed principally at opening up markets for her exports of prepared, rather than raw foodstuffs. This was the crux of her difficulties in negotiating commercial treaties with Austria and Czechoslovakia. She wants to export flour, rather than grain; smoked and dressed meats, rather than cattle, etc. Her neighbors, on the other hand, want raw, rather than worked food products.

Milling is an exceedingly important industry in Hungary, Budapest being, after Minneapolis, the largest milling city in the world. Exports of flour are, therefore, of double advantage to Hungary: both her farmers and her millers profit by it. But one of the interesting results of the post-war developments in the Danubian countries has been the growth of the milling industry in Czechoslovakia and to some extent in Austria. There is almost a

[10] *Hungarian Commerce and Industry in the Year 1925*, p. 32.

direct connection between the rise of textile factories in Hungary and of flour mills in Czechoslovakia. Several attempts at trade negotiations between the two countries broke down primarily because of this. The last Czechoslovak tariff, for example, fixing a ratio of duty 30:70 as between grain and flour, was a great blow to the Hungarian milling industry.

In finally reaching an agreement with Austria and with Czechoslovakia, Hungary had to forego some of the demands she had been putting forth in previous negotiations. At the same time, the other sides also had to make important concessions. The treaties which were signed represent compromises, and although the Hungarians feel that the advantages acquired by them are not as great as they might have desired, on the other hand they realize that the bargains made are probably the best possible under the present circumstances.[11]

III. ATTITUDE TOWARD THE QUESTION OF A LARGER ECONOMIC TERRITORY

With the protection of industries as the keynote of her tariff policy, and with the stimulation of her

[11] For a clear and interesting statement of Hungary's economic policy see *Objects and Methods of Hungary's Economic Policy*, publication of the Federation of Hungarian Industries, Budapest, 1927. See also the section on "Foreign Commerce and Customs Policy" in *Hungarian Commerce and Industry in the Year 1926*. The *Ungarisches Wirtschafts-Jahrbuch* contains several interesting studies bearing on the problem; see especially, Ferenczi, I., "Der neue autonome Zolltariff," and Fenyö, Max, "Die Zukunft der ungarischen Industrie," in the volume for 1925; Ferenczi, I., "Die seit Einführung des neuen Zolltariffes abgeschlossene

agricultural exports as the basis of her commercial treaty negotiations, Hungary is attempting to build, within her present frontiers, an independent economic entity. She faces difficulties in all directions. Apart from her soil, her natural resources are very meager. At the same time she has a population which is too large to subsist only on agriculture.

Hungary's primary interest lies in the development of agriculture and of industries based on agricultural raw materials. Even today with a very low level of per unit yields, Hungarian agricultural production is much too large for the country's own requirements. The exportable surplus can be greatly increased by improvement of the means of cultivation and a diversification and intensification of production.

It is not impossible that Hungary, by increasing her agricultural output and by utilizing her urban population principally for industries concerned with the working of foodstuffs, may be able to maintain productively her present population. But in order to do this she must have an opportunity for greatly increasing her exports of foodstuffs, and in this respect she faces difficulties which lie to a large extent outside her own control.

A Hungarian view of this situation has been phrased as follows: [12]

Handelsverträge," and Barcza, E., "Die Zollpolitik der ungarischen Landwirtschaft," in the volume for 1926.

[12] *Objects and Methods of Hungary's Economic Policy,* pp. 7-8 and 14.

"All the principal agricultural products of present-day Hungary are dependent for a market on the export trade. * * * In consequence of the tendency even of states absolutely industrial in character to develop their own agricultural resources, the sale of these raw products abroad encounters ever increasing difficulties. * * * Hungary's great agricultural industries have suffered a contraction in consequence of competition in the Western states."

The Hungarians further maintain that the difficulties encountered by them along these lines "are of such a nature that it is vain to attempt to eliminate them by granting concessions in the field of industry." [13] This is one of their arguments in favor of the development of general industry. By means of industrialization they hope to be able to create within the country a larger market for their agricultural products.

But the creation of general industry in the absence of essential raw materials is a costly process. There is no lack in Hungary of a realization of this fact. But there is equally no lack of realization of the fact that the extent of agricultural development is a matter of the size of foreign markets that Hungary can hope to obtain in exchange for giving up her attempts at general industrialization. This fact is a basic consideration with her in her attitude toward the question of a larger economic territory.

From the point of view of her agricultural development, Hungary sees little advantage for herself

[13] Ibid., p. 8.

in a Danubian economic union. Her position is that the food requirements of the unified territory cannot provide an adequate outlet for the volume of increased production that she would have to have to compensate her for the loss of her non-agricultural industries.

In an economically unified Danubian territory, the principal industrial centers would be in Czechoslovakia and Austria. The industrial equipment of these two countries is amply sufficient to satisfy the needs of the rest of the territory. Czechoslovakia's coal and timber and Austria's timber and iron ore, in addition to the superior organization of their industrial equipment, would give these two countries sufficient advantage to force out of existence the comparatively weak industries of Hungary. At the same time their requirements of Hungary's foodstuffs, even if Austria and Czechoslovakia should be willing to give up entirely their present efforts in the direction of agricultural development, cannot be extended very much beyond what they are at the present time, when they already depend upon Hungary for a considerable part of their food imports.

Moreover, the Danubian territory would include also Rumania and Yugoslavia, and possibly Bulgaria, all of which, as we shall see below, are primarily agricultural countries, and therefore Hungary's competitors in the Austrian and Czechoslovak markets for foodstuffs. These markets, which Hungary feels would be inadequate for her expanded agriculture alone, would become woefully small if they were to serve as protected outlets for the foodstuffs of the other three Danubian countries as well.

With this as the situation in respect of the whole Danubian territory, there are still two possibilities of a more limited economic union which would involve Hungary, as the country lying between the upper or industrial portion of the Danubian territory and the lower or agricultural one. The first of these possibilities would be an economic union of Austria, Czechoslovakia, and Hungary; the second would be a similar union of Hungary, Rumania, Yugoslavia, and possibly Bulgaria. Both of these possibilities have come under discussion.

The possibility of close economic relations among Austria, Czechoslovakia, and Hungary has been discussed since the end of the war. It will be recalled that the treaties of peace made provisions along these lines. The possibility has not, however, been ever seriously considered, Hungary having strong objections to it for reasons we examined above.

The second possibility might be welcomed by Hungary from the point of view of her general industrial development. True, the three lower Danubian countries are predominantly agricultural. But the four countries combined would constitute a territory with a very substantial exportable surplus of foodstuffs and agricultural materials. They would be in a position to make a strong bid for important concessions for their exports from the large industrial countries of Europe. At the same time the internal market of the combined territory would constitute a valuable outlet for Hungary's manufactured products.

The advantages to Hungary of such a combination would be manifold. She would be in a position of economic leadership. Budapest, with its strong banking and trading organization, would become the economic and financial center of the territory. Her industries would then have a real basis for development. Such a possibility is, however, very remote.

Austro-German union might present distinct advantages to Hungary. In fact, it is not impossible that Hungary might welcome the establishment of a direct frontier and of closer economic relations between herself and Germany. From our analysis of the direction of Hungary's trade it is clear that Germany has been acquiring a larger and larger rôle in the Hungarian foreign trade. Hungary has no political quarrels with Germany; on the contrary, politically they have much in common. And Germany is economically precisely the sort of market that Hungary needs for the development of her agriculture. In order to find adequate outlets for an increased volume of agricultural production, Hungary needs a territory which is now supplied with foodstuffs from other sources. Germany is potentially an almost unlimited market for Hungarian foodstuffs, provided her products can displace those coming from overseas.

PART V

RUMANIA'S EXPERIENCE SINCE THE WAR

CHAPTER XX

THE PROBLEMS OF GREATER RUMANIA

THE character of Rumania's post-war situation has been essentially different from that of Austria, Hungary, or Czechoslovakia. Whereas Austria and Hungary have had to adjust their economic life to a very much diminished territory and population, while Czechoslovakia has had to build up a new economic structure, Rumania has faced the task of extending the economic system of a small pre-war Kingdom to a very much enlarged territory. Bucharest became the economic and financial capital of a territory and a population twice as great as it had served before the war. The problems confronting the Rumanian capital have thus been just the reverse of those faced by Vienna and Budapest, though they have not been unlike, in this respect, those confronting Prague.

Post-war Rumania has a substantially different economic structure from that of the pre-war Kingdom. As we saw in Chapter III, pre-war Rumania was predominantly an agricultural country. The principal pursuit of her population was the production of foodstuffs, which furnished the bulk of her exports. The only other important resource of the country was petroleum, although Rumania also had some timber and a certain amount of minerals. Greater Rumania is no longer primarily a producer and exporter of foodstuffs, although the agricultural resources of the old Kingdom have been greatly increased by the acquisition of Bessarabia and the Banat. But with Transylvania and Bukowina Rumania has also acquired large timber areas, varied mineral wealth, and some industrial equipment.

These new territories were originally parts of Russia, Austria and Hungary. Each was a component part of the economic and financial life of the country to which it belonged. Their inclusion in Greater Rumania has necessitated a reorientation of their trade routes and of their financial affiliations. At the same time their union with the old Kingdom of Rumania has introduced important changes in the economic life of the latter.

Having gained control of the large territory which became Greater Rumania, the government at Bucharest found itself confronted with a large number of immediate and difficult tasks. The administrative machinery of the newly acquired territories had to be reorganized. The various currencies which were in circulation in the different parts of the new Kingdom—the Rumanian leu, the Austro-Hungarian crown, the Russian ruble—had to be consolidated into a single currency. Means of communication had to be established between the various parts of the new Kingdom. The whole complex of economic and financial relationships disorganized by the war and by the separation of the different territories from their former owners had to be reoriented and placed upon a functioning basis.

PRE-WAR SOVEREIGNTY OF LANDS COMPRISING RUMANIA

This work was complicated by the fact that the war did not end for Rumania with the various armistices signed in the first half of November, 1918. On the contrary, the establishment of the communist régime in Hungary in the spring of 1919 and the difficulties which this fact presented for the Rumanian occupation of Transylvania made it necessary for Rumania to remain in a state of war for quite some time after hostilities ceased on all the other war fronts. In fact war with Hungary was reopened in the second half of 1919, and it was only by the end of that year that peace finally came to Rumania.

Still another factor which complicated the work of economic reconstruction in Greater Rumania was the comprehensive and far-reaching agrarian reform, inaugurated during and after the war. This reform transformed Rumania from a country of large landed estates to one of small proprietors. Its immediate effect was to diminish agricultural production, besides saddling the finances of the state with a huge debt due to the expropriation of the land from its former owners.

With every portion of the newly created state exhausted by the war; with the old Kingdom of Rumania pumped dry by almost two years of German occupation; with the gold stocks of the country lost in the vaults of the Russian State Bank, whither large portions of them were transported for safekeeping during the war, it required several years for Greater Rumania to become a fully functioning state. All these factors, superimposed upon the new economic structure of the country, naturally found their expression in Rumania's productive activity, in her foreign trade, in her government and private finance, and in all the other phases of her economic life.

During the first eight post-war years (1919-1926) Rumania faced six major economic problems. These were: (1) currency consolidation; (2) budgetary equilibrium; (3) reconstruction of the system of transportation; (4) restoration and reorganization of production and trade; (5) shortage of liquid capital resources; and (6) readjustment of agriculture, resulting from the agrarian reform. With the exception of the establishment of budgetary equilibrium, she has not as yet achieved a complete solution of any of her major problems, although she has progressed markedly along the road of their eventual solution.

CHAPTER XXI

RUMANIA'S CURRENCY AND FISCAL PROBLEMS

RUMANIA'S currency and fiscal experience since the war falls into two periods. Up to the end of 1922, there was a four-year period of unification and consolidation. These four years were characterized by continued inflation and depreciation of the currency and by budgetary deficits. Starting with 1923, Rumania entered upon a period of balanced budgets which helped in arresting the progress of monetary inflation, and of exchange stability, though within fairly wide limits.

While much has been accomplished in Rumania in the direction of currency and fiscal stability, the process is by no means completed. In this chapter we shall trace the country's experience in this regard and indicate what still remains to be done.

I. THE PROCESS OF CURRENCY CONSOLIDATION

Greater Rumania inherited a large variety of currencies. In the territory of the pre-war Kingdom, there were in circulation the notes issued by the National Bank and also those issued by the Banca Generala during the Austro-German occupation.[1] In

[1] See p. 54.

the formerly Austrian and Hungarian territories of Bukowina and Transylvania, Austro-Hungarian Bank notes were in use. In Bessarabia, which had been acquired from Russia, no less than four different kinds of ruble currency were in circulation. One of the first and pressing tasks confronting the Rumanian government after the war was the unification of all this variegated mass of currency. But this task was not accomplished until 1920-21.

Delay in the accomplishment of currency unification resulted in the creation of a comparatively enormous volume of unsecured paper money. This delay was due mainly to three factors. In the first place, it was not until several months after the end of the war that the Rumanian frontier with Austria and Hungary was finally fixed. In the second place, the government of Greater Rumania was not legally organized for a long time, and the note-issuing privileges of the National Bank did not extend to the new territories. Finally, the inefficiency of the administrative apparatus was responsible for the fact that a considerable period of time elapsed between the announcement of the rates at which crowns and rubles were to be exchanged for lei and the actual stamping of these notes which fixed them as Rumanian currency. All these factors resulted in a large influx into Rumania of crowns and rubles, which, at the announced rate of exchange, were worth more in Rumania than in Austria, Hungary, or Russia.

For the purposes of currency unification, one ruble was declared the equivalent of one leu, while one crown was made equal to one-half leu. It was estimated that the amount of lei necessary for the redemption of these rubles and crowns at the above rates would be about 2,500 millions. Besides, it was considered that the volume of currency issued by the Banca Generala during the war occupation, 2,115 millions in all, could be redeemed for about 1,800 million lei. The note issue of the National Bank on December 31, 1919, was 4,431 million lei. It was expected, therefore, that after the unification of the currency, the total volume of paper money in circulation would be about 8,750 million lei. As a matter of fact, however, the amount of crowns alone that was presented for redemption was almost 9,000 millions, requiring about 4,500 million lei. This was more than twice the amount anticipated.[2]

Altogether, on December 31, 1920, with the work of redemption only partly completed, the circulation of the National Bank stood at 9,486 million lei, as against 4,431 millions a year earlier. On December 31, 1921, when the unification of the currency was practically completed, the total circulation of the National Bank was 13,722 million lei. Thus the redemption of the unsecured crowns and

[2] Adams, A., *Report on Economic Conditions in Rumania*, London, 1921, pp. 24-6. The influx of crown notes was stimulated by the ease with which the stamps used by the Rumanian government could be forged.

rubles necessitated the issue of over 7 billion lei in paper currency.[3]

These billions of paper currency were practically without any cover. On December 31, 1921, the National Bank reported, as its cover reserves, 495 million lei in gold and 4,086 millions in foreign bills and treasury bonds, but both of these items were largely fictitious. Of the gold reserves, 315 millions, or more than three-fifths, represented the stocks of gold removed to Moscow during the war and confiscated by the Soviet government. Foreign bills constituted but a small fraction of the reserves, the rest consisting of bonds, expressed in gold, given to the National Bank by the Treasury, with an obligation to redeem them eventually.

The Rumanian currency depreciated steadily between 1919 and 1922, but thereafter it merely fluctuated, though within comparatively wide limits. In January, 1920, the leu was quoted in New York at 2.17 cents (as against the pre-war parity of 19.39 cents), and this was approximately the average exchange value of the leu through the year 1919. By January, 1921, the leu exchange dropped down to 1.37 cents, and a year later, it was 0.76 cent. In January, 1923, the leu exchange was 0.49 cent. Through the years 1923, 1924 and 1925 the monthly average fluctuated between 0.46 and 0.54 cents.[4]

There were three principal reasons for the depre-

[3] Rumanian Ministry of Finance, *The Monetary Consolidation in Roumania*, Bucharest, 1925, p. 8.

[4] *Les Forces économiques de la Roumanie en 1926*, p. 141.

ciation. They were: (1) increase of unsecured circulation due to the unification of the currency; (2) unbalanced budgets, and (3) excess of outgo over income in the international accounts.

We have already noted that during the years 1920 and 1921, the circulation of the National Bank increased from 4,431 million lei to 13,722 millions, that is, more than three-fold. During the same period the exchange value of the leu dropped by almost two-thirds. During the year 1922, there was a further increase in circulation, the total note issue of the National Bank on December 31 of that year being 15,162 million lei,[5] and a 25 per cent drop in the exchange rate.

This four-year period, 1919-22, was also characterized by general economic and fiscal disorganization. Production within the country was at a very low level, and this was reflected both in the small volume of exports and in a comparatively large volume of imports. The need of imports was further intensified by the post-war economic exhaustion of the country. There is no doubt that the large volume of imports during this period was ill-advised, since the country did not possess the means of paying for them. Maturing bills had to be met by means of payments in paper lei or else be defaulted. Both of these processes took place. As a consequence, there was an increase of inflation within the country and continued depreciation

[5] *The Monetary Consolidation in Rumania,* p. 8.

of the rate of exchange. Unbalanced budgets, with the deficits covered by means of new issues of paper money, exerted a similar influence on the volume of currency and the rate of exchange.

Starting with 1923, however, the situation changed. The achievement of a balanced budget made it unnecessary for the Treasury to have recourse to fiscal inflation. At the same time, the post-war commercial debts began to be funded, and the international accounts were brought to a condition in which they ceased to exert an unfavorable influence on the exchange rate.[6] The note circulation continued to increase, but this was due to expansion of productive activities and did not affect the exchange rate.

The following table shows the increase of circulation and the position of the exchange rate during the years 1920-26:

BANK-NOTE CIRCULATION AND EXCHANGE RATE, 1920-1926

Year	Circulation in Millions of Lei on January 1	Exchange Rate in New York in Cents (Average for Month of January)
1920	4,431	2.17
1921	9,488	1.37
1922	13,722	0.76
1923	15,162	0.49
1924	17,917	0.49
1925	19,356	0.50
1926	20,126	0.44

[6] These developments are discussed in detail later on.

Thus during the years 1923, 1924, and 1925, the increases in the total circulation did not affect the exchange rate. At the end of 1925 and at the beginning of 1926, there was a drop in the rate, which reflected not so much the increase in circulation, as the unfavorable balance of trade in 1925. Toward the end of 1926, in spite of a further increase in circulation, the exchange rate recovered to a level slightly above the average for the preceding three years: in October, 1926, the total circulation was 21 billion lei, but the exchange rate was 0.54 cents.[7]

Rumania is officially committed to a policy of a gradual return to the gold standard through currency deflation. This policy is embodied in two conventions, signed May 19, 1925, between the Ministry of Finance and the National Bank. It contemplates the liquidation of the government debt to the National Bank and the accumulation at the Bank of sufficient cover reserves for the currency to be put on the gold basis.

By virtue of the above conventions, which went into effect on January 1, 1926, the charter of the National Bank has been extended until 1960, and the Bank itself has been restored to the character of a semi-private institution which it had from the time of its establishment in 1880 up to the World War. During the three and one-half decades of its pre-war existence, the Bank made no advances to the government, except for a small loan during the

[7] *Les Forces économiques de la Roumanie*, pp. 117 and 141-42.

crisis of 1901. All through the war, however, and especially during the post-war period, the principal function of the Bank became the issuing of notes for the use of the Treasury. By the terms of the 1925 conventions, the Bank was again freed from the obligation to make loans to the government, while the government, in its turn, undertook to liquidate its debt to the Bank. As before the war, the Bank is now to be operated as a corporation, with the government holding one-third of the stock and enjoying appointative power so far as the Governor of the Bank and a part of its Board of Directors are concerned.[8]

At the time of the signing of the conventions, the total note issue of the Bank (notes in circulation and in the vaults of the Bank) amounted to 21,071 million lei. This figure was fixed as the maximum limit of the Bank's note issue for the period during which the notes are not subject to redemption. This period was made coincident with the period during which the government is to liquidate its indebtedness to the Bank, that is, from 15 to 20 years. The amount of the government indebtedness to the Bank was in 1924 about 12,500 million lei. But this amount was reduced to 10,787 millions by the turning over to the National Bank of the stocks of gold received by Rumania from the liquidation of the Austro-Hungarian National Bank.

[8] For a discussion of the rôle which the National Bank plays in the general financial situation of the country see p. 435.

The government undertook to extinguish this debt of 10,787 million lei by means of a liquidation fund, created at the National Bank out of annual deposits made by the Treasury, amounting to about 700 million lei a year.[9] The administration of the fund is controlled by the Bank and the Ministry of Finance, who decide jointly on the manner of its employment and the degree to which it should be applied to the retirement of notes in circulation.

A part of the fund and especially profits from it are to be employed for the purpose of building up cover reserves at the Bank. No moves toward the establishment of the gold standard are to be taken until the government debt to the Bank is extinguished and cover reserves in gold and foreign bills, equal to one-third of the total note issue, are accumulated. For the immediate purposes of the Bank's accounts, the government authorized it to consider the following items as comprising its cover reserves in millions of gold lei, as of December 31, 1924:

Gold in the vaults of the Bank	135.2
Gold on deposit at the Bank of England	98.1
Gold on deposit at the Reichsbank	14.0
Foreign bills, etc	12.0
Gold in Moscow	315.2
Deposits at the Reichsbank	327.0
Book credits at the Bank of England	302.0
	1,203.5

[9] The sources from which the Treasury is to obtain funds for these deposits are as follows: luxury and turnover taxes; royalties and mining duties; new gold produced in the mines of Transylvania; and government profits from participation in banking, industrial and commercial enterprises.

It is obvious that only the first four of the above items may be considered as real reserves. They aggregate less than one-quarter of the total, or 259.3 million lei. The gold sent to Moscow during the war is lost, at least for the time being. The deposits at the Reichsbank represent the security for the issue of bank notes put out during the war by the armies of occupation, and its validity is disputed by the Germans on the ground that the original deposits were in marks, which became entirely worthless as a result of currency depreciation in Germany. The book credits at the Bank of England do not represent actual funds, and moreover lapse in 1927-28.

With the actual metallic reserves equal to less than 1.5 per cent of the total note issue at the time of the signing of the monetary conventions, it is apparent what a stupendous task the Rumanian government and the Rumanian National Bank faced when they undertook to provide a 33⅓ per cent cover for the total bank-note issue. On December 31, 1926, the stocks of gold in the vaults of the Bank were equal to 160 million lei, while the stocks of foreign bills (including Rumanian rentes expressed in foreign currencies) amounted to 774.8 millions.[10]

[10] Figures from *L'Economiste Roumain,* Bucharest, March 15, 1927. For the details of the Rumanian monetary policy and the text of the conventions see the following documents of the Rumanian Ministry of Finance: *The Monetary Consolidation in Rumania* and *Explanatory Statement concerning the Liquidation of the Issue on Behalf of the State, the Extension of the Privilege of the National Bank,* etc., Bucharest, 1925; also *General Budget of the State* for the years 1924, 1925, and 1926.

There is a strong body of opinion in Rumania which favors immediate stabilization of the currency. The principal argument of the group which favors this view is that lack of currency stability is doing a great injury to the economic life of the country. It is also argued that the pursuance of the policy of gradual currency deflation, carried out by the National Bank under the terms of the 1925 convention, is bound to retard the country's economic development for many years and do much more harm than good.

There seems little doubt that under present conditions the Rumanian currency situation does place a heavy burden on the country's economic life. The effect of these fluctuations has been to create conditions of uncertainty and in that manner to have injurious effects on trade and industry. While the yearly or even the monthly fluctuations of the currency are not large, the variations between the highest and the lowest exchange rates are very great. For example, during the years 1923-25, these fluctuations were as follows:

Exchange Fluctuations, 1923-1925
(Lei to the dollar)

Year	Yearly Average	Maximum Rate	Minimum Rate
1923	209	260	170
1924	203	250	175
1925	208	226	192

It is also pointed out that stabilization need not be delayed because of lack of cover for the notes in circulation. The present stocks of gold, converted into paper lei, represent a cover of almost one-third, and this, together with the stock of foreign bills and currencies and a possible stabilization loan, ought to be sufficient.[11]

II. THE MAINTENANCE OF A BALANCED BUDGET

Greater Rumania inherited a very difficult budgetary situation. The continuation of the war for almost a year after the general armistice rendered it impossible for the government at Bucharest to give its attention to the problems of fiscal organization. Following the final establishment of peace, it was some time before the various territories comprising the post-war Kingdom could be really unified administratively. These initial difficulties were reflected in the country's budgetary situation.

During the first three years, the expenditures of the Rumanian government exceeded its revenues. The deficit was largest during the first year following the end of the World War, and although it decreased progressively during the next two years, it was still very considerable during the fiscal year 1921-22. All through this period, the Rumanian government followed the pre-war practice of using

[11] For a discussion of the view in favor of immediate stabilization see, for example, Popescu, A. I., "The Urgency of Stabilization (in Rumania)," *Manchester Guardian Commercial,* May 26, 1927. See also *L'Indépendance Roumaine,* December 15, 1927.

the period from April 1 to March 31 as the fiscal year.

During the year 1919-20 the budgetary expenditures exceeded the revenues by 3,546 million lei. During the year 1920-21, the deficit was 2,705 million lei.[12]

The budget for 1921-22 closed with a surplus of 30 million lei, the total expenditures being 8,051 millions and the total receipts, 8,081 millions. However, this surplus was only apparent, since further expenditures were made during the year, aggregating approximately 1,957 million lei, principally for work on the railways.[13]

The budget during this three-year period included only the indispensable current expenditures. They excluded such important items as the service of the debts.

The budgetary deficits were covered by means of new issues of paper currency. As during the war, the treasury continued to resort to the discounting of its obligations by the National Bank for the purpose of obtaining the means necessary for the covering of its budgetary deficits.

Starting with the fiscal year 1922-23, the Rumanian budget has been balanced. The budgetary accounts have invariably shown a large excess of revenues over current expenditures, as may be seen

[12] Adams, A., *Report on the Financial, Commercial, and Economic Conditions in Rumania*, London, 1924, p. 7.

[13] Bratiano, Vintila, *Budget général de l'état pour l'exercise* 1924, p. 5.

from the following table, showing the closed accounts for the years 1922-1925: [14]

RUMANIAN STATE BUDGET, 1922-1925
(In millions of lei)

Year	Receipts	Expenditures	Surplus
1922–23	15,113.5	10,032.0	5,081.5
1923 (nine months)..	18,791.5	13,639.0	5,152.5
1924	27,744.0	21,403.6	6,340.4
1925[a]	36,498.8	31,750.0	4,748.8

[a] Provisional closed accounts as of May 31, 1926.

The figures in the above table show the gross revenues and outlays of the government and include the receipts and expenditures of the railways. In the budget for 1926 only the net results of the operation of the railways were included in the budget. The estimates for that year placed the net expenditures of the government at 29,250 million lei, and the net revenues at the same amount.

The surpluses indicated by the closed accounts have been completely absorbed by extraordinary expenditures and supplementary credits. But even so, the expenditures per capita of the population in Greater Rumania are smaller than they were in prewar Rumania. In 1914-15 the per capita budgetary expenditures of the Rumanian government were 14.4 dollars; in 1925, they were 9.5 dollars.[15]

[14] League of Nations *Memorandum on Public Finance*. In 1923 the fiscal year was made coincident with the calendar year.

[15] Figures based on evaluations contained in the memorandum on the budgetary situation in Rumania, prepared by the Rumanian War Debt Commission in Washington in 1925.

The balancing of the budget during the fiscal year 1922-23 made it possible for the Rumanian government to cease having resort to fiscal inflation for the purpose of supplying its budgetary needs. As we saw above, government borrowing from the National Bank ceased during that year. On the contrary, the government has since then undertaken the repayment of its debt to the Bank, and in the budget for 1926 provisions were made for the first payment on this account.

Payments on the public debt and military expenditures are the largest single item in the budget. Both of these items increased considerably during the years 1924-26, although the percentage of total expenditures allocated to them decreased slightly. The table on page 403 shows the principal groups of expenditures in the Rumanian budgets for 1924 and 1926: [16]

Thus we find that between 1924 and 1926 the expenditures for national defense increased by a billion and a half lei, or by 40 per cent. This was due primarily not to any substantial increase in the military establishment, but to larger allowances for the maintenance of the personnel. The increase in the payments on account of the public debts was over a billion lei. This resulted from the funding of the foreign war debts and the inclusion in the 1926 budget of the sum of 623.8 million lei as the first payment to the National Bank under the agree-

[16] League of Nations *Memorandum on Public Finance.*

BUDGETARY EXPENDITURES IN RUMANIA, 1924-1926

Items	1924		1926	
	In Millions of Lei	*As a Percentage of Total*	In Millions of Lei	*As a Percentage of Total*
National defense	3,793.9	*22.39*	5,329.6	*21.78*
Payments on public debt	3,340.9	*19.71*	4,474.2	*18.29*
Pensions and special allowances (military and civil)	1,500.5	*8.85*	4,321.0	*17.67*
Education, religion, and public hygiene	3,180.2	*18.77*	4,480.1	*18.31*
Administration (general, financial and economic)	2,125.1	*12.54*	2,954.9	*12.07*
Net deficit on public enterprises	1,338.6	*7.90*	19.8	*0.08*
Other expenditures	1,667.2	*9.84*	2,886.0	*11.80*
Total	16,946.4	*100.00*	24,465.6	*100.00*

ment for the liquidation of the government debt to it. Altogether, the upkeep of the military establishment and the service of the public debts absorbed in 1926 two-fifths of the total budgetary expenditures.

Next to the national defense and the public debt service, the largest group of expenditure is for education, sanitation, and other social services. This item also increased very substantially between 1924 and 1926. Following this group, come pensions and special allowances, mostly for civil employes, whose regular salaries are extremely low. The expenditures under this head increased almost three-fold between 1924 and 1926.

The table on page 403 indicates important progress in the management of public enterprises. Whereas in 1924 the deficit in the operation of these enterprises, principally the railways, amounted to almost 8 per cent of the total budgetary expenditures, in 1926 it was practically eliminated.

Indirect taxation accounts for over half of the total revenues. The following table shows, in percentages of the total revenue for the year, the rôle played by the various sources of revenue in the total budgetary receipts of Rumania; [17]

BUDGETARY REVENUES IN RUMANIA, 1926
(As percentages of the total for the year)

Direct taxes	17.78
Indirect taxes	54.14
Profits of government monopolies	16.72
Other revenues	11.36
	100.00

While the direct taxes yielded less than one-fifth of the revenues, the indirect taxes accounted for 54 per cent. By far the largest source of indirect taxation revenue was customs duties. Rumania maintains both import and export taxes, and the latter yield more revenue than the former. In the budget for 1926, the import duties accounted for 10.22 per cent of the total, and the export duties, for 16.35

[17] League of Nations *Memorandum on Public Finance.*

per cent. Next in importance were the stamp duties and the luxury taxes.

There are seven government monopolies, namely, tobacco, cigarette paper, matches, playing cards, explosives, salt, and alcohol.[18] These monopolies are important sources of revenue. For example, for the year 1926 the total gross receipts of the monopolies were estimated at 5,980.2 million lei, while the expenditures were estimated at only 1,888.7 millions, leaving a net profit to the government of over 4 billion lei.

The present system of taxation was introduced in Rumania by the law of February 23, 1923. Prior to that each of the territories constituting Greater Rumania retained the taxation system which it had had before the end of the war. The law of 1923 substituted a single system for all these heterogeneous practices.

Before the unification of the taxation system, an attempt was made to reform the fiscal situation in such a way as to increase the emphasis on direct taxation. This reform was embodied in a law, introduced by M. Titulesco, who was Minister of Finance in 1921. The Titulesco plan was based primarily upon a graduated income tax, and a special levy on capital and on war profits. This plan was approved by the Rumanian Parliament, but was never applied.

In 1922, M. Vintila Bratiano became Minister of

[18] The alcohol monopoly is confined to Bessarabia.

Finance. He rejected the Titulesco plan, substituting for it the law of February 23, 1923, which is based primarily on indirect taxation.[19]

[19] For M. Bratiano's explanation of his fiscal policies see his speeches in Parliament, published in *Budget général de l'état pour l'exercise 1924;* for a description of the taxation system in Rumania see Badulesco, V., *Les Finances publiques de la Roumanie,* Chapter IV; and Leon, G. N., "Législation fiscale de la Roumanic," *L'Economiste Roumain,* May, 1926.

CHAPTER XXII

RUMANIA'S INTERNATIONAL ACCOUNTS

RUMANIA's ability to establish and maintain a stabilized currency depends very largely upon the country's international financial position. During the period from 1923 to 1926, as we saw in the preceding chapter, the condition of Rumania's international accounts did not exercise any great influence on the exchange situation. It is apparent, therefore, that during this period the country was able to obtain sufficient means to meet its foreign payments. In this chapter we shall examine Rumania's international accounts with a view of determining how these means were obtained and of what the outlook is for the future.

In her economic and financial relations with other countries, Rumania's main source of international income is her export trade. She has some income from certain classes of service operations, but it is very small. But offsetting these items of income Rumania has a large volume of payments to make on account of her foreign indebtedness.

The Rumanian balance of trade has been favorable since 1922. Prior to that, imports exceeded exports, but from 1922 to 1926, with the sole exception of 1925, the country had an excess of exports over imports. The table below shows Greater Rumania's foreign trade during the first eight post-war years.[1]

RUMANIA'S FOREIGN TRADE, 1919-1926
(In millions of paper lei)

Year	Exports	Imports	Balance
1919	104	3,762	−3,658
1920	3,448	6,980	−3,532
1921	8,185	12,145	−3,960
1922	14,039	12,325	+1,714
1923	24,575	19,514	+5,061
1924	27,824	26,192	+1,632
1925	29,127	29,912	− 785
1926	38,223	37,134	+1,089

The figures in the above table indicate wide fluctuations in the Rumanian balance of trade. During the five years from 1922 to 1926, the balance ranged from an unfavorable one of 800 million lei to a favorable one of five billions. For the whole period, the average favorable balance was 2.2 billion lei a year.

Rumania's large foreign indebtedness requires increasing annual payments. Of her various foreign debts, public and private, some have been funded, and on these payments are now being made. Others still await negotiations for their consolidation.

[1] Figures from *Comertul exterior al României,* official publications of the Rumanian Administration of Statistics.

A part of the public debt was inherited from before the war. This part comprises the pre-war debts of the Kingdom of Rumania and the Rumanian share of the Austro-Hungarian debts, as allocated by the Innsbruck and Prague protocols. The assumption of a share of the Austro-Hungarian debts, as we saw above, is an obligation under the treaties of peace, which also impose upon Rumania a "liberation" debt and an obligation to pay for property in the former Austrian and Hungarian territories, incorporated in Greater Rumania.

During the war and the period immediately following the war, Rumania contracted debts in the United States, Great Britain, France, and Italy. These inter-allied debts constitute a part of her foreign indebtedness. In addition to regular loans, she also received advances during the post-war period against treasury bills, some of which were consolidated in 1922.

As an offsetting item to these obligations of the Rumanian government, the country has a reparation claim against the former enemy powers. Her share of the reparation payments is, however, very small, and the Rumanian government has repeatedly protested against the manner in which the country was treated at the Spa conference, where the reparation receipts were allocated.

The private foreign indebtedness comprises several items. In the first place there are foreign investments which were made before the war in the

Old Kingdom of Rumania. Then there are properties in the former Austrian in Hungarian territories, the ownership of which was retained in Vienna and Budapest. In the third place, there are foreign investments in Greater Rumania made since the war. Finally, there is a considerable body of private commercial debts.

Rumania is not, as yet, making payments on all of her foreign debts. While the payments on the various items of private foreign indebtedness are probably met in full, several important public obligations have not as yet been funded. Practically no payments are made on the debts arising out of the treaties of peace, with the exception of the old Austro-Hungarian debts. Some of the inter-allied debts still await funding. But even the payments actually made at the present time aggregate a very large sum, and since most of the funding agreements are on an ascending scale of annuities, the outlays for foreign debt payments are increasing from year to year.

Other service operations represent net outgo for Rumania. On the income side are the remittances of Rumanian emigrants in other countries, principally in the United States, the expenditures of foreigners in Rumania, and the revenue from Danubian shipping and other transit traffic. On the outgo side are the expenditures of Rumanians in other countries, payments for transport, insurance, etc.

The total income from emigrant remittances and

the services rendered by Rumania to other countries is considerably smaller than the payments which Rumania has to make for services rendered her by foreigners.

Rumania's favorable trade balance has been insufficient to cover the debt payments and the net service outgo. The following summary statement shows the total international income and outgo during the five-year period from 1922 to 1926, in paper lei:[2]

RUMANIA'S INTERNATIONAL INCOME ACCOUNT, 1922-1926
(Total for the five years, in billions of paper lei)

Net outgo for—			
Interest, dividends and profits:			
On public indebtedness	10.6		
On private indebtedness	15.0		
	——	25.6	
Other service operations		4.5	
		——	30.1
Net income from—			
Balance of merchandise trade		8.7	
Emigrant remittances		1.5	
		——	10.2
			——
Net outgo for all items			19.9

Thus during the years 1922-26 Rumania's international outgo exceeded her international income by 19.9 billion paper lei. There was only one year during this whole period, namely, 1923, when the export surplus was sufficient to cover all of the country's debt and service payments. During the

[2] For the sources of materials on which these evaluations are based see Appendix, pp. 597-8.

remainder of the period the deficit had to be made up by the sale to foreigners of securities and domestic enterprises, and by direct borrowing from foreigners.

Rumania cannot continue meeting her foreign debt payments unless her favorable balance of trade is greatly expanded. The two items of net income in her income account are emigrant remittances, which are of minor importance, and the commodity trade balance. In order to meet the payments for which she has already assumed responsibility, she needs a favorable balance of about 6.5 billion lei, or its equivalent in gold. A rise in the exchange rate of the lei will not diminish appreciably the gold value of her payments, since her public debts are expressed in gold or in stable foreign currencies.

When Rumania begins payments on the rest of her foreign obligations, her favorable balance of trade will have to be still larger than at the present time. Moreover, the fact that Rumania is compelled at the present time to cover the deficit in her international accounts by means of new foreign loans will necessitate a still further expansion of her favorable balance in the future. The question whether she can develop a commodity export surplus sufficient to balance her net outgo for other classes of international transactions is one which we shall consider in the next chapter, where her general economic situation is analyzed.

CHAPTER XXIII

TRADE, PRODUCTION, AND BANKING IN RUMANIA

GREATER Rumania is a country of comparatively large and varied natural resources, which constitute the basis of her agricultural and industrial production. She is a large producer of foodstuffs and basic raw materials, and her output of these products is considerably in excess of her own requirements. She is, therefore, in a position to export large quantities of them, both in the form of raw materials and of partly or wholly finished products. In this chapter we shall examine the character of Rumania's foreign trade and of her agricultural and industrial production.

I. CHARACTER AND DIRECTION OF FOREIGN TRADE

While essentially an agricultural country, Rumania is not at the present time predominantly an exporter of foodstuffs. Since the country is richly endowed with natural resources, other products than foodstuffs play an important part in her export trade. At the same time the low level of industrial development is responsible for the importation of large quantities of essential manufactured goods.

Foodstuffs, timber and petroleum are Rumania's chief exports, and textiles and metals are her main imports. The following table shows the principal groups of products that enter the country's foreign trade:[1]

COMPOSITION OF RUMANIA'S FOREIGN TRADE, 1925
(In percentages of the total values for the year)

Exports		*Imports*	
Living animals	14.50	Textiles, textile materials, and clothing	41.97
Animal products	4.25	Metals and metal products	19.77
Cereals and their derivatives	25.22	Machinery and vehicles	12.65
Vegetables, flowers, etc.	4.83	Colonial fruit	3.62
Timber	21.50	Rubber and rubber products	2.30
Petroleum products	19.85	Miscellaneous	19.69
Miscellaneous	9.85		
Total	100.00	Total	100.00

Thus while cereals and their derivatives constitute the largest single group of Rumania's exports, they represent only one-quarter of the total. Living animals and animal products account for almost 19 per cent of the total exports; timber and timber products, for 21.5 per cent; and petroleum and its products, for almost 20 per cent of the total.

Textiles and textile materials represent more than two-fifths of Rumania's imports. The bulk of the imports in this group are cotton and cotton goods, but the country also imports wool and woolen prod-

[1] Figures from *Les Forces économiques de la Roumanie*, pp. 92-3.

ucts, flax, silk, etc. Metals and metal products account for about one-fifth of the total imports, and machinery and vehicles for over 12 per cent of the total.

Rumania trades principally with the countries of central Europe. The following table shows the relative importance of these countries in her export and import trade: [2]

GEOGRAPHICAL DISTRIBUTION OF RUMANIA'S FOREIGN TRADE, 1924
(In percentages of total values for the year)

Exports to:		*Imports from:*	
Austria	14.1	Austria	16.9
Hungary	14.9	Hungary	4.2
Czechoslovakia	9.5	Czechoslovakia	11.5
Poland	3.6	Poland	9.0
Germany	5.8	Germany	19.3
Belgium	5.4	Belgium	1.9
France	6.4	France	8.1
Italy	5.1	Italy	10.0
United Kingdom	5.9	United Kingdom	9.9

No official figures are available as to the geographical distribution of Rumania's foreign trade during any later year than 1924. So far as that year is concerned, however, it is clear that the three principal Danubian countries play a larger rôle in Rumania's export than in her import trade: their purchases during the year were 38.5 per cent of the total value of exports, and only 32.6 per cent of the total imports.

[2] Figures from League of Nations *Memorandum on Balance of Payments and Foreign Trade Balances,* Vol. II.

Important portions of the territory of present-day Rumania were formerly parts of Austria and Hungary, shipping some of their products to other sections of the Monarchy. The trade connections which had thus been established, although interrupted soon after the war, have been gradually restored. Hence the comparatively large share of Rumanian exports going to Austria, Hungary, and Czechoslovakia. With the rest of her Danubian neighbors Rumania has very little trade, Greece being more important to her as a market than Yugoslavia or Bulgaria.

The largest sources of Rumania's imports are Germany, Austria, and Czechoslovakia, followed by the United Kingdom, Poland, Italy and France. All of these countries compete in the Rumanian market in textile products; the largest share of the textile trade falls to Italy, the United Kingdom, Austria, Poland and Czechoslovakia. They all also compete in the Rumanian market in metal products, with Germany and Czechoslovakia as the largest sources of such products.

II. AGRICULTURAL PRODUCTION AND SURPLUS

Rumania has large agricultural resources, especially in the territory of the old Kingdom and in Bessarabia. For the whole of Greater Rumania, arable land represents 41.6 per cent of the total area (46.8 per cent in the old Kingdom and 58.8 per cent in Bessarabia); meadows and pastures occupy 14.1

per cent of the total; orchards, 1.9 per cent; forests, 24.6 per cent; and unproductive lands, 17.8 per cent.[3]

Rumania is a large producer of cereals, although her output of grain is smaller than before the war. Of the total area under cultivation, over 85 per cent are sown to grain, with wheat as the most important product. Both the area devoted to cereals and the total output have been increasing since the war, as may be seen from the following table, although even the 1926 crop was smaller than before the war:

GRAIN PRODUCTION IN RUMANIA, 1921 AND 1926

Grain	1921		1926	
	Area Sown (in Thousands of Hectares)	Output (in Thousands of Quintals)	Area Sown (in Thousands of Hectares)	Output (in Thousands of Quintals)
Wheat	2,488	21,384	3,327	30,445
Rye	327	2,307	296	2,910
Barley	1,569	9,853	1,551	16,633
Oats	1,239	19,632	1,078	11,604
Total for the four grains	5,623	53,176	6,252	61,592
Maize	3,444	28,104	4,075	51,657

[3] *Les Forces économiques de la Roumanie*, p. 10. The data contained in this section are taken primarily from the above publication, and from *Anuarul statistic al României*, annual publication of the Rumanian Administration of Statistics, and the files of *L'Economiste Roumain* and *Argus*.

The figures in the above table indicate an increase in both the area planted to grain and the output of the various cereals. It is interesting to note, however, that the increase in the area planted is attributable entirely to an expansion of the wheat acreage. The other three grains show a contraction of the planting area, although there has been an increase in the output of rye and especially of barley, while oats showed a definite decrease. With regard to maize, there has been some increase in the planting area and a very large expansion of output.

Rumania's largest grain lands are in the territory of the old Kingdom, which produces about one-half of the total output of wheat, and more than one-half of the total barley, oats, and maize crops. The yield per hectare is, however, very low in old Rumania. So far as wheat is concerned, it is slightly higher than in Bessarabia, but appreciably lower than in Transylvania, and much smaller than in Bukowina. For the other three grains, the yield in the old Kingdom is smaller than in any other part of Greater Rumania, although this territory holds the first place so far as the yield of maize is concerned.

The yield of hectare is approximately the pre-war. This is true of the whole country and of its various sections. The following table shows the average yields for the various grains during the years 1921-26, as compared with the average for the years 1911-15 in the old Kingdom of Rumania: [4]

CROP YIELDS IN RUMANIA
(In quintals per hectare)

Grain	Average for 1911-1915			Average for 1921-1926 for the Whole Country	1926 for the Whole Country
	Large Estates	Small Holdings	All Holdings		
Wheat	12.2	10.6	11.9	8.7	9.1
Rye	10.3	8.5	9.0	7.9	9.7
Barley	11.7	10.1	10.5	7.6	10.9
Oats	10.6	8.6	9.2	7.7	10.7
Maize	15.5	12.7	13.6	10.7	14.0

Thus the average yields for Greater Rumania during the years 1921-26 were not only below the general pre-war yields, but even below those on the small farms, which were notoriously less productive than the large estates. And since the territory of the old Kingdom had a generally lower level of yields than the other sections of Greater Rumania, it is clear that the post-war yields in Rumania have been very much lower than the pre-war. It was only in 1926 that the country reached a level of yields which were somewhat higher than the pre-war general average for the Old Kingdom, although in the case of wheat the level is still 23.5 per cent below the pre-war.

[4] *L'Economiste Roumain,* January, 1927.

The agrarian reform and several other factors have been responsible for the decreased yields. During the past decade, Rumania has been transformed from a country of large estates to one of small land properties. A series of legislative measures, enacted between 1917 and 1921, accomplished this transformation.

The results of the agrarian reform, so far as the distribution of land holdings is concerned, are shown in the table on opposite page. All land holdings are divided into two classes: those under 100 hectares (247 acres) and those exceeding 100 hectares.[5]

The radical change in the system of land holdings in Rumania is quite apparent from this table. Whereas before the agrarian reform, 42.4 per cent of the land consisted of large estates, after the reform such estates occupy only 11.2 per cent of the total. On the other hand, the portion of the agricultural land divided into small holdings increased from 57.6 per cent of the total to 88.8 per cent.

As we saw above, the productiveness of the smaller holdings was, before the war, about 20 per cent less than that of the large estates. Differences in the methods of cultivation and in the use of machinery were largely responsible for this. With the passing of the bulk of large estates into the hands

[5] Figures from *Les Forces économiques de la Roumanie*, p. 12. For the details of the agrarian reform in Rumania see *The Agrarian Reform in Rumania and Its Consequences*, Bucharest, 1924; Constantinesco, M., *L'Evolution de la propriété rurale et la réforme agraire en Roumanie*, Bucharest, 1925; and Evans, I. L., *The Agrarian Revolution in Rumania*, Cambridge, 1924.

SHIFT IN SIZE OF LAND HOLDINGS IN RUMANIA

	Area of Holdings of 100 Hectares or Less		Area of Holdings Larger than 100 Hectares	
	In Thousands of Hectares	As Percentage of Total	In Thousands of Hectares	As Percentage of Total
I. *Before the Agrarian Reform.*				
Old Kingdom ...	4,180.6	52.5	3,810.4	47.5
Bessarabia	2,337.8	55.9	1,844.5	44.1
Transylvania ...	4,689.9	63.0	2,751.5	37.0
Bukowina	405.5	78.0	115.0	22.0
Total..........	11,613.8	57.6	8,521.4	42.4
II. *After the Agrarian Reform.*				
Old Kingdom ...	7,293.1	91.5	697.9	8.5
Bessarabia	3,829.7	91.6	352.6	8.4
* Transylvania ..	6,288.3	84.5	1,153.0	15.5
Bukowina	478.0	92.0	42.0	8.0
Total..........	17,889.1	88.8	2,245.5	11.2

* The comparatively large percentage of land in Transylvania still constituting large estates is probably due to the inclusion of timber areas.

of the peasants, who still cultivate the land in a very primitive fashion, there was bound to be a very marked decrease in agricultural production.[6]

There were several other causes which contributed

[6] Rumania's experience in this respect has been different from that of Czechoslovakia, where, as we saw on p. 249, the agricultural output *increased* after the agrarian reform.

to the decrease in agricultural production. One was the general economic disorganization of the country following the war and the process of unification. Another was the introduction of export duties, especially on wheat, of which we shall speak later on, in connection with the commercial policy of Rumania.[7]

Rumania can increase greatly her production and exports of cereals. Next to Russia, she is the largest exporter of grain in Europe. Although the total grain exports of Greater Rumania have been so far smaller than the pre-war exports of the old Kingdom alone, nevertheless Rumania even now surpasses as an exporter Yugoslavia, Bulgaria, Hungary and Poland, which are the other European surplus producers of cereals. And the possibility of increasing the yield of her grain lands renders it possible for her to expand considerably her production and exports.

The reason why the cereal exports of Greater Rumania are smaller than those of the pre-war Kingdom lies partly in the fact that the total production is smaller and partly in the fact that a part of the grain formerly available for export is now used in the domestic market. The industrial sections of Transylvania, which do not feed themselves, are responsible for this to some extent, though the principal factor in the situation is, probably, increased consumption on the part of the peasantry.

[7] See Chapter XXIV.

At the present time, however, with the increase in the total cereal production which we indicated on page 417, the domestic requirements of Greater Rumania are being satisfied at approximately the pre-war level, and the country can still ship abroad a very substantial part of its output. In 1926 the exports of cereals represented 38.5 per cent of the total production.[8] This percentage of the output available for exportation is likely to grow with the increase of production.

The possibilities of increasing the yield per hectare are clear from a comparison of the Rumanian situation in this respect with that of some of the other countries of Central Europe. At the present time, the yield in wheat is, in Rumania, only about three-quarters of what it is in Hungary and only one-half of what it is in Switzerland. Assuming that the intensification of production to the Swiss level of yields would be extremely difficult for some time to come, the increase of yields only to the Hungarian level would still add very greatly to the surplus of cereals available for exportation to other countries.

Rumania is a surplus producer of livestock. All the sections making up the territory of Greater Rumania were before the war exporters of livestock. They all suffered greatly during the war, but have been gradually restoring their livestock population. The figures on page 424 show the situation in this

[8] *L'Economiste Roumain,* January, 1927.

regard for the pre-war period and for the years 1920 and 1926.[9]

LIVESTOCK POPULATION IN RUMANIA
(In thousands)

Livestock	Pre-war [a]	1920	1926
Horses and donkeys......	2,678	1,497	1,890
Horned cattle	6,760	4,875	4,992
Sheep and goats..........	15,250	9,189	14,059
Pigs	4,634	2,513	3,168

[a] 1916 for the old Kingdom and Bessarabia; 1911 for Transylvania; 1910 for Bukowina.

The damage done by the war to the livestock population of the territories comprising Greater Rumania is clear from a comparison of the first two columns of the above table. The number of horses and pigs was reduced by almost one-half; the number of horned cattle and sheep, by about one-third. The figures for 1926 still show smaller numbers of animals than before the war.

The recovery since the war has been quite rapid so far as sheep and goats are concerned. It has been less marked with regard to horses, donkeys, and pigs. The number of horned cattle has remained almost stationary.

The commercial policy of the Rumanian government has been largely responsible for the slow re-

[9] Pre-war and 1920 figures from Adams, A., *Report on Economic Conditions in Rumania,* London, 1923, p. 26; 1926 figures from Humphreys, R. J. E., *Report on Economic Conditions in Rumania,* London, 1927, p. 16.

covery of the livestock population, although crop conditions have also tended to retard it. For example, repeated drouths in Bessarabia, due to deforestation, have been responsible for an actual decrease in the number of cattle in that part of the country. Of far greater importance has been the operation of the export tax on cattle and meat, which was introduced originally for the purpose of keeping supplies within the country and of preventing a rapid rise in prices, but which persisted beyond the period when these measures were really necessary and has been instrumental in retarding the increase of horned cattle.

With the livestock population still considerably below the pre-war figures, Rumania nevertheless exports large quantities of live animals and animal products. As we have already seen, these two export items constitute almost one-fifth of the country's total exports. Since the tendency in Rumania is in the direction of a gradual reduction and final elimination of export duties,[10] that may easily have a favorable effect on the growth of livestock population and an expansion of live animal and animal products exports.

III. INDUSTRIAL DEVELOPMENT AND REQUIREMENTS

In addition to her agricultural resources, Rumania possesses extensive timber areas and a large variety of mineral wealth. She is abundantly supplied with

[10] See p. 453.

both raw materials and fuel, the two indispensable prerequisites of industrial development. Some industrial development existed before the war in the different territories comprising Greater Rumania, especially in the old Kingdom and in Transylvania. Since the war there has been a considerable development of industrial activity.[11]

Rumania's natural wealth provides a basis for industrial activity. The industries now operating in the various parts of the country have grown up mainly as a result of the existence of the necessary raw materials and fuel. The principal industries are those concerned with the preparation of food products, with the working of metals and of wood. Next in importance are the textile, leather, and chemical industries. All of these branches of production, with the exception of the textile industry, use almost exclusively domestic raw materials.

Rumania is abundantly supplied with every kind of fuel. The most important is petroleum, but the country also possesses large quantities of coal, wood, and gas.

Petroleum is obtained in the territory of the old Kingdom, although there are some indications of its presence in Transylvania. The oil fields exploited at the present time extend in a semi-circular strip

[11] The data contained in this section are based primarily on *Les Forces économiques de la Roumanie; Anuarul statistic al României; Statistica miniera a României,* annual publication of the Rumanian Administration of Statistics; the files of *L'Economiste Roumain* and *Argus;* and Angelesco, I. N., *The Increase of Production,* Bucharest, 1924.

along the foothills of the Carpathian mountains. The deposits are very rich, Rumania occupying the second place after Russia as the largest European producer of petroleum.

The production of petroleum was developing very rapidly during the decade immediately preceding

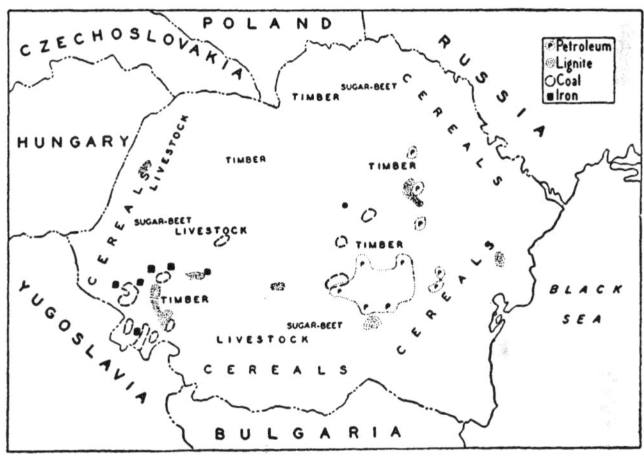

RUMANIA'S PRINCIPAL RESOURCES

the World War. It was interrupted during the war and reached its lowest ebb in 1917, when the oil wells were blown up in order to prevent them from falling into the hands of the Austro-German invaders. The production was resumed after the war, and by 1924 the output surpassed the highest figure attained before the war. The production of petroleum in Rumania has been as follows:

1904	500,561 tons
1913	1,775,225 "
1917	517,491 "
1920	1,034,123 "
1924	1,851,303 "
1925	2,316,504 "

The output of petroleum is now considerably larger than it was before the war. Oil refining represents an important branch of industrial activity, and petroleum exports constitute almost one-fifth of the total exports of the country. These exports are shipped abroad principally in the form of benzine and kerosene.

In spite of the fact that the production of petroleum is larger than before the war, the total exports of petroleum products are much smaller. This is due to increased domestic consumption, since the oil wells of the old Kingdom now have to supply the requirements of Greater Rumania. The following table shows the consumption and the exports of petroleum products (in thousands of tons) before and after the war:

	1913	1925
Consumption	812.9	1,119.5
Exports	1,036.4	788.8

Thus while before the war the exports were 25 per cent larger than domestic consumption, today the domestic consumption exceeds the exports by 50 per cent. With a further increase of production, however, the exports are likely to increase, without infringing upon the country's own requirements of petroleum products for fuel and power purposes.

Coal is mined primarily in Transylvania. There are small reserves of high grade coking coal (about 4 million tons), of which 313,572 tons were extracted in 1925. Rumania has, in addition, large deposits of lignite, of which over 2.5 million tons were extracted in 1925. The coal production is not quite sufficient to meet the country's requirements. This necessitates the annual importation of about 200,000 tons of high grade coal.

Rumania contains very large reserves of natural gas, which is used for light, heat, and power. The consumption of gas has been growing very rapidly since the war, increasing from 48 million cubic meters in 1919 to 146 millions in 1924.

Still another source of energy is water power, which is important because of the mountainous character of the country. It is estimated that Rumania has water power reserves equal to 1,650,000 H.P., of which only 52,592 H.P. are actually in use at the present time.

The enormous forest areas of Rumania represent both a source of fuel and of raw materials. Almost one-quarter of the total area of the country is covered with forests, which are concentrated particularly in Transylvania and Bukowina, with the plains of Bessarabia almost bare. The production of timber is sufficient to satisfy the raw material requirements of the country for the woodworking and paper industries, and to supply over one-fifth of the total exports in the form of logs, half-finished products, furniture, etc.

The deposits of iron ore in Rumania are small, the total known reserves being estimated at 33 million tons. At the present rate of consumption these reserves would be sufficient for only a half century. On the other hand, the country has, in Transylvania, a large metallurgical equipment, which had been formerly supplied with iron ore from the mines of Hungary. In order to employ this equipment, Rumania is compelled to import large quantities of iron ore.

In addition to iron, Rumania produces small quantities of other metals. Notable among these are copper, lead, antimony, manganese, and even some silver and gold. Important deposits of asphalt, amber, and rock salt complete the list of Rumania's principal mineral resources, contributing raw materials for her industries.

The Rumanian industries have undergone considerable development since the war. Before the war the total number of industrial enterprises, using more than 5 HP., in the territory comprising Greater Rumania was 2,747. Many of these enterprises, however, had been destroyed or rendered inoperative during the war, and the first few post-war years were devoted largely to their restoration, which was aided by the need of repairing the general damage done by the war. By the end of 1921 about 3,000 enterprises were in operation.

The work of restoring the industries was also aided by the process of inflation, which ceased in 1922. Nevertheless, in spite of the tightening of financial resources after 1922, the expansion of industries continued. The following table shows the condition of industries by branches of production between 1922 and 1925: [12]

INDUSTRIAL ENTERPRISES IN RUMANIA

Industry	Number of Enterprises		Number of Workmen and Employees	
	1922	1925	1922	1925
Metallurgy and electrotechnical	428	521	36,278	41,567
Woodworking	617	848	47,791	60,648
Chemical [a]	200	281	11,500	9,086
Food-working	536	602	23,105	26,858
Textiles	182	397	15,285	29,326
Tanning industry	164	304	8,916	10,091
Construction materials	561	256	13,277	14,665
Paper and graphic arts	146	167	7,202	10,554
Glass	? [b]	39	? [b]	5,072
Ceramic industry	? [b]	30	? [b]	866
Total	2,834 [c]	3,445	163,354 [c]	208,733

[a] Exclusive of oil refineries.
[b] Not reported.
[c] Exclusive of glass and ceramic industries.

[12] Figures for 1922 from *L'Economiste Roumain,* July, 1926; those for 1925 are from the same publication, December, 1926.

The largest degree of expansion is shown by the textile industry, in which both the number of enterprises and the number of workmen doubled during the four years from 1922 to 1925. All the other industries have increased their equipment, with the sole exception of construction materials. Altogether, the number of enterprises increased by about 15 per cent and the number of workmen and employees by over 20 per cent.

Rumanian industries now supply an appreciable portion of the country's requirements of manufactured goods. Some of the industries, notably those concerned with the working of wood and the preparation of food products, export a part of their output. The others supply exclusively the domestic market. The following table shows in values the production and the imports of Rumania in 1925 classified by principal industrial groups:

INDUSTRIAL PRODUCTION AND IMPORTS, 1925
(In millions of lei)

Industry	Production	Imports
Metallurgy and electrotechnical	6,127.5	9,621.8
Woodworking	5,231.7	481.6
Chemical	2,115.9	1,252.3
Food-working	10,238.9	269.9
Textile	5,643.9	13,531.0
Tanning	2,543.6	784.2
Ceramic	82.5	243.2
Construction materials	837.7	52.9
Paper and graphic arts	1,459.1	359.6
Glass	406.4	442.4

Rumania more than supplies her requirements of prepared foodstuffs, of wood products, leather, construction materials, and paper. She produces 39 per cent of her requirements of metallurgical products and machinery, and 28 per cent of her consumption of textile products. Her domestic production also falls short of her consumption requirements of such commodities as chemical products, glass, and ceramic products.

Flour milling and wood-sawing are the largest single branches of industrial production. Both of these branches have an opportunity for increasing their output and consequently augmenting the country's exports.

IV. BANKING AND CREDIT SITUATION

Greater Rumania, immediately upon the creation of the new country after the war, faced an exceedingly difficult situation in the domain of banking and credit. The old Kingdom was never in a very strong financial position, since the war found it in what were really the initial stages of economic development. The devastation of the war almost destroyed whatever liquid capital resources the country did possess. Yet following the war, Rumania's financial center, Bucharest, found itself compelled to take over the task of satisfying the financial requirements of the newly added territories, which had formerly looked for their financing to the centers of Austria, Hungary, and Russia.

The banks play a dominant rôle in the economic life of Rumania. In this respect, Rumania is in the same situation as all the other countries of central Europe. Her industries are almost entirely "an edifice created by the banks." [13] Her agriculture is also largely dependent on banking credit for its requirements of capital.

The banking resources of Rumania have shown a considerable expansion during the last few years. Between 1919 and 1925 the total number of banks increased from 488 to 928. Between 1923 and 1926 the total volume of bills discounted increased from 8,310 million lei to 15,443 millions; deposits expanded from 8,219 millions to 16,776 millions; and the paid-up capital and surplus of the banks increased from 5,593 millions to 8,414 millions.[14]

Most of the 928 banks operating in Rumania are small. The principal rôle in the banking organization of the country is played by twelve large banks, eleven of which are located in Bucharest. In 1925, these twelve banks had 24.2 per cent of the aggregate paid up capital and 50.3 per cent of the aggregate surplus of all banks in the country. Eight of the twelve banks are controlled by Rumanians, although foreign capital is invested in some of them; three are owned in part by Rumanians and in part

[13] Raducanu, I., "The Financing of Rumanian Industry," *Manchester Guardian Commercial,* May 26, 1927.

[14] The figures given here are from Sitescu, P. M., "A Survey of the Banking Situation (in Rumania)," *Manchester Guardian Commercial,* May 26, 1927, and from *Les Forces économiques de la Roumanie.*

by foreigners, and one is owned entirely by foreigners.[15]

The National Bank plays a very important part in the banking situation. A considerable part of the resources at the disposal of the banks has been obtained by means of advances made to them by the National Bank. In 1923 the total deposits in the banks were smaller than the borrowed funds. By 1925 the deposits doubled in amount, but the borrowed funds also increased substantially.

The operating capital resources of Rumania are very meager. Both industry and agriculture have to be financed very largely by means of banking credit, which, in the case of industrial enterprises, constitutes a much larger amount than their own resources.

In 1925 the paid-up capital and the reserves of the industrial companies in Rumania aggregated 19.4 billion lei. The borrowed capital was 29.7 billions.[16] And even with such preponderance of borrowed funds the liquid capital resources of the Rumanian industries are thoroughly insufficient for their needs.

[15] According to M. Sitescu, article cited above, the Marmorosch Blank Bank is owned by Rumanians to the extent of 78.6 per cent, the remainder being almost exclusively in French hands; the Credit Bank of Rumania is owned by the Rumanians to the extent of about one-half, the remaining shares being in the hands of French and Austrian banks; the Commercial Bank of Rumania is similarly owned by Rumanians to the extent of one-half, with the remaining shares in the hands of French and Belgian banks; the Banca Commerciale Italiana is owned by Italian capital. There is British capital invested in the Banca Romaneasca.

[16] Raducanu, I., article cited above.

The situation in agriculture is even worse. Before the war, the large estates in the old Kingdom alone (which constituted about one-half of the total landed property) carried a mortgage debt of about 600 million gold lei, which had been utilized for agricultural improvement. In 1925 all of the agricultural properties in Greater Rumania carried a mortgage debt of only 4.25 billion paper lei, or a little over 100 million gold lei. Of this amount about 3 billion lei were provided not out of savings, but by means of re-discounts with the Rumanian National Bank.[17]

Rumania's requirements of operating capital are greater today than they were before the war, yet the accumulation of capital is much smaller. In 1913 for the Old Kingdom alone the savings and banking deposits were 39 gold lei per capita. In 1925 for Greater Rumania they were only the equivalent of 25 gold lei.[18]

One of the consequences of this shortage of capital is the high cost of credit. The rate of interest on first-class commercial paper varies between 18 and 22 per cent. On other paper, the rates range from 24 to 30 per cent. To some extent these high rates of interest are, undoubtedly, due to the policy of large profits pursued by the banks. The interest paid on deposits is from 7 to 9 per cent, which

[17] Stoicescu, C., "Opportunities for the Foreign Investor in Rumania," *Manchester Guardian Commercial,* May 26, 1927.

[18] Netta, G., "Le Problème de la petite épargne en Roumanie," *L'Economiste Roumain,* April 1, 1927.

leaves the banks a very large margin of profits.[19] But on the whole the high rates of interest are without any doubt principally attributable to shortage of liquid capital.

Rumania faces the alternative of a slow development with her own means or a more rapid development with the aid of foreign capital. Both views have adherents in the country, although the differences between the two groups is more largely political than economic. The shortage of operating capital in Rumania is so patent, that there is scarcely any difference of opinion as to the need of importing it from abroad, if such importation can be arranged. But there is wide divergence of opinion as to the terms on which foreign capital should enter the country.

The trend of Rumanian legislation with regard to foreign capital so far has been, on the whole, such as to discourage foreign investments. In the next chapter we shall describe the character of this legislation. And so far there has been very little influx of foreign capital into Rumania. Whether or not the situation in this regard is likely to change will depend on a number of factors.

It appears doubtful that Rumania will be able to achieve currency stability without the aid of foreign loans. Yet such stability looms up more and more as an indispensable condition of the country's economic progress and development. It is not im-

[19] Stoicescu, C., article cited above.

possible that in the process of securing stabilization loans, Rumania may modify largely her present attitude toward foreign capital in general.

But Rumania's own attitude toward the question of foreign capital is, naturally, only one element in the situation. Another element is whether or not her international financial position is such that she may safely arrange for foreign credits. The answer to this question depends upon her ability to expand her international income sufficiently to give her the necessary excess of income over outgo to meet the outlays required in the repayment of such credits.

CHAPTER XXIV

RUMANIA'S ECONOMIC POLICY

THE economic policy of Greater Rumania has been an outgrowth of the policy pursued by the small pre-war Kingdom, which had suddenly doubled in size and population and acquired the character of a country endowed with large and varied natural resources. The spirit of nationalism which had wrested political independence from the hands of the Ottoman Empire, persisted through the three and a half decades of Rumania's pre-war existence as a nation. The creation of Greater Rumania intensified this spirit, and the fear of a possible loss of the newly acquired territories to their pre-war overlords has served to keep it at a high pitch.

This spirit of nationalism has been a determining factor in the country's economic policy. It has led Rumania into the path of an uncompromising assertion of economic sovereignty and has imbued her with a fear of foreign economic colonization. All this, in connection with very real economic factors within the country, has shaped the economic policy of Rumania along the lines of pronounced economic nationalism.

I. LINES OF ECONOMIC DEVELOPMENT

Rumania is an overwhelmingly agricultural country. No less than 82 per cent of the total population is rural, and only about 18 per cent is urban.[1] This vast preponderance of rural population, when taken in conjunction with the agricultural resources of the country, has presented for Rumania a problem of first-rate importance. It rendered imperative the radical changes in the system of land holding, introduced by the agrarian reform. It is a factor of great significance in the country's trend toward industrialization, which has been induced both by the existence of large reservoirs of raw materials and fuel and by the desire for a more varied economic development.

The population problem, coupled with the existence of natural resources, indicates for Rumania a policy of industrialization. Judged by the standards of western and central Europe, Rumania is not, in any sense, overpopulated. But taken in relation to her agricultural resources, her rural population is undoubtedly too large. We have already seen that plowlands occupy in Rumania only 42 per cent of the total area of the country. This gives her a very small acreage of arable land per capita of the rural

[1] According to *Osteuropäisches Jahrbuch* for 1923-24, p. 308, the percentage of rural population in the various divisions of Greater Rumania is as follows: the old Kingdom, 82 per cent; Transylvania, 80 per cent; Bukowina, 77 per cent; Bessarabia, 17.5 per cent. For the whole country this works out at approximately 82 per cent.

population—considerably smaller than, for example, in Hungary.

Before the introduction of the agrarian reform, a large part of the peasantry, which constitutes the bulk of the population had no land at all, while the land holdings of the remainder were very small. The reform has improved somewhat the condition of the rural population so far as land holdings are concerned, but it has not solved the problem. In the process of parcelling out the expropriated lands, it was found impossible either to provide land for all the peasants, or even to supply those peasants who have land with fairly large holdings. As a matter of fact, it is estimated that more than half of the rural population today has no land at all, while the remainder have, on the average, very small holdings.[2]

The fact that over half of the peasants in Rumania have no land is a factor of cardinal importance in the economic situation of the country. Prior to the agrarian reform, the large estates provided employment for the bulk of this landless peasantry. At the present time, with only a small part of their number provided with land and with the opportunities of agricultural employment very much diminished because of the disappearance of the estates, nothing but industrial development can provide them with a means of livelihood. And it is

[2] Constantinesco, M., *L'Evolution de la propriété rurale*, etc., pp. 455-60; Evans, I. L., *The Agrarian Revolution in Rumania*, pp. 121-3.

toward industrial development that the country has been tending more and more.

There is one peculiar aspect of the Rumanian industrial situation, and that is that the government is the owner of all the subsoil wealth of the country and of an important part of the existing industrial equipment. This fact has had an important bearing on the manner in which the economic policy of Rumania has developed.

The principal emphasis in the Rumanian economic policy has been in the direction of industrialization through government action. This has found expression in extensive legislation dealing with economic matters and in various measures undertaken by the government.

Under the Rumanian constitution, adopted on March 28, 1923, all subsoil resources are national property. The introduction of this provision into the constitution which provided the legal basis for the unification of the territories comprising Greater Rumania, put an end to the confusion existing prior to that with regard to mining rights and property, which were regulated by more than 15 special laws and decrees in force in various parts of the country. The constitutional provision regarding the nationalization of the mines was given effect by means of a special mining law, which was passed by the Rumanian parliament and was promulgated by the royal decree of July 3, 1924.

The mining law prescribed the manner in which

the Rumanian government intends to exploit the nationalized mining resources of the country. In working out the principles which underlie the provisions of this law, the Rumanian government rejected the system of direct government operation, as well as that of concessions. It adopted the principle of joint public and private exploitation of the mines. The form of organization is to be a corporation, in which the Rumanian government, as well as Rumanian and foreign private capital may participate, in such a way, however, that the majority of shares should always be in the hands of the government and of Rumanian owners. Similarly the majority of the administrative and directing personnel must consist of Rumanian subjects, rather than of foreigners. Provisions are made in the law for the existing vested interests, especially foreign, in the exploitation of mining resources.[3]

Simultaneously with the mining law, three other laws of an economic character were promulgated by the Rumanian government. Two of these laws dealt with the question of sources of energy, and the third was devoted to the problem of the commercialization of state-owned enterprises. By means of this legislation, the Rumanian government is attempting ao coordinate the utilization of the various sources of energy—petroleum, coal, gas, wood, and water power—for the purposes of the general economic

[3] For the text of the law see Rumanian Ministry of Industry and Commerce, *Mining Law,* Bucharest, 1924, or *L'Economiste Roumain,* Nos. 2-6 for 1924.

development of the country, especially in the domain of industry. At the same time, it attempts to place on a commercial basis the various state domains and government-owned enterprises.[4]

The Rumanian government owns nearly all the railways of the country,[5] the system of posts, telegraphs and telephones, and the seven monopolies, enumerated on page 405. In addition to this, it owns five-sixths of the timberlands; most of the fisheries; several mines; some of the largest metallurgical works; two river and maritime shipping companies; docks at the ports of Braila, Galatz, and Constanza; and several important health resorts.[6] All these domains and enterprises are now operated directly by the government.

Under the law for their commercialization, these properties are to be divided into two groups. The railways, posts, telegraphs, telephones, and the fiscal monopolies are to continue to be directly operated by the government. They are, however, to be reorganized on commercial lines and gradually taken out of the general budget of the state.[7] As for the remaining properties, they are to be reorganized in the form of corporations, along the same lines and with the same provisions as to domestic and foreign

[4] For the text of these laws see *L'Economiste Roumain,* Nos. 2-6 for 1924.

[5] There are still some privately owned lines in Transylvania.

[6] *Rumania's Prospective Development within the Scope of the New Economic Laws,* memorandum issued by the Rumanian government in New York in 1925.

[7] This was done in the case of the railways in 1926.

ownership and administration as the mining properties. The laws of 1924 also provide a basis for the organization of similar mixed companies for the exploitation of other government properties, the utilization of which has not as yet been undertaken.

In addition to this intensification of exploitation of government-owned industrial enterprises, the Rumanian government has also taken measures for the stimulation of privately-owned industry. Rumania has a protective tariff policy, of which we shall speak later on. In addition to that she has had on her statute books for a long time legislation providing for the fostering of industries, and has made special provisions for industrial credit facilities.

The first legislation for the fostering of industries was passed in 1912 in the old Kingdom. It was modified in 1919, and in 1921 was extended to the whole of Greater Rumania. Under this legislation, protected industries are permitted to purchase public-owned lands at reduced prices, are exempt from customs duties on imported basic machinery, and are allowed reductions in the transportation tax. In exchange for this they are obligated, during the initial period of protection (from 7 to 10 years), to employ only Rumanian subjects up to not less than 75 per cent of their personnel.[8]

Finally, in order to facilitate the financing of industrial development, the Rumanian government has created, under the law of June 23, 1923, a "Na-

[8] *Les Forces économiques de la Roumanie*, p. 84.

tional Industrial Credit Association." The purpose of this institution is to grant credit to manufacturers, to facilitate commercial credits, and to encourage industrial progress in general. The government owns 20 per cent of its stock, and the National Bank, 30 per cent. The remaining 50 per cent of the stock is in the hands of private investors.[9]

The measures taken for the stimulation of agriculture have not been as extensive as those in the domain of industry. The profound disturbance created in Rumanian agriculture by the agrarian reform rendered it difficult to do anything effective until the new situation had become more or less adjusted to its new forms. In spite of this, attempts were made by the Rumanian government to direct to some extent the course of rural development, although it was not until recently that there has been a growth of emphasis on the problem of agricultural production.

One of the immediate consequences of the agrarian reform was a profound change in the character of the crops. Under the system of large estates, wheat was the most important crop both from the point of view of production and of exports. After the passing of the land into the hands of the peasants, barley and oats, as fodder foods for livestock, became more important. For example, in 1922-23, the area sown to wheat in the Old Kingdom was only 59 per cent of the pre-war, while that sown to

[9] *Rumania's Prospective Development,* etc., pp. 12-13.

barley was 168 per cent and that sown to oats, 165 per cent.[10]

In its anxiety to restore the production of wheat for the sake of the export trade, the Rumanian government attempted to regulate the situation by making it obligatory for the peasants to follow, in the distribution of crops, a plan prescribed annually by the Ministry of Agriculture. A system of district committees was created for the purpose of assisting the Ministry in the working out of the plan. These committees, appointed by the Ministry, were also charged with the duty of supervising the carrying into effect of the provisions of the plan.

The system of the district committees did not bring the desired results, and in 1925 a new scheme was put into operation. This scheme involved the creation of agricultural chambers, representing the agriculturalists themselves, to act in an advisory capacity to the Ministry in the formulation of the annual plan and to stimulate production. The chambers took over such important functions of the district committees as the distribution of government-provided seed and breeding cattle. In order to increase their prestige, the chambers were given representation in the national legislature.

The work of the chambers has proved to be more effective than that of the district committees. As we saw on page 417, the trend of the Rumanian agriculture is now in the direction of increasing the

[10] Evans, I. L., *The Agrarian Revolution in Rumania*, p. 164.

wheat acreage, rather than that of the fodder crops.

There is a strong current of opinion in Rumania which believes that the general emphasis of Rumanian economic policy has been too much in the direction of industrial development and too little in the direction of agriculture. It is urged, for example, that agriculture should be afforded credit facilities at least comparable to those provided for industry, and that more government assistance should be given than hitherto to the work of agricultural education, the creation of experimental stations, and similar activities.[11]

The problem of transportation presents a serious difficulty for the economic development of Rumania. In fact, the need of adequate transport facilities is most acute. This is true of railways, as well as of ports.

Greater Rumania inherited a thoroughly disorganized system of railways. This system comprised the railways of the old Kingdom, which were directed toward Bucharest and the Danubian ports; the lines in Transylvania directed toward Budapest, Vienna, and the Adriatic ports; and the lines of

[11] The principal spokesman for this group, M. Constantin Garoflid, in a speech delivered recently before the General Assembly of the Union of Agricultural Syndicates, said: "It is not normal that our country should have an institution for industrial credit, while agriculture is deprived of a financial institution at the hour of its greatest need for it." As Minister of Agriculture in the last Avarescu Cabinet, M. Garoflid made an attempt to establish such an institution, but did not have an opportunity for putting his plan into effect. He did, however, establish an Institute for Agronomic Research. See *L'Economiste Roumain,* May, 1926, and June 1, 1927.

Bessarabia, directed toward Kiev and Odessa. These were distinct systems, with scarcely any connecting lines. They were in very bad working order, because of the war. This was especially true of the old Kingdom, which in 1919 had but 150 locomotives in complete repair.[12] The country faced at the very beginning the task of repairing the track, of rebuilding bridges and stations, of constructing connecting lines, of relaying the tracks in Bessarabia which, as a part of the Russian system, were of a wider gauge than the railroads of the rest of Europe, of repairing and replacing the rolling stock.

An immense amount of work has been done for the reorganization of the railway system. By 1925 the daily number of trains dispatched daily on the Rumanian railways was over 1,500. Most of the Bessarabian trackage was relaid. Work was begun on four connecting lines in Transylvania and Bukowina and one in Bessarabia. The means for this work of reconstruction were provided out of the budget.

At the present time the Rumanian railway system consists of about 12,000 kilometers of track. But nearly all of this mileage is single-track. The traffic borne over these lines is barely sufficient to satisfy the present requirements. The carrying capacity of the system provides no basis whatever for any expansion of economic activity.

Similarly with regard to port facilities, which are

[12] *Rumania's Prospective Development,* etc., p. 11.

essential for the export trade, Rumania's present equipment is thoroughly inadequate. A great deal of new construction is necessary in order to provide the ports with adequate warehouses, docks, etc.

II. TARIFF POLICY AND COMMERCIAL TREATY ARRANGEMENTS

In her commercial policy, Greater Rumania has followed, from the very beginning, a system of far-reaching government regulation of foreign trade. Not unlike Hungary and Czechoslovakia, Rumania has been inclined to regard her export and import trade largely from the point of view of the monetary problems confronting the country, and to some extent from that of considerations concerned with the internal cost of living. Starting with the complete government reglementations of foreign trade during 1919, and on through the various stages of export and import regulation, the foreign trade of Roumania has been developing in these abnormal conditions.

The export trade was placed under rigid government control immediately after the end of the war. As early as January, 1919, regulations were issued prohibiting all exports, with the exception of petroleum and wood products. The exportation of these products could be carried on only under government licenses and on the following conditions: (1) that the proceeds in foreign currencies be turned over to the government in exchange for the equivalent amount of paper lei; (2) that an export duty of

20 per cent and a commission of 2 per cent be paid to the government on all exports. These conditions applied only to the old Kingdom; in the new territories other prohibitive and restrictive regulations were in force.

In 1920 a system was created to cover the whole country. Under this system, no goods were permitted to leave the country without the permission of the Ministry of Industry and Commerce. The export duties were fixed by a special Export Commission. The government retained its right to share in the profits of the export trade, although in practice this right was exercised only in the case of petroleum products. By the law of November 27, 1920, the Cabinet was empowered to make from time to time the necessary regulations as to the categories of goods which could be exported.

Under this system all exports were divided into four groups: (1) products the exportation of which was entirely forbidden; (2) products which could be exported on the basis of "compensation" arrangements made by the Rumanian government with other governments; (3) products for which special licenses were required; (4) products which could be exported freely upon payment of the export duty.

This intricate system remained in full force until the middle of 1922 when the government began to relinquish its control. By 1923 the license system was almost completely given up, and the Export Commission was abolished. The export duties have, however, remained, although they have been gradually reduced. The law of November 27, 1920, is still in force, but it is applied only in case of real necessity.[13]

There were several reasons for the introduction of export regulations and export duties. The restriction of exports facilitated the process of directing the trade of the territories acquired from Austria, Hungary, and Russia away from their former markets and into the domestic market of Greater Rumania. Moreover, because of the economic exhaustion resulting from the war, the retention within the country of goods which otherwise would have been sold abroad helped to keep down domestic prices and prevented the cost of living from rising too rapidly. Export taxes also operated in the same direction, besides providing for the government an important source of fiscal revenue. Since they have been from the start payable in gold or foreign currency, these export duties have had the special significance of supplying the government with the means of making foreign debt payments. As a matter of fact, when the short-term debts of the Rumanian government were consolidated in 1922, the annuities were guaranteed by the proceeds of export duties.[14]

[13] "Le Régime de l'exportation en Roumanie après la guerre," *L'Economiste Roumain*, October 15, 1927.
[14] Gheorghiu, D. I., "The Tariff Policy of Rumania," *Manchester Guardian Commercial: Reconstruction in Europe Series*, July 27, 1922.

But while the export duties were of advantage to the Rumanian government, they also worked to a disadvantage by retarding the economic recovery of the country. We have already seen what effect they had on the development of agriculture. As a result, Rumania has been moving gradually toward their complete suppression, which, however, is complicated by the fact that they serve as a guarantee for the consolidated loan of 1922.

The regulation of the import trade has not been nearly as far-reaching as that of the export trade. As a matter of fact, during the period immediately following the war there was such a dearth of supplies in the country, that very little was done to restrict the import trade. The result of this was that the volume of imports during the years 1919-21 was much larger, when reckoned in gold values, than during the three years following.[15] The large unfavorable balances of trade during these three years were the consequence of very large imports, as well as of very small exports.

The tariff began to be utilized early as the principal means of regulating the imports. During the

[15] According to Iliescu, L., "The Distribution of External Trade," *Manchester Guardian Commercial*, May 26, 1927, the Rumanian imports in gold lei (official paper lei figures, converted into gold at the average rate of exchange) have been as follows:

1919	830
1920	696
1921	782
1922	447
1923	495
1924	673

year 1919 and the first few months of 1920 the Rumanian tariff of 1906 remained in force, with the original rates of duty. These rates were increased five-fold in May, 1920, because of the depreciation of the currency. In October, 1920, the Rumanian Parliament passed an important law, whereby the government was authorized to make changes in the existing tariff rates merely by royal decree. In this matter tariff policy was taken largely out of the hands of parliament and became an instrument in the hands of the executive branch of government for regulating the import trade.

In 1921, frightened by the large adverse trade balances, the Rumanian government introduced important changes in the tariff system. Many duties were greatly increased, and provisions were made for curtailing the importation of superfluous goods and articles of luxury. A list of import prohibitions was prepared and put into effect. Payments of duty in gold, rather than in paper currency began to be required in the case of articles of luxury.[16]

On August 1, 1924, a new tariff went into effect. It introduced many important modifications into the existing tariff, the most important of which were the general raising of customs duties and the provision that thenceforth all duties were to be payable in gold. Under this tariff, the relation between gold and paper lei was to be fixed by the Council of

[16] Halchiopol, G., "La Législation douanière de la Roumanie," *L'Economiste Roumain*, September, 1926. See also Gheorghiu, D. I., "The Tariff Policy of Rumania," cited above.

Ministers. The 1924 tariff remained in force until April 1, 1926, when new increases were made in several groups of customs duties. Still further increases were made in 1927.

In her tariff policy Greater Rumania has followed the old Kingdom's policy of protection. The protection of industries by means of the tariff began in Rumania as early as 1874, although it was not until the tariff of 1906 that the country had really adopted an effective protectionist system. Under this system, which was carried into the post-war period, lower duties were levied on machinery necessary for factory installations and on raw materials than on finished products.

The tariff of 1924 gave the Rumanian industries a higher degree of protection than they had enjoyed before the war. This protection, especially in the case of the textile and the metallurgical industries, was very greatly increased by the tariff of 1926, and raised still more by the tariff of 1927. In connection with the promulgation of the 1927 tariff, the Rumanian government issued an explanatory memorandum, in which it was announced that in fixing the new rates, the Tariff Commission was guided by the following principles:

(1) An import duty of from 1 to 10 per cent of the value of raw materials imported for industrial use, the duty varying from 1 to 10 per cent according to the necessity for the product.

(2) An import duty of from 10 to 20 per cent of the

value of partly manufactured goods imported for completion in Roumania. This includes tools and accessories needed for industrial purposes.

(3) An import duty of from 20 to 30 per cent of the value of manufactured articles, edible products, etc., ready for immediate use or consumption.

(4) An import duty in excess of 30 per cent of the value of the article has been applied only in exceptional cases—that is, to offset the removal of the luxury surtaxes or to afford the maximum amount of protection to industries the prosperity of which is essential to the peace and prosperity of the country.[17]

Under her present tariff system Rumania has the highest protective system of any of the Danubian countries. The group of commodities which has the largest degree of protection is the textiles, for which the customs duty is equal to almost three times the import price. Paper products bear a duty of 49.6 per cent; glass and glassware, 46.8 per cent; iron and iron products, 39.6 per cent. Altogether, because of the very high duty on textiles, the Rumanian imports bear a customs duty equal to 98.4 per cent.[18] All these are maximum duties.

Greater Rumania has not concluded as yet a single tariff treaty. In April, 1921, the Rumanian government denounced all pre-war commercial treaties and conventions, and consistently refused up to 1927 to engage in negotiations for the conclusion of tariff

[17] *Manchester Guardian Commercial,* May 26, 1927.
[18] *Zollhöhe und Warenwerte,* Table I.

treaties. The farthest it would go in this direction has been the negotiation of provisional arrangements and conventions, usually based simply on the most-favored-nation treatment principle. Under its tariffs of 1924 and 1927, nations according Rumania such treatment received in exchange the benefits of the minimum tariff; all other nations were compelled to submit to the maximum tariff.

By the beginning of 1927 Rumania had concluded provisional arrangements with sixteen European nations and with the United States. It is interesting that of her six immediate neighbors she had most-favored-nation relations only with Poland and Czechoslovakia (since 1921) and with Hungary (since 1925). Her commercial relations with Yugoslavia, Bulgaria and Russia were not regulated by any agreement or convention.[19]

In connection with the promulgation of the 1927 tariff, an important change took place in the commercial treaty policy of the Rumanian government. A note was addressed to all countries, with the exception of Russia, inviting them to enter into negotiations with Rumania for the purpose of concluding commercial treaties based on the new tariff, in which the difference between the minimum and the maximum rates was fixed in such a way that the latter are 50 per cent higher than the former. The period during which such negotiations were to be inaugu-

[19] For a list of Rumania's trade agreements see Humphreys, R. J. E., *Report on Economic Conditions in Rumania*, 1927, Appendix IV.

rated was to expire on July 1, 1927, on which date all existing agreements and conventions were to expire.[20]

The Avarescu government, which was responsible for the passage of the 1927 tariff, fell soon after the tariff went into effect, and the governments which succeeded it have expressed a determination to modify this tariff. A commission is now at work preparing a new draft. And since new commercial treaties have to be based on a definitive tariff, their negotiation has been postponed until the work of tariff revision is completed.[21]

There is a general feeling in Rumania that neither a definitive tariff, nor a system of long-term tariff treaties is possible until the currency of the country is placed on a thoroughly stable basis. As an important Rumanian publication puts it, "first a sound money system, and then a definitive tariff." [22]

III. ATTITUDE TOWARD THE QUESTION OF A LARGER ECONOMIC TERRITORY

It is clear from the foregoing discussion that Rumania's principal preoccupation in the domain of economic policy has been along the lines of internal development. The existence within her boundaries of rich natural resources and of a large available

[20] See Tranco-Iaşi, G., and Stoe, G., *La Roumanie en travail*, Bucharest, 1917, pp. 24-27, and *L'Economiste Roumain*, April 15, 1927.

[21] *L'Economiste Roumain*, July 1, 1927, and *The Economist*, London, August 13, 1927.

[22] *Les Forces économiques de la Roumanie*, p. 96.

labor force provides her with a basis for a fairly extensive and varied scope of economic activity. In spite of the difficulties which she encounters because of a paucity of financial resources, Rumania is nevertheless determinedly directing her policy toward this aim.

The characteristic feature of Rumania's economic policy is its intense nationalism. This aspect of her situation is most sharply demonstrated by her attitude toward foreign capital, but it also colors and determines other phases of Rumania's activities and policy.

The economic legislation of 1924, which we described in an earlier part of this chapter, was the expression of the view that foreign capital must not be permitted to acquire a dominant position in the economic life of Rumania. In accordance with this view, the controlling ownership and management of enterprises in which foreign capital is invested must be in the hands of Rumanian nationals. Article 33 of the mining law gives an excellent picture of how this system is expected to work out in practice. The principal provisions of this article in this respect are as follows:

(a) Shares to be of a nominal value not exceeding 500 lei and to be registered, transfers other than between Rumanian citizens to require the authorisation of the board of directors.

(d) Capital belonging to Rumanian citizens to be at least 60 per cent of the whole. An exception is allowed in favor of existing mining enterprises, which are given ten years from the date of promulgation of the law to acquire national character; in these cases the limit of national capital is reduced to 55 per cent.

(e) Two-thirds of the board of directors, the managing committee, and the auditors, as well as the chairman to be Rumanians.

It is readily recognized that the influx of foreign capital into Rumania on these terms cannot be as large as it might have been under a régime of complete equality between foreign and domestic capital, and that consequently the country's economic development must necessarily be slower than if foreign capital were permitted complete freedom of action. Nevertheless, the proponents of this view maintain that Rumania's national interests would be served best if the evil of slow development be preferred to that of a possible domination by foreign capital.

There exists in Rumania also the view that this choice of evils is injurious, rather than beneficial, to Rumania, that the danger of a possible acquisition by foreign capital of a dominant position in the economic life of the country is exaggerated, while the injurious effects of slow developments are underemphasized. For the time being, however, the first view has much more powerful support than the second. And while it is not impossible that the uncompromising attitude toward the question which has predominated so far may become moderated, its essential influence on the economic policy of the country is likely to remain strong for some time to come.[23]

In this connection it is important also to bear in mind that the extraordinary efforts made by Rumania to keep the management of economic activity under national control is, in part at least, dictated by the fear of Hungarian penetration in Transylvania. The policy of "nostrification" there has by no means lost its virulence with the passage of time. And on the question concerned with the fear of Hungarian penetration there is scarcely any dissension of opinion among the various groups in Rumania.

Rumania's whole position with regard to foreign capital is excellently summed up in a speech by a prominent Rumanian statesman,[24] in which he said:

> Our policy does not exclude the participation of foreign capital in our economic life, because we are fully conscious of the fact that a country like ours, without any great accumulation of capital, cannot, with its own means, develop the large natural wealth, which exists above and below our soil.

But at the same time, the form in which foreign capital should enter the country is not, by any means, a matter of indifference:

[23] For a discussion of the existing legislative provisions with regard to foreign capital see Dascovici, D. N., "Restrictions on the Use of Foreign Capital in Rumania: a Legal Examination," *Manchester Guardian Commercial*, May 26, 1927.

[24] I. G. Duca, former Minister of Foreign Affairs, before the Rumanian Economic Institute. See *L'Economiste Roumain*, June 1, 1927.

Foreign capital cannot be truly beneficial to our national economy, unless it enters the country, not for the purpose of draining our economic resources, but for the purpose of collaborating with Rumanian initiative, labor, and capital.

In her trade relations with other nations Rumania considers that her interests are amply served by favorable commercial treaties. Neither the commodity composition, nor the geographical distribution of her export trade indicate the need for her of a more intimate economic intercourse with her neighbors than that provided by treaty relations. And even in her negotiations for such treaties she has so far shown a great deal of independence of action, refusing to make anything approaching permanent arrangements until she succeeds in placing her internal economic and currency situation on a more stable basis than hitherto.

Rumania is very fortunately situated so far as the bases of her commercial policy are concerned. Her principal exports—cereals, livestock, petroleum, and timber—are products in which there is not nearly as much competition in the world markets as there is in such products as textiles and metal goods, which constitute her principal imports. With the exception of cereals and their derivatives, she really encounters no difficulty in disposing of her exports. As for cereals, she is in a position to increase her markets by granting privileges for the importation into her market of the highly competitive products which constitute the bulk of her purchases abroad.

Rumania is now entering upon a period during which she expects to place her commercial relations on a treaty basis. In the course of the negotiations which will be involved, she expects to make concessions and to receive them. But she envisages neither a desire nor a necessity to go beyond that.

From Rumania's point of view there is no reason for the creation of a Danubian economic union. She sees no advantage that would accrue to herself from the consummation of such a union, but a good many disadvantages. Politically, her objections are very much similar to those offered by Czechoslovakia, namely, the incompatibility of any such arrangements with national sovereignty. Economically, the other Danubian countries offer very little opportunity for increase of markets so far as her agricultural exports are concerned. She looks for her enlarged markets in the countries of northern and western Europe, rather than in the nations which are her Danubian neighbors. At the same time, she hopes for an expansion of her trade with the Near East.

The problem of Austro-German union is economically remote so far as Rumania is concerned. Politically, this question concerns her much more closely, since it involves an important change in the situation established by the treaties of peace. On this ground, she might be inclined to oppose it. But economically, she has no fear of Germany and might, like Hungary, even welcome the expansion of Germany to the middle reaches of the Danube. Her trade with Germany has been on the increase, and she has lately even begun to look to the German money market for financial assistance. In Germany she has a distinct possibility for enlarged exports of foodstuffs to take the place of a part of that country's imports from overseas. But since these advantages might almost as easily be obtained simply by means of commercial treaties, the whole problem does not present to her any immediate and serious concern.

PART VI

YUGOSLAVIA'S EXPERIENCE SINCE THE WAR

CHAPTER XXV

THE PROBLEMS OF THE SERB-CROAT-SLOVENE KINGDOM

YUGOSLAVIA, or the Kingdom of the Serbs, Croats, and Slovenes, has been faced with a situation similar to that which has confronted Rumania, although some of her problems have been even more complicated. Here, too, the state which came into existence after the war was legally the expansion of a small pre-war Kingdom, but whereas the pre-war Kingdom of Rumania became from the start the dominant factor in Greater Rumania, Serbia found her position in this respect challenged by some of the other territories incorporated in the triune Kingdom. At the same time the economic organization of Yugoslavia is substantially different from that of pre-war Serbia.

The triple name of the Kingdom of the southern Slavs reflects the fact that each of the three main groups comprising it considers itself an entity. While the Serbians, Croatians, and Slovenes come of the same racial stock and use practically the same language, each group had its own development prior to the war. When they united to form a single country, the question came to the fore as to whether they should be organized as a federated or a unitary state. The Serbians were in favor of a unitary state with a strongly centralized government; the Croatians and the Slovenes stood for a federal system and territorial autonomy. The matter remained unsettled for nearly three years, until, on June 28, 1921, the National Assembly adopted a constitution, which settled the question. Yugoslavia became a triune Kingdom under the rule of the Serbian dynasty, but provisions were made for a certain amount of administrative decentralization.

But while the adoption of the constitution disposed of the question formally, in reality it still remained, especially since the constitutional provisions regarding administrative decentralization were being put into effect very slowly. It assumed its most acute form in Croatia, where a peasant movement, led by Stepan Radič, kept it alive for several years. Not until 1925 did the Croatian opposition subside sufficiently for its leader to become a member of the government at Belgrade, thus removing, for the time being, the most formidable element of internal political dissension.

This aspect of the internal situation served to aggravate the problem of organizing the administration of the country. Even apart from this, the task of creating an administrative system to take the place of that maintained formerly by the governments of Austria and Hungary was formidable enough in itself. It has been a difficult and costly process, many phases of which still await final regularization.

In her external relations, Yugoslavia has had important controversies with three of her neighbors, namely, Bulgaria, Italy, and Greece. The center of

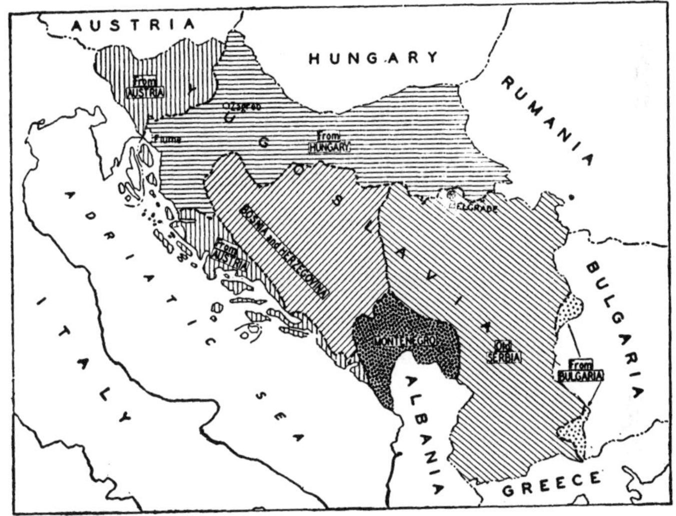

PRE-WAR SOVEREIGNTY OF LANDS COMPRISING YUGOSLAVIA

her differences with Bulgaria has been the Macedonian question, which antedates the World War. The pacification and regularization of the Macedonian situation has cost the Yugoslav government a great deal of effort.[1]

[1] See Ancel, J., *Les Balkans face a l'Italie,* Paris, 1928, Chapter IV.

Apart from the Bulgarian question, Yugoslavia's principal difficulties in the realm of international relations have been with Italy. The two countries came to a clash at the peace conference in Paris over the disposition of the port of Fiume, which was claimed by both. The D'Annunzio raid placed the port in the physical possession of Italy, and it has remained there ever since. The controversy was finally terminated by the conclusion of an agreement between Italy and Yugoslavia in January, 1924, whereby Yugoslavia recognized Italy's claim to the port, while Italy handed over to Yugoslavia the port of Sušak, which lies across the river from that of Fiume and was originally united with it.

Fiume has not been the only point at which Yugoslavia's interests have clashed with those of Italy. In addition to the former Hungarian port, Italy also laid claim to the Dalmatian littoral, although she eventually relinquished her claims to the whole coast, with the exception of the city of Zara, which is now in her possession. Equally sharp has been the controversy between the two countries over Albania, the strategic position of which at the mouth of the Adriatic Sea is a matter of vital importance to both Italy and Yugoslavia. This controversy has not as yet approached the point of amicable agreement.

Finally, Yugoslavia has had an important controversy with Greece over the port of Saloniki. The peace treaties assigned this port to Greece, but they made provisions for a Yugoslav free zone there. The establishment of this zone has been a matter of protracted negotiations and still awaits a definitive and mutually satisfactory solution.

In the realm of economic activity, Yugoslavia faced truly stupendous problems immediately after the creation of the new Kingdom. Serbia and Montenegro had been completely overrun during the war and were left after the cessation of hostilities in a condition of utter exhaustion and devastation. One of the first tasks of the Yugoslav government was the reestablishment of more or less normal economic life in these territories. At the same time the Yugoslav government faced the task of coordinating the economic life of all the heterogeneous territories that had united to form the triune Kingdom.

Serbia and Montenegro had before the war economic systems of their own. Slovenia and Dalmatia had been parts of the Austrian economic system. Croatia-Slavonia and the provinces which were organized into Voivodina had been parts of the economic life of Hungary. Bosnia and Herzegovina had been controlled jointly by Austria and Hungary. Communications, trade routes, and financial affiliations had to be reorganized and redirected, if the new Kingdom was to function economically as a unified state.

During the first eight years of her post-war existence (1919-26), Yugoslavia faced six major economic problems. These were: (1) the repair of the devastations caused by the war; (2) the establishment of a currency system and the stabilization of the currency; (3) the achievement of budgetary equilibrium; (4) the organization of production and trade; (5) the building of a banking system; and (6) the alleviation of the situation created by shortage of operating capital. The solution of these problems has been complicated by political difficulties, but during the eight years under review Yugoslavia has gone far toward their eventual solution.

CHAPTER XXVI

YUGOSLAVIA'S CURRENCY AND FISCAL SITUATION

THE process of rehabilitating and reorganizing the economic life of Yugoslavia placed a heavy burden on the currency and fiscal resources of the triune Kingdom. The government budget was at the beginning practically the only source from which means could be obtained for the reestablishment of the normal processes of life, disrupted by the war and by territorial readjustments. And the Treasury itself had to resort to new issues of paper money for the meeting of budgetary expenditures.

In its currency experience, Yugoslavia has passed through the stages of depreciation, appreciation, and stabilization. She has not, as yet, placed her currency on a definitely stable basis. In her budgetary experience, Yugoslavia has passed through a period of unbalanced budgets, which roughly coincided with that of currency depreciation, and a period of budgetary equilibrium. In both of these phases of her national life she is still facing many unsolved problems, the nature of which will be apparent from the discussion in this chapter.

I. CURRENCY UNIFICATION AND STABILIZATION

Yugoslavia inherited four currencies. The monetary unit in the territory of the Kingdom of Serbia was the dinar; in the territories formerly belonging to Austria and Hungary, the crown; in Montenegro, the perper; in the districts acquired from Bulgaria, the lev. The difficulty of unifying these currencies after the creation of the Kingdom of the Serbs, Croats, and Slovenes was complicated by the fact that during the war Serbia and Montenegro had been under complete occupation and administration of the enemy armies. In the course of this administration, the dinar and the perper were driven out of circulation, and the Austro-Hungarian crown was the currency in both of these countries, with the Bulgarian lev also circulating in the districts occupied by Bulgarian troops. It was only after the Serbian government returned to Belgrade at the end of the war that the dinar currency was reintroduced. Following the creation of the triune Kingdom, the dinar became the basis of the Yugoslav currency.

The establishment of a unified Yugoslav currency was accomplished by the introduction of the dinar throughout the new kingdom. This required a long and complicated process, in the course of which it was first necessary for Yugoslavia to separate the crowns circulating in her territory from the authority of the Austro-Hungarian Bank, and then to replace these crowns with newly printed dinars. The question of the valuation of the crowns for the purpose of exchange caused considerable difficulty.

The first action of the Yugoslav government was to divide the country into two zones, so far as the circulating medium was concerned. The Serbian dinar was declared legal tender in the territory lying southeast of the Save and the Drina rivers, while the crown was made legal tender in the territory lying northwest of these two rivers. All importation of crowns into Serbia proper was forbidden. In January, 1919, the Yugoslav government ordered the stamping of all crowns found in the country. An adhesive stamp, affixed to the bank notes and cancelled by means of a rubber stamp, was considered sufficient protection against forgery, but in practice a certain amount of falsification occurred. While about 7 billions of crowns were presented for stamping, the amount which was actually replaced by dinars was almost 8 billions.

The replacing of the stamped crowns with dinars was not decreed until the end of 1919. During the year the relation between the value of the crown and that of the dinar was changed three times. At first, 2.5 crowns were declared the equivalent of one dinar; later on, the value of the dinar was raised to 3 crowns, and soon after that, to 3.5 crowns. Finally, in connection with the replacement decree, the relation between the two currencies was definitely fixed at 4:1. Eight billion crowns thus became two billion dinars.[1] The perper currency was replaced at the rate of one dinar to one perper for persons who possessed sums under 5,000 perpers, and at the rate of two perpers to one dinar for persons with larger amounts.[2]

By the law of January, 1920, the Yugoslav government transformed the National Bank of Serbia into the National Bank of the Serb-Croat-Slovene Kingdom, and the notes of the new Bank, which replaced all other currencies, became the Yugoslav currency. When the operations for the introduction of the new currency began, the note issue of the Bank was 711 million dinars. By December 31, 1920, the amount of notes in circulation was 3,344 millions.

The exchange value of the dinar depreciated through the years 1919-23, but began to appreciate in 1924. The increase of circulation for the purpose of replacing the crowns which had no covering of any kind was partly responsible for this. But the depreciation was also the result of budgetary, trade, and political conditions.

Immediately after the war the exchange value of the dinar was almost at par, that is, a little over five to the dollar. By March, 1919, it was quoted at ten to the dollar, and by January, 1920, at 22. By the end of 1920 the exchange value of the dinar fell to

[1] Djermekow, D., "The Exchanges of Yugoslavia," *Manchester Guardian Commercial: Reconstruction in Europe Series,* p. 183.

[2] Nedeljkovič, M., "The Monetary System (of Yugoslavia)," *The Near East Year Book,* pp. 49-52.

34.[3] As we have already noted, the amount of currency in circulation during the year 1920 increased almost five-fold, and this sudden increase of unsecured paper money was, undoubtedly, the principal initial factor in the downward course of the dinar. However, although the amount of currency in circulation continued to increase after 1922, this fact was not always reflected in the course of the dinar exchange, as may be seen from the table below.[4]

CURRENCY CIRCULATION AND DINAR EXCHANGE, 1921-1925

Year	Total Circulation on December 31 in Millions of Dinars	Annual Average Value of Dollar in Dinars on Belgrade Bourse
1921	4,688	46.6
1922	5,040	75.7
1923	5,190	94.0
1924	6,002	76.7
1925	6,063	58.8

During the year 1922 the total circulation increased by only 7.5 per cent, but the exchange value of the dinar depreciated by almost 40 per cent. During the year 1923 there was a very slight increase of circulation, but the exchange value fell by almost one-third. In 1924 there was a marked increase in circulation, but a marked appreciation

[3] *The Near East Yearbook*, pp. 52-53.
[4] Figures from *The Near East Yearbook*, pp. 53 and 71.

of the exchange. By comparison with the end of 1922, the circulation at the end of 1924 was 20 per cent larger, but the average exchange rate during 1924 was almost the same as during 1922. In 1925 the circulation remained practically what it had been in 1924, but the exchange value of the dinar again appreciated very greatly.

As a general thing, therefore, there has been very little connection, after 1920, between the currency circulation and the rate of exchange. The rapid depreciation of the dinar during the years 1921, 1922, and 1923 was primarily the result of budgetary deficits, of an excess of imports over exports, and of political conditions. The government budget during this period was unbalanced, but while the deficits, as we shall see, were not very large, their mere presence reacted unfavorably on the condition of the exchange. The adverse trade balances operated even more powerfully in the same direction. The effects of these two factors were greatly magnified by the uncertain political situation of Yugoslavia, both internally and externally.

There seems little doubt that the exchange rate was over-depressed by the above factors. There was a very large spread between the purchasing power of the dinar at home and abroad. The rapidity with which the dinar began to appreciate in 1924, under the influence of the balancing of the budget, a marked improvement in the foreign trade situation, and a growing stabilization of political conditions, reflects this situation. As a matter of fact, during the year 1924 Yugoslavia witnessed the peculiar phenomenon of a simultaneous appreciation of the exchange and rise of domestic prices. It was only in 1925, following a still further appreciation of the dinar, that the prices and the exchange became adjusted to each other.[5]

The question of the legal stabilization of the dinar is still in abeyance. In fact, the dinar has been stable since 1925. And while there is little disagreement in Yugoslavia as to the need of placing the country's currency legally on a stable gold basis, there has been a marked difference of opinion on the question of whether or not legal stabilization should be undertaken at the present rate of exchange.

This question was especially acute in 1924 and 1925, during the period of appreciation. Confronted with the crisis incident upon the sudden change from depreciation to appreciation, the Yugoslav government adopted the policy of slow deflation. This policy was stated in the following terms by Dr. Milan Stojadinović, then Minister of Finance:

> Our aim must not be a rapid improvement of the dinar, but relative stabilization with a tendency to a further steady improvement of the rate of the dinar.

In pursuance of this policy, the government and the National Bank intervened periodically in the money

[5] See *Economic Yugoslavia,* Belgrade, 1927, Chart III, and *The Near East Year Book,* pp. 99-100.

market with the view of preventing excessive exchange fluctuations.

On the other hand, it was felt in many quarters, especially in some banking groups, that the appreciation of the dinar should be permitted to go on unchecked. This body of opinion maintained that a complete deflation of the currency to the pre-war parity was not only possible, but was greatly to be preferred to a definite stabilization at a lower gold value.[6]

The policy of stabilization has apparently prevailed. Starting with the second half of 1925, the exchange value of the dinar has been stable at about 56.5 to the dollar, that is, at approximately one-eleventh of the pre-war parity. The course pursued at the present time by the Yugoslav government and by the National Bank was summed up as follows by a former Yugoslav Minister of Finance: [7]

> We shall follow a monetary policy which will have for its tendency the maintenance of the dinar at its present exchange level, by preventing its fluctuation either above or below this level.

[6] For a discussion of the government policy see Dr. Stojadinović's speeches in Parliament, contained in the following pamphlets: *The Financial Position of The Kingdom of the Serbs, Croats, and Slovenes,* Belgrade, 1924, and *Expose Ministra Finansija,* Belgrade, 1925. For a defense of the deflation policy see Marković, V. T., *Deflaciona valutna politika,* Belgrade, 1925.

[7] Dr. Bogdan Marković in his *Exposé sur la situation financière et économique* (speech delivered in Parliament in the course the discussion of the budget for 1927-28), Belgrade, 1927.

It is believed that the present exchange rate of the dinar corresponds with the essential economic interests of the country, and the government takes the position that all possible measures should be taken to ensure its stability. These measures are to be directed toward the maintenance of fiscal stability and the establishment of a proper balance between the fiscal needs of the state and the economic and social interests of the country.

The National Bank has at the present time sufficient resources for maintaining currency stability. The Bank has a monopoly of note-issue, and is also charged with the duty of regulating the exchange rate of the dinar. It does this by means of its foreign bill policy, which enables it to have at its disposal sufficient means for preventing exchange fluctuations.

As a result of a convention concluded in July, 1921, between the National Bank and the Ministry of Finance, the Bank undertakes to purchase each year one-third of the foreign bills resulting from the country's export trade. Since the Bank acts as the state treasurer, a portion of these bills is used for government payments abroad. Another portion is sold in the money market, but the Bank always retains a supply of bills as its own reserve.

In order to facilitate its foreign bill operations, the National Bank has been empowered to issue paper currency for the purchase of such bills, without counting the amounts thus used as a part of the total authorized bank-note circulation. By an act of Parliament, article 20 of the Bank Law has been given the following interpretation:

> The bank notes issued for the purchase of foreign bills are not to be counted as a part of the total amount of bank notes which the Bank is authorized to issue, provided that such purchases are made for the account of the state.

In this manner the Bank is enabled to have at its disposal all the time the necessary amounts of dinars required for its intervention in the money market, whenever an appreciation of the exchange rate sets in. At the same time, by having in its hands a sufficient volume of foreign bills, the Bank is in a position through its sale of bills, to prevent a depreciation of the exchange.[8]

At the end of 1926, the National Bank had at its disposal a volume of foreign bills, amounting to 615 million dinars. A year before that, the amount was 805 millions. Thus during the year 1926, the Bank found it necessary to diminish its stocks of foreign bills by nearly 200 million dinars for the purpose of maintaining the stability of the exchange rate. As we shall find, this was necessitated by the exigencies of the balance of international accounts. The

[8] Hantos, E., *La Monnaie en Europe Centrale,* pp. 190-192. It is interesting to note that the practice with regard to bank-note issues for the purpose of purchasing foreign bills was adopted by France in 1926; by the act of Parliament, passed in August of that year, the Bank of France was authorized to exclude the bank notes issued for that purpose from the total amount of issue authorized by law.

officials of the Bank consider the volume of bills held at the present time adequate for the purposes of currency stability. In his report for the year 1926, the Governor of the Bank said:

> Experience up to date enables us to state that the stocks of bills held by the National Bank is quite sufficient to resist any attack on the dinar and to prevent speculation having the lowering of its value for its end.

A definite stabilization of the dinar will be difficult before the reserve resources of the Bank are strengthened. At the present time, these resources, while sufficient to enable the Bank to maintain a stable exchange rate, can scarcely be considered adequate for the establishment of a gold currency. As a matter of fact a large portion of the metal cover shown in the Bank statement is fictitious.

On December 31, 1926, the National Bank showed a total metal and foreign currency cover of 438.8 million gold dinars. Of this amount, however, actual gold represented only 86 millions, and silver amounted to 17.5 millions. The remainder, or 335.3 million dinars, was designated as "deposits abroad." But of this amount, 261.5 millions represented book credits in France, while the conversion of some of the other deposits in foreign currencies into gold dinars was made at too high a rate.[9] As a result,

[9] For example, in a detailed statement of the metal and foreign currency cover given on p. 41 of the *Report of the National Bank* for 1926, Austrian schillings, Belgian and French francs, Italian lire, and Czechoslovak crowns are shown as the equivalents of gold dinars. This is obviously incorrect.

the actual cover of the Yugoslav currency is scarcely over 150 million gold dinars, or between 1.6 and 1.7 billion paper dinars.

On the same date, the amount of bank notes in circulation was 5 billion dinars, and the sight liabilities of the Bank were approximately the same amount. Thus the reserve ratio was only 16-17 per cent.

The reserves of the Bank increased considerably in 1927, as a result of foreign loans. But these resources, like the stocks of foreign bills held by the Bank, are subject to fluctuations in the process of maintaining currency stability. It is therefore necessary for the Bank to assure for itself larger permanent cover reserves than it has at the present time, before Yugoslavia can proceed to a definite stabilization of the currency.

Another difficulty in placing the dinar on a permanently stable basis is the existence of a large government debt to the National Bank. On December 31, 1926, this debt amounted to 4.4 billion dinars. The only provision made thus far for its extinguishment is out of the state's share in the profits of the Bank, which, for the year 1926, amounted to only 36.7 million dinars.

II. ACHIEVEMENT OF BUDGETARY EQUILIBRIUM

The conditions in which Yugoslavia began to function as a nation after the end of the war were entirely chaotic so far as public finances were concerned. Serbia and Montenegro, when freed from the régime of enemy occupation, presented almost a mass of ruins. The collection of taxes was practically impossible. On the contrary, the government, upon its return to Belgrade, found itself compelled to provide for the maintenance of the population and the economic reconstruction of the country. Nor were the former Austrian and Hungarian provinces, which joined with Serbia and Montenegro to form the new state, productive of revenues. This was due to the fact that nearly the whole tax-gathering personnel in these provinces had to be replaced. Moreover, the taxes that were collected were paid in constantly depreciating crowns. Even after the economic life of the new country became more or less re-established, it was not for some years that a regular budgetary system was organized.

Political conditions impeded the organization of Yugoslav public finances for several years following the war. In its budgetary practice, the new Kingdom took over the system that existed in Serbia before the war. This system was notoriously difficult of application, because it had been only in rare years that the Serbian Parliament voted the budget before the beginning of the fiscal year which was intended to be covered by the estimates. Usually the voting of the budget was delayed until long after the beginning of the year, and in the interval it was necessary to resort to the system of monthly budgets for the financing of the government. Precisely the same difficulty confronted Yugoslavia after the war, and it was handled in the same manner.

During the war Serbia had no budgets at all. Her government and her army, which remained through almost the whole period of the war outside the country, were maintained by means of subventions from the Allied Powers. Upon the return of the government to Belgrade, an attempt was made, in the summer of 1919, to draw up a budget. This budget, however, not only failed of being voted in time by the Parliament, but its estimates were entirely provisional and did not correspond in the least with the actual expenditures and revenues.[10]

An attempt to meet the difficulty presented by the delay in the parliamentary handling of the budget was made when the beginning of the fiscal year was changed from January 1, which was the pre-war practice, to July 1. But even under this system, the budget for 1920-21 was not voted in time, and resort had to be had to the system of monthly budgets, or the so-called budgetary "twelfths."

A budget was prepared for the year 1922, but it never came up for vote in Parliament, and during the first seven months of that year the government operated on the basis of monthly budgets. On July 29, 1922, the Parliament passed a budget for the fiscal year from July 1, 1922, to June 30, 1923, and this budget remained in force for the remaining eleven months of that year. The budget for the

[10] Société de Banque Suisse, *Bulletin mensuel,* April, 1924.

following fiscal year was delayed by parliamentary elections, and came up before the Parliament only at the beginning of 1924, when the Minister of Finance proposed that this draft budget, with some modifications, be adopted as the budget for the year 1924-25. At the same time, the beginning of the fiscal year was changed once more, this time to April 1. Thus the budget for 1924-25 was the first budget since the war actually passed by Parliament before the beginning of the fiscal year for which it was designed.[11]

For over five years, therefore, following the end of the war, Yugoslavia financed her government on the basis of monthly budgets. This system was readily recognized as unsatisfactory. As a prominent Yugoslav Minister of Finance[12] put it, "the 'twelfths' always mean disorder in state financing: they hinder the normal course of state business, and thus injure not only the finances, but the economic life of the people." Nevertheless unsettled political conditions, resulting in frequent changes of government and dissolutions of the Parliament, rendered impossible normal budgetary procedure.

The Yugoslav budget has been balanced since the middle of 1923. Prior to that, the expenditures generally exceeded the revenues. Closed accounts are

[11] See Šečerov, Slavko, *Naše finansije—1918-1925,* Belgrade, 1926, and Harvey, E. M., *Report on the Economic and Industrial Conditions in the Serb-Croat-Slovene Kingdom,* London, 1922, 1923, and 1924.

[12] Dr. Stojadinović in his speech delivered in Parliament on January 30, 1924.

not available for the whole post-war period, but sufficient information has been made public to indicate the general nature of the budgetary problem confronting the Yugoslav government.

During the fiscal year extending from July, 1919, to June, 1920, budgetary expenditures exceeded the total revenues by about two billion dinars.[13] During the fiscal year 1920-21, the budgetary deficit was 901 million dinars.[14] No figures are available for the remainder of 1921 and the first half of 1922. During the period from August, 1922, to June, 1923, the deficit was 841 millions. This deficit, however, was due to extraordinary outlays for military equipment.[15] Starting with July, 1923, revenues have been in excess of budgetary expenditures, as may be seen from the following table: [16]

Yugoslav State Budget, 1923-1926
(Closed accounts, in millions of dinars)

Period	Expenditures	Revenues	Surplus
August, 1923, to March, 1924	6,376	7,414	1,038
April, 1924, to March, 1925	10,579	11,190	611
April, 1925, to June, 1926	11,494	11,974	480

[13] Harvey, E. M., *Report,* etc., for 1922, p. 6.

[14] Stojadinović, M., "The National Finances of Yugoslavia," *Manchester Guardian Commercial: Reconstruction in Europe Series,* pp. 291-292.

[15] Šećerov, S., *Naše finansije,* pp. 60-1.

[16] Figures for the period from July, 1923, to March, 1925, from Šećerov, S., *Naše finansije,* pp. 90-91 and 132-133; for the period from April, 1925, to June, 1926, from *Belgrade Economic Review,* November, 1926.

The deficits during the years 1919-23 were covered principally by means of borrowings from the National Bank, that is, by means of currency inflation. A small portion of the deficits was covered out of the proceeds of internal loans. Moreover, the years of budgetary deficits resulted in an accumulation of floating indebtedness, principally in the form of unpaid arrears. The surpluses since 1923 have been used largely for railroad construction and the liquidation of the accumulated floating indebtedness.

The Yugoslav budget includes the gross receipts and expenditures of railways and of government enterprises. For this reason it is difficult, in dealing with budgetary figures, to determine the relative importance of the various items of expenditure and the different sources of revenue. In the draft budget for 1927-28, however, an attempt was made for the first time to distinguish between expenditures for the general need of the state and the operating budgets of the government-owned enterprises. The table on page 490 shows the relative importance of the various items of expenditure.[17]

Thus almost one-third of the total expenditures for the general needs of the state goes for the upkeep of the military establishment. Education is the next largest item of expenditure, followed, in importance, by the requirements of the Ministry of the Interior

[17] *Exposé des motifs du Ministre des Finances pour le projet du budget pour l'exercice 1927-28*, p. 9.

BUDGETARY EXPENDITURES IN YUGOSLAVIA, 1927-1928

Classification	Amount in Millions of Dinars	*As Percentage of Total for the Group*
I. FOR THE GENERAL NEEDS OF THE STATE		
Supreme administration of the State	130	*1.71*
Pensions	604	*7.91*
Public debt	602	*7.88*
Ministry of War and the Navy	2,350	*30.78*
" " Education	813	*10.64*
" " the Interior	606	*7.93*
" " Finance[a]	409	*5.35*
" " Public Works	387	*5.08*
" " Social Policy	371	*4.86*
" " Justice	294	*3.84*
" " Public Health	288	*3.76*
" " Agriculture	197	*2.58*
" " Foreign Affairs	161	*2.11*
Other Ministries	252	*3.30*
Budgetary Reserves	174	*2.27*
Total for the group	7,638	*100.00*
II. FOR THE OPERATION OF GOVERNMENT ENTERPRISES		
Means of transportation	2,530	*62.45*
Posts and Telegraphs	426	*10.50*
Other government enterprises	545	*13.46*
Monopolies	551	*13.59*
Total for the group	4,052	*100.00*

[a] Exclusive of monopolies.

and the outlays for pensions and for the public debt payments.

The sources from which budgetary revenues are obtained in Yugoslavia are as follows: [18]

BUDGETARY RECEIPTS IN YUGOSLAVIA, 1927-1928

Classification	Amount in Millions of Dinars	*As Percentage of Total*
Direct taxes	1,828	*15.64*
Indirect taxes	3,531	*30.21*
Government enterprises	3,848	*32.91*
Monopolies	2,362	*20.21*
Miscellaneous receipts	121	*1.03*
Total	11,690	*100.00*

A comparison of the above two tables shows at a glance that the expenditures required for the general needs of the state are covered only in part by means of taxation. With expenditures estimated at 7,638 million dinars, the revenues from direct and indirect taxation are only 5,359 millions. The remainder is made up out of the profits of government monopolies and enterprises. The government-owned railways and the other enterprises yield a net profit of only 347 millions, but the monopolies (chief among them being the tobacco monopoly) [19] bring in a gross revenue of 2,362 million dinars while their expenditures amount to only 551 millions.

[18] *Exposé des motifs,* etc., p. 11.

[19] The monopolies are seven in number: tobacco, salt, petroleum, matches, cigarette paper, alcohol, and saccharine. For a description of their operation see Djouknić, M., "State Monopolies," *Belgrade Economic and Financial Review,* January, 1924.

Yugoslav public finances are still in a process of reform. There are three principal lines along which changes are considered necessary: (1) there is an unequal distribution of the burden of taxation as among the various parts of the country; (2) the incidence of taxation as of among the various groups of the population is disproportionate to their income; and (3) the general burden of taxation is too high. Many complaints are made in the country along these three lines.

Yugoslavia inherited six different systems of direct taxation. In the Kingdom of Serbia the taxation régime of the territories acquired during the Balkan wars had not, at the outbreak of the World War, as yet been unified with that existing in the older part of the Kingdom. Provinces acquired from Austria and Hungary lived under two different régimes. Montenegro had a system of her own, while Bosnia-Herzegovina had a special taxation régime. The unification of all these systems has been slow for many reasons. Fiscal reform could not be undertaken until the promulgation of a new constitution, which did not take place until 1921. The requirements of the budget forced the government to have recourse primarily to indirect taxation, as the easiest method of obtaining revenue. Finally, conditions in the various parts of the new Kingdom were so different that the process of adopting a unified system of taxation was most difficult.

Several steps have been taken in the direction

of creating a unified system. In 1919 and 1920 the fiscal legislation of the Kingdom of Serbia was extended to the whole Serbian territory and to Montenegro. A provision was incorporated in the constitution (Article 116) laying down the principle of equal taxation throughout the Kingdom. In 1922 a special commission was appointed to study the question of fiscal reform. In 1923 extraordinary super-taxes were introduced on the total amount of direct taxation in order to increase the rôle of direct taxes in the government budget and thus provide a basis for fiscal reform. These supertaxes amounted to 500 per cent on land taxes and 30 per cent on all other categories. In 1925 a scheme of fiscal reform was worked out.[20]

In spite of all these attempts, the problem of a unified system of taxation still remains unsolved. It is accentuated by a large variety of systems of local taxation as among the various parts of the country.

The disproportionality of taxation is due primarily to the preponderance of indirect taxes. As we saw on page 491, direct taxes represent only 15 per cent of the gross budgetary receipts. The bulk of government revenue comes from indirect taxation and monopolies, that is, from levies on consumption, which constitute a proportionately heavier burden for the poorer than for the wealthier groups of the population.

[20] Milojević, D. M., "On the Eve of the Reform of Direct Taxation in Yugoslavia," *Belgrade Economic and Financial Review,* April and July, 1925.

Taking the national income as about 75 billion dinars[21] and local taxation as 1,124 million dinars,[22] the burden of taxation in Yugoslavia works out at about 12 per cent of the national income. Compared with the post-war taxation burdens of other European countries, this figure is not high, although its relative size is somewhat increased by the absence of a large national debt.

The Yugoslav government is fully conscious of a need of fiscal reform. In his speech on the 1927-28 budget, cited above, Finance Minister Marković said:

> There is a pressing need of eliminating the regional inequalities of taxation and of instituting a real control over local finances. There is an equally pressing need for fiscal reform that would diminish the disproportionality of taxation. Finally, it is necessary to decrease budgetary expenditures: the large volume of undercollections, accumulated from previous years, and the frequent instances of forcible collections bear witness to the crushing burden of fiscal charges.

Reforms along these lines are in process of preparation. Their need is fully realized as being on a par with that of a legally stabilized currency.

[21] Professor Gini, in a study kindly placed by him at our disposal in manuscript form, estimates the net national income at 6-6.5 billion gold francs, that is between 66 and 72 billion dinars; in *Naša narodna privreda,* a study of Yugoslav national wealth and national income by a group of Yugoslav economists, Sarajevo, 1927, the national income is estimated at 80 billions.

[22] Estimated by Finance Minister Marković in his speech on the 1927-28 budget, cited above.

CHAPTER XXVII

YUGOSLAVIA'S INTERNATIONAL ACCOUNTS

As we saw in the preceding chapter, the fluctuations in the exchange rate of the dinar have been very closely connected with the foreign trade situation of Yugoslavia. In this chapter we shall examine the country's international accounts, in order to see the conditions with which Yugoslavia has been confronted in the process of meeting her foreign payments, and what her future outlook is for maintaining a balance between her international outgo and income.

Yugoslavia's balance of trade changed in 1924 from an import to an export surplus. The table on page 496 shows the country's exports and imports during the post-war period: [1]

During the years 1919-22, Yugoslavia had a large excess of imports over exports. This situation was due not so much to excessive imports, as to very small exports, resulting mainly from a series of poor crops. In 1923 imports were considerably larger than in 1922, but during that year the export trade

[1] Figures of the Customs Administration of the Ministry of Finance, published in *Statistika spoljašnje trgovine,* official organ of the Administration.

YUGOSLAVIA'S FOREIGN TRADE, 1919-1926
(In millions of dinars)

Year	Exports	Imports	Balance
1919	687	2,982	−2,295
1920	1,321	3,466	−2,145
1921	2,461	4,122	−1,661
1922	3,691	6,442	−2,751
1923	8,049	8,310	− 261
1924	9,539	8,222	+1,317
1925	8,905	8,753	+ 152
1926	7,818	7,632	+ 186

of the country made a remarkable recovery, with the result that the adverse balance of trade for that year was very small. During the following year, there was again a substantial increase of exports, which resulted in a comparatively large export surplus. During the years 1925 and 1926 Yugoslavia maintained a small excess of exports over imports.

The year 1924, during which the trade balance shifted from an import to an export surplus, marked an important change in the whole economic situation of the country. It was during that year that the exchange rate of the dinar stopped depreciating and began to appreciate under the influence of the availability of a large volume of foreign bills, resulting from a favorable balance of trade.

Yugoslavia has large payments of interest and dividends to make to foreigners each year. The foreign public debt of Yugoslavia consists of pre-war debts, war debts, post-war debts, and the country's share of the Austro-Hungarian pre-war debts, allocated under the Innsbruck protocol. Almost two-thirds of the total debt resulted from the war, the creditors being the United States, Great Britain, and France. The country has now funded her debts to the United States and Great Britain, and at present is making interest payments on all of her foreign debts, with the exception of her debt to France, which still remains to be funded.

Offsetting Yugoslavia's payments on the foreign debts of the government are her receipts on reparation account. Under the Spa protocol, the country is entitled to a small percentage of Germany's payments and to a somewhat larger share of the Hungarian and Bulgarian payments.

The bulk of foreign private investments in Yugoslavia is in enterprises located in the territories detached from Austria and Hungary. These investments are held by the nationals of present Austria, Hungary, and Czechoslovakia, and require payment to them of large annual sums in interest and dividends. Some western European capital is also invested in the country, and recently Yugoslavia has received some loans from the United States.

Other service operations represent net income for Yugoslavia. In this group of transactions, income from the one item of emigrant remittances and sums earned by migratory workers is considerably larger than net outgo for other items. There are more than 600,000 Yugoslav emigrants in the United

States alone, besides smaller numbers in other countries. The remittances which these people send to friends and relatives in Yugoslavia amount to very considerable sums in the course of a year. Moreover, a large number of migratory laborers from Yugoslavia find seasonal employment in other countries, particularly in France. The money which they send or take back home provides the country with a certain additional amount of foreign purchasing power.

Offsetting these receipts to some extent are the fairly large payments that must be made each year for a variety of services rendered by foreigners to the people of Yugoslavia. While shipping and transportation charges paid to other countries are somewhat smaller than the country's own receipts from the transit trade, the expenditures of Yugoslav subjects in other countries are larger than foreign tourist expenditures in Yugoslavia. Another item of net outgo in the accounts is the net amount paid to foreigners for banking and insurance services.

In only one year has Yugoslavia's international income exceeded the total required for her foreign payments for goods and services. The table opposite shows the country's international income account and outgo during the three-year period 1924-26, a period during which the exchange value of the dinar was more or less stable.[2]

[2] For the sources of the figures given here, see Appendix, p. 598.

YUGOSLAVIA'S INTERNATIONAL INCOME ACCOUNT, 1924-1926

(Totals for the three-year period, in millions of dinars)

Net income from—			
Net exports of commodities		1,655	
Emigrant remittances		1,900	
			3,555
Net outgo for—			
Interest and dividends:			
On public debts	1,000		
On private investments	1,800	2,800	
Other service operations		150	2,950
Net income from all items			605

It will be seen that for the whole three-year period the country's income from net exports of commodities and from emigrant remittances was more than sufficient to meet outgo for interest and dividends and for all other service operations. This result, however, was largely attributable to the large favorable trade balance of the single year 1924.

During the three-year period, income from emigrant remittances averaged about 650 million dinars a year. All other service items in the account resulted in net international outgo averaging about 975 millions a year. Income from emigrant remittances thus fell short of meeting outgo for other services by about 325 millions a year. In 1924, the commodity export surplus amounted to 1,317 millions, a sum that was far in excess of the amount required to offset the year's net outgo on service account. The detailed trade figures are given in the table on page

496. In 1925 and 1926, however, the export surplus was only 152 and 186 million dinars respectively, thus failing to meet the deficit from service operations. And it will be recalled that during the years preceding 1924, imports of commodities persistently exceeded exports. However, when the data for the three years 1924-26 are brought together into a single income account, as they are on page 499, total income exceeds total outgo by 605 million dinars, thanks to the large export surplus of the year 1924.

For the future Yugoslavia must increase her export surplus if she is to meet her foreign obligations without borrowing abroad. Interest and dividends on foreign indebtedness, the most important of the outgo items, is practically certain to increase in the future. By funding her debt to the United States in 1926, and to Great Britain in 1927, the country has already augmented the sums which she must transfer abroad each year. The funding of her debt to France will still further increase this amount. Moreover, recent borrowings abroad for railroad construction and other economic developments are increasing the total of her foreign indebtedness, and interest on these new loans will add to the foreign payments she will have to meet in the future.

If further foreign borrowing for the purpose of meeting foreign payments is to be avoided, this increase in the country's foreign debt service will have to be offset by an increase in international income from other services or from the commodity trade. But among the service items there is none that can be expected to provide any appreciable increase in net income. Emigrant remittances, the one income-producing item in the service accounts, cannot be expected to show any great future expansion, if, indeed, any expansion may be expected.

The need for increasing the excess of commodity exports over imports thus becomes imperative. Theoretically this may be brought about by an expansion of exports, or by a contraction of imports. The outlook for such changes in the country's foreign trade is a subject discussed in the following chapter.

CHAPTER XXVIII

TRADE, PRODUCTION, AND BANKING IN YUGOSLAVIA

THE possibility for Yugoslavia to increase her favorable balance of trade depends on her situation with regard to production and requirements. In this chapter we shall examine the character and direction of the country's foreign trade and the condition of her production in the domain of agriculture and industry, with a view to setting forth the factors which are involved in a possible improvement in the country's foreign trade balance. At the same time we shall examine Yugoslavia's banking and credit situation, which is an important element in the problem of trade and production.

I. CHARACTER AND DIRECTION OF FOREIGN TRADE

The general economic character of Yugoslavia is reflected in the commodity composition of the country's foreign trade. Agriculture and stock-raising supply the major portions of its exports, and manufactured goods constitute the bulk of its imports.

Yugoslavia is primarily an exporter of foodstuffs and an importer of finished products. Her exports are chiefly in the form of raw, rather than prepared products, while her imports are mainly finished, rather than raw or semi-manufactured goods.

In 1925 the products of agriculture and stock-raising constituted more than three-quarters of Yugoslavia's exports. Cereals, exported almost exclusively in the form of grain, made up 32 per cent of the total exports,.with maize as by far the most important cereal exported. Besides, Yugoslavia shipped across her frontiers comparatively large quantities of other foodstuffs, such as vegetables, sugar, prunes, etc. Live cattle and meat products were also important items of export, furnishing about 22 per cent of the total. The remainder of the exports was made up principally of forest products and of small amounts of minerals.

So far as the imports were concerned, textiles constituted by far the largest items. They made up no less than 38 per cent of the total imports. Next in importance came machinery and other metal manufactures. They represented about 18 per cent of the total. The remainder of the imports consisted of a large variety of manufactured goods. The figures for 1926 show an approximately similar commodity composition of the export and import trade.[1]

The bulk of Yugoslavia's foreign trade is with other Danubian States and Italy. The following table shows the distribution of the country's exports and imports in 1926: [2]

[1] *The Belgrade Economic Review*, May, 1927.
[2] *Ibid.*

Geographic Distribution of Exports and Imports, 1926
(In percentages of total values for the year)

Exports to:		Imports from:	
Austria	20.59	Austria	20.08
Czechoslovakia	12.01	Czechoslovakia	18.70
Rumania	10.00	Hungary	4.65
Hungary	4.74	Rumania	4.35
Italy	25.07	Italy	13.82
Germany	9.27	Germany	12.03
Greece	7.39	Great Britain	5.75
Switzerland	3.79	France	4.63
France	2.41	U. S. A.	4.05
Other countries	4.73	Brazil	2.46
		Other countries	9.48
Total	100.00	Total	100.00

Thus the four Danubian countries took in 1926 about 47 per cent of Yugoslavia's exports and supplied her with 48 per cent of her imports. Of these four countries, Austria is the most important so far as Yugoslavia's foreign trade is concerned. She occupies the second place after Italy as the market for Yugoslav products and the first place as the source of Yugoslavia's imports.

Austria takes the bulk of Yugoslavia's exports of live cattle and meat products, while Italy is her most important customer for cereals and wood. Austria, Czechoslovakia, and Italy supply Yugoslavia with the bulk of her textile imports, while her imports of machinery and other metal products come primarily from Austria, Czechoslovakia, and Germany. Rumania supplies Yugoslavia with petroleum, and Hungary ships her coal.

II. AGRICULTURAL PRODUCTION AND SURPLUS

While Yugoslavia is primarily an agricultural country, her agricultural resources are by no means great in relation to the total area. Only 26.2 per cent of the total area represents land under cultivation; meadows and pastures occupy 16.8 per cent; vineyards and orchards, 2.4 per cent; forests, 30.9 per cent; and unproductive lands, 23.7 per cent.[3] Thus Yugoslavia has the largest percentage of unproductive lands of any of the Danubian countries, and the lowest percentage, with the exception of Austria, of land under cultivation. In spite of this fact agriculture is the principal source of livelihood for more than three-quarters of the total population of the country.

Agricultural production in Yugoslavia is larger today than it was before the war. While there are no official figures for the pre-war output of the territories comprising the country, several careful estimates are available, and even on the basis of the highest of these estimates the production for 1925 appears to be larger than the pre-war figures.

The table on page 506 shows the production of the principal grains in 1925, as compared with the pre-war figures: [4]

[3] *Agricultural Survey of Europe*, p. 94.

[4] League of Nations *International Statistical Yearbook, 1926;* pre-war figures based on the estimates of the International Institute of Agriculture. In *Agricultural Survey of Europe* the pre-war output is estimated as somewhat higher than in this table, but still below the 1925 figures.

PRODUCTION OF GRAIN IN YUGOSLAVIA
(In thousands of quintals)

Grain	Pre-war	1925
Wheat	20,850	21,404
Rye	1,500	1,998
Barley	3,500	3,951
Oats	3,250	3,450
Maize	28,000	37,907
Total	57,100	68,710

Even assuming that the pre-war production was somewhat higher than is indicated by the table above, the output of the five principal grains in 1925 was still appreciably larger than it was before the war. The rapidity with which agricultural production has recovered and expanded in Yugoslavia during the post-war years may be seen from the following table, showing the development of crop yields: [5]

CROP YIELDS IN YUGOSLAVIA, 1920-1925
(In quintals per hectare)

Grain	1920	1923	1924	1925
Winter wheat	8.17	10.87	9.26	11.83
Winter rye	8.01	8.24	7.36	10.70
Winter barley	8.19	9.22	8.55	11.90
Oats	7.75	8.36	8.56	10.05
Maize	14.15	11.95	19.31	18.30

[5] Figures for 1920-1924 from *Obradjena zemlia i žetveni prinos,* official publication of the Yugoslav Ministry of Agriculture; for 1925, from *Economic Yugoslavia,* pp. 7-8.

For wheat, rye, and barley we have an increase of yield between 1920 and 1923, a drop in 1924 on account of bad crop conditions, and again a substantial increase in 1925. For oats we have a steady increase through the whole period. For maize, there is a drop between 1920 and 1923, an exceptional increase in 1924, followed by a slight drop in 1925. On the whole, the yields in 1925 are larger than before the war.

The agrarian reform did not retard the process of agricultural recovery in Yugoslavia. In this respect, Yugoslavia's experience has been similar to that of Czechoslovakia, rather than of Rumania.

Immediately upon the unification of the country, Yugoslavia faced an exceedingly complicated system of land tenure. In Serbia proper there were practically no large estates; nearly all the land was held by peasants in comparatively small holdings. On the other hand, in the territories that had formerly belonged to Austria and Hungary, there was a prevalence of large landed estates. In addition to that, in Dalmatia, Bosnia, and Herzegovina there still existed remnants of the Turkish feudal régime. This was also true of Macedonia and the other provinces acquired by Serbia after the Balkan wars.

The problem that confronted Yugoslavia consisted of the final suppression of all vestiges of feudalism and of an equalization of land holdings. By means of a series of measures, a far-reaching agrarian reform was introduced, providing for a gradual expropriation of large estates and the distribution of land among the poorer peasantry. The reform also provided for a removal of peasant population from the poorer and the overcrowded sections of the Kingdom to those sections in which large tracts of land could be expropriated and made available for colonization.[6]

So far as may be judged by agricultural output, the effects of the agrarian reform in Yugoslavia have been far from detrimental. While there is no doubt that the breaking up of large estates affected adversely the output in some sections of the Kingdom, the new incentive toward increased production received by the peasants after their liberation from the feudal and near-feudal régimes formerly existing in some of the provinces and their acquisition of the expropriated lands has more than overcome the injurious effects of the breaking up of the larger units.

Yugoslavia is a surplus producer of cereals and other agricultural products. Her production is more than sufficient to satisfy her requirements of all cereals; and in the case of wheat, barley, oats, and maize she has a substantial exportable surplus. In addition, she produces an exportable surplus of potatoes, beans, and other vegetables.

On the basis of the production of the first three

[6] For the details of the agrarian reform see Nedeljković, M., "Agrarian Reform in Yugoslavia," *The Near East Year Book*, and the same author's *Economic and Financial Review of the Kingdom of the Serbs, Croats, and Slovenes,* Paris, 1924; also Šećerov, S., *Problemi agrarne reforme,* Belgrade, 1925.

post-war years, it has been calculated that Yugoslavia's exportable surplus of wheat ought to be about 4 million quintals a year; of maize, 8 millions; of barley, 1.5 millions; of oats, 1.5 millions; and of potatoes, 2 millions.[7] As a matter of fact, Yugoslavia has not as yet reached these export figures, except in the case of maize. The actual export of maize in 1925 was over 10 million quintals, and in 1926 about 9 millions. On the other hand, the exports of wheat in 1925, in the form of grain and flour, were about 2.2 million quintals, and in 1926, 3.4 millions. The exports of potatoes in 1925 were only 65,137 quintals.

Yugoslavia is in a position to expand still further her output of cereals and other products. She can increase her planting area somewhat at the expense of the pasture lands. And she can at the same time increase the yields by an intensification of cultivation. While the yield per unit in Yugoslavia is larger than in Rumania, it is not as large as in Hungary, in spite of the fact that some of the best Hungarian wheat and maize areas have been incorporated in Yugoslavia. The principal reason for this lies in the fact that the yields per unit in Serbia proper were extremely low before the war. Although the productivity of the soil outside the well-developed agricultural areas formerly comprised in Hungary has been increasing since the war, there is still

[7] Franguesch, Otto, "The Main Features of Agricultural Production in the S. H. S. Kingdom," *Belgrade Economic and Commercial Review,* November, 1923.

considerable opportunity for improvement in methods and for increase in productivity. This expansion, however, will be possible only if Yugoslavia succeeds in finding new outlets for her exports of foodstuffs.[8]

Yugoslavia is a surplus producer and exporter of fruit and vegetables, of wine, and of a number of industrial plants. The most important of the latter is the sugar-beet. We shall deal with the production of industrial plants later in connection with the industrial situation of the country.

Yugoslavia is a surplus producer of livestock. Although the war had destroyed a substantial part of the livestock population of the territories now included in Yugoslavia and although the post-war recovery in this field has been slow, the exportation of the products of stock-raising has played an important rôle in the country's export trade since the war.

The following table shows the livestock population of Yugoslavia before and after the war: [9]

LIVESTOCK POPULATION IN YUGOSLAVIA
(In thousands)

Livestock	1914	1919	1925
Horses	1,556	1,009	1,106
Cattle	6,277	4,555	3,796
Pigs	5,234	2,973	2,802
Sheep	11,570	5,250	7,807

[8] See pp. 523-4.
[9] *Naša narodna privreda,* p. 63.

The figures for 1919, as compared with those for 1914, show the devastation wrought by the war in the livestock population of Yugoslavia. The number of horses and cattle decreased by about one-third, the number of pigs and sheep by about one-half. The figures for 1925 show a slight recovery with regard to horses, a substantial recovery with regard to sheep, but a further decrease in the number of cattle and of pigs.

The Yugoslav government has made serious efforts to stimulate stock-raising. It has insisted on receiving a part of the country's share of German, Hungarian, and Bulgarian reparation payments in live animals. It has established several breeding centers and studs.[10] In spite of this, the number of horses and sheep, while larger than immediately after the war, is still far below the pre-war figures, while the number of cattle and pigs is actually smaller than in 1919. This latter fact is due partly to small fodder crops, and partly to the condition of the export markets; although as compared with 1924, the figures for 1925 show an improvement in all classes of the livestock population.

With the condition of the livestock population as we have just described it, stock-raising nevertheless furnished in 1925 about 22 per cent of the total exports of Yugoslavia. As the livestock population approaches nearer to the pre-war figures, there is bound to be a larger export surplus.

[10] See *The Near East Year Book,* pp. 159-162.

III. INDUSTRIAL PRODUCTION AND REQUIREMENTS

Although, as we saw in the preceding section, agriculture provides the principal source of livelihood for about three-quarters of the total population of Yugoslavia, the country also has some industrial equipment, especially in the areas which had formerly constituted a part of the Austro-Hungarian Monarchy. These industries, which are for the most part primitive, have for their basis the availability of agricultural raw materials, as well as the existence of large forest areas and of other natural resources.

Yugoslavia possesses large, though undeveloped, natural resources. This is true of fuel, mineral wealth, and timber resources. With her present small industrial development, she is able to supply the major portion of her requirements of fuel and raw materials and to export fairly large quantities of some of them.

The coal deposits of Yugoslavia are rather extensive, although they consist for the most part of brown coal (lignite). The extraction of coal has been developing since the war. In 1919 the total output was about 2.5 million tons; in 1925 it was 4.2 millions. With this output, Yugoslavia is in a position to satisfy a large part of her present very small coal requirements. In 1925, out of the total consumption of 4.6 million tons, home production supplied almost 90 per cent.[11] The imports of coal

[11] *Economic Yugoslavia,* p. 16.

have been mostly in the form of reparation receipts from Hungary.

In addition to coal, as a source of power, Yugoslavia also has large unutilized water power resources. It is estimated that the potential water power resources of the country are 3.5 million HP,

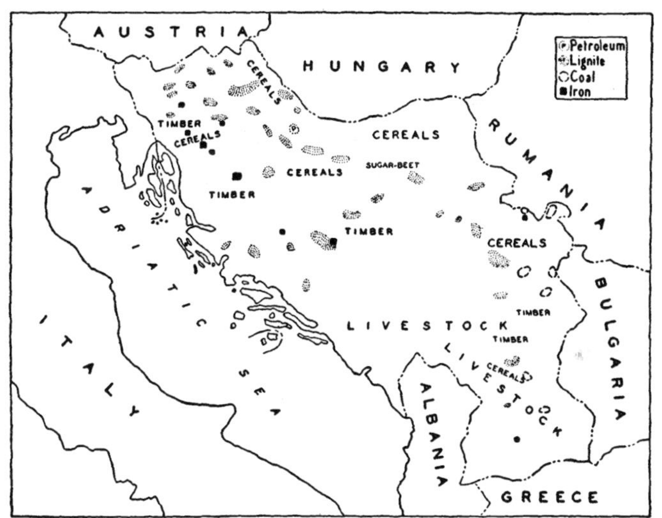

YUGOSLAVIA'S PRINCIPAL RESOURCES

of which at the present time only 160,000 HP are actually utilized.[12]

The timber lands of Yugoslavia occupy 30 per cent of the total area of the country, making her the most important of the Danubian countries as regards timber resources and the seventh most im-

[12] *Ibid.*, p. 26.

portant in Europe. It is estimated that about one-half of the annual output of forest products is exported.[13] Between 1921 and 1925 the volume of timber exports more than quadrupled.

The most important mineral ores mined in Yugoslavia are iron and copper. Although the output of both of these products has been increasing rapidly since the war, it is still small by comparison with the known resources. The extraction of iron ore increased between 1920 and 1924 from 18.9 thousand tons to 330.1 thousands; the extraction of copper increased from 42.1 thousand tons to 143.3 thousands. The bulk of the extracted ore is exported in raw form. Of the other minerals, Yugoslavia produces lead, zinc, manganese, bauxite, chrome, antimony, etc.[14]

Small-scale production predominates in the Yugoslav industries. The country's industrial enterprises, classified according to the number of workmen employed, are as follows: [15]

Employing less than 10 workmen	7,419
11 to 20 workmen	653
21 to 50 "	600
51 to 100 "	218
101 to 200 "	153
201 to 500 "	120
501 to 1,000 "	37
more than 1,000 "	22
Total	9,222

[13] *Naša narodna privreda,* pp. 116-146.

[14] For a description of the mineral resources of Yugoslavia see *Economic Yugoslavia,* pp. 16-21, and *The Near East Year Book,* pp. 125-135.

[15] *Naša narodna privreda,* p. 182.

Thus out of a total of over nine thousand industrial enterprises, only about 350 employ over 100 workmen each. Most of the industrial production in the country is done in small factories. The output of these factories is supplemented by that of small craft-shops, of which, it is estimated, there are no less than two hundred thousand scattered throughout the whole country.[16] For example, in the most important branch of industry, that connected with the exploitation of timber, there are in the country about 2,750 sawmills, of which, however, only 350 are operated on anything like an extensive scale. The rest of the mills are very small. A similar situation exists in other branches of production.

Generally speaking, the Yugoslav industries are of recent origin. Only about 40 per cent of the existing equipment dates to the pre-war period. The other 60 per cent grew up during the war, and especially during the first four years following the cessation of hostilities.[17] While a great deal has been done for the expansion and development of industrial activity, the predominance of small-scale production is still marked.

Yugoslavia is largely dependent upon importation for her requirements of finished products. While her industries based on timber resources and on raw foodstuffs produce, for the most part, an exportable surplus, other manufactured goods are produced

[16] *Economic Yugoslavia,* p. 24.
[17] *Statement,* submitted to the International Economic Conference by the Serb-Croat-Slovene members.

within the country in insufficient quantities to satisfy the consumption requirements.

The timber industry is concerned principally with the production of construction timber. There are, however, in addition to the sawmills, about 150 factories devoted to the manufacture of furniture, packing cases, and other wooden products. There are also 14 pulp mills, nine paper mills, six cardboard factories, and over 80 factories, most of them small, turning out articles made of paper. A substantial part of the construction timber and about half of the paper output are exported.

Chief among the industries devoted to food products are the milling of flour, the preparation of meat, and the manufacture of sugar. The milling industry is sufficient to meet the domestic requirements and to export about 10 per cent of the output. The meat industry exports a part of its output of fresh and prepared meat and of lard. The sugar industry exported in 1924-25 about one-third of its production.

Of the other agricultural industries, the breweries of the country supply the domestic requirements. The alcohol distilleries produce a substantial export surplus. Fruit and vegetable products are also turned out in sufficient quantities to provide an export. surplus.

The country has a fairly well developed leather industry, which turns out sufficient quantities of its product to supply the domestic requirements and to provide some special kinds of leather for the export trade. The foot-wear factories, of which there are 70 operating on a fairly large scale in addition to numerous craft-shops, produce almost enough shoes for the home market.

The situation in the textile industry is quite different. While Yugoslavia exports small amounts of flax and hemp products, which are manufactured out of domestic raw materials, her consumption requirements of cotton and woolen goods are supplied only to a small extent from home production. The cotton industry has been growing since the war, and possesses at the present time 112,000 spindles and 5,500 looms—an equipment only slightly smaller, especially as regards spindles, than that of Hungary. Its output, however, is not nearly sufficient for the country's needs. This is true also of the woolen industry.

The metallurgical industry is very small, in spite of the existence of the necessary mineral wealth. As a result, Yugoslavia exports a large part of its mining output in raw or semi-manufactured form, and imports large quantities of metal manufactures. The machine industry is just beginning to develop.

Classified by production groups, Yugoslavia's exports and imports were in 1925 as shown in table on following page.

This table indicates the country's dependence upon imports for the satisfaction of its requirements of manufactured goods.

YUGOSLAVIA'S EXPORTS AND IMPORTS BY INDUSTRIAL GROUPS, 1925
(In millions of dinars)

Commodities	Exports	Imports	Net
Agricultural	388.5	370.5	+ 18.0
Textile and textile materials	1,291.0	4,637.5	−3,346.5
Glass and glassware	3.3	118.4	− 115.1
Metals and metal goods	459.1	980.7	− 521.6
Machinery and vehicles	31.9	630.9	− 599.0

IV. BANKING AND CREDIT SITUATION

Yugoslavia, at the time of the unification of the new Kingdom, received a very meager legacy, so far as banking facilities and operating capital resources were concerned. The financial organization of the Kingdom of Serbia, never very strong before the war, was completely disrupted by the years of enemy occupation. The territories which had formerly belonged to Austria and Hungary, depended for their financial facilities primarily on Vienna and Budapest. The problem which confronted the new Kingdom was the creation of a national banking system. This involved the rehabilitation of old banks, the establishment of new ones, and the reorganization into independent institutions of what had formerly been branches of large Austrian and Hungarian banks.

The banking system of Yugoslavia is still poorly developed. In 1926 there were in the country 639 financial institutions classified as banks, although most of them were merely small credit associations and cooperatives. The most important of the larger banks are located in Zagreb (the capital of Croatia) and in Belgrade, with Zagreb as the largest financial center of the Kingdom. Six of the larger banks are owned entirely by foreigners.[18]

The combined paid-up capital of the Yugoslav banks was, at the beginning of 1926, 2,011 million dinars. In addition to this, they had reserves amounting to 543 millions. The growth of the banking organization in the country may be seen from the following table: [19]

Capital and Reserves of Yugoslav Banks
(In millions of dinars)

Year	Amount
1920	733.3
1921	1,098.4
1922	1,803.8
1923	2,283.6
1924	2,450.9

To some extent the increase indicated in the table above was due to the depreciation of the currency. But even making allowance for this factor, there has been an unmistakable growth in the banking organization, although it is still considered inadequate for the needs of the country.

Most of the banks receive savings and other de-

[18] The banking statistics given here are taken primarily from *Economic Yugoslavia, The Near East Year Book,* and *Report of the National Bank of the Kingdom of Serbs, Croats, and Slovenes* for 1926.

[19] *Privredni Pregled,* Nos. 43 and 44 for 1925.

posits. At the beginning of 1926 the amount of deposits in all the banks was 5,732 million dinars. Moreover, 327 banks were borrowers from the National Bank. The combined operating capital resources of the banks were estimated at about 14 billion dinars.

The banks in the Serbian portion of the Kingdom are engaged primarily in financing agriculture and trade. Industry is financed largely by the Zagreb banks. In accordance with this, the Belgrade banks operate mainly by means of discounts, while the Zagreb banks by means of current accounts. The Serbian banks account for over one-half of all discounts, while the Zagreb banks hold nearly two-thirds of all current accounts.

Yugoslavia has no purely industrial banks, although some of the larger institutions are engaged in financing industry to some extent. The National Bank is also active in promoting industrial credit. Generally speaking, Yugoslavia is still in the process of developing adequate banking facilities for the financing of industry. As regards credit for small-scale or craft industry, the government has attempted to alleviate the situation by the creation of a Crafts Bank, partly financed out of government funds. Similarly, the Yugoslav government has founded an Agricultural Bank for the purpose of promoting agricultural credit.[20]

[20] See "Industrial Credits," *Belgrade Economic and Financial Review,* July, 1925, and "The Foundation of an Agricultural Bank," same publication, July-August, 1924.

The problem of operating capital is very pressing in Yugoslavia. The liquid capital resources of the existing banking institutions are barely sufficient for the current needs of agriculture, industry, and trade. The foreign trade of the country depends to some extent on seasonal credits from abroad. The resources available for long-term investment and for general economic development are very meager.

This meagerness of liquid capital is reflected in very high interest rates. According to an investigation made by the National Bank of 223 banks, the rates of interest charged by them are as follows: 12 banks reported as their maximum rate 16 per cent; 68 banks reported 18 per cent; 47 banks reported 20 per cent; 6 banks reported 21 per cent; 20 banks reported 22 per cent, and 70 banks reported 24 per cent. For the whole banking system, the interest rates are undoubtedly much higher. The rates of interest paid on deposits range between 5 and 12 per cent.

The accumulation of savings increase from year to year, but at an insufficiently rapid rate to provide for the needs of the country. Yugoslavia has therefore been turning her attention to the problem of the importation of capital, and this question has been a factor of some importance in the country's economic policy.

CHAPTER XXIX

YUGOSLAVIA'S ECONOMIC POLICY

THE economic policy of Yugoslavia owed its nationalist character at the beginning very largely to the same factors that were responsible for a similar policy in Czechoslovakia and Rumania. Here, too, the new Kingdom was confronted with the problem of welding into a functioning state several heterogeneous territories. Here, too, the fear of a possible reversal of the situation created by the treaties of peace stimulated nationalism.

The strong nationalism of pre-war Serbia became even stronger in post-war Yugoslavia. Moreover, the transformation of a small agricultural state into a much larger country, endowed with a greater variety of natural resources and some industrial equipment, served both as a temptation and a stimulus to a more rounded economic development. It led Yugoslavia into attempts at rapid industrialization. All this found expression in the manner in which the economic life of the country has been developing since the war.

I. LINES OF ECONOMIC DEVELOPMENT

We have already noted the fact that the agricultural resources of Yugoslavia are not very great, in spite of the fact that the country is overwhelmingly agricultural in character. With about 75 per cent of the population on the land, the amount of land under cultivation per capita of the rural population is smaller in Yugoslavia than in Rumania, although the per capita amount of grasslands is somewhat larger. A large part of the country represents barren or non-cultivated lands, with the result that an extension of arable land is difficult. Land allotments can scarcely be provided for the natural increase of the population. It is estimated that even in the best agricultural section of Yugoslavia, the Banat, there is an annual surplus of 15,000 persons for whom employment must be found outside agricultural pursuits.

Yugoslavia is face to face with the necessity of a more intensive economic activity. The manner in which this can be accomplished is a question on which the country has not as yet developed a definite policy, although there are strong indications of the path which it is likely to follow.

The first need that confronts Yugoslavia is an intensification of agricultural production. A responsible Yugoslav view of this phase of the situation runs as follows: [1]

[1] *Statement* presented to the International Economic Conference, cited above.

Yugoslavia, in her economic structure, is essentially an agricultural country. She has large surpluses of agricultural produce which are exported to the world markets, particularly those of Central Europe. Here our agriculture has to face the competition of similar products of overseas countries. The cost of agricultural production in overseas countries is below our own, and this difference is not compensated by costs of transport, which, furthermore, are steadily decreasing. Thanks to their low costs of production, overseas countries can offer their agricultural produce at prices which are below our cost of production. This means that our agriculture, in so far as it has to place its produce on the world market, is ceasing to yield a return. . . . Faced with this apparently insoluble problem, our agriculture is attempting to set its production on a new footing. It is reducing those forms of cultivation (such as cereals) in which overseas competition is most severe, and is passing over to the forms of cultivation in which this competition is weaker, such as cattle-raising, horticulture, fruit-farming, and the cultivation of plants for industrial purposes.

Without analyzing the arguments set forth in the above quotation, it is clear that Yugoslavia is contemplating a reorganization of her agricultural production on a basis of more intensive cultivation. It is improbable, however, that the output of cereals will be seriously curtailed. While there undoubtedly exists a tendency to use some of the present cereal acreage for industrial plants, efforts are also being made to improve the methods of grain cultivation. Yugoslavia appears to be fully conscious of the need of making her agriculture more productive and more profitable.

But a reorganization of the kind indicated here involves more than a change of crops. It means also the extension and creation of industries for the purpose of working up the agricultural materials thus produced. And in the long-run it points to a general industrial development accompanied, perhaps, by a certain curtailment of agricultural activities.

In the field of industrial activity, Yugoslavia is gradually adapting herself to stable conditions. A large part of her present industrial equipment owes its existence to the inflation and reconstruction boom of the first few years following the end of the war. Built on the insecure foundation of currency inflation, a good deal of the industrial edifice was bound to collapse with the coming of stable financial conditions. This is precisely what happened in 1925 and 1926, and the economic crisis of these two years served as a decidedly sobering influence on the tendency toward too rapid and indiscriminate industrialization.

Yugoslavia undoubtedly has a basis for a very real industrial development. The existence within her territory of very considerable raw material and fuel resources and of an abundant supply of labor indicate for her the possibility of industrialization. But at the same time the difficulties which confront the Yugoslav industries are also very real.

The pre-war industrial equipment was reorganized and the post-war equipment constructed mainly with borrowed funds, obtained at very high rates of interest. As a result the industries are burdened with excessive interest and amortization charges, which are reflected in their production costs. These costs are further increased by the fact that Yugoslav labor has not as yet developed even a fair degree of efficiency in industrial pursuits. The costs of production even in industries which are based on domestic raw materials are so high that the products of these industries find it difficult to compete with similar products imported from better developed countries. When it comes to industries which have to depend on imported raw materials, the situation is still more difficult.[2]

Nevertheless, Yugoslavia is reluctant to give up entirely her efforts in the direction of some industrialization. She is neither willing nor able, because of the problem of providing employment for her population, to become merely an exporter of raw materials. Her aim is to create an organization which would enable her to export her foodstuffs and raw materials as far as possible in finished or at least semi-manufactured form.

The general tendency in Yugoslavia at the present time is toward weeding out such industrial growths as do not appear to have any chance of

[2] See discussion of the industrial crisis in Yugoslavia in *Statement* presented to the International Economic Conference, cited above, and *Report of the National Bank* for 1926, pp. 27-33.

survival, except at the cost of exorbitant customs protection, and to concentrate attention on the industries which have a reason for their existence. The policy of the National Bank and of the government is directed toward this aim. The latter sees its primary duty in adapting the fiscal policy of the state to the economic needs of the country, and first of all in freeing the national economy from "the excessive fiscal burden which at the present time paralyzes all activity and impedes economic rehabilitation." [3]

The problem of transportation is an important factor in the economic situation of Yugoslavia. The United Kingdom inherited five railway systems of four different gauges. Each of these systems was directed to a different center. They were practically unconnected with each other. For example, the only railway connection between Serbia and the Austro-Hungarian Monarchy was the trunk line running through to Constantinople. The problem of reorganizing the railroad lines into a unified system has occupied the attention of the Yugoslav government from the very beginning, and is by no means solved.[4]

[3] Budget speech delivered by Finance Minister Marković, cited above.

[4] The following is an excellent illustration of the railway situation in Yugoslavia: "Panchevo, the terminus of the Banat railway system on the left bank of the Danube, is only 15 kms. in a straight line from Belgrade (on the right bank of the river). By boat the journey is 23 kms. In winter, if the river is frozen, the railway journey between the two towns is 403 kms. Even this route has been in operation only since the war; in Austro-Hungarian days the railway journey between the two towns was over

Yugoslavia has two great problems of railway construction. The first is the providing of adequate railroad facilities within the country. The second is the establishment of railway communication between the inland centers and the Adriatic ports.

The first problem has several phases. The existing railways in various sections of the country have to be joined together in order to provide uninterrupted railway connections within the Kingdom. New lines have to be constructed to serve those sections of the country which have never had adequate rail transportation. Many narrow-gauge lines have to be relaid. A considerable portion of the permanent way has to be relaid with heavier rails in order to increase the speed of transportation.

The second problem is largely a matter of new construction. Yugoslavia has over 600 kilometers of the Adriatic coast, but the only important railway connection with the ports is in the northern part of the country, through a line that runs from Zagreb to Sušak and Fiume. Recently this line has been extended to the ports of Šibenik and Split. But there is still no rail connection between the central and southern parts of Yugoslavia and the Adriatic coast, except a difficult, narrow-gauge line running through Bosnia and Herzegovina.

Yugoslavia has at the present time 10,265 kilo-

600 kms. The completion of the Titel-Orlovat line will reduce the journey to 205 kms., and when the Danube has been bridged at Belgrade, the rail transit would be 18 kms." *The Near East Year Book,* p. 188.

meters of railway lines, or about one kilometer to every 24 kilometers of territory. Moreover, most of her railways are single-track. This makes her one of the least developed countries of Europe from the point of view of railway transportation. The plans of railroad construction at present under consideration contemplate an increase in the system that would nearly double its present size.[5]

The Yugoslav government has been devoting large means to the requirements of the railway system. Altogether up to the end of 1925 about 2,750 million dinars were spent for repair and construction. About half of this sum came from the budget and the proceeds of an internal loan. The remainder was provided out of the Blair loan, floated in the United States.

The problem of foreign capital is paramount in the Yugoslav situation. Domestic accumulations of liquid funds cannot provide for the large tasks which Yugoslavia sets herself. Neither agricultural reorganization, nor industrial expansion, nor the carrying out of a program of railway construction can be accomplished without foreign capital.

During the first years after the establishment of the new Kingdom, there was a strong feeling in Yugoslavia against foreign capital. This feeling was directed primarily against Austria and Hungary. The policy of "nostrification" was in full swing. Strenuous attempts were made to place every enterprise on the basis of domestic ownership.

[5] Vasković, Z., *Plan buduće željezničke mreže*, Belgrade, 1924.

This program proved impossible of achievement. Foreign ownership became merely disguised, instead of disappearing, while at the same time it was not long before the meager financial resources of the country showed themselves utterly inadequate. Then the Yugoslav business interests began to seek foreign capital in the money markets of Great Britain, France, and Switzerland, but encountered immediately one very important difficulty. In the absence of any large banking institutions in Yugoslavia, the foreign investors found it difficult to deal with Yugoslav industry directly, and foreign funds began to percolate into the country through the intermediary of the Vienna banks.[6]

Thus Yugoslavia found herself in precisely the situation she tried so strenuously to avoid: she found it necessary to rely on Vienna for the financing of her industry. Economic need has, however, overcome to some extent the fear of possible foreign domination, although as yet very little foreign capital has found its way into Yugoslavia, either directly or through the intermediary of Vienna.

II. TARIFF POLICY AND COMMERCIAL TREATY ARRANGEMENTS

In her commercial policy, Yugoslavia began her independent existence as a successor of Serbia. The Serbian tariff of 1904 was made applicable to the

[6] Todorović, M., "Investment of Foreign Capital in Our Industrial Enterprises," *Belgrade Economic and Financial Review*, January, 1924.

triune Kingdom, and the commercial treaties between Serbia and other powers which still remained in force were made applicable to Yugoslavia. But the exigencies of the post-war period imposed many new factors upon this structure. These factors moulded the commercial policy of the country into forms far removed from the arrangements and practices of the pre-war period.

Yugoslavia's commercial policy was highly unstable during the first few post-war years. Various factors dominated it at different times. At first the need of restocking the country with the necessities of life, after the exhaustion caused by the war, was preeminent in the situation. Later on, considerations of currency and exchange became prominent, and conflicts arose between policies based on these considerations and those looking toward the need of keeping the country adequately supplied with prime necessities. Still later, the element of industrial protection entered into the picture. All this resulted in a veritable stream of confusing regulations and counter-regulations.

From the termination of the war to the end of 1919 the principal preoccupation of Yugoslavia in the domain of commercial policy was the stimulation of imports and the restriction of exports. As early as August 30, 1918, the exportation of almost all classes of commodities was forbidden by government decree. Exceptions were made only in the case of commodities which were not considered essential or of which there was an abundance. In March, 1919, a Central Bureau of Foreign Trade was established, for the purpose of regulating the export trade. On the other hand, because of an acute need of commodities within the country, imports were stimulated by means of a lowering or a complete removal of customs duties on some classes of merchandise and by the granting of government credits to importers.

Special restrictions were applied to the countries formed out of the territory of the former Austro-Hungarian Monarchy with the view to preventing the introduction into Yugoslavia of large amounts of paper crowns. Trade with Austria, Hungary, and Czechoslovakia was regulated on the basis of barter treaties, concluded during the year.

After 1919 the currency situation began to exercise a very marked influence on commercial policy. Under the pressure of fiscal inflation, the exchange rate of the dinar began to depreciate, and the Ministry of Finance sought to remedy this situation by forcing the foreign trade into a condition of balance. With this in view, export restrictions were lightened, while imports began to be restricted by means of increased customs duties and prohibitions of luxury imports.

But at the same time, the Ministry of Food, alarmed lest supplies within the country be unduly decreased by large exports, began to take measures for a continued restriction of exports. In the chaotic political conditions in which the Yugoslav government operated during these early years, these conflicting policies were permitted to function side by side.[7]

This period of confusion lasted for some time, with the currency aspect of the situation playing an increasingly important rôle. The maintenance of import restrictions by means of high tariff duties was moreover influenced by the growing reliance of the government budget upon customs receipts and the demands of industry for a large degree of protection. It was to some extent responsible for Yugoslavia's refusal to ratify the Portorose protocol, although the principal reason for that refusal was the feeling on the part of the Yugoslav leaders that the general condition of the country was too unstable for the government to relinquish its control of the foreign trade.

It was only gradually that the period of confusion yielded to more stable commercial policies. The feeling in favor of tariff protection crystallized more and more, and work was begun on a new and definitive customs tariff, which could serve as the basis for regular commercial treaties. At the same time negotiations were opened with Italy for the conclusion of a tariff treaty.

The treaty with Italy and the tariff of 1925 marked the beginning of a stable commercial policy. Al-

[7] Todorović, M., "The Commercial Policy of Yugoslavia," *Manchester Guardian Commercial: Reconstruction in Europe Series,* July 27, 1922.

though the Italian treaty was signed in 1924, its ratification by the Yugoslav Parliament was delayed, pending the introduction of the new tariff, which went into effect on June 30, 1925. Since then Yugoslavia has entered into negotiations with a number of countries for the conclusion of tariff treaties.

Prior to that Yugoslavia had commercial treaty relations with a large number of European powers. These treaties embodied the most-favored-nation treatment principle, but were mostly of short duration and did not provide a stable basis for commercial relations.

A tariff treaty with Austria was negotiated fairly soon after the new tariff went into effect. In this manner Yugoslavia has so far established regular commercial treaty relations with the two countries which play the largest part in her foreign trade. Several other important negotiations, notably those with Germany, are still pending.

The tariff of 1925 is distinctly protectionist in character. It is based on maximum and minimum duties, and in this manner operates as an instrument for bargaining in negotiations. But it is constructed in such a way that its principal object is to afford protection to the country's industries.

The customs duties provided in the tariff are considerably higher than those which were in operation under the 1904 tariff, and even under the amended tariff of 1921. The maximum tariff adds 34.8 per cent to the value of imports. The group of commodities which carries the highest protection is glass and glassware; the tariff adds 53.3 per cent to the cost of these commodities. Next comes the stone and clay products group with 48.6 per cent; foodstuffs with 48.3 per cent; forest products, with 44.7 per cent; and iron products with 41.1 per cent. The duty on textiles is 29.9 per cent; on metal products, other than iron, 25 per cent; and on machinery, 22.8 per cent.[8]

The minimum tariff is somewhat below these maximum rates. It includes at the present time primarily concessions given to Italy and Austria in the tariff treaties signed with these two countries, and is extended to all the countries with which Yugoslavia has commercial treaties based on most-favored-nation treatment principle.

III. ATTITUDE TOWARD THE QUESTION OF A LARGER ECONOMIC TERRITORY

The economic policy of Yugoslavia, as we have seen from the foregoing discussion, is directed primarily towards an internal development and intensification of economic activity. The task that lies before the triune Kingdom is one of organizing its economic life in such a way as to provide for a greater utilization than heretofore of its very considerable natural resources. In the nature of the situation, the accomplishment of this task can be only gradual. The country's primary interest, so

[8] *Zollhöhe und Warenwerte,* Table I.

far as its economic relations with the rest of the world are concerned, lies in the finding of markets for the exports of foodstuffs, forest products, and some minerals. And this consideration is of great importance in Yugoslavia's attitude toward the question of a Danubian union.

Yugoslavia does not consider that her interests would be served best by the formation of a Danubian economic union. In this respect the same considerations apply in her case as in the case of Hungary and Rumania. So far as her exports of foodstuffs are concerned, Austria and Czechoslovakia, the two food-importing countries of the Danubian group, can scarcely provide her with any larger markets than at present, especially with Hungary and Rumania also expecting larger markets for foodstuffs within the union. As for forest and mineral products, their exportation cannot be greatly advanced by the formation of a Danubian economic combination.

Just as the other two agricultural exporters of the Danubian group, Yugoslavia can look for larger food markets only in the countries which are at the present time purchasers of overseas supplies. Even if she really succeeded in accomplishing the transformation of her agriculture along the lines which we indicated on page 524, she would still have to seek her increased markets in countries which have large requirements of agricultural products.

Favorable treaty arrangements with her Danubian neighbors are considered in Yugoslavia amply sufficient to serve her interests in trade intercourse with these countries. It is true that she has been rather slow in placing her commercial relations on a basis of regular treaties. But this has been due primarily to difficult political conditions at home.

Fear of foreign economic domination is a strong factor in Yugoslavia's attitude toward the question of a regional economic union. This is especially true with regard to a possible increase of Austrian financial influence in Yugoslavia. Vienna is still the most important financial center with which Yugoslavia can deal. She acts as a middleman in the matter of obtaining foreign loans, as well as in respect of foreign trade. While the general attitude of Yugoslavia on the question of foreign capital has been undergoing a change in the direction away from uncompromising nationalism, she is still anxious to build up her own international trade and financial connections.

Yugoslavia fears Budapest much less than Vienna. On the contrary, there appears to be a movement both in Yugoslavia and in Hungary for the establishment of closer relations between the two countries. The basis of this movement is, however, political, rather than economic. From the point of view of her foreign trade, Yugoslavia has little to gain from a close cooperation with Hungary.

Similarly the problem of a possible union between Yugoslavia and Bulgaria is a political, rather than economic, question. The two countries are much too similar in their economic characteristics to have any advantages to offer each other, while the trade between them is negligible.

The question of a possible Austro-German union is of close concern to Yugoslavia. While from the point of view of its possible bearing on the problem of changes in the peace treaties, Yugoslavia is as vitally interested in the question as Czechoslovakia and Rumania, she has a peculiar problem of her own which may influence her attitude toward the question of the union. This problem is her relations with Italy.

Italy is the largest market for Yugoslav exports, but she is also Yugoslavia's most powerful neighbor and one with whom the triune Kingdom has had differences almost continuously since the end of the war. The final solution of the Fiume problem, after five years of intermittent negotiations, opened the way for the conclusion between the two countries of a regular commercial treaty. But the outstanding differences between Italy and Yugoslavia have not been solved. Their interests clash in Albania, and the existence of this complicated problem creates an enduring strain in their relations.

There is a current of opinion in Yugoslavia which is inclined to regard the question of an Austro-German union in the light of its possible bearing on the problem of the country's relations with Italy. According to this view, Yugoslavia might feel rather safer with two powerful neighbors than with one.

It is interesting to note that Serbia was never, before the war, as antagonistic toward Germany as toward Austria. This feeling appears to be still in evidence in present-day Yugoslavia.

Apart from these political considerations, which contemplate at best merely a choice between two evils, there is also a feeling in some Yugoslav circles that the establishment of a common frontier between Germany and Yugoslavia (political or economic) might prove to be of advantage to Yugoslavia economically. The establishment of closer relations with Germany might open up real opportunities for an increase of Yugoslavia's agricultural exports. With Germany and Italy as her immediate neighbors, Yugoslavia might reap the advantages of proximity for her export trade, provided, of course, she succeeded in maintaining amicable relations with both of them.

PART VII

NATIONALISM VERSUS UNITY

CHAPTER XXX

FACTORS IN THE SITUATION

In the foregoing chapters we dealt with the economic experience of the Danubian countries since the war and indicated the major problems and interests of each of them. We saw that during the years that elapsed since the termination of the war, each of the five countries under discussion faced and overcame many of the difficulties that had confronted it and went far in its emergence from the disorganization and chaos of the first post-war years into varying degrees of organization and well-being. Each of the five countries still faces grave problems, and each of them has developed a more or less thorough-going economic policy, in the light of which it is contemplating these problems. With this in mind we may now turn to a more general consideration of the Danubian countries as a group.

In this chapter we shall examine the major factors which appear to be operative so far as the whole group of Danubian States is concerned—what may be termed the Danubian problem, as distinguished from the problems of each of the Danubian States. On the basis of our discussion of the experience and policy of each of the five countries, we shall attempt to disclose the outstanding features of the situation existing in the Danubian territory as a whole, rather than in any one of its component parts. In the chapter which follows, we shall examine the possibilities of the plans proposed for the improvement of the situation in the Danubian countries, dealt with as a group, and make an appraisal of these possibilities.

I. MALADJUSTMENTS CREATED BY THE TREATIES OF PEACE

The Danubian States came into existence as a result of the break-up of the Austro-Hungarian Monarchy, although formally they owe their status as independent nations to the treaties of peace. The question of the justice or the injustice of these treaties is outside the scope of this study. What is of importance to us in this connection is the fact that these treaties constitute the international basis of the present-day Danubian States.

The forces which led to the break-up of the Monarchy were originally set into motion by the struggle of the subject national groups against the two dominant groups, the Austrian and the Hungarian. In their idealistic aspects, the liberation movements of the formerly subject groups sought to eliminate the abuses of which these groups considered themselves the victims. In the practical working out of the arrangements, which, after the war, supplanted the

Monarchy, it was found impossible to eliminate the abuses and yet leave the new scheme of things free from maladjustments and dissatisfaction.

Of the five heirs of the Austro-Hungarian Monarchy here under consideration, the treaties of peace left three contented and two discontented nations. In the natural order of things, the formerly subject, now liberated, peoples—constituting Czechoslovakia, Rumania, and Yugoslavia—belong to the first group; the defeated and dismembered Austria and Hungary belong to the second. The reader will recall, from our previous discussion of the Danubian States as national entities [1] how important a rôle this element in the situation has played in the development of their nationalism.

The fortunes of war and of revolution shaped this aspect of the Danubian situation. It is idle to attempt an appraisal of the extent to which the peace settlement might or might not have been more mutually satisfactory. Time will show whether the arrangements embodied in the treaties of St. Germain and Trianon are permanently workable or not. It is not impossible that at some future date they may be changed in such a way as to allay the discontent of the defeated countries, without impairing too much what the victor states have come to regard as their essential interests.

In the meantime, the discontent of the defeated countries in the Danubian basin, although it has lost

[1] See Chapter IV.

some of the uncompromising virulence which characterized it during the first post-war years, remains an important maladjustment created by the treaties of peace. Despite the passage of years, this discontent still retains its character as one of the outstanding factors in all discussions concerned with the establishment of closer economic collaboration among the Danubian countries. Apart from its purely political aspects, such as the loss of prestige, etc., it is fed largely by two tangible grievances, concerned with the disposition of population and the disruption of economic relationships.

The treaties of peace failed to solve the problem of racial minorities. The Slavic and the Rumanian minorities of the Monarchy were freed from their former Austrian and Hungarian overlords, but in the process of adjusting frontiers, large groups of Austrians and Hungarians were placed under the overlordship of the liberated groups. True, the treaties made provisions for the protection of the rights of minorities. To the extent to which these provisions are being carried out, the present arrangement represents, in this respect, a great advance over the situation that existed in the Monarchy. But the minority problem still remains.

Here again it is a question of the fortunes of war. There are nowhere in Europe sharply differentiated ethnic frontiers. Areas of racially mixed populations are the rule, rather than the exception. Moreover, in the case of the former Monarchy, there was a strong element of the so-called "historic wrongs." In the course of their long subjection, the territories of the now liberated groups were colonized by Germans and Hungarians. In Bohemia, for example, the last revolt against the Habsburg rule over three centuries ago, gave the Austrian government a pretext for taking some of the best lands away from the Bohemian nobility and giving them into Austrian ownership. The large natural resources of the Bohemian territory attracted large numbers of Austrian Germans, who, with the aid of Vienna, became a numerically large and economically powerful group of the population. Therefore, in reclaiming at the time of the break-up of the Monarchy, the historic frontiers of the ancient Kingdom of Bohemia, the Czechoslovaks inevitably had to include in their newly constituted country a large number of Austrian Germans. They faced a similar problem in Slovakia and Sub-Carpathian Ruthenia with respect to Hungarians.

On the other hand, the defeated nations have claimed consistently that more has been taken from them than they had originally attached to themselves—that portions of their own ancient territory have been detached from them. Such, for example, is the Hungarian argument against the loss of several cities on the Danube, which, they claim, Czechoslovakia took from Hungary in order to gain access to the river. Of the same nature is Hungary's resentment against the loss of several districts in

Transylvania, and Austria's protests against her present frontier in the Tyrol. A new set of "historic wrongs" has thus been created, with the grievances reversed.

Without going into the merits of these claims and counterclaims as to old or new "historic wrongs," it is quite clear that their existence and the emphasis they acquire in the minds of the peoples concerned represent an important element in the Danubian situation. Finding their expression in the minority problem, they constitute an indubitable maladjustment, which has an important bearing on the problem of economic relations.

The frontiers established by the treaties of peace cut across economically interdependent areas. With principal emphasis placed on ethnic delimitation and the re-establishment of historic frontiers, the question of economic interrelations was left almost entirely out of account in the defining of the territorial limits of the newly created and reconstituted states. Each of the countries received whatever resources and equipment happened to be located in the territory assigned to it. The result of all this was that factories were often cut off from their supplies of raw materials and fuel, and vice versa. Mutually dependent industries, in some instances, branches of the same industry, became separated by frontiers. A good example of this kind is furnished by the textile industry of Austria: the spindles of its equipment were located principally in Bohemia and Moravia, now parts of Czechoslovakia, while the weaving looms were mainly in and about Vienna.

This, perhaps the most serious of the maladjustments created by the treaties of peace, was also very largely unavoidable. The economic system of the Austro-Hungarian Monarchy was not and could not have been built with any special reference to a possible dissolution of the country along more or less definite ethnic lines. On the contrary, in the process of its development it had cut across these lines, and when the territory of the Monarchy became reorganized on the basis of ethnic boundaries, the new frontiers cut the existing economic system into fragments.

Both the victor and the vanquished states of the Danubian group have felt the burden of this maladjustment. Each of them has sought in its own way to overcome the difficulties thus placed before it.

II. SITUATION RESULTING FROM A DECADE OF POST-WAR EXPERIENCE

Each of the three Danubian countries which were carved wholly out of the territory of the former Monarchy was confronted with the task of organizing a new economic system within its territory out of segments of what had formerly been larger units. The other two, Rumania and Yugoslavia, faced the task of coördinating the segments that had fallen to their share with the economic system each of them had had as an independent Kingdom. Now, after almost a decade of experience as national entities, these countries are confronted with a situation which has a number of outstanding features.

A system of restrictions against mutual economic intercourse is a prominent feature of the present situation in the Danubian countries. These restrictions arose, for the most part, out of the necessities of the abnormal conditions in which the war and the process of their formation left the heirs of the Austro-Hungarian Monarchy. Their existence to this day, when many of these abnormal conditions have disappeared, is the result of developments to which they themselves have given rise.

Very much the same factors operated in all of the Danubian countries as regards economic restrictions. Furthermore, these same factors existed also in other European countries. The rigid regulation of foreign trade which was adopted by the Danubian countries at the beginning existed as well in such countries as Germany and Poland. Owing its origin largely to the exhaustion produced by the war, this system of trade restrictions was intensified in the Danubian countries by the process whereby they sought to build themselves up as national entities. The use of the system as an instrument for the regulation of currency problems was another important factor in stimulating its application.

The system of trade restrictions operated primarily in the direction of protecting domestic production.

It created in each country economic interests in the form of enterprises and developments, which absorbed large investments of capital and effort. Once created, these interests came to depend for their survival upon continued protection, principally by means of customs tariffs. This has been an important obstacle in preventing the removal of the economic barriers which separate these countries.

Another important obstacle is the fact that none of the countries concerned feels strong enough to take the initiative in freeing itself from a system which came into existence as a result of abnormal conditions and persists after these conditions have ceased to exist. All international attempts to remove this system have failed, largely because of the impossibility of obtaining concerted action. This was the fate of the Portorose protocol. This, so far, has been the fate of the convention drawn up by the International Diplomatic Conference on the Removal of Export and Import Prohibitions and Restrictions, which was held at Geneva, in October, 1927.

The best example of the difficulty in approaching this problem from the point of view of action by individual countries is found in the development of Austria's policy. Austria's interests lie overwhelmingly in the direction of freer trade intercourse. Yet her policy has been developing in exactly the opposite direction, because of her feeling that in the absence of a concerted agreement and action the only thing that remains is bargaining for trade advantages.

It is primarily in the field of industry that the effects of the system of trade restrictions have been most strongly felt. Here, more than in any other field, we have the manifestations of economic interests, which, while their creation might have been to some extent wasteful and unnecessary, nevertheless exist and cannot be disregarded.

The outstanding result of post-war experience in the Danubian countries has been the growth of industry in the formerly non-industrial areas. Whatever the reasons that have been responsible for this phenomenon, the fact is that during the years that have elapsed since the war, Hungary, Rumania, and Yugoslavia have definitely embarked upon a career of industrialization. Whether pushed into this development by the difficulties of commercial intercourse during the early post-war years, or actuated by such considerations as the population problem, a desire for a more varied economic activity within its frontiers, needs of national defense in case of war, or general national prestige, each of these countries has, in the course of the past decade, developed a will toward industrialization.

The greatest expansion of industrial activity in formerly non-industrial areas came during the years of the most widespread restrictions of economic intercourse. These were also the years when monetary inflation was stimulating the construction of new equipment. With the stabilization of currencies and the development of freer commercial relations, the growth of new industrial equipment slowed down, while some of the mushroom growths of the inflation period disappeared. But the impulse toward industrial activity has not subsided. The process of industrialization has assumed somewhat more rational forms, but the will toward it appears firmly implanted.

It is impossible to tell how much actually additional equipment has been constructed. Many new plants had to be put up merely to replace those destroyed or damaged by the war. In the case of some industries there has been a good deal of redistribution of equipment. For example, the machinery of the textile industry that has grown up in Hungary, Rumania, and Yugoslavia has come, to some extent, from the dismantled textile mills of Czechoslovakia. On the other hand, there has undoubtedly been some genuinely new construction.

Conflicts between the industrialized and the industrializing areas have exercised an important influence on the Danubian situation. The reader will recall from our discussion in Chapter I that similar conflicts existed before the war in the Austro-Hungarian Monarchy. Under post-war conditions, these conflicts have become much sharper, and their effects during the decade that has elapsed since the war have been very real. Back of these conflicts now is the authority of sovereign states, which is freely exercised toward a definite end in the industrializing countries. Once the government of such a country decides upon the desirability of promoting industrial activity, it can do much in this direction. The measures taken since the war by the governments of Hungary, Rumania, and Yugoslavia bear ample witness to this.

The rise of industrialism in what had formerly been primarily agricultural countries has had interesting repercussions in the industrialized countries. It has stimulated in them an intensification of agricultural activities. This is especially true of Czechoslovakia, which has done a great deal during the past decade toward increasing her domestic production of essential foodstuffs.

From this point of view the industrial development in Hungary, Rumania, and Yugoslavia affected adversely some of the markets for their surplus agricultural products. Moreover, industrial development has been and continues to be a very costly process. The cost of initial installation is high, because the liquid capital resources of these countries are very meager. The costs of operation are also high, because of lack of experience and the comparatively small scale of operations. The need of giving the developing industries tariff protection on the basis of high costs of domestic production places a very appreciable burden of high prices on the consumer. In the case of the agricultural population, this burden is increased by the fact that agricultural products are turned out in quantities much too large for home consumption, requiring the exportation of the surplus and thus placing the price of these products under the influence of general world prices.

Thus the rise of industrialism in what had formerly been primarily agricultural areas and the consequent conflict between industrialized and industrializing countries appears at first sight to be a development detrimental to everybody concerned. Czechoslovakia and Austria find themselves unable to utilize their industrial equipment and compelled, in order to make up for the loss of industrial exports, to curtail their agricultural imports by protecting their own agriculture. In this manner they have to pay higher prices for foodstuffs, without benefiting their industry. Hungary, Rumania, and Yugoslavia maintain industries at a large cost to the domestic consumers, and at the same time find their agriculture in a more or less critical condition. These effects do not, however, reveal the whole story, nor do they prove existing policies necessarily wrong.

The population problem is a profoundly important factor in the Danubian situation. The Austro-Hungarian Monarchy was confronted with this problem, and sought to solve it partly by emigration and partly by industrialization. It was still far from a more or less adequate solution of this problem when the holocaust of war shattered the Monarchy itself. But broken into segments, the territory of the former Monarchy still faces the same problem, which confronts alike the primarily industrial and the primarily agricultural countries of the group.

During the ten years of their post-war existence, the Danubian countries have discovered no other basic way of dealing with their population problem than that followed by the Monarchy. It is true that the agrarian reform, introduced with a fair degree of thoroughness in Czechoslovakia, Rumania, and Yugoslavia, has provided a certain amount of relief. A reorganization of land holdings in Austria and a thorough-going agrarian reform in Hungary would accomplish similar results. But the relief thus provided has not been adequate. Emigration and industrialization still appear to be the only effective approaches to the population problem.[2]

The emigration possibilities of the Danubian countries are much smaller than had been those of the Monarchy. The United States, which during the last pre-war decade absorbed each year over 200,000 emigrants from the Monarchy alone, now admits very few. There is comparatively little migration to other parts of the world.

Industrialization, therefore, remains as the principal method of providing a livelihood for the whole of the population. From our discussion of the situation in each of the Danubian countries, we have seen how important a rôle this problem plays. It explains in large measure not only the reluctance of

[2] The problem of restriction of population through birth control is left out of account, principally because the effects of such a policy would emerge too slowly to affect the present situation.

Austria and Czechoslovakia to reduce their industrial activities, but also the determination on the part of Hungary, and to a smaller degree of Rumania and Yugoslavia, to continue the process of industrialization.

Can the situation be aided by some sort of concerted action by the whole group of the Danubian States? Before turning, in the next chapter, to the possibilities of what might be termed a "Danubian solution," we have to consider still another factor in the Danubian situation, this time one which transcends their territory as a group.

III. INTERESTS OF OTHER POWERS

So far we have dealt with the factors in the Danubian situation which pertain primarily to the Danubian States themselves. But the question of what happens to these countries is of direct interest to other European powers as well, since they too are more or less vitally concerned with what takes place in the basin of the Danube.

The four great powers of central and western Europe, namely Great Britain, France, Germany, and Italy, all have an interest in the Danubian situation.[3] There are two principal ways in which the Danubian situation affects these powers. In the first place, the three great former allies are signa-

[3] Russia is here left out of account, because she is not as yet an important factor in the European situation, though there is no doubt, of course, that sooner or later she will resume her rôle of first-rate importance.

tories of the treaties of peace which affect the Danubian countries. They must, therefore, be consulted in any projects that have a bearing on the basic terms laid down in these treaties. In the second place, all four of these powers have most-favored-nation commercial treaties with the Danubian States, and their consent must therefore be sought in the negotiation of any arrangement that would involve an exception to the principle underlying these treaties. On this latter point such powers as the United States and Japan must also be consulted. Finally, there are some European powers which may be said to have special interests in the situation.

Steps tending toward any changes in the situation created by the treaties of peace are a matter of vital concern to all European powers. To what extent the establishment of close economic relations among the Danubian countries would involve such changes would depend upon how broad an interpretation could be placed on the provisions of the treaties. In any event no steps in this direction could be definitely undertaken by the Danubian countries alone.

So far as the most-favored-nation principle is concerned, any exceptions from it are clearly matters that concern other powers than the Danubian States alone. Such exceptions as regional preferential arrangements have been recognized.[4] But before ne-

[4] For example the Resolution on Commerce, adopted by the International Economic Conference, states: "It is highly desir-

gotiations for such an arrangement can be opened among the Danubian countries consent must first be obtained from all the countries having most-favored-nation treaties with the countries of the Danubian group.

The principal country that has what might be termed "special interests" is Italy. As one of the heirs of the Austro-Hungarian Monarchy, Italy has consistently maintained that she is entitled to special consideration in any preferential arrangement that is based on the fact that the Danubian States have common economic interests in view of their derivation from the former Monarchy. Poland, the seventh heir of the Monarchy, might make similar claims.

able that the widest and most unconditional interpretation should be given to the most-favored-nation clause. This is not inconsistent with the insertion in any particular treaty of special provisions to meet local needs, so long as such provisions are clearly expressed and do not injure the interests of other States." *Final Report of the Conference*, Geneva, 1927, p. 32.

CHAPTER XXXI

APPRAISAL OF POSSIBILITIES

THREE distinct possibilities are open to the Danubian States. They may constitute themselves into isolated units, each striving toward self-sufficiency. They may unite into a single economic territory. They may continue their existence as national entities, tending toward closer and mutually beneficent relations with each other and with other countries. We may rule out at once the first possibility, because it has never been seriously entertained by any responsible group in any one of the countries under discussion. In this chapter we shall examine and appraise the two remaining possibilities.

The principal reason why in all discussions of what may, for the sake of convenience, be called the Danubian problem, the possibility of a Danubian economic union is so often suggested, is that the bulk of the territory comprising the five countries of the group constituted, before the war, an economically more or less unified area. The advantages of a large economic union over five small units are urged in favor of such a development. Here we have a plausible analogy, which we shall examine in the light of the discussion contained in our chapters on the economic policy of each of the five countries and on the principal factors involved in the Danubian situation taken as a whole.

I. DIFFICULTIES IN THE CREATION OF A DANUBIAN ECONOMIC UNION

There are three main sets of difficulties inherent in the process of combining the five Danubian States into an economically unified territory. The first is concerned with national sovereignty and with political apprehensions on the part of some of these states. The second lies in the need of finding a suitable form into which the unification could be molded. The third is the attitude of the outside powers.

Considerations of national sovereignty constitute a factor of paramount importance. The formerly subject groups of the Austro-Hungarian Monarchy, having become independent states, are not disposed to regard sovereignty as a purely political matter, quite apart from economic factors. On the contrary, their experience in the Monarchy leads them to an opposite conclusion.

There is no doubt that the concentration of economic and financial power in Vienna, for the whole Monarchy as well as for the Austrian Empire proper, and in Budapest for the Kingdom of Hungary, was no accident. The whole economic development of the Monarchy revolved around these two pivotal points. While such concentration had its indubitable advantages, it also inevitably reacted to the advantage of the dominant groups and to the disadvantage of the subject groups. In fact these latter consistently directed their efforts toward liberation, not only from the political rule of Habsburg dynasty, but also from the economic domination of the powerful capitals. The efforts of the Czechs to create their own financial and economic center in Prague and of the Croatians to do the same in Zagreb were indicative of this. And even Budapest strove for economic and financial independence from Vienna.

It is true that today the political power of Vienna is negligible, while that of Budapest is not very much greater. But the economic and financial power of Vienna still remains very great. Moreover, one of the objects in the creation of an economically unified Danubian territory would be to make the advantages of the financial and trade apparatus built up in Vienna available once more to the whole territory, giving Vienna at the same time an opportunity to derive benefits from the exercise of these functions. To a smaller extent, the same considerations apply to Budapest as regards the territories detached from Hungary.

Czechoslovakia, Rumania, Yugoslavia, and even Hungary are frankly apprehensive of a renewed concentration of economic and financial power in Vienna. While conditions are different politically from what they were before the break-up of the

Monarchy, these countries still feel that such a concentration might constitute a potential threat to their hard-won sovereignty.

The form of an economic union presents a serious difficulty. As a matter of fact, no serious discussions of the question have ever gone beyond the scope of some sort of trade arrangement, with a customs union as the ultimate limit. Of the adequacy of such an arrangement we shall speak further on. But there are real difficulties even in the achievement of this degree of unity.

The Austro-Hungarian Monarchy, while a free trade area within its frontiers, was surrounded by a tariff wall which separated it from the rest of the world. Within this wall were economically conflicting areas. The character and the scope of tariff protection was determined by means of a compromise between the interests of the Empire of Austria and the Kingdom of Hungary, and such compromise was not always easy to achieve or to maintain over a long period of time.

A Danubian customs union would re-establish a free-trade area. But the difficulties of providing this area with adequate protection from the competition of the rest of the world would be very much greater than those which confronted the Monarchy. In place of a compromise between sovereign Austria and autonomous Hungary, it would be necessary to reconcile the views and interests of five fully sovereign states.

A form of economic union going beyond the limits of a customs arrangement would present still greater difficulties. It is very symptomatic that no discussion of the problem, except that concerned with the admittedly illusory Danubian confederation, has ever set forth a definite form for such a union.

The attitude of outside powers renders unification difficult. As they are, the five Danubian countries constitute important markets, especially so far as trade in manufactured goods is concerned. The areas which import such goods are now open to competition, on equal terms, between the industrial centers of the former Monarchy which had supplied them before the war and the industries of other countries. Recombined into a single, customs-protected territory, they would cease to be such markets. The result of this would be that the other industrial countries would have to renounce the relative privilege which they now enjoy in favor of the industries of Austria and Czechoslovakia. And they have not as yet shown any great willingness to do this.

Perhaps the greatest opposition in this respect has come from Italy. The difficulties of her own economic situation are so great that she cannot afford to give up any trade advantage that she may possess. True, her exports to the Danubian countries are not very great, but they are increasing in volume. She is thus acquiring in the Danubian countries growing markets for her exports of manufactured goods, which constitute an essential element in her economic improvement.[1] These advantages would be greatly curtailed at least for the time being by an economic unification of the Danubian countries. Italy's status as one of the heirs of the Austro-Hungarian Monarchy gives her an opportunity for insisting upon being a participant in any trade arrangements that are made, as among themselves, by the other heirs.

The other industrial countries of Europe, while they are not as outspoken on the matter as Italy, are also loath to forego their advantages. Italy's attitude in the matter simply saves them the necessity of voicing their objections, while making it possible for them to look askance at any trade arrangement among the Danubian countries which may also include Italy.

On the other hand, it is argued that the Danubian countries, combined into a single economic territory, will eventually represent a much larger market for the other European countries than they will as separate entities. It is pointed out that the five Danubian countries today purchase from the rest of the world scarcely three-quarters of what this same territory purchased before the war. But so far, the exigencies of the present have outweighed the possible advantages of the future.

[1] For a discussion of Italy's general economic situation see McGuire, Constantine E., *Italy's International Economic Position* (Investigations in International Economic Reconstruction, Institute of Economics, Washington), 1926.

II. ADEQUACY OF A DANUBIAN CUSTOMS UNION

On the whole it must be admitted that a customs union represents approximately the furthest limit to which considerations of national sovereignty and the technical difficulties involved in finding a form of more far-reaching collaboration would permit the development of economic unity among the Danubian countries. Clearly, there are serious obstacles in the way of achieving even this degree of unity. But all things considered, these obstacles might, probably, not prove insuperable, were there a real desire on the part of all the countries of the Danubian group for economic unity—were they all really convinced that such a development would be to their best advantage. There is, however, no such agreement among the Danubian countries. The reason is to be found in the different effects such a union would have on the several countries.

The establishment of a customs union would aid the industrial, but not the agricultural, countries. As we have already seen, Austria and Czechoslovakia would welcome the establishment of freer trade relations among the Danubian countries, the first in any form whatever, the second, in the form of a preferential customs régime, rather than as a full-fledged customs union. Freedom from the competition of other industrial countries in the markets of the industrially under-developed countries of the Danubian basin would give Austria and Czechoslovakia an opportunity for utilizing more fully than at the present time their industrial equipment for the trade requirements of the territory for which this equipment was originally built up. But even that would not restore to them entirely their former markets. The establishment of a customs union or of freer trade relations in some other form could not undo altogether the results of post-war experience. The industries which have grown up in the formerly non-industrial areas would not be altogether swept out of existence by the withdrawal of customs protection, for they would doubtless continue to have administrative protection of some sort.

For example, countries like Rumania and Yugoslavia, which possess both mineral and fuel resources necessary for the development of a metallurgical industry, would not be unlikely to promote these industries by placing with them the orders of state-owned enterprises. Use of home-produced rails in the construction of government-owned railways is an instance of this kind.

In the case of Austria, more than in that of Czechoslovakia, the regaining of some of the former Danubian markets would meet only a part of the present difficulties. Austria needs not only an opportunity for a fuller utilization of her industrial equipment, but also an opportunity for deriving a fuller benefit from the trade and financial apparatus of the city of Vienna. To this end the establishment of freer trade relations would contribute comparatively little. For this the Danubian countries would have to become not merely a free-trade, but also an economically unified territory in a much wider sense, with Vienna as a voluntarily accepted financial and trade center.

To the primarily agricultural countries, the disadvantages of a union appear to outweigh the advantages. The foremost interest of Hungary, Rumania, and Yugoslavia lies in the development of their agricultural resources. Even at present each of these countries is an exporter of foodstuffs and agricultural raw materials, and each is capable of expanding production considerably beyond the present level. But increased foreign markets necessary to absorb the extra output cannot be developed in the Danubian territory.

The primarily industrial countries of the Danubian group now depend for their importations of foodstuffs largely on their Danubian neighbors. They cannot substantially increase their purchases of these products from the primarily agricultural countries of the group. Freedom of commercial intercourse among the Danubian States would therefore offer but little benefit to the agricultural countries from the point of view of an expansion of their production.

It is true that with the lowering or the abolition of the tariff walls that separate the primarily industrial from the primarily agricultural countries the latter would have the benefit of lower prices on manufactured goods of mass consumption. But these prices would still be higher than the general level of world prices, since the whole territory would have to have tariff protection against the competition of larger and industrially better equipped countries.

The creation of a free-trade area comprising the five Danubian States would thus mean for the primarily agricultural countries the destruction of a large share of the industrial equipment that they have created since the war, without giving them in exchange opportunities for an adequate development of their agricultural activities. It would reduce the possibility of relief for their population problem through industrialization, without offering them as large a benefit in the form of lower prices for manufactured goods of general consumption as they might obtain by facilitating imports of such commodities from all industrial countries, and not from Austria and Czechoslovakia alone.

III. IS THERE A DANUBIAN SOLUTION?

Our discussion of the various problems and interests of the five Danubian States discloses the fact that there exist among them very real divergencies of interests, and that these numerous and various divergencies are not altogether of post-war origin. They are both political and economic in character, and it is just as impossible to separate the one from the other as it was impossible to segregate them in the affairs of the former Dual Monarchy. Freedom of trade within the Monarchy failed to allay the regional conflicts that were fast gathering momentum there. These regional conflicts have now become transformed into clashes of interests among five sovereign nations. Can these interests be either reconciled or adequately advanced by the creation of an economically united Danubian territory? In other words, is there a Danubian solution for the problems confronting each of the Danubian States?

In its most pressing aspects, the present Danubian problem appears to be that of Vienna and to a lesser degree of Budapest. The two capitals of the former Austro-Hungarian Monarchy suffered more than any other portions of the Habsburg domains as a result of the break-up of the Dual Monarchy. But we have to bear in mind the fact that to some extent the regional conflicts within the Monarchy were directed against the concentration of economic and financial power in the two capitals, especially in Vienna, which was partly the result of natural advantages, and partly of political factors.

If we look at the foreign trade of the five Danubian countries, we find that Czechoslovakia, Rumania, and Yugoslavia have an excess of exports over imports, while Austria and Hungary have an excess of imports over exports. The cities of Vienna and Budapest are largely responsible for this condition. In the Monarchy they paid for their material requirements with the services they were able to perform in trade and finance. They were the wealth centers of the Monarchy. Today they possess but a small part of their pre-war sources of income and in consequence constitute real burdens for the two small countries for which they serve as disproportionately large capital cities.

Vienna is a much more serious problem than Budapest. It is by far the larger of the two cities, and moreover it comprises a much larger proportion of the total population of Austria than does Budapest of the population of Hungary. It is the capital of a country which does not produce its own food supply and which has to depend for its well-being upon the exportation of manufactured goods, mostly in a highly competitive field, and upon the financial and trade services rendered by Vienna itself to other countries. Budapest is the capital of a country which has opportunities for development along less competitive lines. On the whole, Hungary with Budapest appears to be basically in a less precarious economic position than Austria with Vienna.

Any reconstruction of economic unity among the Danubian countries along lines analogous to those of the pre-war situation must therefore result, first of all, in a restoration to Vienna of its pre-war position as a trade and financial center. But in the meantime each of the other four countries of the group has developed its own facilities along these lines. Vienna's former predominant position in this respect has been definitely weakened, though it has retained it to some degree. A resumption by it of its pre-war rôle in full measure would have to be at the expense of very real developments in the other Danubian countries, and it is doubtful whether Vienna can offer them adequate compensation for this. Therefore, apart from other considerations, it appears unlikely that the other Danubian countries would consent to any economic unification in which Austria and Vienna would be the principal beneficiaries.

Outside of Austria, the trend of development in the Danubian States points in the direction of nationalism, rather than unity. This does not mean that Czechoslovakia, Hungary, Rumania, and Yugoslavia have not outlived or are not fast outliving the extreme isolationist ideas that pervaded their national policies during the early post-war years. On the contrary, they have made substantial advance toward freer economic intercourse among themselves and with the rest of the world. But none of these countries considers that its national interests impel it in the direction of seeking economic unity with the other countries of the group.

The first three of these countries are abundantly supplied with natural resources. Their populations, freed by the war from political subjection or from the confines of small, more or less primitive countries, are eager for economic development within their national frontiers. By dint of better utilization of their material resources and their labor force they have before them considerable opportunities for advancing their economic well-being beyond the pre-war level. They are not confronted with the choice, as is Austria, of becoming a part of a larger economic territory or falling into economic retrogression.

Hungary's future appears less bright than that of the other three countries, but it is better than that of Austria. Her people are somewhat handicapped by the psychological difficulty of accepting their post-war situation as the masters of a much smaller country than before the war. Her natural wealth is not nearly as extensive or varied as that of Czechoslovakia, Rumania, or Yugoslavia. Nevertheless her resources are probably sufficient to save her from the contemplation of the alternative that confronts Austria.

None of these countries can be an economically self-contained area. Indeed, except perhaps for a few extremists, no one in them contemplates such a possibility. Each of them is fully alive to the need of economic intercourse with other countries. Each is confronted with the task of defining its national interests and formulating its economic and commercial policies in such a way as to serve these interests best.

The growth of industrial activity in the formerly non-industrial areas is a part of this process. It would be difficult and futile to attempt an evaluation of the extent to which this growth is wasteful and unnecessary or of how far it is based on the real needs of the situation. In the course of our discussion we have indicated the character and scope of these industrial developments and of the importance of such considerations as the population factor in influencing the rise of industries.

The development of commercial policy is another phase of the same process. The past decade has witnessed great modifications in the commercial policy of the Danubian States. With the gradual subsidence of the acute animosities aroused by the war and the whole complex of circumstances in which the Danubian countries came into existence, with the more or less complete disappearance of such abnormal conditions as currency disorganization, budgetary chaos, and general economic exhaustion, the commercial policies of the Danubian States have been tending toward forms which would insure greater and greater mutual benefits from international trade.

Taken in its broad implications, commercial policy is concerned not only with tariff arrangements and concessions, but also with such important questions as frontier formalities, discriminatory transportation rates, technical financial arrangements, etc. With regard to all of these features of the situation there has been gradual improvement.

To be sure, a great deal still remains to be done in this field. But in this respect the situation in the

Danubian States is no different from that obtaining in other parts of Europe. The discussions at the International Economic Conference, held in May, 1927, bear ample witness to that. Further improvements along these lines would be of indubitable value to all countries concerned, and any improvement in the economic relations among the Danubian States would be a step toward a general betterment of the European situation as a whole. But such improvement need not necessarily be incompatible with the preservation by the Danubian States of their character as national entities. Their unification is too fundamental a change to be undertaken except for reasons of compelling necessity. And in the opinion of four out of the five Danubian States such reasons do not really exist.

The weight of argument is against the creation of a Danubian economic union. The possible advantages of such a union do not appear sufficiently great to outweigh the efforts involved in overcoming the obstacles inherent in the process of its organization. The fact that the bulk of the territory comprised in the five Danubian countries constituted before the war a politically united free-trade area fails to lend substance to the argument in favor of unity based on analogy with the pre-war situation. Even this powerful factor did not provide the Monarchy with the necessary basis for a reconciliation of regional interests and a real economic advancement. The political dissociation of the Monarchy and the developments which have taken place in each of the five countries that have risen out of its fragments have added new difficulties and created new obstacles to unity.

Our analysis of the problems and interests of these five countries, whether taken singly or as a group, points to the conclusion that these problems cannot be solved and these interests cannot be either reconciled or adequately advanced by the creation of an economically united Danubian territory. It indicates rather the need of considering the situation in each of the Danubian countries as a part of the general economic situation of Europe as a whole, and of seeking the solution of the problems involved on a European, rather than regional, scale.

In concluding that the creation of an economically unified Danubian territory does not provide an adequate solution for the problems confronting the five states concerned, we do not mean to question the advantages of large economic areas over small ones. But in applying this general proposition to any group of already existing national entities, functioning as economic units, it is necessary to consider the character of the area to be unified, and the effects of the unification on the basic economic interests involved. What these effects are likely to be in the case of the Danubian economic territory we have indicated in the course of our discussion.

IV. DANUBIAN PROBLEM AS A PART OF THE GENERAL EUROPEAN SITUATION

Of the five Danubian States discussed in this book, four—Czechoslovakia, Rumania, Yugoslavia, and Hungary—do not feel impelling reasons for amalgamation into a larger economic territory. It is true that their economic outlook, after a decade of existence as separate entities, is not free from difficulties. Each of them encounters obstacles in its efforts to find larger markets for commodities of which it is a surplus producer. But each feels that such markets are to be sought outside, rather than within, the Danubian territory.

The solution of the economic difficulties of these countries can come only with the general economic improvement of the whole of Europe and the establishment of freer commercial intercourse among European countries generally. Czechoslovakia may find more adequate outlets for the surplus of her manufactured products as the internal market of Europe expands. Only an increased demand for foodstuffs and agricultural raw materials on the part of the large, industrially developed countries of Europe can furnish the three primarily agricultural countries of the Danubian group with increased markets for their exports.

Austria alone of the countries of this group, feels impelling reasons for her incorporation in a larger economic territory. She, too, would undoubtedly gain from a general European improvement and the establishment of closer commercial relations among European countries generally. But it appears that even such improvement would not be sufficient to meet her economic requirements. As to the larger economic territory, in which Austria might be incorporated, there are two principal alternatives. One is the creation of a Danubian economic union; the other is an Austro-German union. The first of these plans is, on the whole, more difficult of achievement than the second. It is much easier to find a form in which a smaller territory can unite with a larger, than that in which five small territories, more or less approximating each other in size, can band together into a unified area.

However, the obstacles in the way of the establishment of an Austro-German union are by no means small or unimportant. Whether or not primarily industrial Austria would gain economically from a union with even more overwhelmingly industrial Germany is open to question. It is not impossible that as a part of the German economic system, Austria might become more efficiently organized and thereby be a substantial gainer. It is also not impossible that, incorporated in the German system, Austria would assume a decidedly secondary position and gain comparatively little. The Austrians argue that at the worst their situation after union with Germany could not be worse than it is today, and that at least the danger of further impoverishment would be removed. While a leap in the dark, union with Germany might hold out some hope for Austria where today she sees no hope at all.

But Austria realizes that until Germany becomes actively interested in the accomplishment of a union between them, she herself is powerless to bring the question to a definite issue. Germany has not as yet taken a definite stand on the question of union with Austria. Neither her political nor her economic situation has reached the stage at which she can really turn her attention to this problem. It is not unlikely, however, that some day she may be in a position to do so. When this happens, Germany's recrudescent prestige and weight in European affairs may do much toward overcoming the opposition which exists today, especially on the part of France, Italy, and Czechoslovakia, against Austro-German union. As time goes on, this opposition may become less determined, especially if Europe as a whole really develops a trend toward that closer economic association which has been slowly emerging from the chaos of post-war years.

What we have, for the sake of convenience, termed the Danubian problem, is thus in reality a part of the general problem that confronts Europe as a whole. Its solution in terms of some regional arrangement is difficult of achievement and offers little hope of advance if achieved. The economic well-being of each of the five countries with which we have dealt in this study is bound up, not so much with their mutual interrelations, as with the much larger problem of the trend of development likely to be followed by Europe as a whole.

APPENDIX

DATA ON THE INTERNATIONAL ACCOUNTS OF THE DANUBIAN COUNTRIES

In presenting the international accounts of the countries discussed in this book, we gave summary figures for the various items, covering, in the case of each country, only the period during which that country's currency has been more or less stable. The methods by which we arrived at these figures and the materials on which our evaluations are based are described in this Appendix.

The reader will note that in none of the countries under discussion is there a thoroughly complete and reliable statement of international accounts. Czechoslovakia and Hungary offer the closest approach to such a statement, and even for them many of the estimates are open to doubt.

As regards export and import figures, we have used the official statistics of the countries concerned. These figures are often questioned as to their reliability. On the whole, however, they appear to be sufficiently accurate for the purposes of appraising, in a more or less general way, the international financial relations of the Danubian countries.

Our estimates of the service items are necessarily approximations, based on the best evidence we have been able to obtain. As methods of research in this particular field are perfected in various countries, it will no doubt be possible to obtain more precise information on the subject. In the meantime, however, we believe that the data given in this book are not too far removed from reality to give a more or less undistorted view of this phase of the economic situation that has confronted the Danubian countries since the war.

I. AUSTRIA

There is no complete estimate of Austria's international accounts prepared either by the Austrian government or by any other institution or individual. The only fairly comprehensive study on the subject is one made by Dr. Friedrich Hertz of Vienna, published under the title, *Zahlungsbilanz und Lebensfähigkeit Oesterreichs,* Munich, 1925. Brief discussions of the subject are also found in A. Basch and J. Dvořáček, *Austria and Its Economic Existence,* Prague, 1925; in the Layton and Rist report on Austria, quoted elsewhere in this book; and in "Das oesterreichische Wirtschaftsproblem: Denkschrift der Oesterreichisch-Deutschen Arbeitsgemeinschaft," published in *Der oesterreichische Volkswirt,* Vienna, July 18, 1925. Materials contained in these publications were supplemented by the author's conversations with a large number of Austrian economists and bankers, and by reference to isolated data appearing in periodic publications.

A. Income from Foreign Investments

Austrian investments abroad are located principally in those countries which had formerly constituted a part of the Austro-Hungarian Monarchy. They fall into several categories, the most important of them being in the form of ownership of various industrial, trading, and banking enterprises. The returns from foreign investments comprise, therefore, profits from such enterprises, as well as from lands owned by Austrians; and also dividends, directors' fees, and bonuses, accruing from ownership and control of stocks and bonds.

Prior to the war the returns from these properties were very considerable. Dr. Hertz has made an evaluation of the portion of these returns which represented the share of the territory of present-day Austria. As his basis he used pre-war data showing the distribution of production, income tax, etc., between the various districts of the Monarchy, and arrived at the following conclusions: [1]

1. The yield of foreign securities with fixed dividends held in Austria he estimates at no less than 200 million crowns.
2. The profits from private undertakings located outside the territory of present-day Austria but accruing to persons living within this territory he places about 470 million crowns.
3. Profits from agricultural undertakings he puts at 55 million crowns.
4. Dividends, directors' fees, etc., he estimates at 97 millions.

We thus get a total of 822 million crowns as the prewar income derived by the territory of present-day Austria from investments outside its frontiers. But in using this figure as a basis for estimating Austria's postwar income, account must be taken of important changes that have occurred during the past ten years. There is

[1] *Zahlungsbilanz und Lebensfähigkeit,* ibid., pp. 46-57.

no doubt that Austria has lost a part of her investments. The amount of this loss cannot be precisely determined, but by taking account of the various factors involved, a rough estimate of the total may be made.

Practically all of the fixed-dividend securities (the net income from which amounted before the war to 200 million crowns) have disappeared. Some of them were sold during the war for the purchase of supplies. Some —those of the Allied countries—were taken away by the treaties of peace. Russian and Balkan securities have become practically worthless because of the inflation through which these countries have passed. On the whole, therefore, present income from these securities is probably only a very small part of pre-war income.

Austrian participation in industrial, commercial, and banking enterprises in the other Danubian States is still considerable. In Czechoslovakia Austrian banks still participate in the ownership of no less than three important banks, eight metal and engineering enterprises, seven textile and clothing factories, seven sugar refineries, four alcohol distilleries, and a number of breweries, chemical works, and other enterprises. Most of these enterprises are among the largest in Czechoslovakia. In Hungary Austrian banks have proprietary interests in no less than twenty-one important business enterprises of various kinds; in Poland, fourteen; in Yugoslavia, twelve. They also share in the ownership of two important banks in Bulgaria, and a considerable number of various types of enterprises in Rumania; and even in several enterprises as far afield as Holland and Italy.[2]

[2] *Austria and Its Economic Existence*, ibid., pp. 26-29.

It is impossible to determine the exact extent to which Austria's income from ownership in these various business enterprises in other countries falls below the prewar figure. While the list that we have given above undoubtedly is incomplete, there seems no doubt that such holdings are smaller than before the war During the first years of the country's independent existence, the Austrian people sold a large part of this class of their investments abroad. But in 1923, when there was a large influx of foreign funds into Austria, they repurchased some of these investments, while in 1924 they probably again sold some of them to foreigners. There is another factor which has contributed to the diminution of the returns from direct investments in foreign enterprises. Prior to the breakup of the Austro-Hungarian Monarchy the main office of many enterprises in which Austrians participated as whole or part owners were located in Vienna. After the break-up, under the influence of the policies of "nostrification," most of them were removed to the countries in which the enterprises are located, thus certainly curtailing the flow of funds into Vienna. On the whole, there seems little doubt that the actual returns from this category of investments outside the present frontiers of Austria are not nearly so large as they were before the war.

Returns from investments in agricultural property outside of Austria are also much smaller today than they were before the war. Some such investments have been altogether lost in connection with the agrarian reforms inaugurated all through central and eastern Europe.

Dr. Hertz believes that the permanent loss in industrial investments reduces returns from them by forty to fifty per cent. In the case of other investments, the loss is much greater. Altogether, he estimates that in the future the returns from all remaining Austrian investments abroad can scarcely exceed 400 million gold crowns.

While this figure may represent a correct estimate of Austria's potential income from investments, our investigations in Vienna, as well as in other Danubian States, leads us to believe that actual income at the present time is nowhere near this figure. The best estimates we have been able to obtain for the years since the stabilization of the Austrian currency (1923-1926) place the returns from Austrian investments in other countries at about 300 million gold crowns, or a little over 400 million schillings a year.

B. Payments on Foreign Debts

The public foreign debt of Austria, as of January 1, 1926, was as follows (in millions of schillings):[3]

League of Nations Loan	1,034
Other funded debts	120
Floating debt	806
Share of the Austro-Hungarian pre-war debts	470
	2,430

Austria has been paying interest and some amortization charges on the League of Nations Loan, and the other funded debts, and is making payments on the share of the Austro-Hungarian pre-war debts assigned to her by the Innsbruck and Prague protocols. The total amount paid out by the Austrian Treasury on account

[3] League of Nations *Memorandum on Public Finance,* 1922-1926.

of the public debt during the years 1923-26 was as follows (in millions of schillings): [4]

1923	233
1924	192
1925	160
1926	155
	740

These payments were made on account of both the domestic and the foreign public debt. Since the foreign funded debts constitute about 85 per cent of all the debts on which payments are being made at the present time, the amount actually paid abroad during the four years under consideration was about 630 million schillings.

During these years, Austria also floated a number of publicly offered loans, in addition to the League of Nations loan. The amount thus borrowed amounted to 21 million schillings in 1924; 160 million in 1925; and 50 million in 1926. The average rate of interest on these loans is slightly under 7.5 per cent.[5] In addition to these publicly offered loans, Austria has a short-term indebtedness, the interest payments on which are estimated at no less than 40 million schillings a year. Thus for the whole four-year period from 1923 to 1926 a total of approximately 200 million schillings was paid out as interest on other foreign debts than those owed by the State.

C. Trade Commissions and Banking Profits

Before the war Vienna derived considerable revenue from its position as a trade and financial middleman.

[4] Ibid.

[5] *Mitteilungen des Direktoriums der oesterreichischen Nationalbank,* April 30, 1927, p. 156.

The bulk of foreign investments in the whole territory of the Austro-Hungarian Monarchy passed through the Vienna banks. Vienna also took an important part in financing the Balkan countries. At the same time, the great Vienna banks served as depositories for large amounts of working capital of enterprise operating throughout this immense territory, principally in the Monarchy itself.

Vienna was not only the financial, but also the trading center of south-central Europe. A great deal of both the domestic and the foreign trade of the Monarchy was done through Vienna. Some of this goods traffic passed through the capital city; but most of it consisted of transactions, which, so far as physical deliveries were concerned, passed entirely outside the city itself, and yet yielded Vienna appreciable profits. For example, Vienna firms might purchase coffee in Brazil or cotton at Charleston, and deliver the former to Budapest through Trieste or the latter to Moravia through Hamburg, and yet derive a profit from the transaction.

Both of these sources of revenue still exist for Vienna, though in reduced dimensions. Vienna has lost its position as the overwhelmingly important financial and banking center of south-central Europe. Each of the new States has developed its own banking system and has made every effort to establish its own international connections. Much of the working capital that had formerly concentrated in Vienna is now found in the banking institutions of the countries to whose industries it belongs. Nevertheless, the great prestige and long-established international connections of the Vienna banks still affords them an opportunity to handle many of the international financial transactions in which the Danubian States are concerned.

Similarly, with regard to trade operations, the new states have been strenuously developing their own facilities and connections. But here again Vienna still plays an important rôle. As a source of *international* revenue this activity is very important. Much of the trade which had formerly represented transactions within the frontiers of the Monarchy is now foreign trade, and whatever revenue Vienna derives from it is international revenue. Viennese firms still purchase goods in all parts of the world and sell them to, say, Czechoslovakia or Yugoslavia, or sell Czechoslovak or Yugoslav products in, say, Belgium or South America, without any of the physical deliveries passing through Austrian territory.

The best estimates we have been able to obtain place Austria's revenue from these two sources at about 200 million schillings a year.[6]

D. Tourist Traffic

Large numbers of foreigners are attracted every year to various parts of Austria. Vienna is still the great scientific, artistic, and cultural center of central Europe, and many visitors come to it from other parts of Europe and from overseas. The mountainous portions of Austria, especially the Tyrolian Alps, constitute one of the most important vacation areas of Europe. Tourist traffic in Austria is, therefore, very considerable.

According to official figures, 647,179 foreigners visited Austria in the year 1923. During 1924 the number was

[6] In *Austria and Its Economic Existence*, ibid., p. 74, the amount for 1924 is estimated at 100 million gold crowns; in this estimate, however, banking profits are not taken into account.

much larger, reaching the figure of about 1,100,000. The average stay of each foreigner is estimated at 5½ days. On this basis it is calculated that the amount of money spent by foreign tourists and visitors in Austria during 1924 was about 170 million schillings. Austrian tourists abroad were much fewer in number. Their expenditures during the year probably did not exceed 30 million crowns, which would leave Austria in 1924 a net income from tourist expenditures of about 140 million schillings.[7]

But that is not all. So far we have been considering merely the living and travelling expenses of foreign visitors to Austria. We must now consider their purchases of goods, particularly in Vienna, where many articles of apparel and numberless specialties attract the attention of tourists. Vienna has enormous facilities for catering to this sort of trade. To the visitors coming from the countries to the south and east of Austria, Vienna offers a large assortment of articles which are either unavailable in their own countries or else much more expensive. As a Czechoslovak writer puts it, "Czech visitors to Austria leave their own country with empty trunks and return with their trunks filled to overflowing." [8]

To some extent this is true of nearly all foreign visitors to Austria, particularly to Vienna. This "pocket" or "trunk" export naturally escapes inclusion in the general export figures, and yet it represents a fairly consid-

[7] Hertz, op. cit., p. 53, estimates that before the war the territory of present-day Austria derived about 110 million crowns a year from tourist traffic. Layton and Rist (p. 18) say, "It has been estimated that Austria earns a revenue of something between 100 and 200 million crowns from this source." Basch and Dvořáček (p. 74) say, "The country's income from tourist traffic in 1924 was between 100 and 120 million gold crowns."

[8] Dr. Karl Uhlig, in a study of the Czechoslovak balance of payments, placed at the author's disposal in manuscript form.

erable item. In fact, in view of the special conditions of Austria's tourist traffic and of the fact that a fairly large part of this export is in the form of rather expensive articles, such as jewelry, leather goods, books, etc., it is quite possible that "pocket" export adds to the country's international revenue about one-half as much as the living and travelling expenditures of the tourists. For the four-year period from 1923 to 1926 we estimate Austria's total income from these two sources at 800 million schillings.

E. Other Invisible Items

There are several other sources of international revenue. Austrian emigrants and residents abroad transmit money to their relatives at home. Before the war the territory of present-day Austria received 20 million schillings a year from emigrant remittances.[9] Assuming that the remittances in post-war years remained approximately the same, we must add to this figure something for the earning of Austrian musicians, actors, scientists, etc., both in the form of actual salaries paid them abroad and in the form of royalties. This would bring the figure up to about 30 millions a year.

Finally, we have the earnings of the Austrian railways, river boats, and the port of Vienna from international transit of goods and passengers. Railroad earnings were estimated at about 14 million gold crowns a year, with a total for all transit services of 25 million schillings.[10] Later estimates, however, place the annual

[9] Figure arrived at by R. Riemer on the basis of investigations conducted by the Ministry of Finance; quoted in Hertz, p. 54.

[10] See *Statistische Nachrichten,* April 25, 1924.

earnings of the Austrian transit services at 100 million schillings.

II. CZECHOSLOVAKIA

The first complete study of Czechoslovakia's international accounts, covering the year 1925, was made by Dr. Pavel Smutný, of the Czechoslovak Central Statistical Office. The results of this study appeared in Dr. Smutný's pamphlet, *Naše platezní bilance a její methoda,* Prague, 1927, and in *Bulletin of the National Bank of Czechoslovakia,* February, 1927. An earlier study on the subject of international accounts was made by Dr. Karl Uhlig; his study, entitled, *Allgemeine Charakteristik der tschechoslovakischen Zahlungsbilanz,* was kindly placed at our disposal in manuscript form. Still another study, made by Mr. K. Karásek, a prominent Prague banker, was published in the *Central European Observer,* April 3, 1925. Our evaluations are based on these studies and on our own investigations.

A. Payments on Foreign Obligations

There is no precise estimate of the extent of foreign investments in Czechoslovakia. Mr. Karásek places it at a little over 5 billion crowns. On the basis of Dr. Smutný's figures for interest and dividend payments, the total works out at a somewhat higher figure. Our own investigations, both in Prague and in Vienna, lead us to the conclusion that the total is considerably higher. We estimate the total of interest, dividends, and profits paid to foreign investors by Czechoslovak industrial, banking, and agricultural enterprises at 800-900 million crowns a year, with 800 million crowns as the approximate net payments after deducting the country's own income from foreign investments.

Total interest payments made by the Czechoslovak government on account of the public debt, during the years 1922-26, amounted to about 11 billion crowns.[1] The foreign public debt of Czechoslovakia is equal to a little over one-quarter of the total public debt. Considering the fact that payments on some of the debts were not begun until the latter part of the period under consideration, the amount attributable to the foreign debt prior to 1926 was under 25 per cent of the total payments. On the other hand, in 1926, Czechoslovakia began payments on her share of the pre-war debts. Therefore, we estimate that the total amount paid out on account of public foreign debts during the five-year period was about 2.5 billion crowns.

In addition to the debts owed by the central government, there are also local or communal debts. The payments on these debts, added to payments on private loans obtained since the war, probably amount to about 100 million crowns a year, or 500 million crowns for the whole period.

B. Service Operations

Czechoslovakia's income from transit traffic was estimated by Dr. Smutný for 1925 as 440 million crowns, and by Mr. Karásek for 1924 as 400 millions. We take the average income from this source during the five-year period as somewhere between the above two figures, or a total of 2.1 billion crowns.

Emigrant remittances to Czechoslovakia are estimated

[11] *Státni závěrečný účet republiky československé.*

by Dr. Smutný for 1925 as 452.8 million crowns. Offsetting this item, there are remittances sent out of Czechoslovakia by foreign laborers, as well as funds taken out of the country by new emigrants, doweries, bequests, etc., altogether totalling for 1925 the sum of 149.9 million crowns. This leaves a net income from this source equal to 302.9 million crowns. Mr. Karásek's estimate for 1924 is only 150 million crowns. We are inclined to accept Dr. Smutný's figure and use it as the approximate annual income from this source.

The health resorts of Czechoslovakia attract to the country a large tourist trade, the income from which is estimated by both Dr. Smutný and Mr. Karásek as 400 million crowns a year. On the other hand, however, according to Dr. Smutný's estimate, Czechoslovak tourists and travellers in other countries spend no less than 725 million crowns annually. Tourist traffic, therefore, represents for the country a net outgo of about 325 million crowns a year.

There are several other items of net outgo, such as commissions, insurance, patent fees, film royalties, the difference between the expenditures of foreign representatives in Czechoslovakia and Czechoslovak representatives in other countries, etc. They aggregated for 1925, according to Dr. Smutný, about 300 million crowns. We take this as the annual figure for the period.

III. HUNGARY

A great deal of work on Hungary's international accounts has been done by Professor Friedrich von Fellner of the University of Budapest, and by Dr. Julius Szigeti, director of the Royal Hungarian Statistical Office. Professor Fellner's studies cover the pre-war period and the first few post-war years, while those of Dr. Szigeti deal with the years 1923, 1924, and 1926. Our evaluations, since they refer to the period since stabilization, that is to the years 1924-26, are based primarily on Dr. Szigeti's studies, published in *Magyar Statistikai Szemle* (Hungarian Review of Statistics), October, 1925, and June, 1927, and on our own investigations in Budapest.

A. Payments on Foreign Obligations

In Dr. Szigeti's study on the international accounts of Hungary for the year 1926, the total interest and amortization payments on Hungary's foreign obligations are estimated at 133 million gold crowns. This amount includes the payments on the League of Nations Reconstruction loan, on all the other foreign debts of the government, and on all municipal and private long-term and short-term borrowing, as well as payments on account of Hungary's share of the pre-war debts and the charges resulting from the treaties of peace. In the Final Report of the Commissioner-General of the League of Nations for Hungary, issued on July 16, 1926, Hungary's annual payments on long-term obligations alone, are estimated as 93.8 millions. On the basis of this last figure, we estimate the foreign debt payments in 1925 as about 120 million crowns, and for the year 1924 at approximately 55 millions. Thus for the three-year period from 1924 to 1926, Hungary's total payments on foreign obligations were equal to about 308 million gold crowns.

Offsetting these payments, was the income received by the country from Hungarian investments in other countries. Dr. Szigeti places the amount of this income at 9.4 millions in 1924 and at 7.1 millions for 1926. Our investigations lead us to believe that these figures are too low. We estimate the income from this source at about 15 million crowns a year, or 45 millions for the three-year period.

B. Service Operations

Hungary's income from emigrant remittances is estimated by Dr. Szigeti at 21.2 million crowns for 1924 and 29.5 millions for 1926. When a deduction is made for the value of the property taken out of the country by new emigrants, the net income from this source amounts to 21.0 million crowns in 1924 and 25.2 millions in 1926. For the three-year period we estimate the total income at 69 millions.

On the basis of Dr. Szigeti's figures and information from other sources, we estimate the net income from transit traffic and shipping at about 10 million crowns a year, or 30 millions for the three-year period.

The expenditures of foreign tourists and visitors in Hungary are estimated by Dr. Szigeti at 3.5 million crowns for 1924 and 2.6 millions for 1926. The expenditures of Hungarian tourists and travellers in other countries are estimated respectively at 10.8 millions and 11.4 millions. On the basis of these figures we estimate Hungary's net outgo on account of tourist traffic at 25 million crowns for the three-year period.

For the smaller items in the international accounts, such as commissions and insurance, diplomatic services, etc., we estimate the net outgo at 5 million crowns a year, or 15 millions for the whole period.

IV. RUMANIA

Several studies have been made in Rumania on the international accounts of the country. The most important among them are those of Professor I. N. Angelescu, published in *Analele Statistice ši Economice* (Rumanian Statistical and Economic Annals), January-February, 1925, and of the Research Department of the Bank of Marmorosch, Blank and Co., published in *Les Forces économiques de la Roumanie* for 1926 and 1927. Very valuable materials on Rumania's foreign payments are contained in *The Economic Review* of London, January and February, 1927. Our estimates are based largely on these studies and on our own investigations.

A. Payments on Foreign Obligations

The total figure of payments on foreign public debts, appearing in the summary statement on p. 411, is based on data found in the budgets. It is smaller, however, than the latter by about 20 per cent. The explanation for this is that there is reason to believe that not all of the debt payments inscribed in the budgets are actually being met.

As regards interest and dividend payments on foreign investments and private debts, the estimates of Professor Angelescu and of the authors of *Les Forces économiques* differ widely. The former places the annual payments on these accounts at 2.3 billion lei; the latter, at 3.9 billions. Our investigations lead us to believe that the actual payments are about 3 billions, making the total payments for the five-year period under consideration 15 billion lei.

B. *Service Operations*

According to *Les Forces économiques*, the expenditures of foreigners in Rumania are equal to 700 million lei a year, while the expenditures of Rumanians in other countries aggregate 1.5 billions. This indicates a net outgo for the country of 800 million lei a year on this account. In addition to this the net outgo for transport and other services amounts to approximately 200 millions. Altogether, therefore, the country's net outgo for international services aggregated, during the years 1922-26, no less than 5 billion lei.

Emigrant remittances are estimated in *Les Forces économiques* at 300 million lei a year, making a total of 1.5 billions for the five-year period.

V. YUGOSLAVIA

The only published estimate of the various items in Yugoslavia's international accounts is contained in *La Balance des paiements du Royaume des Serbes, Croates et Slovènes en 1926*, by Mil. Tošić, A. Vegner, P. J. Rudčenko and G. Strekačev, Belgrade, 1928. The figures contained in the summary statement on page 499 differ somewhat from these estimates. They are based on these estimates and also on data supplied to us in Belgrade by economists and financiers. The figure for the payments on the public foreign debts is based on the budget.

INDEX

K

L

P

R

Printed and bound by CPI Group (UK) Ltd, Croydon, CR0 4YY

16/10/2024

01774962-0016